Studies in Political Economy

Series Editors: Gregory Albo and Pat Armstrong

This series, sponsored by *Studies in Political Economy: A Socialist Review,* and Canadian Scholars' Press, publishes contributions to contemporary political economy. The series is intended to advance progressive education, to disseminate research, and to foster public debate.

Other Titles in the Series

Feminism in Action: Studies in Political Economy
P. Connelly and P. Armstrong (eds.)

For more information write:

Studies in Political Economy
Social Science Research Building, Rm. 303
Carleton University
1125 Colonel By Drive
Ottawa, Ontario K1S 5B6

To order titles please write to:

Canadian Scholars' Press Inc.,
180 Bloor Street West
Suite 402
Toronto, Ontario
M5S 2V6

Production, Space, Identity:

Political Economy Faces the 21st Century

Edited By

Jane Jenson
Rianne Mahon
Manfred Bienefeld

Canadian Scholars' Press Inc.   Toronto   1993

Production, Space, Identity: Political Economy
Faces the 21st Century

First published in 1993 by
Canadian Scholars' Press Inc.
180 Bloor St. W., Ste. 402
Toronto, Ontario
M5S 2V6

Canadian Cataloguing in Publication Data

(Studies in Political Economy)
Includes bibliographical references.
ISBN   1-55130-024-9

1. Canada - Economic conditions - 1991-. 2. Economic history - 1990-. I. Jenson, Jane, 1946-. II. Mahon, Rianne, 1948-. III. Bienefeld, M.A.   IV.   Series: Studies in Political Economy (Toronto, Ont.).

HC115.P76   1993   330'.971'064   C93-094573-5

Printed and bound in Canada

Book design by Steven Hain Associates, Toronto.

TABLE OF CONTENTS

PART III:
SPATIAL HORIZONS: RECONFIGURING THE MAP

LIST OF CONTRIBUTORS

Gregory ALBO teaches political science at York University and is a member of the editorial board of *Studies in Political Economy*.

Caroline ANDREW is a professor of Political Science at the University of Ottawa and a member of the editorial board of *Studies in Political Economy*.

Manfred BIENEFELD is a professor in the School of Public Administration, Carleton University and a member of the editorial board of *Studies in Political Economy*.

Gérard BOISMENU is a professor in the Département de science politique, Université de Montréal.

Harriet FRIEDMANN is a professor of Sociology at the University of Toronto and a member of the editorial board of *Studies in Political Economy*.

John HOLMES teaches geography at Queen's University.

François HOULE teaches in the Département de science politique, Université d'Ottawa and is a former member of the editorial board of *Studies in Political Economy*.

Lizette JALBERT taught in the Département de science politique, Université de Québéc à Montréal.

Jane JENSON is a professor of Political Science at Carleton University and a member of the editorial board of *Studies in Political Economy*.

Raphael KAPLINSKY teaches in the Institute of Development Studies, University of Sussex, England.

Pradeep KUMAR teaches in the Industrial Relations Centre, Queen's University.

Carla LIPSIG-MUMMÉ is the co-ordinator of the Labour Studies Programme in the Division of Social Science of York University.

John LOXLEY teaches Economics at the University of Manitoba and is a former member of the editorial board of *Studies in Political Economy*.

Rianne MAHON is a professor in the School of Public Administration, Carleton University and a member of the editorial board of *Studies in Political Economy*.

Lynn Krieger MYTELKA is a professor of Political Science at Carleton University.

Barbara NEIS teaches Sociology at the Memorial University of Newfoundland and is a member of the editorial board of *Studies in Political Economy*.

Alain NOËL teaches in the Département de science politique, Université de Montréal.

George ROSS is a professor of Sociology at Brandeis University.

Glen WILLIAMS is a professor of Political Science at Carleton University.

J. Yvon THÉRIAULT teaches in the Département de sociologie, Université d'Ottawa.

PREFACE

These essays represent part of a widespread effort to rethink Canadian political economy in the light of changes in the world that it attempts to understand—and to transform. In this volume we situate domestic challenges such as those posed by the formation of a North American free trade area, the constitutional debates over the Meech Lake and Charlottetown accords, and the 1990 events at Oka/Kanesatake, in relation to broader changes in the organisation of production, the future of the nation-state, and re-configurations of collective actors and political sites. Together, these developments entail changes in the parameters, content, and locus of effective policy initiatives designed to promote sustainable growth and the equitable sharing of its product. Such rethinking is not, of course, unique to the authors of this volume. Others have preceded us and more will, we hope, follow.

Our approach has been to focus each chapter on a particular theme. The thread knitting together the whole is the need for new conceptual maps and strategic horizons if we are to comprehend the forces currently at work and the possible futures to which they might give rise. Such an analysis does not imply by any means that the rich and indigenous tradition of Canadian political economy is about to be jettisoned. Nevertheless, this volume does suggest that its original core concepts—dependency, class, state—and the strategic horizon of the nation-state need to be reworked to incorporate the insights contained in the more recent work by Canadian and non-Canadian political economists on production, identity and space. Some of the latter are represented in the volume; others are frequently cited. Indeed, one of the novelties of this volume on the new Canadian political economy is that several of the authors in this volume are not Canadian. They are here, however, because intellectual dialogue across national borders is on the increase.

This book has its roots in a conference on Canadian Political Economy in the Era of Free Tradeheld at Carleton University in April 1990. That institution provided the ideal setting for evaluating the legacy of the vibrant political economy tradition, which it has encouraged and sustained throughout the last two decades, as well as for launching a process of re-thinking. We are grateful for the contributions and encouragement of the Dean of Social Sciences, Marilyn Marshall, the School of Public Administration and the Department of Political Science. In addition, substantial support came from the Social Science and Humanities Research Council and the Douglas-Coldwell Foundation, and we take this opportunity to thank them again and in public. For her editorial wisdom and general support, we want to acknowledge with thanks the contribution of Emer Killean to making this book, and the special issue before it, happen. Finally, while the editors take responsibility for the volume, it has always been a project generated and supported by *Studies in Political Economy*. The intellectual and material sustenance so generously provided by our fellow "editorial" board members have made it possible to imagine and complete this project.

| | CHAPTER |
| | 1 |

| The "New" Canadian Political Economy Revisited: Production, Space, Identity | Rianne Mahon |

To be condemned to live in interesting times: the Chinese proverb seems to fit the twilight years of the twentieth century. The collapse of "actually existing socialism" in Eastern Europe, and with it the rationale for Cold War politics; the decomposition of the Keynesian class compromise and the apparent triumph of neo-conservativism with its celebration of market forces; the reshaping of continents via the movement to form supra-national trading blocs and the resurgence of nationalisms asserted against existing nation states; the degradation of life conditions in much of the Third World; the growing signs of impending ecological disaster: these trends are reshaping the world as we have known it. To think and to act in such "interesting times" is indeed a challenge. For some, meeting the challenge means jettisoning the conceptual and political baggage of the past. For the Left, in Canada and elsewhere, it means a time of confusion over what constitutes a progressive project, who the agents of change may be and even what the spatial horizons of action are.

Although history is indeed marked by crises and disjunctures that call for different theoretical lenses through which the unfamiliar can be understood, the world is not made anew with each upheaval. The continuities and discontinuities of the present can only be grasped when older ideas are brought into a creative tension with the new. Thus, as the Canadian Left confronts these interesting times, it can look to the "new" Canadian political economy (NCPE), forged in the early twilight years of the postwar order, as an important intellectual tradition, one capable of renewal.

The NCPE is marked by the context in which it was "reborn."[1] At that time, the Viet Nam war and other Third World struggles were beginning to reveal serious cracks in the foundations of American economic and military hegemony. In the relatively privileged North, worker and student revolts gave voice to dissatisfaction with the "American way of life" based on mass consumption—a way of life spread not only by transnational corporations but also through the consolidation of the Keynesian welfare state within each national society. In Quebec, the New Left quickly took an explictly anti-imperialist, "independentist" expression. In the rest of Canada, the Waffle—which began as a ginger group within the New Democratic Party (NDP)—became the standard-bearer of a left-nationalist challenge to American dominance.

These political challenges spawned new theoretical work. Third World struggles inspired a reconceptualization of underdevelopment as a process resulting from trade, aid and investment links between North and South. The European worker and student revolts contributed to a rethinking of the classic Marxist concepts "class" and "state." Like the Waffle from which it drew much of its inspiration, the new Canadian political economy concocted its own rich intellectual brew, combining the concepts developed by the Left in Latin America and Europe with the work of an earlier generation of Canadian political economists. While the NCPE was certainly enlivened by internal debate, most practitioners accepted the core problematic—Canada as a "rich dependency"—and the politico-strategic horizons which followed therefrom—struggle for an independent, socialist Canada.

In many respects, the serious challenges that Canada faces today seem to bear out the Waffle-NCPE analysis of the accelerating tendency toward the subordinate integration of Canada into a structure of continental corporate power and the balkanization of the Canadian state. The Canada-U.S. Free Trade Agreement (FTA) and its successor, the North American Free Trade Agreement (NAFTA), can thus be seen as merely hastening the deindustrialization process that had already begun in the seventies. The failure of government efforts to settle the constitutional question seems to confirm the inability of a regionalised bourgeoisie, fixated on continental trade, either to halt the balkanization of the Canadian state or to recognise Quebec as a distinct society. Aboriginal peoples' fight for control over their lands and their demand for recognition as a sovereign people are but further evidence of the contradictions embedded in the Canadian model of development.

NCPE thus still seems to make sense of contemporary reality: the web of dependency and uneven development, woven by a continental bourgeoisie, is becoming more visible as the various parts of Canada are differentially incorporated into the North American economic bloc, while the Canadian state fragments as a result of centrifugal forces. Yet the NCPE's very prescience should not be allowed to give rise to theoretical complacency. Assumptions that still seemed warranted in the early years of the crisis are being called into question by broader developments. Just as in its formative years, the NCPE needs to engage in a process of rethinking its core concepts—dependency, class and state—in relation to newer ideas designed to probe the broader set of changes in the realm of *production*, in the collective *identities* that have constituted the stuff of politics, and in the nation-state as the basic principle of *spatial organisation* and the horizon of political action.

These themes will be explored in greater depth throughout this volume. It is the task of this chapter to begin to integrate the new ideas about production, identity and space into a political economy centred on dependency, class and state.

DEPENDENCY, CLASS AND STATE

Three concepts—"dependency," "class" and "state"—were central to the NCPE's problematic.[2] The literature on dependency, which stressed the process of systematic underdevelopment resulting from the unequal exchange between resource-producing peripheries and industrial centres, seemed to make sense of Canada's status as a country of "hewers of wood and drawers of water." In re-interpreting Canadian history from this perspective, the work of Harold Innis, Donald Creighton and others proved indispensable, revealing the roots of Canada's position as a dependent, staples-exporting economy. Innis had highlighted the uneven and crisis-prone development of the Canadian economy via the exploitation of a series of staples, beginning with cod and fur. For Innis, too, it was the path traced by the extraction and export of these staples that mapped the frontiers of what would become Canada. Creighton's *Empire of the St Lawrence* explained the creation of Canada—a national boundary based on neither geography nor culture—in terms of the spatial horizons of an indigenous merchant elite, formed in the era of the fur trade.

The concept of dependency also merged with earlier work by Stanley Ryerson, Vernon Fowke and C.B. Macpherson to shed light on regional inequality within Canada. Western political economists could draw on Macpherson's work on the political struggle of prairie farmers to illuminate the forces behind their region's dependence on central Canada and imperial centres.[3] Analyses of subsequent western initiatives—notably the "province building" strategies launched in the midst of the seventies—challenged the Central Canadian focus of many political economists.[4] A vibrant Atlantic wing of the school looked in part to the specific relations of production and consumption linked to the dominant staples (especially fishing) of that region to explain its relative poverty and the particular forms which resistance took.[5]

Quebec intellectuals produced their own left nationalist synthesis of then-new ideas and older indigenous sources. Some of the key debates in Quebec were published in English-language books and journals like *Studies in Political Economy (SPE)*, contributing to a sense of commonality as well as difference.[6] Thus, like Canada, Quebec was understood as a dependent capitalist society in which the national and class questions were necessarily linked. At the same time, it was a subordinate nation whose struggle for independence and socialism had to be recognised and supported by the left nationalist movement in Canada.

While the concept of dependency was easily grafted onto the older political economy tradition, the new political economists gave the concept of class a more central role in their attempts to explain the roots of Canada's distorted economy. The role played by classes in shaping Canadian history was in fact central to the debates within the NCPE where it often constituted the dividing line between various tendencies within the New Left.

One aspect of the debate—that which focused on the nature of the dominant class—put flesh on the seemingly abstract conceptions of "class fractions" and "power bloc" associated with the work of Nicos Poulantzas. Here debate centred on which fraction was responsible for the overdevelopment of the resource sector and the truncated character of Canadian manufacturing. Was it the early victory of Canada's merchant-financiers over indigenous industrial capital, or was it the nature of the compromise between the two which gave the latter a relatively protected home market in exchange for its acceptance of the hegemony of the staples fraction? Was the whole conception of "fractions" of limited relevance now that finance capital—the synthesis of industrial and financial capital which Lenin and Hilferding associated with the dawn of imperialism—had become paramount?[7] This debate was no mere scholastic exercise. Rather it was central to the politics of the time. It dealt with the question of who was to blame for Canada's industrial weakness and it touched on the whole problem of potential alliances for change. Was there a domestic bourgeoisie who could be rallied to the call for independence or was the latter thoroughly implicated in a system of continental corporate power?

The debate on class did not, of course, focus on one class alone. The subordinate classes also played their part in shaping Canada's historical trajectory. The Waffle put part of the blame for Canada's dependent position on the domination of the Canadian labour movement by the so-called international unions, which functioned to instill into the organised working class acceptance, not only of capitalism but also of American dominance of the Canadian economy. Labour historians did much to provide a more nuanced picture of the formation and development of the Canadian working class but they generally rejected the whole dependency problematic and thus split off from NCPE to engage in their own debates in the pages of *Labour/Le Travail*.[8] Others, however, directly challenged explanations that made the dominant class the critical actor shaping Canada's historical trajectory, arguing that Canada became a *rich* (and liberal democratic) dependency precisely because of the role played by family farmers and the working class.[9]

The NCPE debates on the role of the Canadian state mirrored the debates elsewhere, while acknowledging the specificity of the Canadian state, notably a federal structure which reflected a balkanised, dependent economy.[10] Thus those who saw the Canadian state as an "instrument" of foreign capital (or a comprador bourgeoisie) were pitted against those who argued that its "relative autonomy" forced or permitted it to organise the intra- and inter-class compromises essential to hegemonic class domination. These theoretical differences reflected divergent strategic orientations: to capture or to transform the (federal or provincial) state? what kind of alliance to construct toward this end? Nevertheless, both sides in the debate shared a sense that the struggle for change was a struggle that would take place within *national* boundaries—with greater or lesser room for provincially-based strategies.

These debates certainly contributed to the vitality of the NCPE in the seventies. While some rejected its left-nationalist problematic, many accepted its dominant themes: the importance of industrial or technological "sovereignty" to the struggle for independence and socialism; the centrality of class or class alliances forged on the basis of a common national interest to explanations of, and efforts to transform, Canada's position within the global economy; and the critical role played by the national (and/or provincial) state in reproducing or challenging the status quo. In the eighties, however, dissident voices were to come to the fore, challenging these certitudes.

A feminist political economy, which had developed alongside the NCPE, launched a direct attack on its gender-blind analysis of Canadian development.[11] Others pointed to its silences on questions of race.[12] Environmentalists criticised the "productivist" insensitivity to nature, embedded in the emphasis on (re)industrialization which the NCPE shared with the very bourgeoisie it sought to challenge (see Williams in this volume). More broadly, the NCPE proved as vulnerable to the critiques of structuralism as the European and Latin American theories on which it drew: it could illuminate certain structures of domination but largely in ways that left little analytical room for human agency.[13]

These theoretical and political challenges are important and they form a significant part of the impetus to "rethink" the NCPE which motivates this and other contributions. Yet what of the old problematic? At one level, it does help to make sense of contemporary reality. The accelerating collapse of the domestic manufacturing base, the secular rise in unemployment and the corresponding rise of welfare dependency certainly can be understood as effects of the deindustrialization process decried by the Waffle and the NCPE. Its "break-up of Canada" scenario also rings true. And yet there is more to understanding the crisis and the forces that it has brought to the fore than this.

Therefore this volume offers a new way of thinking about the long-standing concerns of the NCPE. First, class still matters. But other social forces, whose aims are "historically progressive" but whose social base, demands and terrains of struggle are not reducible to class, also require recognition. Here the concept of *identity*, used by feminists and students of the new social movements, has real insight to offer. It helps to focus attention on the multiple structures of oppression and the way that collective actors capable of challenging these, come into being. Second, while the nation state has not been superceded by other political institutions, we do need new ways of thinking about how political *spaces* are configured and reconfigured. Third, new conceptions of *production* need to be incorporated into the NCPE's analysis of the process of restructuring ongoing. Such new ways of thinking must not only offer insight into what is happening but must be able to suggest viable alternatives to the dominant trends—alternatives based simultaneously on human needs and respect for nature.

PRODUCTION

The NCPE's "deindustrialization" scenario was a first attempt to spell out the possible consequences of economic restructuring under the aegis of transnational corporations. Multilateral or continental trade liberalization would entail a rather drastic pruning of Canada's branch plant economy as Canadian markets could be more efficiently served by larger plants in the United States. In the FTA era, deindustrialization—and the use of the threat of deindustrialization to extract concessions from workers and governments—seems all too real. The extension of the trade pact to Mexico, moreover, is expected to accelerate the process as firms move to take advantage of low wages in the "maquilladora" along the U.S.-Mexican border. Here the original NCPE has been reworked to incorporate the insights offered by theorists of the "new international division of labour" (NIDL) who predicted the shift of production to low wage sites all over the world. From this standpoint, Canada is caught in a double bind: it shares a high wage disadvantage with other northern countries (it is a "rich" country) but it lacks the latters' capacity for retaining at least some good jobs through technological leadership (it is "dependent").

Relocation to low wage sites is a threat which seems all too real these days, but there is another important dimension that this scenario misses: the shift to new forms of production highlighted in a growing body of literature that began to appear in the mid-eighties.[14] This literature points to other dangerous trends, including polarized growth, as well as suggesting how industrial renewal might be pursued in advanced capitalist countries.

Briefly put, the argument is that we are in the midst of an epochal shift, from the "Fordist" logic of accumulation which drove the postwar boom to "post-Fordism," the precise parameters of which remain unclear although its broad outlines can be sketched. Fordism was based on mass production of standardized goods, by semi-skilled workers using dedicated equipment. The mass markets for which these goods were destined, in turn, were sustained by collective bargaining and the Keynesian welfare state. As the boom came to an end in the seventies, capital began to explore various routes to recovery, one of which was relocation to low wage sites. Technological innovation, in the form of hard automation (i.e. the "workerless factory") also seemed promising but more careful scrutiny of the basis for Japan's successful challenge gradually began to shift the focus to "flexible automation." The latter is facilitated by developments in microelectronics and telecommunications, but it is organizational innovations—on the shopfloor and in intra- and inter-firm relations—that lie at the core of the emergent model of production. It is the latter line of exploration that is most often associated with post-Fordism.

It is possible to sketch, as Kaplinsky does in this volume, certain features that fit the economic logic of post-Fordism. Many theorists agree, for instance, that flexible automation requires a break with the Taylorist division between conception and execution that lies at the heart of Fordist relations in production. Forms of intra-firm relations that eliminate functional specialization and promote an interactive, multidimensional planning process are also emphasised, as are forms of inter-firm co-operation associated with "just-in-time" production and a new interest in quality.

In certain countries, some of these changes will be difficult to make, although success need not rest on the kind of capacity for "high tech" innovation difficult for smaller countries to sustain. Rather, success is linked to the ability to promote the rapid diffusion of the new logic of production to all parts of the country. This depends, in turn, on a country's capacity for social innovation, i.e. innovation in the realm of social relations. The latter are particularly important not only in determining whether a given economy can make the transition to post-Fordism; they are the decisive factor in deciding whether post-Fordism marks an advance on Fordism—socially and ecologically—or whether post-Fordism takes an historically regressive form.

In other words, post-Fordism may deliver what enthusiasts promise.[15] It could provide the basis for an ecologically sustainable industrial renewal in the North where skilled workers are engaged in the production of high quality, socially useful goods and services. As both Kaplinsky and Albo argue here, however, it can also mean increased polarization between a smaller core of (re-)skilled workers and a growing mass of temporary and part-time workers who give the system what is euphemistically called "numerical flexibility."[16] It could also offer new opportunities for regionally balanced growth within and between countries.[17] Yet, as Mytelka's analysis of global developments in the textile and clothing industries suggests, post-Fordism can also mean new forms of dependency and exploitation. The reassertion of dependency, she argues, cannot be explained simply by reference to unequal relations between capitals in the North and the South, nor even by comparison of the skills and relative strength of the working class in these two zones. Gender relations in many Third World countries also inhibit the development of progressive forms of post-Fordist production.

Possible limits to the progressive potential of post-Fordism certainly include the interests of capital. While capitalists may want "involved workers" to breach the barriers to productivity growth (and quality) inherent to Fordism, they are also aware that this increases their dependence on those very workers. In order to restore the balance of power, they seek a version of post-Fordism in which core workers come to identify with the firm rather than as members of a class.[18] In addition, current managerial practices and relations between industrial and finance capital in particular countries may constitute barriers to any form of post-Fordism. Yet the "interests of capital," whether defined at the abstract level of class interests or more specifically in terms of its "habits" within a particular economy, are not the only barriers to the transition.

As Neis argues, existing social relations and even barriers in nature itself can block or severely constrain the progressive potential of post-Fordism. Her contribution shows that even traditional resource industries, like fishing, have experienced a turn toward craft production, initially prompted by increasingly regulated access to the decline in natural sources of supply. The revival of artisanal production, however, proved short-lived. Continued depletion of natural sources of supply are combining with government intervention on the side of the large, vertically integrated fish companies, and revisions to unemployment insurance legislation that are consistent with the regressive version of post-Fordism to threaten the very survival of these artisans.

Thus, the concept "post-Fordism" draws attention to significant shifts occurring in the realm of economic relations. Yet post-Fordism should not be treated as a new economic system whose contours are well-defined and which can be embraced as a solution to inequality within and between nations. The concept draws attention to certain novel features of the restructuring process but it cannot tell us which of these, if any, will become the new norm. Nor can it tell us whether a post-Fordist world will be a better one. At best, the concept helps to identify certain (contradictory) tendencies and provides some insight into strategic options.

Understood in this way, the concept can make a useful addition to NCPE's arsenal. It gives us a somewhat different angle on the "Americanization" of the Canadian economy, alerts us to the prospect of uneven growth, and provides a sense of where to begin to look for progressive alternatives to polarization and deindustrialization.

IDENTITY

The NCPE had a conception of the kind of struggles required to challenge existing relations of dependency and class exploitation. Behind the debates internal to the NCPE were shared assumptions that change involved some form of alliance between workers and farmers, and perhaps a fraction of the bourgeoisie, and that such an alliance could be constituted around a common interest in nation (or region). "Nation" certainly provided the glue that held together the opposition to the FTA, and trade unions and the National Farmers' Union constituted important elements of that coalition.[19] Yet the coalition's composition and the tenuous nature of the links which held it together (opposition to the FTA) suggest that the politics of transformation have become more complex. This is not to suggest a return to the liberal pluralist conception that was the object of the NCPE's critique. It does mean finding ways to think about how class, nation, gender, race, and "nature" can be brought together to constitute an effective challenge to the dominant forces.[20] The concept of the politics of identity can be of help here.[21]

The politics of identity is a politics that aims to break open existing definitions of the issues subject to political contestation, by making visible the multiplicity of relations of oppression previously hidden from view. The politics of identity is also a politics of "difference" in that no single relation of domination/resistance, such as class, is seen to subsume the rest. Its emphasis on the recognition of difference and the refusal to assign a priority to a particular identity in abstraction from the concrete situation are to be welcomed. At the same time, there is a real danger that its celebration of difference will contribute to the fragmentation of opposition to the dominant forces. In other words, politics needs to be thought about in ways that recognise the diverse identities which constitute resistance to domination and at the same time contribute to solidarity among the oppressed.

In this volume, Jenson integrates insights derived from thinking about the politics of identity into an analysis of Fordism and post-Fordism inspired by the regulation approach. For Jenson, "politics is conflict about collective identities—about *who* has a right to make claims—as much as it is conflict among groups and organizations over disputed claims about who gets what, when and how." In other words, struggles over difference, about who the actors are, affect the definition of which issues are to be considered open to political contestation, and the acceptable arenas of struggle as well as the resulting claims. And if the names the actors bear shape political issues, they also condition the state's policy choices.

Yet although politics always involves identity politics, there are whole periods during which new collective actors find it hard to assert their presence. Such periods of relative political closure tend, in turn, to coincide with periods of economic stability. As regulation theorists have argued, economic stability can be (temporarily) secured through the institutionalization of a model of development, including a "mode of regulation"—a collection of norms and institutions that bring about a rough conformity to the requirements of a regime of accumulation such as Fordism. No mode of regulation, however, is capable of permanently overcoming the contradictions inherent in capitalist growth and periods of stable growth will be followed by periods of crisis. Economic crises need not coincide precisely with a political crisis but they can only be resolved if political struggles result in the discovery and stabilization of a new model of development. The process of discovery, however, is likely to be messy for it often occurs at a moment of political crisis when the very boundaries of politics are especially fluid.

In many Western European countries, Fordist politics centred around the "democratic class struggle"—within national boundaries. As Ross argues in this volume, however, the search for post-Fordist solutions is taking place in a context marked by the decline of the kind of class politics associated with Western European Fordism. To some extent, the decline is an effect of the very process of postwar development in that the latter brought in train the rapid expansion of a corps of white-collar workers who often remained outside traditional class organizations like unions and social democratic parties. It is also linked to capital's drive—often aided by the neo-liberal policies adopted by states—to restructure by devaluing the "power resources" which unions may have accumulated at the national level. To some extent, the crisis of post-war class politics constitutes an opening for the politics of identity, within each nation and in the European Community as a whole. Yet, as Ross cautions, there is also the all too real prospect that identity politics will take the form of the politics of fragmentation. In Europe, the "left of the Left" has yet to discover a new socialist politics capable of bringing labour and the new social movements together.

In certain respects, Canada's postwar politics was constructed along similar lines to those of Western Europe. Thus collective bargaining and a form of Keynesian-welfare policies did help to secure a certain balance in a system geared to mass production (as well as staples exports) and mass consumption. Yet, much as in the United States, class identities were weakly rooted in federal politics as inter-party strife took the form of brokerage politics. In Canada, moreover, the Keynesian welfare state was represented as a contribution to "nation-building" and the details of its architecture were worked out not in the sphere of partisan class struggle but through a series of federal-provincial bargains.[22]

As Noël, Boismenu and Jalbert argue, however, Canada began to abandon what might be described as its "branch plant" model of American-style

Fordist politics as the U.S. model itself began to go into crisis. The divergence remains visible in the area of social policy but it has become especially marked in the two countries' industrial relations systems, as Holmes and Kumar's careful comparison of collective bargaining patterns in the North American auto industry shows. The Canadian Autoworkers have been more successful in retaining the progressive features of Fordist capital-labour relations which strengthen the union's hand in negotiating the terms of any future relation in the workplace.[23]

Both articles, however, are careful to stress that it would be premature to conclude that Canada's future will be any more progressive than that taking shape south of the border. The very dynamics unleashed by the FTA are making it more difficult to retain what was won in the past, let alone to follow a truly divergent course. At the same time, it would be a mistake to fall back into the de facto fatalism to which the earlier structuralist analyses were prone: politics can make a difference.[24] Certainly, the popular coalition formed to oppose the FTA has had difficulty moving beyond the defensive and elaborating an alternative vision of the future that could turn the coalition into an organic alliance capable of exercising hegemony. Nevertheless, capital has yet to establish a new basis for its hegemony. The future remains an object of struggle.

One of the barriers to the formation of an organic alliance of popular forces is the gulf that divides progressive groups in Quebec from those in the rest of Canada. If the Waffle and the NCPE could detect the parallel between their struggle for independence and socialism and the Québécois' struggle for self-determination, the links seem more difficult to maintain today. This can, in part, be attributed to the way in which the crisis has affected the Quebec labour movement. Lipsig-Mummé argues that the very traditions which once made the latter seem so much in advance of the rest of Canada are now the source of a paralysis that has left the definition of Quebec nationalism largely to neo-liberal forces. The latter, like their counterparts in the rest of Canada, favour the creation of the very North American economic bloc which the Action Canada Network was created to resist.[25]

What all these contributions suggest is that class remains an important social relation and thus a basis for political contestation. Yet the concept of "identity" makes explicit what many Canadian political economists implicitly recognised: politics cannot be read off from social relations. Like most societies, Canada is traversed by various relations of oppression—class, nation, race and gender. Sometimes these jostle with each other as potential bases of political organization and resistance, but they can also form the basis for coalition politics.

SPACE

The NCPE's problematic took for granted a particular world order and the role and nature of the nation state within it. This assumption is understandable, for the NCPE was formed before the rise of neo-liberalism which has helped to put the future of the nation state itself in question. In the late seventies, the deepening economic crisis provoked a crisis of faith in the Keynesian paradigm, but it was only with the victories of Thatcher and Reagan that deregulation, privatization and contracting out became the order of the day. Until recently, moreover, much of the Left's critique of neo-liberalism has rightly focused on its domestic social consequences. One of the effects of neo-liberalism, however, has been to disarm the nation state, as Bienefeld's analysis of the consequences of financial deregulation in this volume shows. In this respect, neo-liberalism reinforces already extant tendencies toward globalization, unleashed by the growth of transnational corporations.

Increased consciousness of the crisis of the nation state, however, does not stem from economic developments alone. Contemporary feminism is a transnational phenomenon even if national specificities have shaped the forms of struggle. Even more than in the sixties, the peace movement of the eighties blended local mobilization with a transnational horizon. The ecological movement has helped to drive home the point that nation states cannot hope to operate as some kind of protective bubble, keeping pollution generated elsewhere from national territory. Aboriginal peoples are using extra-national strategies in order to press their claims.

The qualitative shift in the direction of globalization, which the spread of neo-liberalism has only hastened, puts in question one of the core organising concepts not only of the NCPE but of the whole modern era: the coherence of national "societies," territorially-rooted entities whose boundaries coincide with those of the nation state. Analyses of the formation of nation states, moreover, remind us that other ways of organising space—empires and networks of city states—co-existed with the nation-state form until (and even after) the postwar period.[26] The nation state thus by no means represents the final form of political evolution.

This does not mean that we have to fall back into the icy void of world systems theory: the world has more depth than a global network of economic power extending from the centre(s) to the periphery. To problematise the coherence and durability of national societies and states, however, does call for new ways of thinking about the way that social space is organised and reorganised over time. One of the most promising images is offered by geographer Edward Soja, who suggests that

> the intelligible lifeworld...is always and everywhere comprised of a multilayered system of socially created nodal regions, *a configuration of differentiated and hierarchically organized locales.... The topological structure is mutable and permutable*, but it is always there to envelope and comprise, to situate and constitute all human action, to concretize the making of both history and geography.[27]

Soja's notion of a mutable hierarchy of nested locales—from the home and workplace through the city, region and nation state to the earth as a whole—can be used to situate the changing place of the nation state within this hierarchy. It also helps to open up new strategic horizons by rendering visible the multiplicity of sites of action that have simultaneously to be considered, especially in periods like the present when the old hierarchy is breaking down and the relation among these sites has become much more fluid. Loxley takes up the question of the formation of relatively closed regional blocs. From this perspective, the Canada-U.S. Free Trade Agreement is but the first step toward the constitution of a continental proto-state of the sort which seems to be forming in Western Europe. Loxley takes issue with this, however, arguing that powerful counter-tendencies are likely to result in significant cross-regional connections. The nation state will remain an important factor although there is little to indicate that national policies will be deployed in such a way as to counter the forces behind globalization.

Friedmann takes a more historical approach, tracing the changing forms of inter-state and market relations from the free trade era (1846-1870) to the present. For her, the globalization of capital does not mean the death of the nation state. An alternative is the formation of "transnational states" which would involve the restructuring of state apparatuses such that those ministries with the closest links to supra/international institutions, would be systematically favoured relative to those parts of the national state apparatus with closer links to domestic forces. Another is the subordination of national states to supra-national units continental in scope. While Friedmann focuses on the restructuring of space from "above" the nation state, her preferred alternative would give greatest weight to sub-national sites based on, and geared to the development of, regional economies much smaller in scale than the typical Canadian province.

There is also a strong strand in the literature on post-Fordism that would link the new importance of micro-regional sites of intervention, the impact of the crisis on the nation state and the emergent logic of production. It is argued that regions can indeed become critical sites for nurturing a progressive variant of post-Fordism. Yet, as Andrew, Houle and Thériault argue, federal and provincial interest in fostering local "networks of innovation" is as much connected with neo-liberal desires to off-load responsibilities as it is with any interest in creating new industrial capacity. That neo-liberalism is one of the forces behind decentralization in Canada does not mean that Friedmann's preferred scenario (a new relation between the local, national, continental and global, in which the local is the core unit) is impossible to realise, for, as Andrew *et al.* suggest, crises *are* moments of openness and opportunity for the Left as well as the Right. Nevertheless, for the progressive potential of such moves toward decentralization to be realised, new relations among the levels of government need to be worked out. In other words, progressive forces need to devise strategies that recognise the new potential for democratic planning at the local level without losing sight of the fact that the extent of local gains will be severely circumscribed in the absence of a fundamental challenge to the existing "global hierarchy of nested locales."

Cities, in other words, continue to exist within a political universe still structured by national (and, in Canada's case, provincial) states. The latter not only affect the potential scope and character of local interventions but can also foster or hinder the transition to post-Fordism in a more direct way. For instance, as Bienefeld's analysis suggests, the fate of potential "industrial districts" is contingent upon the capacity and willingness of nation-states to establish a monetary environment conducive to bold local initiatives. National policies are also needed to inhibit destructive inter-city competition and to promote regional equality.

Yet neither the Fordist state, with its rigid bureaucratic hierarchies that mirrored social relations in industry, nor the laissez-faire, state celebrated by the neo-liberalism of the eighties, are likely to prove adequate to the task. For Kaplinsky, what is needed is an "enabling state," one capable of fostering those very changes in social relations necessary for making the successful transition to post-Fordism. The state's relation to the realm of production needs to be more direct than that admitted within the Keynesian (or pre-Keynesian) universe, but at the same time it needs to disavow the top-down planning model favoured, albeit in different ways, by the Soviet Union and by certain advanced capitalist states. For Kaplinsky, industrial strategy should be structured as a participative process that sets out the broad arenas for restructuring and identifies an institutional framework within which it can occur. The state also has a particularly important role to play in revamping education and training structures if polarised restructuring is to be avoided.

Training policy has been very much at the centre of Canadian debates. Yet, Albo cautions, it is a mistake for labour and the Left to embrace training as the new panacea. What has to be recognised and confronted is the state's (and business,) reliance on defensive forms of flexibility, centred on wage and cost competition. If the more progressive forms of flexibility associated with the requalification of work are to extend beyond a few islands of high quality production, progressive forces need also to insist on a new version of full employment policy, one which includes a reduction in working hours, as Albo argues. A redefinition of the working day is not only a concrete expression of solidarity with the jobless. It also provides a means for beginning to integrate feminist and ecological concerns into an alternative vision of the future.

The national form of state thus has not become redundant, but what should its relationship be to supra-national institutions, especially the continental structures currently in the making? According to Kaplinsky, the old economies of scale associated with capital's drive beyond the national boundaries continue. While it is the new economies of scope in production that have fed images of flexible specialization and the new industrial district, there remain important economies of scale especially in the areas of research and marketing. Supra-national entities are better placed to facilitate the kind of strategic alliances among large and small capitals thus required than are individual nation states. They may also contribute to providing a framework for "co-operative competition" amongst the micro-regions.[28]

The European Community has gone much farther than other continental entitites toward the creation of a supra-national structure. Ross' assessment of the progressive potential of the European Community, however, is decidedly cautious. The Community has begun to acquire the formal trappings of democracy, although progressive forces are still engaged in a struggle to win responsible government. Thus the goal of really democratising state structures, so that the latter can promote the kind of re-alignment Friedmann favours, remains a distant dream. In addition, Jacques Delors, the President of the European Commission, has pushed the notion of a "social democratic Europe," with rights enshrined in a European social charter. Nevertheless, the most likely outcome of post-Maastricht Europe is neo-liberalism, unless the Left finds a way to establish an organic alliance among progressive forces, old and new. In North America, the prospects seem even dimmer to the extent that the FTA remains an agreement whose implementation will be overseen by state managers and continental capitalists. Certainly, as Williams argues, progressive forces can learn to manoeuvre in the cracks of an "inter-federal" system just as they have had to learn to manoeuvre within the intra-federal system. Here too, however, they can only do so with effect if the "politics of identity" can be translated into the "politics of solidarity." Such solidarity, moreover, can no longer afford to stop at national boundaries but must extend across the continent and beyond.[29]

What these essays suggest is that Canadian political economy's concern with the spatial dimension of development remains as appropriate as ever. Yet from the standpoint of the horizons of political action, the NCPE tended to emphasise the centrality of the national (or provincial) state. In Canada as elsewhere the political map is becoming more complex. Regions, both sub-provincial and continental, seem to be gaining a new importance. This does not mean that the national and provincial states are no longer important sites, but they need to be located in the changing hierarchy of nested locales.

The chapters of this book do not pretend to provide a set of ready-made answers to the challenges Canadian political economists have to confront in these "interesting" times. They do, however, aim to contribute to the process of rethinking that has been going on for over a decade. In general, they agree that the older concepts—class, nation, state and dependency—continue to offer insight because they illuminate social relations which remain important. At the same time, the tradition is in need of renewal: things have changed since the NCPE was formed and the conception of the world which organised the way it combined class, nation, and state to explain—and to contribute to the transformation of—reality is no longer adequate.

Three theses, outlined in this introduction, will be explored in the pages of this book. First, post-Fordism is a concept that helps us to think critically about the reorganization of production that is occurring. It alerts us to certain regressive tendencies while at the same time rendering visible the outlines of a viable, non-utopian, strategy that could contribute to unity among progressive forces. Second, class remains an important social relation and workers and their organizations form a critical component of any progressive alliance. Yet there are a multiplicity of relations of oppression, and the movements that spring up to challenge these cannot be reduced to mere appendages. The ideas they give voice to have to be woven into the core problematic if the politics of identity is to produce a politics of solidarity rather than a return to liberal pluralism. Third, the nation state is not dead but strategic horizons have to be expanded to render visible other layers of action. We have to be aware of changes occuring at all levels and the ways in which such changes could be used to democratise politics.

ENDNOTES

I would like to thank Greg Albo, Amy Bartholomew, Jane Jenson, Anne Showstack Sassoon, Donald Swartz, Rob Ryan and Rosemary Warskett for their comments on an earlier draft of this chapter.

1.   It is called the "new" Canadian political economy because it succeeded in establishing a creative dialogue between the theoretical innovations of the late 1960s and early 1970s and the critical tradition developed in the formative years of the postwar order by intellectuals like Harold Innis, Donald Creighton, Vernon Fowke, Stanley Ryerson, C.B. Macpherson and H.C. Pentland.

2.   It is fair to argue that a feminist political economy grew up *alongside*, rather than as part of, the NCPE, despite their common origins in the New Left. See below for a brief discussion of this and other lacunae.

3.   For an overview of these classic works and their influence on the NCPE see Wallace Clement and Glen Williams (eds.), *The New Canadian Political Economy* (Montreal: McGill-Queen's, 1989), pp. 7-11.

4.   See, for example, John Richards and Larry Pratt, *Prairie Capitalism: Power and Influence in the New West* (Toronto: McClelland and Stewart, 1979).

5.   The first major collection of the work of the Atlantic wing of the school was Robert Brym and James Sacouman (eds.), *Underdevelopment and Social Movements in Atlantic Canada* (Toronto: New Hogtown Press, 1979). Several articles addressed the politics of Atlantic underdevelopment, notably the failure of petty commodity producers there to produce a party equivalent to the western farmers' protest parties.

6.   Essays by Québécois political economists appeared in books such as Gary Teeple's edited NCPE classic, *Capitalism and the National Question in Canada* (Toronto: University of Toronto Press, 1972) as well as in the early issues of *SPE*. The journal published translations of certain articles which originally appeared in *Cahiers du Socialisme* and vice versa.

7.   For overviews of these debates see Rianne Mahon, *The Politics of Industrial Restructuring: Canadian Textiles* (Toronto: University of Toronto Press, 1984) and William Carroll, *Corporate Power and Canadian Capitalism* (Vancouver, UBC Press, 1986).

8.   Labour historians were more influenced by E.P. Thompson's richly detailed history of the "making" of the English working class. See, for example, G.S. Kealey, *Toronto Workers Respond to Industrial Capitalism* (Toronto: University of Toronto Press, 1980) and Bryan Palmer, *Working Class Experience: The Rise and Constitution of Canadian Labour* (Toronto:

Butterworth, 1983). Unfortunately, because the labour historians so quickly rejected the NCPE's core problematic, the latter remained largely indifferent to the important question of class formation in a context of regional and ethnic diversity, although Janine Brodie and Jane Jenson, *Crisis, Challenge and Change: Party and Class in Canada* (Toronto: Methuen, 1980) is an exception in this regard.

9.   See, *inter alia*, L.V. Panitch, "Dependency and Class in Canadian Political Economy," *Studies in Political Economy* 6 (Autumn 1981).

10.   See L.V. Panitch, "The Role and Nature of the Canadian State" in L.V. Panitch, (ed.), *The Canadian State: Political Economy and Political Power* (Toronto: University of Toronto Press, 1977) for a first overview of debates. For more recent discussions see Gregory Albo and Jane Jenson, "A Contested Concept: The Relative Autonomy of the State" in Clement and Williams, *The New Canadian Political Economy* and David Wolfe, "The Canadian State in Comparative Perspective," *Canadian Review of Sociology and Anthropology*, 26 (1) (February 1989).

11.   See, *inter alia*., Heather Jon Maroney and Meg Luxton (eds.), *Feminism and Political Economy: Women's Work and Women's Struggles* (Toronto: Methuen, 1987); Roberta Hamilton and Michèle Barrett (eds.), *The Politics of Diversity: Feminism, Marxism and Nationalism* (Montreal: Book Centre, 1986); and Pat Armstrong and Patricia Connolly (eds.), *Feminism in Action: Studies in Political Economy* (Toronto: Canadian Scholars' Press, 1993).

12.   Frances Abele and Daiva Stasiulis, "Canada as a 'White Settler Colony': What about Natives and Immigrants?," in Clement and Williams, *The New Canadian Political Economy.*

13.   In other words, while NCPEists shared Marx's commitment to "understanding reality in order to change it" there was a tendency to bend the stick too far in the direction of structural forces and pay too little attention to the question of how the subordinate forces themselves contributed both to reproduction and to change. For a good discussion of this point see Albo and Jenson, "The Relative Autonomy of the State, in Clement and Williams, *The New Canadian Political Economy.*"

14.   For a review of this literature see Rianne Mahon, "From Fordism to ?: New Technology, Labour Markets and Unions," *Economic and Industrial Democracy*, (1987). Of the various approaches, the regulation school has had the most impact on Canadian political economy. In addition to essays in this volume see Gérard Boismenu and Daniel Drache (eds.), *Politique et régulation : Modèle de développement et trajectoire canadienne* (Montreal: Méridien, 1990); Jane Jenson, "'Different' but not 'exceptional': Canada's Permeable Fordism," *Canadian Review of Sociology and Anthropology*, vol 26:1, 1989; and Daniel Drache and Maric Gertler (eds.), *The New Era of Global Competition* (Montreal: McGill-Queen's, 1991).

15.   For an example of one such enthusiastic scenario see Michael Piore and Charles

Sabel, *The Second Industrial Divide* (New York: Basic Books, 1984).

16.   There is some evidence that Canada is entering post-Fordism via this route. See, *inter alia*, the Economic Council of Canada, *Good Jobs: Bad Jobs* (Ottawa: 1990) and Rianne Mahon, "Post-Fordism: Some Issues for Labour," in Drache and Gertler, *The New Era of Global Competition*.

17.   Several authors in this volume, for instance Kaplinsky and Andrew *et al.*, argue that there is room for decentralised growth, promoted at the regional level but the question of how to promote greater inter-regional equality is less often addressed.

18.   For an elaboration this argument see Mahon, "Post-Fordism: Some Issues for Labour," which draws on the work of Danielle Leborgne and Alain Lipietz.

19.   For a discussion of the Pro-Canada Network, later Action Canada, which opposed the FTA see Peter Bleyer, "Coalitions of Social Movements as Agencies for Social Change: The Action Canada Network," in W.K. Carroll (ed.), *Organizing Dissent: Contemporary Social Movements in Theory and Practice* (Toronto: Garamond, 1992).

20.   The debate on how to fit these pieces together has already begun. Each of these is the basis for a distinct element in a popular coalition for Daniel Drache and Duncan Cameron (eds.), *The Other Macdonald Report* (Toronto: Lorimer, 1985). In contrast, the new ideas can be encompassed within a new class politics for L.V. Panitch and Donald Swartz, *The Assault on Trade Union Freedoms* (Toronto: Garamond, 1988). See also the debate in Warren Magnusson and Rob Walker, "De-Centring the State: Political Theory and Canadian Political Economy," *Studies in Political Economy* 26, (1988); Jane Jenson and E. Fuat Keyman, "Must we all be post-modern?," *Studies in Political Economy* 31, (Spring 1990); and Warren Magnusson and Rob Walker, "Socialism and Monotheism: A Reply to Jenson and Keyman," *Studies in Political Economy* 34 (Spring 1991).

21.   This concept comes from the work of feminists, Marxists involved in cultural studies, and theorists of the new social movements. See Jenson in this volume for a more detailed discussion.

22.   See Jenson, "'Different' but not 'exceptional'," in *Canadian Review of Sociology and Anty,* Vol. 26:1 (1989).

23.   On the CAW, see Sam Gindin, "Breaking Away: The Formation of the Canadian Auto Workers," *Studies in Political Economy* 29, (Summer 1989) and Charlotte A.B. Yates, "From Plant to Politics, The Canadian UAW 1936-1984." (Ph.D dissertation, Carleton University, Ottawa, 1988).

24.   Mahon, "Post-Fordism: Some Issues for Labour," in Drache and Gertler, *The New Era of Global Competition*.

25.   See also Jane Jenson and Gilles Breton, "After Free Trade and Meech Lake: Quoi de neuf?," *Studies in Political Economy* 34, (Spring 1991).

26. For example, Charles Tilly, *Coercion, Capital and European States, AD 990-1992* (Oxford: Blackwell, 1992).

27. Edward Soja, *Post-Modern Geography* (Berkeley: University of California, 1989), p. 148; emphasis added.

28. It can be argued that supra-national entities may be more favourably disposed to micro-regions in that they see the latter as a means of circumventing national states and establishing a more direct connection to the people.

29. This is actually beginning to happen in North America. Thus Common Frontiers, a coalition that includes many of the forces grouped under the Action Canada banner, is explicitly oriented to making such links with progressive forces in Mexico and the United States. There are also the beginnings of a discussion of the notion of a "social charter" for North America. See, for instance, *CUPE Facts* 13:1, 1991.

PART
I

Post-Fordist Production: Threat and Promise

	CHAPTER 2
POST-FORDIST INDUSTRIAL RESTRUCTURING: SOME POLICY IMPLICATIONS	RAPHAEL KAPLINSKY

INTRODUCTION

This chapter considers the policy challenge of restructuring the industrial sector to accomplish the transition from the Fordist to the post-Fordist mode of accumulation.[1] I shall argue that in order to move to new international best practice, restructuring is required at three levels: the micro (enterprise), the meso (the region and the sector) and the macro (national).[2] There is no unique path to post-Fordist restructuring. Individual countries, regions, sectors and firms find themselves in different circumstances and their policy responses will reflect—and reinforce—their particular constellations of power relations. Thus, the restructuring response is simultaneously both a normative and positive issue.

The chapter addresses these issues as if the only policy challenge is that involved in epochal transition and as if there is a binary opposition between two distinct types of production system. Both of these assumptions are problematic. Clearly, many of the social, economic and political problems of the past four decades do not have their roots in the degradation of the Fordist mode of accumulation. It is equally evident that many elements of post-Fordist production were prefigured in Fordist structures just as post-Fordism can coexist with features remaining from Fordist organization and technology. This said, I believe that it is heuristically valuable to proceed on the basis of these assumptions since I have little doubt that a substantive structural change has occurred in the ground rules of accumulation. Too much stress on caveats might easily lead to a dulled strategic vision. For this reason readers are asked to overlook what might at times seem oversimplification.

Industrial accumulation is best seen as occurring in epochs, each of which is characterised by a close fit between social and technical relations, referred to variously as socio-techno systems or production systems.[3] Transition between epochs thus requires restructuring in both the social and technical domains, although historically there is no "rule of primacy" between them.[4]

I shall argue that we are currently witnessing such a transition in production systems. This transition has been linked to the discussion of long-waves, to the shift from mass production to flexible specialization, and to the transition from machinofacture to systemofacture.[5] Each of these approaches offers particular insights and provides manifold opportunities for academic (and, more likely, polemical) debate. Nevertheless, I believe that it is more productive to focus on their similarities, which lie in their recognition of epochal change involving both technical and social relations. Hence a broad characterization of epochal change will be adopted in this paper, distinguishing between the Fordist and post-Fordist mode of accumulation.

Four major systemic differences between the two epochs inform this analysis. First, Fordist production focuses upon reaping the benefits of scale, and involves the production of standardised products by dedicated machinery in an hierarchically and functionally specialised labour process.[6] In contrast, post-Fordist production places the emphasis on *flexibility*—of product, of work, of machinery and of production scheduling. Associated with this transition from standardization to flexibility is the *altered nature of competition*. In Fordism it is primarily price which determines competitiveness; in post-Fordism, innovation and product characteristics are to the forefront.[7] A third difference between these two epochs relates to the general relationship between what might be called "the parts and the whole." In Fordism, optimization takes place at the level of the individual machine, the individual firm and the individual worker. In post-Fordism it is the *systemic* interlinkage between groups of individual units which assumes primary importance. The fourth and final contrasting feature concerns *the role of labour.* In the epoch of price-competition the primary focus on labour lay in relation to its cost of production, which had to be minimised. By contrast, in the new epoch, labour is primarily seen as a resource whose potential has to be maximised.

Common experience suggests that the market has proven a poor disseminator of these elements of restructuring and that there is a key role to be played by an enabling state, especially in helping to restructure social relations. These changes in attitudes and organization have been particularly difficult to command. This poses problems as they, rather than new production technologies, appear to be the primary initial requirement for epochal change. However, as will be discussed below, there is more than one route to post-Fordism and the nature of the social change which results will be affected by important political struggles. These clearly affect the distribution of the rewards arising from industrial restructuring.

Discussion of these issues will take the following form. The next section addresses the restructuring responses arising at the micro level. This is followed by a discussion of changes at the meso level and the macro level. The chapter concludes with a brief evaluation of the major policy conclusions which arise for an industrially advanced country (IAC) such as Canada.

My intent is to provide an overall outline of the issues involved in industrial restructuring. Consequently the discussion is wide-ranging and individual issues can only be sketched in broad outline. Therefore, references are provided for more detailed consideration.

RESTRUCTURING AT THE MICRO LEVEL[8]

Awareness at the corporate level of the need to restructure has been driven less by the erosion of profit rates (which were in fact buoyant in many IACs during the 1980s) than by the loss of market share. Market share is an important strategic objective since it provides the opportunity to spread the growing indirect costs of production over larger sales. Across a range of sectors, firms in the old industrial centre have confronted the loss of market position to firms which have adopted many features of post-Fordist production. This phenomenon has been most clearly documented for firms in the United States. For example, between 1962 and 1979 its global share of markets fell from 23 to 14 percent for motor vehicles, 71 to 58 percent for aircraft, 29 to 12 percent for telecommunications, 33 to 22 percent for metal working machinery, 40 to 23 percent for agricultural machinery, 21 to 14 percent for hand- and machine-tools, 16 to seven percent for textile and leather machinery, and 35 to 12 percent for railway vehicles.[9]

The initial response of most firms was to introduce new technology. But repeated experience across a number of sectors has shown that the introduction of new technology alone does not ensure competitive positioning. The global automobile industry provides a telling example of this response.[10] Between 1969 and 1981, the Japanese share of the U.S. market rose from three to 23 percent. Faced with this growing import penetration, the U.S. industry commissioned comparative studies which showed higher output/capital and output/labour ratios in Japanese firms. This was consistent with their notion that the Japanese had introduced a higher level of automation, so the U.S. firms responded with a heavy program of capital investment—over $50bn between 1975 and 1984—in new automation technologies. Despite this large and sustained investment, the share of the market accounted for by imports from Japan rose from nine to 18 percent over the same time period. Further market penetration by the Japanese was only limited by the restrictions imposed on Japanese exports to the U.S.

A series of detailed studies were thus undertaken to compare performance at the corporate level. Almost without exception they concluded that: (a) by the early 1980s the Japanese industry was less mechanised than its American and European competitors; (b) its primary competitive advantage arose from changes in labour process, inter-firm linkages and factory organization; and (c) having concentrated in the first instance on these organizational changes, the Japanese were proceeding with the very rapid diffusion of new flexible automation technology. These studies for autos were replicated in a series of other sectors, each of which concluded that organizational restructuring was of primary importance, and that only after this was completed could advantage be taken of the new electronics-based automation technologies.[11] This inability to achieve competitiveness through the introduction of new technology makes it apparent that there is a transition between production systems.

With the lessons of these various empirical studies in mind, it is possible to distinguish three areas in which corporate restructuring is required in the transition to post-Fordism: the adoption of computer integrated manufacturing (CIM); the introduction of a new labour process and factory layout; and the development of new inter-firm relationships. Each of these areas of restructuring is briefly considered, beginning with the introduction of CIM, not because it is the first and most important element, but because it is often perceived as being an adequate competitive response on its own. My concern in describing this flexible technology is limited to showing that its successful introduction is associated with a change in production organization and philosophy. This places the emphasis on the technology's systemic capability, its contribution to flexible production and its link with product innovation.

THE ADOPTION OF CIM[12] *Computer Integrated Manufacturing*

The recounting of epochal change offered by the long-wave theorists is insightful in helping to understand the key potential role to be played by CIM in post-Fordist accumulation. They identify the importance of what they call *"heartland technologies,"* those which are of sufficient import to alter the trajectory of technological change and the balance of accumulation. For a technology to fulfil this key role it must have pervasive applications, be clearly seen to have descending costs, and be in practically unlimited supply. Historically, key technologies have been textiles, steel, railroads and the internal combustion engine. Most recently the role of the heartland technology has been played by electronics.

The importance of electronics-based automation technologies can best be gauged in relation to previous phases of mechanization. The development of modern industry saw the mechanization of manufacturing in which the tool was manipulated by machines rather than human beings. In most cases this involved more rapid, regular and accurate transformation of materials. Towards the end of the nineteenth century the next major development was the mechanization of transfer, that is the carriage of work-in-progress between work-stations. In the third phase of mechanization automated controls were introduced, beginning in the 1920s with electrical relays. These various developments provided for a high level of labour productivity in plants ideally geared to producing standardised products—often referred to as "hard automation."

Electronic controls first entered the production process in the 1960s and 1970s with the advent of numerical controls and then computer numerical controls for machine tools.[13] Other important areas of production—design and co-ordination—had barely encountered mechanization and it was only with the development and diffusion of computers, utilized in activities such as stock and wage-control and design, that improvements to traditional methods began to spread. Diffusion proceeded rapidly so that by the mid-1980s electronic control mechanisms were widely used in all areas.

This widespread diffusion of electronic control mechanisms provides the potential for reaping a number of competitive advantages. They provide for systemic gains so that the operations of different electronically-controlled machines can be easily linked. For example, machine-tools can be automatically and precisely programed by design equipment; designs can be translated into parts-lists or production schedules without human or paper-based intervention. A second competitive attribute offered by these technologies is the flexibility arising from their programmability and their systemic interlinking. With electronic controls, machine-resetting is much more rapid and precise than with electro-mechanical or manual controls and can be rapidly extended to a number of linked machines. This reduces the costs of producing a diversified range of products. Third, the application of computers to design significantly enhances the ability to introduce new products—or variations of existing products—with shorter leadtimes. As we have seen, product competition is one of the defining characteristics of post-Fordist accumulation. Fourth, CIM—especially when electronically controlled machines are linked together—often enhances labour productivity. And, finally, the precision in their controls means that the quality of their products is often much higher than that produced with electro-mechanically controlled equipment.

In each of these cases effective utilization of flexible automation technology promotes a different mode of competitive response, but requires prior changes in organization and operating procedure. This conclusion emerges most clearly from a series of recent studies on the diffusion of flexible manufacturing systems which found that unless prior organizational change was undertaken, few competitive benefits were achieved through flexible automation.[14]

The Adoption of a New Labour Process[15]

The Fordist labour process was forged over a long period with its origins in the first factories described by Adam Smith. Its operations can be reduced to four principles. The first saw the increasing division of labour and specialization of tasks. As this proceeded, it became clear that further profit was to be obtained through the separation of skilled from unskilled workers. The existence of the reserve army of labour meant the costs of labour could be reduced, both by paying lower wages for the unskilled content of work and by exercising greater control. Labour turnover thus became a central component of the Fordist labour process.

The second element in this evolving labour process was the application of Taylor's principles of scientific management. Management had to absorb and codify the traditional skills of workers and to reduce these to rules; conception ("brain-work") was removed from the shop-floor and lodged with management; direct and indirect tasks (such as quality-control, machine set-up and maintenance) were separated; and this schema was implemented by a stratified managerial taskforce. In the early 20th century the introduction of dedicated machinery in a moving transfer line allowed for the further consolidation of managerial control. Large stocks of inventories acted as a buffer—the "just-in-case" philosophy—to ensure the uninterrupted operation of the production line. The final element of this Fordist labour process saw the translation of these four principles to the global level. Firms used "world factories" to produce "world products" for "world markets." It was a highly stratified system at all levels—authority was paramount and information flowed from top to bottom at the global level.[16]

As the postwar Golden Age began to run out of steam in the late 1960s and productivity growth began both to slow and to become more uneven, it was within this Fordist labour process that the degradation of the production epoch was becoming most evident. Shopfloor capital-management relations were riven with conflict while work-stoppages and absenteeism became widespread; defect rates were high, despite the mushrooming of quality control departments to rectify complex products after final manufacture; the growth of indirect labour was eroding productivity gains in direct labour; innovation was poor, product leadtimes were growing longer and raw materials were taking months to pass through manufacturing processes. Compounding matters was the fact that ever-larger scale factories were producing homogeneous products either in numbers too large for markets, or too unattractive for consumers who were more discerning of quality and more desirous of individual variety.

It is in this context that the rise of a post-Fordist labour process must be seen. Of course there is no single post-Fordist labour process and there are important differences between national systems and between firms. Nevertheless common responses are emerging which suggest an overturning of Fordist principles of work organization. In Japan, the driving force for change was the concern with inventory reduction and with the need to produce more flexibly to satisfy an increasingly varied and discerning final market.

In the case of flexible production, the need to change the composition of output required the resetting of machinery. The time involved in this had to be cut in order to reduce the costs of changeover. For this to occur, the single-tasking of work and the single-skilling of workers had to give way to multi-tasking and multi-skilling. These changing work practices significantly reduced the costs of flexibility but such savings could only be achieved through major changes in attitude and work practices. In many countries they also necessitated changes in industrial relations, with new unions supplanting the inherited unions of Fordist production, in part because inter-union rivalry impeded flexible work practices.

The requirement for lower inventories—"just in time" production—means that there are no buffer stocks to cushion the production line "just in case" anything goes wrong. Hence quality-at-source assumes critical importance. Three important and related conclusions follow from this. First, labour can no longer be treated in an authoritarian manner. Its co-operation is essential, because with low inventories it has an enhanced power to disrupt production and also because direct operatives assume responsibility for quality control. Second, Taylor's schema saw the separation of direct and indirect tasks as being desirable; in post-Fordist production multi-skilling and multi-tasking makes this unnecessary and, indeed, undesirable. Finally, and perhaps most significantly, the labour force has come to be an important source of innovation, an essential element in competition. The Japanese firms' ability to harness this source of technical change—in a process of *kaizen* (continuous improvement)—has proved to be an especially significant source of innovation in recent years.

Thus the basic politics of production are altered and this is especially significant with respect to capital's attitude to labour. In Fordism, management's prime requirement was to sustain its dominance over the labour force. Now, while management finds it necessary to exercise control over production, this can only be achieved with the active co-operation of its labour force. This has important implications for labour, since there are elements within the post-Fordist labour process which inherently enhance the quality of work and other elements which inherently empower labour. Moreover, investment by capital in a multi-skilled labour force able to contribute actively to innovation means that labour turnover is likely to be lower, with labour increasingly seen as a fixed cost of production.[17]

THE DEVELOPMENT OF NEW INTER-FIRM RELATIONS[18]

The principles of separation and specialization are also reflected in the pattern of inter-firm relations which developed during Fordism. The innovations of Alfred Sloan in the 1920s enshrined the division of labour within the firm, as well as between firms. Arms-length negotiations were pursued and suppliers were held at bay to ensure acquisition of the lowest-cost components. In general this meant dual-sourcing, playing off different suppliers against each other, and short-term contracts.

Chandler illustrates the benefits reaped by the expanding multinational producers from this rationalization of inter-firm relations.[19] It facilitated the capturing of scale economies and global markets and, for a time, provided low-cost inputs. But with time, this climate of inter-firm hostility proved to be increasingly dysfunctional, giving way to various forms of closer inter-firm links.

A number of factors explain the atrophy of the old pattern. The specialization of tasks in arm's length relationships slowed down innovation. Design and production changes at each stage of the production chain required the prior completion of changes in the previous link. By contrast, simultaneous and coordinated innovation in different parts of the chain proved to be much more rapid, and much more flexible. The transition to networking and close cooperation between firms is also mirrored in the merging of the various stages of design within firms, which is proving to be a necessary requirement to shorten product leadtime.[20] Both these developments are referred to as a process of "simultaneous engineering."

Associated with the part which close inter-firm links play in speeding up innovation is their role in improving the quality of innovation. Many modern production products and processes are becoming so complex that no single firm can hope to cover the spectrum of required capabilities. Increasingly, final assemblers are seeing themselves as sub-system integrators. But for this to be effective, close co-operation is required between different units so that the various components of the system fit together with maximum synergy. The importance of this inter-firm collaboration is especially evident in the automobile sector.

Closer inter-firm (and inter-affiliate) linkages are a necessary component of just-in-time production, which works optimally when deliveries are made to the factory floor itself, "just in time" for incorporation in assembly. In Toyota's case, for example, most component suppliers are located within Toyota City and deliver at regular intervals—sometimes up to sixteen times a day, one hour before use. Working to such tight delivery schedules obviously requires close co-ordination in production scheduling. However, there is little point in reducing raw material stocks if the burden is instead pushed on to the supplier.[21]

Just-in-time production also necessitates closer inter-firm and inter-affiliate linkages to ensure a zero-defect component supply. As described above, the introduction of a low-inventory strategy requires a quality-at-source program.

This not only encompasses worker responsibility within the plant, but also a predictable performance by component suppliers. It is not merely quality which is important; incoming goods also have to be packed in predictable numbers in specially-designed containers.[22] Ensuring this level of supplier predictability involves close interaction along the production chain. Typically, Japanese enterprises and those following Japanese practices monitor input-quality on a 100 percent basis for the first few months. If performance is acceptable, they then progressively reduce the proportion of incoming components checked. Only after acceptable quality levels are attained for a defined period are these audits removed. However, and perhaps more importantly, the auditing of component-quality is only part of the total quality program. When defects are found, engineers are sent to component suppliers to analyse the source of the defects, and through interaction with the suppliers' technical staff, to correct them.

In the face of these various pressures for change, inter-firm and inter-affiliate linkages have begun to alter. The number of component suppliers is being reduced; production schedules are closely co-ordinated to ensure inventory-reduction throughout the productive chain; long-term relationships (instead of two-year competitive bidding) are being forged between suppliers and assemblers; quality, predictability and innovative capability are becoming more important than price in choosing suppliers; a cross-flow of design engineers is being promoted to speed up and improve the innovative process; and assemblers are actively assisting suppliers with quality and process technology. For all these reasons the relationship between various production units in the vertical chain of production has become much closer. This co-operation takes various forms. In some cases (such as the Western European and North American electronics and automobile sectors) this involves more intimate links between independent firms. While this is clearly an improvement on past practice, problems of trust and confidentiality remain. Japanese practice is to develop groups of subcontractors tied together by cross-equity links. In the auto industry, both Toyota and Nissan have developed two networked "subcontracting systems." Each of these contains various tiers, and in general each tier is responsible for networking with the level immediately above and below itself.

Such a system of interlinkage between firms seems to have functioned very effectively in recent years. But as technology has become more complex, the dangers inherent in close interdependence have become more acute. Many Japanese firms are thus actively exploring a loosening of historic ties, although there is no question of them moving to the arms-length distancing of Fordism.

The discussion of inter-firm linkages has so far focussed on the vertical chain of production and on networking systems in which large firms are dominant. This pattern is not the only alternative. The development of horizontal linkages between small firms has proved especially fruitful in Northern Italy and other industrial districts in Europe, a process often referred to as flexible specialization.[23] Close collaboration between small firms has occurred, especially in the sharing of indirect costs of production. These include activities such as design intelligence and marketing which are firm, rather than plant-scaled. In some cases, as in the garment industry, small firms also share expensive capital equipment for computer aided design and grading, for example. Such collaboration allows these small firms to retain the flexibility arising from their size without sacrificing the advantages of knowledge intensity which arises from indirect investments in production.

RESTRUCTURING AT THE MESO LEVEL

There are a range of restructuring issues which are relevant at the meso level, but because many of these are relatively new phenomena there is no existing power base which has a vested interest in bringing them to the fore. Thus in many countries a regional power vacuum is in danger of creating a regional industrial vacuum.

Regional-level industrial development is not a new issue in economic thought. Renewed concern about it as a policy issue follows from the globalization of production in Fordism, in which optimum location was seen to arise from the pursuit of scale economies in dispersed "world factories," rather than through clusters of proximate enterprises. The renewed importance of industrial districts—and, hence, a program of intervention by the regional state— arises from the demonstrated success of these agglomerations in various countries. In Europe, Italian industry has flourished during the 1980s. This success rests on an uneasy balance between five very large corporations acting at the national and transnational level (the Fiat Group alone accounts for around four percent of Italy's GDP) and a mass of small-sized firms acting at the local level. This latter segment of industry has made Italy the world's largest net exporter in a series of traditional industries such as garments, shoes and furniture. It has also played an influential role in metal-working and food-processing. Most of these small firms produce in agglomerations which are focussed at the regional level—the Emilia Romagna area has been especially important. In Germany regional industrial development has flourished in Baden-Würtemburg. In the

U.K., the M4 corridor between London and Bristol has become a focus for the information industry. In the U.S., Route 128 around Boston and Silicon Valley south of San Francisco have at various times displayed similar characteristics. In Spain, regional agglomerations are to be found around Barcelona and in Valencia. Even in Japan it is argued that district-level agglomeration economies have been one of the major factors explaining rapid industrial growth.[24] The phenomenon is not confined to the modern sector, nor to the industrially advanced countries. Experience with the informal sector in both Kenya and Ghana shows a similar pattern of clustering.[25]

Three major factors relevant to post-Fordist competitiveness account for the growing importance of regional industrial development. The first arises from the locational logic of just-in-time production. Here there is an inherent advantage in proximity—it makes little sense to reduce intra-plant inventories and then to find that inter-plant inventories stretch to weeks, and sometimes even to months. A second factor is especially relevant in high-precision industries. In sectors characterised by one-off or small batch production and in sectors with many bought-in components and sub-assemblies, proximity to suppliers plays an important role in attaining competitiveness. Proximity to final consumers is a further factor explaining the rise of industrial districts. This has become especially important as the final markets have become less price-sensitive and more product-sensitive. Allied to the move towards reduced inventories, this has placed a premium on locating production near final markets rather than at the site of lowest labour costs. However, the policy environment is seldom geared to maximising these local-level linkages. An exception is Italy, where the Left-dominated municipalities have produced a legislative regime encouraging the formation of *consorzia*.[26] These provide assistance and financial incentives which promote the sharing of indirect costs (such as design and marketing) described earlier. There are, however, a range of other potential interventions—including networking between industrial districts in different countries—which remain to be explored.[27] But for these to emerge, a political basis of regional power, including the ability to allocate resources, will be required.

Another element of meso restructuring operates at the sectoral level. Many constraints and opportunities at the enterprise level are common to those faced by other enterprises operating in the same sector. Because of this it is often most effective to group specific restructuring interventions at this meso tier of activity, especially when production occurs within small firms.[28] Thus in Northern Italy, the *consorzia* jointly share the costs of design intelligence, marketing, training, finance and often also minimum-scale equipment.

A similar pattern of sectoral specialization is observed in the Japanese machine-tool sector.[29]

As both the Italian and Japanese experiences with small firms have shown, while a program designed to promote post-Fordist restructuring will require attention to both the regional and sectoral levels of accumulation, these often are conflated in a common package of policies. This is because industrial districts are most often composed of firms operating in the same sector.

RESTRUCTURING AT THE MACRO LEVEL

Although real resource allocation occurs at the corporate and district levels, it is at the macro level where interventions have to be rationalised, since this is the locus of state power and the arena in which state-controlled resources are allocated. Interventions at the macro level are relevant not only because of the central state's control over budgetary appropriation and expenditure, but also because there are a variety of policy issues which are best tackled at the centre rather than at the level of the firm or local government.

The first and most important point to make concerns the role of the market in epochal transition, since it is sometimes argued that, if post-Fordism is really so much more efficient, the new practices and technologies will diffuse most rapidly if left to a smoothly functioning market. Within the literature on technical change it is widely accepted that capitalist markets are imperfect allocators of resources with respect to technical change.[30] This is because technology is a public good and is hence inherently difficult to appropriate. In respect to epochal change, the inadequacy of market allocation is even more marked. Added to the problem of technical change are the social barriers to diffusion of new attitudes and work practices. There is widespread evidence that such barriers are the major impediment to change. An example is the difficulty of diffusion of quality-at-source managerial practices.[31]

Since market failure is endemic to technical change in general, and to epochal change in particular, this suggests there is a critical role for an enabling state. Obviously, not all state interventions are conducive to industrial restructuring. But the experience of those countries and regions which have made a successful transition to post-Fordism suggests that an enabling state is clearly a necessary requirement for restructuring.

Here the discussion is confined to those areas which are relevant to the new production system so that areas of policy which are relevant to all industrial strategy—for example, a sectoral focus, support for research and development and industrial training—are taken as given. The discussion which follows is problematic since many of the keys for moving successfully to post-Fordism require altered social relations. These are difficult to address. Policy discussions of habituation, the work relation, and corporate strategies are not only inherently intangible, but also make uneasy bedfellows. But this situation only emphasizes the difficulties involved in the transition between production systems.

One of the major problems in the development of successful policies is that the state apparatus is itself often an extreme example of Fordist organization, with layered hierarchies, top-down flows of information, much centralization and structured inflexibility. Thus it is questionable how significant a role the state can play in promoting industrial reorganization if it does not address its own internal organization.[32]

The state needs to adjust.

THE SOCIAL CONSTRUCTION OF WORK

The social construction of work (referred to by Burawoy and others as "habituation") in Fordism was premised on a particular pattern of power relations on the shopfloor.[33] It was one in which, having applied the precepts of Taylor, managerial authority was crucial. Workers were expected to do as they were told; managers were expected to govern. Henry Ford II believed that "[t]he average worker wants a job in which he does not have to put in much physical effort. Above all, he wants a job in which he does not have to think."[34] In terms of production culture, the line-worker was ascribed a reactive rather than a proactive role. Indirect labour was given the task of exercising control over production, although even here its domain of intervention was heavily limited by senior management. Furthermore, as observed earlier, the separation of skills meant that wages could be kept low, as long as the reserve army of labour could be tapped and labour turnover was an important part of the social construction of work.

By contrast, the post-Fordist labour process necessarily sees its multi-tasking and multi-skilled labour force as a resource whose potential has to be maximised, rather than a cost which has to be minimised. Far from labour turnover being a desirable systemic attribute, the emphasis is placed on continuity and commitment. Clearly this requires fundamental attitudinal changes by the whole workforce. Perhaps more important is the manner in which the workforce's proactive participation in the labour process is mediated. As we have seen, both quality-at-source and innovation require that detailed line workers initiate interventions in the process of production. But how is management to give workers the right and the power to intervene in production without these being "abused"?

The answer lies in a work relation which is not seen as one of conflict, but one of accommodation and co-operation. Consider, for example, the role of the *Andon lights* in Toyota's assembly plants. This is a system whereby each worker has the power to communicate progress to management: a green light means all is well, an orange light means that the worker is under pressure, and a red light indicates that the worker cannot cope, or has spotted a defect in the manufacturing process. When the red light goes on, the whole production line comes to a halt. Management's objective is to have the whole plant lit with orange lights, that is, maximum pressure without any interruption to production. Yet despite this pressure, it is very unusual for labour actually to bring the line to a halt.

There are particular features of this Japanese system which suggest the feudal roots of this social construction of work.[35] Yet, as will be suggested below, this is not the only path to a post-Fordist labour process. Other patterns of work relation, more in tune with the Western European tradition of social democracy, are beginning to emerge. Whichever form emerges, the state has a role to play, perhaps within tripartite negotiations, in the redefinition of capital-labour relations on the shopfloor; there is widespread evidence of the failure of both organised labour and management to appreciate the significance of the changes which are required.

This redefinition of the work relation cannot be confined to the shopfloor alone. There is an important interaction between social relations at the point of production and those in the wider social sphere, including between the core and peripheral segments of the labour force.[36] It is important to bear in mind that there is no unique set of policy prescriptions which can be laid out for all states. The reconstruction of the work relation will necessarily reflect individual firm, regional and state trajectories as well as those of organised labour. But within this political process, there is some room for autonomous state intervention.

CORPORATE RESTRUCTURING STRATEGIES

Another important set of attitudes which require change in the transition from Fordism to post-Fordism is the strategic perspective of management. In North America and large parts of Western Europe, "best-practice management" has been concerned with volume rather than quality, with supply—rather than demand-imperatives; with scale economies rather than flexibility; and, in their links with other firms, with arm's-length relationships and conflict rather than co-ordination and co-operation. These are no longer optimal in a post-Fordist world, and require reorientation if the conditions of best-practice are to be met.

Corporate strategic attitudes are not easily adjusted, and within this the state can only play a limited role. But there are nevertheless steps which it can take that are conducive to promoting the necessary changes. To be effective, the state's role has to be proactive and it should initiate discussions (including with organised labour), seminars, demonstrations and a process of "learning-by-visiting."[37] As will be discussed below, changes are also required in the incentive and banking system if the restructuring is to proceed effectively.

TRADE POLICIES[38]

The transition to post-Fordism has particular implications for comparative advantage and trade. The emphasis given to product flexibility and innovation suggests a strategy of developing niches in market positioning; the required investment in labour, systems and CIM entails heavy expenditure. Thus comparative advantage implies the search for what might loosely be called "technological rents," and in many countries this represents a departure from previous eras of specialization in resource-based sectors or in systems designed to achieve price-competitiveness in commodity markets. This is not confined to the choice between sectors but also within sectors. For example, as the Italian garment and the German kitchen furniture industries have shown to their benefit (and to the detriment of their British rivals), post-Fordist industry trajectories have proved critical to sustaining international comparative advantage.

This reorientation of production has a number of implications for trade policy which might not be immediately obvious. Trade policies are simultaneously becoming more important and more complex. On the one hand, the necessity of producing for global markets continues as growing indirect costs of production (such as R&D and marketing) must be spread over a large market. Similarly, in many sectors (as the Japanese and Korean semiconductor industries have found) the rising fixed costs of production also require international markets for production scale economies to be met. Moreover, there is abundant evidence that "learning-by-exporting" is an important tool for acquiring technological capabilities.[39]

On the other hand, market access is becoming increasingly problematic (as a consequence of the transition to post-Fordism). This epochal change is an inherently uneven process. Differentials in productivity growth have become accentuated and trade imbalances have become endemic, with Japan, West Germany, Korea and Taiwan in structural surplus, and the U.S., the U.K., Canada, Eastern Europe and most of the Third World being in structural deficit. This leads to a more complex international trading environment. The post-Bretton Woods trading system involved a sustained reduction in tariff barriers, promoting a growth in world trade consistently exceeding output growth. Now, given these structural trade imbalances, new forms of non-price protection are rapidly being introduced and the ratio of trade to output growth has been falling since the early 1980s.

It would appear that in many sectors investment at the margin is shifting to the final market. This tendency to locate production in final markets is not merely a consequence of the growth of non-price barriers to trade. The increasing importance of product flexibility and market segmentation means that proximity to final demand is an important competitive attribute. Moreover, the logic of just-in-time production means that once final assembly is located near the market, it is increasingly rational for component suppliers also to produce there, rather than at their home base or, if relevant, in the Third World where labour costs are lowest. It appears that, at least in the early stages of transition to post-Fordism, the organising principle of location is likely to be at the site of the final market, whereas in Fordism it was more likely to be at the site of least cost.

All these factors affect trade policies. Whereas in Fordism the need to spread sales over a global market often meant the construction of world factories, in the neo-protectionist environment of post-Fordism, and with the new imperative to be close to final consumers, trade assumes a lesser importance. Moreover, with just-in-time production, even where trade continues to be the most efficient determinant of investment location, this is more likely to be the case with final products than intermediate components and sub-assemblies. The overall implication of these trends is a move to what the head of Sony first called "global localization." By this he meant that instead of producing in Japan for world markets, Sony would aim for a three-way split: production in Japan, North America and Europe of products specifically tailored to regional needs. This strategy of global market segmentation is now being pursued by a large number of corporations, especially Japanese and U.S. transnational corporations, and is a development which European ones will inevitably follow as well.

Implicit in this strategic restructuring is a significant change in the pattern of global trade. First, regional trading blocs are growing in importance. Canada and the U.S. have signed the 1988 Free Trade Agreement and the North American Free Trade Agreement is in the works. The European Community has moved to greater integration and there is growing talk of co-operation among the Asian countries. Clearly these represent important issues of trade policy which have to be tackled, and which are direct outcomes of epochal transition.

Second, strategic alliances between firms are becoming a significant mechanism for spreading indirect costs of production and coping with technological complexity. For example, in the auto industry, GM has taken over Saab, Ford, Jaguar, Renault and Volvo have entered a complex alliance and various parties are scrambling to link up with Eastern European producers. While these strategic alliances often occur independently of state intervention, this is not always the case. Moreover, especially in the European context, there are grounds for concern over the absence of suitable alliances in some sectors. And since market forces are not bringing about this restructuring, it probably requires state-led facilitation for these to take place, perhaps by the European Community rather than individual nation states. It should also not be forgotten that within Japan, in earlier periods of technical change, the state was an important actor in mobilising strategic alliances between firms. Finally, the Italian experience shows co-operative sharing of the indirect costs necessary to facilitate international competitiveness need not be confined to large firms; networking among small firms has an important role to play. Most often the inherited policies of Fordism are not especially supportive to these *consorzia*-like activities. This has clear implications for revising industrial policy, as the Labour Party in the U.K. recognizes.

Production Incentives

Given its emphasis on hard mechanization and the capital intensification of production, Fordism developed a series of appropriate investment and production incentives. The primary inducement to enhancing productivity was that of depreciation allowances which provided tax breaks on new fixed investment. As the Fordist mode of accumulation began to slow down, many countries tried to encourage restructuring by promoting the introduction of electronics technologies. This was done by providing further depreciation incentives, or subsidies, for the acquisition of electronics-based automation technologies or for the development of new products utilising the technology.

If the difference between Fordism and post-Fordism is best characterised as a contrast between inflexible and systemic flexible automation, in the period of epochal transition the major area of change lies in social relations and organization. Indeed, investments in new automation may often represent a mistaken path to industrial restructuring since they divert attention from the necessity of restructuring organization. Hence the inherited system of production incentives may be wholly inappropriate to epochal transition. Instead, enterprises should be assisted in adopting new labour processes, developing new forms of inter-firm linkages and in restructuring factory layouts. These types of incentives are more difficult to administer since they are seldom backed by tangible investments in equipment. This may lead to particularly acute problems when loans are involved and may often affect the operations of development banks.[40]

Thus a restructuring of incentives will be required to promote the demand for appropriate skills in reorganising production. But, in itself, this will be an inadequate policy response since it only addresses the demand for what has come to be called the "productive service sector," incorporating various types of consulting advice. Specific attention needs to be paid to the creation of a sector able to provide the services demanded. This, too, lends itself to intervention by an enabling state, for example by subsidising the acquisition of design services, just-in-time production know-how, total quality control procedures and so on.

There are also implications for the banking community: two are especially important. First, the need for longer term and closer networked relationships between firms needs to be mirrored in the relationships between banks and their clients. Instead of liquidating firms in difficulty, banks should be encouraged to assist in the process of restructuring. A case in point is the key role played by Mazda's banking affiliate in the reconstruction necessitated by an unwise commitment to energy-inefficient rotary engine cars in the early 1970s.[41] This is not an exception; in general both German and Japanese large firms have developed close links with a group banking affiliate. Second, banks are geared to lending for the acquisition of fixed assets against which security can easily be raised; lending for investment in people and organization generally creates difficulty with existing procedures, and may raise difficulties in providing tangible securities against loans. This only emphasizes the need for longer term and closer relationships between banks and their clients.

INDUSTRIAL RELATIONS

The Fordist labour process had a matching form of industrial relations. Since management was primarily focused on wage minimization and control, the role of the unions in defending worker rights was generally accomplished through concentrating on wages and job demarcation. As a reflection of the separation of skills in this Fordist labour process, the trade union movement was often divided between those unions representing craft workers and those representing unskilled production workers. Inter-union conflict over job demarcation and wage leap-frogging was an endemic feature of this system. Both the labour process and industrial relations were built around the existence of a reserve army of labour and easy entry into and exit from employment.

As we have seen, this inherited labour process is no longer effective and has instead given way to the development of a new form of work organization. This is one which stresses co-operation on the shopfloor, draws on the creativity of the labour force, reduces polarization between skills (encouraging multi-skilling), moves away from the fragmentation of tasks, and promotes long-term employment (which is crucial if labour is to be treated as a resource, rather than a cost). To function effectively this new labour process requires an altered form of industrial relations.

A frequent response of capital to this changing labour process is to try to individualise work contracts and to operate in a union-free environment. Where workers have been able to defend their interests effectively, capital has attempted to achieve single-union status at the plant level. This may be considered a necessary requirement for the transition to flexibility, multi-tasking and multi-skilling since it removes inter-union conflict over job demarcation.

In this context, organised labour faces familiar and unfamiliar issues. Unchanged concerns are defence of the right to organise and to bargain over wages and working issues. But in addition, capital's dependence on its labour force opens space for organised labour to intervene on three new fronts. First, total-quality-control procedures and the promotion of incremental technical change promote worker involvement in management and provide access to strategic planning. This access could be used to influence a corporate orientation which is not inimical to the interests of labour. Second, organised labour can enhance capital's commitment to treat its labour force as a resource to be augmented through investment, by pressing for long-term, and perhaps life-time employment. And, third. a key emerging problem with the post-Fordist labour process concerns the danger of segmentation between the core and peripheral labour forces,[42] a development that undermines the overall interests of labour, particularly with respect to the provision of the social wage. In Fordism the desire to facilitate labour mobility meant the costs of reproduction of labour (including health and education) were borne by the state. In post-Fordism long-term investment in the labour force has often meant the "corporatization" of the social wage, with the firm becoming responsible for pension, training and private health care, reducing state provision of these services. Responding to these challenges of privatization often represents a substantial problem for labour and requires a class consciousness in which the struggle transcends the narrow confines of the workplace. By responding proactively to the emerging labour process, organised labour will be in a position to help set the agenda.

From the state's point of view, these changes in industrial relations require a significant alteration in attitudes and institutions. As with technical change, it is unlikely that these developments will occur spontaneously or diffuse at optimal speed. Policy interventions are thus likely to be critical to rapid transition.

CONCLUSIONS

It is in this context of epochal change that an industrially advanced country such as Canada has to consider the development of a strategic policy response to the challenges of the 1990s, a policy which has to be informed by Canada's past history of industrial development. Restructuring, thus, often has to be considered in relation to "brown field" rather than "green field" sites; similarly, the social construction of the work relation must take into account a long history of Fordist habituation and industrial relations.

Many of the major policy implications have been sketched out above: at the micro (corporate), meso (district) and macro (national) levels. But a *sine qua non* of industrial restructuring is the development of an industrial strategy. In many countries this not only runs counter to the dominant ideology (which, at least in the U.K. during the 1980s, attempted to reimpose the conditions for successful Fordist accumulation), but is also hindered by the failures of past episodes of industrial policy. Hence it will be important to make the distinction between industrial strategy as a participative process setting out the broad areas of restructuring, the principles on which this will occur and identifying an institutional framework within which this can occur, and industrial policy as a myriad of detailed *dirigiste* interventions confronting the productive sector. In addition, the process in which industrial strategy is formulated is more important than its content. A strategic document from on high—although important in focusing attention—is inadequate. Industrial strategy has to emerge from an interplay between actors at the micro, meso, and macro levels.

Although many of the policy responses required involve issues of an essentially technical nature, there are critical political and social dimensions of industrial restructuring which have to be considered. Crudely put, it is possible to identify at least two major routes to post-Fordism—the quasi-feudal corporatist one of Japan and a more social democratic one such as in the Nordic countries. In part this is evident in the social construction of work, and the politics of work on the shopfloor.

In Japan there is a complex web of consensual legitimation interwoven with hierarchical domination. This arguably has its roots in feudal Japan. In Sweden the pattern of technological innovation is much more cooperative and democratic and increases the ability to introduce flexible automation technology productively.[43] In Norway, there has long been legislation which requires that innovation have the consent of the labour force. The Japanese route is predominantly corporatist, one in which the social wage is largely provided at the firm level (to ensure the retention of a multi-skilled labour force) rather than through the welfare state. This creates dangers of social segmentation and will not be attractive to many schooled in the western social democratic tradition.

Finally, technical training is a key component of restructuring which has implications not just at the technical but also at the normative level. Industrially advanced western economies with a long tradition of Fordist production have tended to evolve highly polarised educational systems which exclude large segments of the population from education and skills. These systems may have been appropriate to the Fordist labour process, but dysfunctional to post-Fordism. If continued, they will not only reduce economic competitiveness, but also exclude a large segment of the population from participation in the modern sector. It is an issue—perhaps *the* issue—of fundamental policy importance.

ENDNOTES

I am grateful to Manfred Bienefeld and Stuart Holland for insightful comments on an earlier draft.

1. Similar factors arise with respect to the agricultural and services sector although this chapter does not consider them.

2. The term "meso" is used in its loosest sense to refer to the intermediate level of decision making between the national and firm level. This usage is different to that contained in other, related texts, for instance S. Holland, *The Market Economy: From Micro to Meso-economics* (London: Weidenfeld and Nicholson, 1987) and S. Holland, *The Global Economy: From Meso to Macro-economics* (London: Weidenfeld and Nicholson, 1987).

3. C. Perez, "Microelectronics, Long Waves and Structural Change: New Perspectives for Developing Countries," *World Development*, 13/1 (1985).

4. In earlier work, we have identified four such periods in industrial history—handicrafts, manufacture, machinofacture and systemofacture—each of which involves a matching combination of social and technical relations. The point of transition between these epochs has sometimes involved the prior introduction of new social relations, and at other times the prior adoption of new production technologies. See K. Hoffman and R. Kaplinsky, *Driving Force: The Global Restructuring of Technology, Labour, and Investment in the Automobile and Components Industries* (Boulder, CO: Westview Press, 1988), Chapter 2.

5. Hoffman and Kaplinsky, *Driving Force*; M. Piore and C.F. Sabel, *The Second Industrial Divide* (New York: Basic Books, 1984); C. Freeman *et al.*, *Unemployment and Technical Innovation: A Study of Long Waves and Economic Development* (London: Frances Pinter, 1982).

6. This focus on standardization often reflected a production ideology rather than reality. Some sectors, especially those producing capital goods, necessarily manufactured one-off or small batch goods; other sectors (notably garments and shoes) proved to be inherently difficult to mechanise, thus allowing for differentiated output.

7. An interesting pattern appears to be emerging in this change in competitive environment. Under Fordist relations there appeared to be a trade-off between price and quality/shorter leadtime product characteristics. By contrast, in many post-Fordist factory regimes of total-quality-management it appears that the pursuit of product characteristics often also results in lower cost output. The trade-off between price and quality thus appears to have narrowed, and often even to have disappeared.

8.   Restructuring at the micro level is considered (for reasons of convenience) as being synonymous with the corporate level. This might appear to exclude non-capitalist modes of ownership, but in fact the transition from Fordism to post-Fordism transcends the capitalist mode of production. If anything "socialism-as-we-knew-it" was even more determinedly Fordist than capitalism.

9.   *Business Week*, 30 June, 1980.

10. A. Altshuler *et al.*, *The Future of the Automobile* (Cambridge, MA: MIT Press, 1984); Hoffman and Kaplinsky, *Driving Force*.

11. M.L. Dertouzos, R. K. Lester and R. M. Solow, *Made in America: Regaining the Productive Edge* (Cambridge, MA: MIT Press, 1989).

12. For a more detailed discussion of the nature and diffusion of CIM see R. Kaplinsky, *Automation: The Technology and Society* (Harlow: Longmans, 1984); J. Bessant and B. Haywood, "The Introduction of Flexible Manufacturing Systems as an Example of Computer Integrated Manufacturing," *Operations Management Review*, Part 1-3, 1988; C. Edquist and S. Jacobson, *Flexible Automation: The Global Diffusion of New Technology in the Engineering Industry* (Oxford: Blackwell, 1988).

13. The primary reason for the introduction of NC and CNC was product quality (especially in the aerospace industry) rather than flexibility. Despite public belief, the displacement of labour and the desire to control labour were not primary factors driving the diffusion of these technologies. See D.F. Noble, "Social Choice in Machine Design: The Case of Numerically Controlled Machine Tools," in A. Zimbalist (ed.), *Case Studies in the Labour Process* (New York: Monthly Review Press, 1979).

14. Reported in J. Bessant, *Managing Advanced Manufacturing Technology* (London: Hutchinson, 1991). Care must be taken in reading this conclusion. The point is that, at this period of epochal transition, it is in the realm of social relations that the primary changes are required. However in the long run it will be in the transition to CIM that the most significant benefits will probably be found.

15. A more detailed discussion of these issues can be found in R. Kaplinsky, "Changes in the Capitalist Labour Process: Some Lessons from the Auto Industry," *Cambridge Journal of Economics* 12/4 (1988) and J. Mathews, *Tools of Change: New technology and the democratization of work* (Sydney: Pluto Press, 1989).

16. S. Hymer, "The Multinational Corporation and the Law of Uneven Development," in H. Radice (ed.), *International Firms and Modern Imperialism* (London: Penguin, 1975).

17. Of course this tendency for labour to be seen as a fixed cost is not new. However in the past it has in large part been due to the power of organised labour as reflected in labour law. In post-Fordism capital has come to be an active proponent of long-term employment, at least for the core labour force.

So what is emerging is both a change in degree and a change in material interest.

18. These issues are treated in more detail in Piore and Sabel, *The Second Industrial Divide*; Hoffman and Kaplinsky, *Driving Force*; and A. Amin, "Flexible specialization and small firms in Italy: myths and realities," *Antipode*, 21/1 (1989).

19. A.D. Chandler, *The Visible Hand* (Cambridge, MA: Harvard University Press, 1977).

20. Dertouzos *et al.*, *Made in America*.

21. For example, one British firm making industrial fasteners delivers in a predicted time directly to an IBM production line 400 miles away. It ensures reliability by keeping three months worth of stock. Caterpillar Tractor in the U.K. virtually eliminated its incoming stock of components, but now requires its suppliers to keep a minimum of three weeks final stock.

22. This is discussed in detail in R.J. Schonberger, *Japanese Manufacturing Techniques: Nine Hidden Lessons in Simplicity* (New York: The Free Press, 1982).

23. For the argument see Piore and Sabel, *The Second Industrial Divide*. For a dissenting note, Amin, "Flexible specialization."

24. D. Friedman, *The Misunderstood Miracle* (Ithaca, NY: Cornell University Press, 1988).

25. H. Schmitz, "Flexible Specialization—A New Paradigm for Small Scale Industrialization?" *IDS Discussion Paper 261*, May 1989 and R. Kaplinsky, "Small Scale Enterprise, Non-Agricultural Rural Employment and Appropriate Technology in Kenya," (Report prepared for International Fund for Agricultural Development, Rome, 1989), p. 77.

26. M. Best, *The New Competition* (Oxford: Polity Press, 1990).

27. S. Holland, "The Promotion of Networking by Regional Development Agencies and Small and Medium Enterprise within the European Community," (Paper prepared for European Commission, Florence, European University Institute, 1990).

28. For this reason Holland argues that where very large TNCs are involved, they are best seen as a meso-level of economic activity since they incorporate many of the common interventions which occur at the meso level when small firms are involved. See *The Market Economy* and *The Global Economy*.

29. See Friedman, *The Misunderstood Miracle*.

30. K.J. Arrow, "Economic Welfare and the Allocation of Resources for Invention," in *The Rate and Direction of Inventive Activity: Economic and Social Factors* (Princeton, NJ: National Bureau of Economic Research and Princeton University Press, 1962). Socialist social relations probably have even greater problems in getting the "Schumpeterian motor" to function effectively.

L. Balcerowicz, "Enterprises and Economic Systems: Organizational Adaptability and Technical Innovativeness," in H. Leipold and A. Schuller (eds.), *Zur Interdependenz von Unternehmens-und Wirtschaftsordnung, Schriften zum Vergleich von Wirtschaftsordnungen*, Band 38 (Stuttgart: Gustav Fischer Verlag, 1986).

31.   The logic of these procedures was understood in the 1930s, but taken up by the Japanese only in the 1950s. Yet, despite the demonstrated effectiveness of this approach to quality in Japan, western corporations only began to adopt these procedures in the late 1980s.

32.   Although not germane to the central discussion in this paper, these strictures are directly relevant to state-owned enterprises. Most commonly they have pursued the logic of mass production, operating in a monopolistic and low-innovation environment (for example in hydro generation). Thus the supposed "inefficiency" of state-owned enterprises is not so much a feature of a particular relation of ownership, but rather of the organizational model in which this control has been exercised.

33.   M. Burawoy, *Manufacturing Consent: Changes in the Labour Process under Monopoly Capitalism* (Chicago: University of Chicago Press, 1979).

34.   Cited in R. Sobel, *Car Wars: Why Japan is Building the All-American Car* (New York: McGraw Hill, 1982).

35.   See S. Kamata, *Japan in the Passing Lane* (London: Penguin, 1982), including the introduction by R. Dore. See also Kaplinsky, "Changes in the Capitalist Labour Process" and J. Humphrey, "Adapting the 'Japanese Model' in Brazil," (mimeo, Institute of Development Studies, University of Sussex, 1990).

36.   An example of the experience of a prominent South African industrialist is insightful. Having read the literature on Japan he attempted to introduce quality-at-source procedures but failed miserably, wasting $75,000 in the process. His explanation for this failure was that the "broader political problems of Apartheid" stood in the way of work-process reform. Significantly, it was largely for this reason, rather than any ethical objection, that he came to oppose apartheid. For the link between apartheid and Fordism see R. Kaplinsky, "The Role of Labour in South Africa's Economic Future," (paper presented to Lausanne Colloquium on the Future of the South African Economy, 1989).

37.   There is increasing evidence of the role which "learning-by-visiting" has to play in promoting corporate restructuring. In fact it stands to reason that since the primary arena of change lies in organization and attitudes rather than the introduction of new embodied technologies, this form of learning will be of increased significance. Were embodied technical change to be the fulcrum of change then it would be investments in fixed capital and learning-by-doing which would be most important.

38.   For a discussion of many of these issues, see D.E. Evans, *Comparative Advantage and Growth: Trade and Development in Theory and Practice* (Hemel Hempstead: Harvester/Wheatsheaf, 1989).

39. L.E. Westphal, Y.W. Rhee and G. Pursell, "Sources of Technological Capability in South Korea," in Fransman and King (eds.), *Technological Capability in the Third World* (London: Macmillan, 1984).

40. Institute of Development Studies, *Cyprus Industrial Strategy: Report of UNDP/UNIDO Mission* (Brighton: Institute of Development Studies, University of Sussex, 1988) and D. Costa, "Appraising and Financing Flexible Manufacturing Methods: Lessons from Cyprus," IDS.

41. Altshuler *et al.*, *The Future of the Automobile*.

42. A. Sayer, "Post-Fordism in Question," *International Journal of Urban and Regional Research*, 1989.

43. Edquist and Jacobson, *Flexible Automation*; B. Haywood and J. Bessant, "The Swedish Approach to the Use of Flexible Manufacturing Systems," *Innovation Research Group Occasional Paper No. 3*, Brighton Polytechnic, 1988.

Technological Change and the Global Relocation of Production in Textiles and Clothing

Lynn Krieger Mytelka

The 1970s and 1980s were turbulent times for the textile and clothing industries. Shifts in demand, the emergence of new actors and the diffusion of new technology contributed in a major way to the intensification of competition in this industry world-wide. As part of that process, dynamic firms in the advanced industrial countries pursued a dual strategy in which the delocalization of production served as a complement to rapid technological change transforming the production cycle from conception to the market. The first section analyzes these changes and their initial impact on the relocation of production to the Third World. The next section examines the strategies developed by firms in the newly industrialized economies (NIEs) in response to these changes. The last section discusses the limitations on the ability of indigenous manufacturers in the NIEs and in second-tier Asian industrializing countries to become competitive, independent[1] textile and clothing producers.

To appreciate the extent to which current changes in technology potentially constrain the emergence of Third World producers as independent competitors, it is necessary to focus on the knowledge components that dominate the process of technological change. For the textile and clothing industry this includes design, engineering, problem-solving, maintenance, management and marketing capabilities that, for the most part, are still lacking in all but a handful of Third World countries.

Much of the conventional literature on technological change[2] ignores these hard-to-measure "immaterial" elements in the production process, preferring to emphasize embodied technological characteristics, particularly those associated with shifts in the method of production or in the production function[3] which occurred as spinning, weaving and knitting became more capital-intensive. In this context, both theoreticians and practitioners fell prey to the belief that the mere displacement of machinery to the Third World provided the basis for internationally competitive textile and clothing production. Yet the evidence shows that such transfers do not automatically lead to the efficient operation of modern machinery and equipment and that Third World firms frequently fail to achieve best practice. Among the factors that account for low and sometimes declining levels of productivity in Third World firms are poor maintenance, leading to lower volumes and poorer quality output; inappropriate product and process choices that give rise to a lack of specialization and to underutilized capacity; and higher costs resulting from the need to import a high proportion of both material and non-material inputs from a wide variety of sources and from frequent infrastructural, engineering, management and marketing failures.[4]

In some product lines, particularly those standardized products with a high labour content, low labour costs can compensate for these inefficiencies. But cost competitiveness is a less important part of the story today because the transformation of textiles and clothing into "knowledge-intensive" industries is only partly focused on knowledge embodied in machinery and in the software needed to operate and integrate it. Increasingly important is the knowledge required for the design, marketing and manufacture of products embodied in the wide variety of organizational changes subsumed under the label of "flexible specialization".

As this alters the form of international competition from one based largely on price to one based more on innovation and price, new barriers to entry are created for Third World firms. In managing such continuous adjustment to changing prices, products and processes, the ability to acquire, master and integrate knowledge inputs will largely determine the extent to which indigenous independent producers may succeed.

SHIFTS IN DEMAND AND THEIR IMPACT ON THE MODE OF COMPETITION

As late as the 1960s, textiles and clothing could be described as relatively labour-intensive industries in which technology was stable, goods were largely standardized, competition was based primarily on price, and economies of scale were relatively important. Each of these features has since undergone considerable change, in part stimulated by changes in demand resulting from the crisis of the 1970s.

The 1970s were already marked by a secular decline in the rate of growth of consumer spending on clothing as incomes in the advanced industrial countries (AICs) rose.[5] In Japan, for example, the annual increase in consumer spending on clothing fell from 6.9 percent in 1963-73 to 0.3 percent in 1973-82, with negative growth rates in the early 1980s. Though consumer spending on all goods and services was increasing at an average annual rate of 4.3 percent towards the 1980s, expenditure on clothing barely rose by 1 percent annually over the same period.

The economic crisis of the 1970s accelerated this decline, particularly in the European Community (EC) where the annual rate of growth in consumer spending on clothing fell from an average of 3.9 percent in 1963-73 to 0.9 percent in 1973-82. It then continued to grow at around 1 percent over the period 1983-86, rising slightly to 2.1 percent per annum in 1987-89. Only in the United States, the United Kingdom and Sweden, where the relative price of clothing remained well below that of other consumer goods, did the rate of increase in consumer expenditure on clothing remain above that of consumer expenditure as a whole over the period 1973-1982.[6] Moreover, for the period 1980-86, U.S. consumer expenditure on clothing rose by 5 percent per year, making that country the world's most buoyant textile and clothing market, although the EC remained the world's largest importer of clothing.

This continued strong sensitivity to price changes obscured important changes in price-quality relationships resulting from the differential impact of the crisis on various income groups. This became increasingly important over the 1970s and 1980s, and emerged clearly from a series of standardized surveys of household consumer spending patterns in Germany, France, the U.K. and Italy.[7] Significant differences in price elasticities of demand, across income categories and within product categories, had led to a far more complex pattern of market segmentation. As a result there was continued growth both in the substantial market for cheaper textile and clothing, generally manufactured in low wage countries and marketed through large chain and discount stores, as well as in the much smaller upscale segments of the market where demand was far less sensitive to price increases. This was accompanied by slower growth in the mid-price segment of the market. At the same time, domestic demand in many Third World countries collapsed as a result of the imposition of austerity measures necessitated by structural adjustment programs. This contributed to the increasingly zero-sum nature of international competition in the industry.

Slow growth of total demand for textiles and clothing combined with the market segmenting effect of the crisis had two major consequences for the mode of competition. First, it focused greater attention on the need to maintain market shares, especially in the face of rising import penetration by low-cost clothing manufacturers. This had already begun in the late 1960s and early 1970s. See Table 3.1

TABLE 3.1

AREA DISTRIBUTION OF WORLD EXPORT
OF TEXTILES AND CLOTHING

TEXTILES	1955	1963	1973	1982	1986	1988
World [U.S.$bn]	4.7	7.0	23.2	51.5	66.3	92.9
Developed area (%)	79	76	74	65	65	59
Developing area (%)	15	16	18	25	25	29
East. trading area (%)	6	8	8	10	10	13
CLOTHING						
World [U.S.$bn]	0.8	2.2	12.7	41.0	61.8	89.5
Developed area (%)	71	69	56	44	46	41
Developing area (%)	10	13	30	42	41	45
East. trading area (%)	19	18	14	14	13	14

Sources: Refer to GATT—Textiles and Clothing in the World Economy (Geneva: July 1984) pp. 40-41 for the 1955, 1963, and 1973 figures. Refer to GATT—International Trade 86-87 (Geneva: 1987) p. 17 for the 1982 and 1986 figures. Refer to GATT—International Trade 89-90 (Geneva: 1990) p. 61 for the 1988 figure.

Second, it called into question earlier strategies based exclusively on mass produced, standardized products, thus giving rise to a change in the mode of competition from one based primarily on price to one based more on price and creativity. Beginning in the 1970s, large firms in the advanced industrial countries adopted a dual strategy. They aimed at reducing cost by modernizing plant and equipment, and reorganizing production via international subcontracting. At the same time these firms concentrated on product innovation. This involved increasing both the number of collections produced in a year and the number of items per collection, further development of producer and distributors' trademarks and brand names, commercial franchising, shorter production runs of more differentiated products, the use of domestic subcontracting and greater attention to quality control. Each of these responses has tended to stimulate the demand for new innovations.

KNOWLEDGE INTENSITY AND DYNAMIC COMPARATIVE ADVANTAGE IN TEXTILES AND CLOTHING

The late 1970s and early 1980s thus witnessed a tremendous acceleration in the demand for new innovations coming from the textile and clothing industries, as well as increased state support for their modernization.[8] The pull of textile demand, moreover, was accompanied by a push from the electronics, computer and some of the metalworking industries then facing a slowdown in the growth of demand from established markets. The more intense application of these new, advanced technologies to the textile and clothing industry led to: the development of automated pattern cutting (the *American Gerber* method finding its inspiration in metal cutting techniques developed for the aerospace industry, the French *Lectra Systems* technique drawing upon laser technology); the wider incorporation of electronic devices into spinning, weaving and knitting machines; and the computerization of the design and management processes, including inventory control. These changes are continuing to transform production processes in each of the major branches of this industry.

TEXTILES

From its earliest beginnings, the industrial development of textile and later clothing production was predicated upon the growth of a mass market. As a result, early technological change in these industries focused primarily on the lengthening of production runs for standardized products and to a lesser extent on labour reduction strategies associated with increased machine speeds, reduced machine down-time and the elimination of steps in the production process. The latter issues, together with international subcontracting, became more important in the 1960s when trade liberalization, within the context of GATT, and the creation of a European Economic Community coincided with rising textile exports from low-cost Asian producers, notably Japan, Hong Kong, China, Korea, Taiwan, India and Pakistan.

While the major technological innovations of the 1950s and 1960s (e.g. open-end spinning, shuttleless looms and circular knitting machines) had much more productive potential than their predecessors, they were initially quite limited in the number of applications and range of products for which they were suited.[9] As a result the cost advantages to be gained from modernization were relatively small so that many countries responded to the pressure from rising imports by opting for protectionism. Resort to protection through the Short Term Cotton arrangement in 1961 and the Long Term Arrangement a year later slowed the diffusion of new spinning and weaving techniques in many of the industrialized countries during the 1960s.[10] This further intensified the pressure from lower cost producers, who were mainly, but not exclusively, NIEs. (See Table 3.2.) There were exceptions, however. Within Europe, Germany and Italy emerged as formidable competitors, following the adoption of a dual strategy of textile modernization and domestic subcontracting in the case of Italy.[11] So successful was this two-pronged strategy that by the early 1970s, Germany had catapulted into first place among the world's textile exporters while Italy moved from fifth place in 1973 to third in 1982 and second in 1986.

Not until the late 1970s did the new technologies become more widely diffused within the advanced industrial countries. (See Table 3.3) Thus, between 1977 and 1983 the share of shuttleless looms in total installed weaving capacity in the OECD countries rose from 7.6 percent to 19 percent and by 1986 it had reached 29.9 percent. This still lagged far behind France, Germany and Italy where the share was over 50 percent in 1986. While total installed production capacity in the Third World continued to grow rapidly, so that by 1986 it accounted for roughly 60 percent of world spinning and weaving capacity, the OECD and the former COMECON countries maintained an impressive lead over the Third World in their share of both open-end spinning machines and shuttleless looms. (See Table 3.3.)

TABLE 3.2

TOP 15 WORLD EXPORTERS OF TEXTILES (BILLION U.S. DOLLARS)

1963		1973		1982		1986		1989	
Japan	0.90	Germany	3.0	Germany	5.5	Germany	8.1	Germany	11.1
U.K.	0.71	Japan	2.5	Japan	5.1	Italy	5.9	Italy	8.0
France	0.63	France	1.7	Italy	4.0	Japan	5.5	H.K.	7.6
India	0.54	Benelux	1.7	U.S.	2.8	China	4.3	China	7.0
Germany	0.53	Italy	1.5	Benelux	2.7	H.K.	3.9	Japan	5.5
Italy	0.53	U.K.	1.5	France	2.7	Benelux	3.9	Taiwan	5.4
Benelux	0.51	Neth.	1.3	Korea	2.5	France	3.6	Korea	5.4
U.S.	0.49	U.S.	1.2	China	2.2	Korea	3.2	Benelux	5.3
Neth.	0.36	India	0.7	U.K.	2.0	Taiwan	3.1	France	5.0
Switz.	0.21	Switz.	0.6	Neth.	1.8	U.S.	2.6	U.S.	4.4
H.K.	0.11	China	0.6	Taiwan	1.8	Neth.	2.5	U.K.	3.6
Austria	0.11	Taiwan	0.6	Switz.	1.4	U.K.	2.4	Neth.	2.4
China	0.09	H.K.	0.5	India	1.1	Switz.	1.9	Switz.	2.0
Portugal	0.09	Austria	0.5	Austria	1.0	Pakistan	1.3	Pakistan	2.0
Pakistan	0.09	Pakistan	0.4	Pakistan	0.9	Austria	1.2	India	1.8

Share of top 15 in total world exports:

84%	78%	73%	80%	78%

Share of LDCs in top 15:

14.1%	15.1%	22.6%	29.5%	38.1%

Source: GATT—*Textiles and Clothing*, p. 43; GATT—*International Trade 86-87* p.18; GATT—*International Trade 89-90* p. 62.

TABLE 3

REGIONAL DISTRIBUTION OF WORLD SPINNING AND WEAVING CAPACITY

SPINNING: (IN MILLIONS OF UNITS)

Region	1963 Spindles	1973 Spindles	1980 Spindles	Rotors[b]	1983[ab] Spindles	Rotors	1986 Spindles	Rotors
Total World	128.2	143.5	158.3	3.6	151.7	5.3	151.7	7.07
%	100.0	100.0	100.0	100.0	100.0	100.0	100.0	100.0
OECD	65.7	56.0	47.4	0.9	42.5	1.1	39.8	1.34
%	51.3	39.0	30.0	25.3	28.0	21.2	26.2	19.0
East. Trading Area (c)	19.8	24.0	24.4	2.3	23.9	3.5	21.4	4.8
%	15.5	16.5	15.4	63.5	15.8	65.8	14.1	67.9
LDCs(d)	42.7	53.5	84.5	0.4	85.3	0.69	90.5	0.93
%	33.3	44.3	54.5	11.1	56.2	13.0	59.7	13.1

WEAVING: (IN '000 LOOMS)

	1963 Total	1973 Total	1980 Total	Shuttle-less	1983 Total	Shuttle-less	1986 Total	Shuttle-less
Ttl. World	2,697.6	2,820.6	1,975.7	231.3	2,877.1	306.7	2,779.8	429.1
%	100.0	100.0	100.0	100.0	100.0	100.0	100.0	100.0
OECD	1,335.5	1,073.8	598.8	94.1	728.4	138.8	652.9	187.4
%	49.5	38.1	30.3	40.7	25.3	45.3	23.5	43.7
East. Trading Area(c)	728.7	921.7	363.4	92.8	432.5	102.1	382.0	132.7
%	27.0	32.7	18.4	40.1	15.0	33.3	13.7	30.9
LDCs(e)	633.5	825.1	1,013.5	44.4	1,716.2	65.7	1,744.9	109.0
%	23.5	29.3	51.3	19.2	59.7	21.4	62.8	25.4

Notes: [a] open-end rotors
[b] Investa [Czech] did not report its shipments in 1983.
[c] Europe-Comecon
[d] The Asian developing countries accounted for between 75 and 78 percent of the LDC total over the period 1963-1986.
[e] The share of the Asian developing countries which had remained at 58-59 percent between 1963 and 1973, rose to 69 percent in 1980 and to 75 percent in 1983 and 1986.

Sources: For the years 1963, 1973 refer to GATT—Textiles and Clothing, Appendices I-IV, Tables 4 and 8. For the 1980s, refer to ITMF, International Textile Machinery Shipment Statistics (Zurich: ITMF), diverse years.

Two or three of the NIEs have, however, kept pace with the OECD countries in their drive to modernize the spinning and weaving branches of the textile industry. Thus cumulative shipments of shuttleless looms in the period 1977-86 amounted to 22,201 units in Taiwan and 15,059 units in Korea as compared with 16,098 units in Germany and 12,153 units in France.[12] At the same time, attention to quality and increased productivity of traditional looms coupled with exceedingly low wages catapulted China into the front ranks of textile exporters by 1986.

These developments give some support to the hypothesis that the relative accessibility of spinning and weaving technology will make it possible for NIEs and would-be NIEs to catch up over the next decade. However, three factors suggest that a word of caution should be appended to this prognosis. First, the Multi-Fibre Agreement (MFA) with its increasingly restrictive quotas has contributed to concentration in an industry which had been characterized, until recently, by large numbers of small firms and a relatively accessible technology. This effect is reflected in the limited number of significant new market entrants from among Third World textile producers. Thus, over the nearly three decades from 1963 to 1989 covered in Table 2, only six Third World countries have ever figured among the top 15 exporters and their share in world exports has steadily increased in value. Moreover, despite a steadily declining share of textiles in their total exports, Taiwan, Hong Kong and Korea have steadily improved their ranking among the world's top textile exporters.

Second, rapid modernization of the spinning industry in the period 1977-86 was very costly. In Germany, Japan and the United States the cost of depreciation and interest had risen from between 12 and 15 percent in 1983 to 20-24 percent of total production costs in 1987. However, this was still considerably below the 36 percent registered in Brazil and the 29 percent recorded in India in 1987. Only in Korea was the share of capital costs in total costs comparable to that in the OECD countries. In weaving, where raw material inputs have a smaller weight, capital costs in the three OECD countries for which data were available from the International Textile Manufacturers Federation rose from 21-26 percent of total costs in 1983 to 30-35 percent in 1987. In the latter year, comparable shares in Third World producing countries were 34 percent for Korea, 42 percent for India and 53 percent for Brazil.[13]

Rising capital costs under conditions of slow demand growth have intensified competition and accelerated the process of concentration among textile firms in the OECD countries. Mergers and acquisitions are producing larger firms better able to finance the higher costs of RandD and technological change.[14] In the Third World, however, rising capital costs have begun to constrain the diffusion of new technology and new machinery purchases in many countries. Indeed, in Africa high financial charges and the debt crisis are making even the purchase of spare parts difficult.[15]

Third, there are the enormous gains in productivity resulting from the now rapid diffusion of new technology in the already highly automated spinning, weaving and dyeing branches of the textile industry. During the 1980s, the introduction of electronic controls remarkably improved diagnostic and monitoring capabilities and reduced down-time to change models, patterns or colours or to repair broken threads. This has produced major cost savings by significantly reducing labour time, energy consumption and materials wastage, while improving product quality. Thus, in Japan operating manpower requirements in spinning were reduced from 76.6 to 43.5 workers per 10,000 spindles between 1975 and 1982.[16] In Germany, the productivity of capital in the spinning industry rose from 62.8 kg to 122 kg of yarn per spindle between 1960 and 1983, while labour productivity rose from 6,100 kg per employee to 16,000 kg over the same period.[17] In weaving the gains were even more remarkable—an increase from 14,300 square metres of cloth per loom in 1960 to 43,700 in 1982.[18] This does not yet take into consideration the impact of newer, more productive weaving techniques, such as airjet looms, whose speed is 4.5 times faster than traditional looms and half as fast again as earlier shuttleless looms of the projectile and lance type. Because the efficiency of these looms depends upon careful maintenance and fine adjustments, Japan's traditional strength in quality control has produced additional productivity gains in their use. Thus, whereas airjet looms are down on average 1.5 to 2 times an hour in the U.S., this average has fallen to one stop per hour in Japan.[19]

In addition to cost savings, new spinning and weaving technologies have considerably improved product quality and reduced throughput time. Thus the newest open-end spinning machines splice rather than knot yarn breaks, producing longer lengths without faults and allowing the use of higher speed weaving techniques because there is less risk of breaks as the weft is inserted into the warp. With regard to throughput, the time from bale opening to finished product has been reduced from 30 to 20 days and is expected to drop to 18 days in the near future. In yarn dyeing the fall in throughput time has been even greater, going from 24 to four days.[20] The just-in-time system has thus become possible in textiles and clothing.

Computerized design systems have also permitted textile firms to participate in the shift to design-intensive products. *SAIC-Velcorex*, a leading French producer of corduroy, for example, now employs between 15 and 20 persons in its design unit and a further four percent of its workforce is engaged in doing up samples for the marketing staff to show buyers from the major distribution chains.[21] *DMC*, the world's eleventh largest textile company, now produces 2,000 new designs a year, each presented in five different colour combinations.[22] What formerly took over three weeks to put together can now be done with a CAD (Computer Aided Design) system in six hours.

In knitting, major new labour saving technologies that also enhance flexibility in model changes and design only became available in the 1980s, but their appearance has now revolutionized the industry by reducing the time needed to change over to a new model from three hours to 13 minutes. The newest knitting machines significantly reduce materials wastage and dramatically increase throughput from design to production by combining computerized pattern design, the electronic selection of needles and "knitting to form". The speed of response to changes in demand for seasonal merchandise has thus considerably accelerated and the knitwear industry, under pressure from low-wage imports, has become a highly design-intensive industry. From two collections a year the industry has moved, on average, to four or five collections, and in the case of *Liz Claiborne*, a major American mid-priced clothing firm with annual sales of $800 million, to six collections a year.[23] Where in the past the same basic design for a skirt or a sweater would be made up into 100,000 articles, today 30,000 articles is a goodly number, and at the upper end of the mid-price range that figure falls to under 20,000. Quality has also improved dramatically, so that *Marks and Spencer*, which takes nearly half of the output of cotton jersey knit at *Courtaulds'* plant in the U.K., expects about one fault per ten metres of cloth. At *Courtaulds'*, however, managers using the new machinery now expect only one fault in every 25 metres.[24]

For a number of knitwear products, notably socks, certain types of pullovers and T-shirts, the amount of assembly (sewing) time, the only labour-intensive segment of the production process left, has been reduced to under five minutes. Moreover, because the new knitting machines can be easily and cheaply programed to produce a variety of items, economies of scale have become less important. These two factors have created new possibilities for small, modernized firms in the advanced industrial countries to play the role of domestic subcontractors in those markets where segmentation favours the production of more diversified and design-intensive products.

Increasing the design and marketing intensity of products, adopting highly automated knitting machinery and introducing managerial innovations such as closer inventory control and local subcontracting have already had a notable effect on the competitiveness of Europe's knitwear industry. By 1983, for the European Community as a whole, the unit value of imports coming from other EC countries, particularly Italy, was below that of imports from the Third World for some 50 articles, notably stockings, socks, children's clothes, T-shirts, and pullovers.[25] Nevertheless, knitwear exports from Asian and Caribbean countries have continued to increase, largely stimulated by subcontracting, especially from American ready-to-wear companies that have already abandoned local sourcing for international subcontracting and would do even more work abroad were it not for the MFA. The relationship between *Liz Claiborne* and the global knitwear interests of the Hong Kong-based Fang family, discussed below, is illustrative of a model which covers both subcontracting by manufacturers and by the large distribution chains such as *Montgomery Wards* and *Sears* in the United States, *CandA*, *Marks and Spencer* and *Carrefour* in Europe.

In sum, although the OECD countries' share of world installed capacity of spinning and weaving machinery declined between 1973 and 1986 (Table 3), output in the OECD countries has not fallen.[26] With 1973 as the base year, the 1989 volume of textile output stood at 100 for the EC countries and 114 for the U.S.[27] Moreover, many OECD countries have been able to maintain their position as leading textile exporters (Table 2) and international production cost comparisons reveal an erosion of the cost advantage of producing in the newly industrialized economies as firms in the OECD countries continue to modernize.[28] The increasing availability of relatively cheap, good quality fabrics in the NIEs will thus most likely have an impact over the next decade not in the textile but in the clothing branch of the industry. As the NIEs move into higher value added garments, using more design-intensive fabrics, they will increasingly subcontract more of the clothing assembly stage to lower wage countries that have preferential access to European and American markets.

CLOTHING

If the picture in spinning, weaving and knitting is one of considerable technological change accompanied by a growing ability of firms in some of the advanced industrial countries to retain or regain international competitiveness, the same cannot be said for garments assembled from woven fabrics. No "weaving-to-form" techniques have yet been developed and the small pieces into which a pattern is cut require a large number of manipulations as they are transferred from one workstation (sewing machine) to another. Major innovations, however, have been introduced in product design and in the organization of production and marketing which create new barriers to entry for Third World firms seeking to become independent producers in this part of the industry.

As in textiles and knitwear, clothing firms have successfully increased the design-intensity and the quality of their products. Fashion is king in this industry across all product categories. In home furnishings (bedlinen, towels, etc.) "where there was once a commodity market, there is now a fashion market where colour and pattern sell a product and where consumers expect coordination to a sophisticated degree."[29] Adjusting to this new creative and flexible world has not been easy. At *Gossard* and *Berlei*, the two firms that make up *Courtaulds'* foundation garment division, the CEO John Hall described a major reorganization that has just been undertaken in order to pull the division

> out of the frowzy foundation garment market into the kind of fashion underwear pioneered by *Janet Reger*... [R]edesigning the product range was one thing, tightening up the company's reflexes to keep pace with accelerating trends in the fashion world was quite another. Closer contact with customers and faster reading of product trends have allowed a quicker response from the production floor. Warehousing was reorganized to "respond overnight."[30]

Getting feedback from the market and responding with speed are key strategies even in the medium-priced garment industry. *Benetton*, a medium-priced Italian sportswear manufacturer, is typical here. Built around a combination of an ultramodern factory (20 percent of output) and local subcontracting (80 percent of the piecework is farmed out to 250 subcontractors employing a total of 25,000 people), *Benetton's* productivity is estimated to be very close to that of producers in Asia.[31] In 1972 producing-to-order, the clothing version of Japan's just-in-time system, was made possible by improved methods for dyeing assembled garments. This operation, centralized in *Benetton's* factory in Ponzano Veneto, is linked by computer to headquarters and to a world-wide network of franchised stores, thus making possible a more rapid response to market demand. In this way *Benetton* is able to keep its clothing shops stocked and to increase its total sales by at least 15 percent per year.[32] Distinctive *Benetton* boutiques selling over 1,000 brand name designs per collection have become "best practice" in the sportswear industry and have found numerous imitators in Europe and North America.

Unlike *Benetton*, *Steilmann*, Germany's leading ready-to-wear company, has not moved downstream towards the market and its biggest customers remain *Marks and Spencer* and the *CandA* group. Though we might expect such a company to be a candidate for massive international subcontracting, in 1987 47 percent of *Steilmann's* output came from its own factories in Germany and a further 17 percent from German subcontractors. Only 36 percent came from international subcontractors in Southern Europe and Asia. Here, too, as Klaus Steilmann, founder and President pointed out, reliance on home production has continued because the fashion industry is too fast-moving and unpredictable.

> If people suddenly want green, and we can provide green very quickly, then they'll pay an extra DM20 to have it... the problem is getting the right things to the market at the right time. You can't do that in the Far East.[33]

Recognizing the importance of creating "brand loyalty", *Steilmann* is also positioning itself as a bridge between mass market and high fashion, creating new "labelled" collections and bringing in prominent fashion designers to design an upmarket line.

While design and marketing intensity have become prominent characteristics of the garment industry, reducing labour time (and hence costs) through the application of electronics to production, and through automation has not been as extensive as in knitwear or textiles. Thus far it has only been possible to automate the pre-assembly stage—product design, pattern grading, pattern marking and fabric cutting—but the diffusion of these new innovations has been truly remarkable. Although the kind of three-dimensional systems needed for clothing design are still not perfected, the CAD systems that are currently available have permitted collections to grow, and model changes have become more frequent. As in knitwear, the two-season year in clothing has been replaced by a four-collection year and collection sizes have grown from 50 to well over 200 articles. Moreover, many of the larger manufacturers engage in a continuous process of creation throughout the year, doing up samples and working closely with large retailers well in advance of each salon.[34] In addition to materials savings of some ten percent, the integration of design, pattern marking, grading and cutting processes has resulted in a 40 percent reduction in the number of persons previously performing these operations a reduction in the time needed to gradate and make patterns from roughly three days to one hour and a 50 percent cut in the time it takes to move a product from the decision stage to production.[35] Thus, turnaround time has been shortened and the number of models that can be introduced has increased dramatically. In the case of *Levi Strauss*, for example, it took only 16 weeks to mark and gradate the patterns for the 442 models that made up its fall collection in

1986, using 500 different fabrics and 700 different sizes. The most labour intensive activity and the one that accounts for nearly 90 percent of the labour costs in garment manufacturing is sewing and it is still largely a one machine, one operator affair although individual machines have become more highly automated and versatile.[36] The use of overhead systems to move pieces between workstations is expensive—between $2000 and $4000 per post with an average system linking anywhere from 60 to 150 posts. But they have significantly reduced non-productive time and speeded up throughput. Thus by combining computer aided design, pattern marking and gradating and cutting systems with automatic transfers, *Moynaton-Roy* reduced the production time of a shift from 30 minutes 56 seconds to 19 minutes two seconds. As a result, labour costs fell from 50 percent of total manufacturing costs to 30 percent.[37] Shirt manufacturing has also benefited from one of the rare, successful attempts at automation and in France, fifteen shirtmakers regrouped into *France Chemise* now have access to a multistation industrial robot.[38] As in knitting, therefore, the tradeoff in the clothing industry is between labour time and the elasticities of demand for different products, where the nature of what constitutes a product combines function (men's outerwear, women's underwear, household textiles), fashion (design intensity, brand naming) and price.

If automation has not yet achieved the gains in productivity in the clothing industry that it has in the textile industry, innovations at the level of management and the organization of production have become primary strategies in this industry. For certain product categories, the need to develop flexible production systems with close ties to the market is leading large firms in France and Germany to make greater use of domestic subcontracting.[39] In other instances, large firms are being broken down into smaller independent profit centres; in still others, cost considerations are leading firms to engage in outward processing or to subcontract work to Asian manufacturers.

Meanwhile, some of the process, product, organizational and marketing innovations, by increasing the speed of response to changes in demand, give a competitive edge to firms that are in close contact with their market.[40] In most instances this favours firms located in the advanced industrial countries. U.S. coat and suit makers, for example, have reduced the time from design to market to six weeks, compared to the six to eight months it takes foreign producers. This was largely accomplished by improving the management of fabric purchasing and garment manufacture. Suit manufacturers in OECD countries that have modernized their factories and work closely with local, innovative fabric manufacturers are thus at a considerable advantage at the fashion end of the market, and increasingly in the middle-price ranges as well. In other instances the tradeoff will continue to give greater weight to cost considerations and in these cases increased international subcontracting is likely to expand. Thus, *The Limited*, a medium-priced American clothing chain store and competitor to *Benetton*, uses satellite communications to transmit high-definition pictures of its latest designs to factories in southern China. Six weeks later, clothing is on the shelf in American stores."[41]

The point is that there is not one single competitive way to produce a given product in this industry. Rather, as Figure 3.1 illustrates, because the calculus is complex, several production systems may coexist. Even within a single firm, as the *Benetton* and *Steilmann* cases show, different production systems may, in fact, complement each other by permitting the firm to retain flexibility and bring down average costs.

FIGURE 3.1

COMPETITIVE PRODUCTION SYSTEMS IN THE MANUFACTURE OF WOMEN'S DRESSES

	Low Priced (150-250FF)	Medium-Priced (250-700FF)	High Priced (> 700FF)
CLASSIC [1,000-10,000 articles]	large firms using nearby OTP suppliers	large firms with a strong brandname using OTP	
Long Circuit [six months]	medium-sized firms using Asian sub-contracting		large firms with a strong image using local sub-contracting
FASHION [<2,2000 articles]	large firms using local subcontractors	large firms with a strong brandname using local subcontracting	
Short Circuit [<six weeks]	small local enterprises with good market links		

Source: Adapted from The Boston Consulting Group, *Les Mechanismes de la Competitivité dans les Industries du Textile et de l'habillement de la CEE* (June 1984) pp.93-101 (Rapport de synthèse préparé pour la Direction Generale III de la commission des Communautés Européennes).

IMPLICATIONS FOR THE NIES

From the OECD producers' perspective, therefore, the current situation appears quite fluid, with opportunities for domestic and international subcontracting likely to grow. From a Third World perspective, however, these changes constitute a new challenge. For the more advanced Third World producers, at issue is the ability to master the knowledge-intensive aspects of this newly transformed industry. The relationship of *Liz Claiborne* to *Fang Bros.*, its major Asian subcontractor, is illustrative.

Liz Claiborne, like many of the middle- and lower-priced ready-to-wear enterprises engaged in overseas subcontracting,

> bases the quantity of its production runs on the number of garments it expects to sell in the two-month period that each season typically stays in the stores. Most items are sellouts, and sometimes they sell out very quickly, but there is no provision for increasing output in response to demand, nor is a garment ever repeated in a subsequent season...[42]

Thus a senior company official and the firm's local agent, working with their preferred East Asian subcontractor, plan each collection—in terms of costs and delivery dates—at least six months in advance. Because quota limitations can interfere with delivery dates, working with an internationalized Hong Kong, Taiwanese or Korean firm provides both the cost and quota flexibility needed. The division of labour in these arrangements is thus quite distinct. In the case of *Liz Claiborne* and the Fang family enterprises, designs are provided by *Liz Claiborne* and the Fangs manage the production end, shifting production among their clothing factories in Hong Kong, Thailand, Malaysia, Ireland and Panama as quotas fill up and as the amount of labour time required increases relative to the price elasticity of demand for the product. Thus, baby clothes, for which demand is relatively price inelastic, mark-ups are small and quality workmanship is less important, are delegated to their overseas factories, while men's jackets and suits, which require more tailoring, are kept at home, at least until the Hong Kong quota fills up. When that happens, the factories closest to Hong Kong with the highest skill levels will be next in line.[43]

As this example demonstrates, the established NIEs, because of their long apprenticeship in the industry and the considerable managerial and production capabilities they have amassed, are in a favoured position to take advantage of the new competitive environment.[44] But even they are now coming up against limits on their ability to adjust. In large part this is due to the shift within the industry from a labour- to a knowledge-intensive mode of production, and from competition based solely on price to competition based more equally on price and creativity.

Throughout the 1960s and 1970s, the ability of textile and clothing firms in the NIEs to respond to these changes hinged critically upon their mastery of *production* technology. Thus as textile and clothing quotas, based on volume rather than value, tightened and were extended to more fabrics and product categories, these firms absorbed the new production techniques in spinning, weaving and knitting, used them to increase efficiency, and gradually moved downstream—away from textiles and towards clothing. In the late 1970s and early 1980s this led to a number of managerial errors, notably over-investment in waterjet looms for the synthetic fabric industry in Korea,[45] and to some bankruptcies. But on the whole, accelerated rates of modernization combined with a far higher annual rate of machine utilization, considerably lower salaries, and longer working weeks in the Asian NIEs than in the advanced industrial countries, enabled these NIEs to compete successfully in price terms with the advanced industrial countries over a wide range of standardized products that benefit from economies of scale through mass production. That period is now coming to an end.

A recent study by Mody and Wheeler, for example, points to the erosion of Korea's competitive advantage *vis-à-vis* the United States in standardized products, as the American clothing industry automates and becomes more flexible.[46] Currently, U.S. firms come close to their Korean counterparts in costs for only two of the products studied. Yet speed has increasingly become more of a determinant in the choice of production sites. Integrated production by American firms within the U.S. market, and subcontracting by U.S. firms to nearby countries, such as Jamaica, where turnaround time is roughly 36 days, will outcompete Korean integrated production and Korean-Jamaican production which require 66 and 71 days, respectively.[47] Added to this is the fact that Korea's competitive advantage *vis-à-vis* lower cost Asian producers is also fast disappearing as its own labour costs rise.[48]

To compensate, firms from the Asian NIEs have moved into higher value added products within the garment industry. This, however, requires considerable improvement in product design and variety, and the development of marketing expertise along with continued modernization of textile and clothing production itself. Such a dual strategy is currently being pursued in Korea where some $4 billion in new credits has been allocated by the Ministry of Industry for plant modernization that will reduce labour content through automation, upgrade quality, and improve flexibility.[49]

At the same time, universities and companies have set up programs in fashion design. However, this effort to strengthen design capabilities in Korea has encountered social constraints that may prove more intractable than acquiring high speed automated machinery and learning to operate it efficiently. The central problem is the quasi-impossibility for educated women to work after marriage. Fashion designers, who apart from their creative capabilities are principally forecasters, require from seven to ten years of post-university experience to hone this skill. The absence of experienced fashion designers, most of whom are women, is thus a limiting factor on the ability of Korea's clothing manufacturers to export Korean fashions.

Proximity to the local market has enabled a domestic fashion industry to develop and a small number of firms have recently begun to design for foreign markets. Further expansion of this sector, however, is slowed by the lack of marketing capabilities among firms whose growth was based primarily upon subcontracting. Few are the Asian firms which, following upon the *Benetton* example, have launched their own sales networks in the United States as the *Fang Brothers* or the Korean firm *Non-No Fashions* have recently done.[50] Instead, most firms in the NIEs have sought to maintain their competitive advantage as managers of the production process by attempting to develop longer term relationships with North American, Japanese and European subcontractors and by reducing production costs through internationalization.

Stable relationships with preferred Far Eastern companies who organize production to meet pre-arranged deadlines and price terms and who bear the risks of direct foreign investment and of trade embargos, provide numerous cost advantages for large firms in the advanced industrial countries. They also reinforce the market power of these large firms in the NIEs, contributing to an increase in concentration in the Asian industry and to the creation of additional barriers to entry for newcomers. Among Hong Kong manufacturers, for example, small firms are already losing out to the larger companies. In Korea, MFA quotas are allocated on the basis of past export performance, a procedure that discriminates against smaller independent companies and favours established large firms which are usually affiliates of the Chaebol.[51]

During the 1980s, however, as the MFA became more restrictive and as domestic export production reached the limits of various national quotas, the large NIE firms could grow further only if they could secure a share of the quotas available in other Third World countries. This has led to dramatic increases in the extension of production by NIE companies to countries with unused quotas or to countries covered by special agreements ensuring access to the

U.S. or European Community market. The list of overseas holdings is already extensive for many Hong Kong firms particularly in Macao, Mauritius, Thailand and Malaysia. Many more have subcontracted spinning and weaving operations to China and four Hong Kong firms have jumped the EC's protective barriers and established factories in Ireland, France and Italy.[52] *Fang Bros.*, for example, has a plant in Ireland and *Peninsula Knitters Ltd.*, another major Hong Kong knitwear firm, has established itself in Northern England. Although Henry Y.Y. Tang, managing director of *Peninsula*, acknowledged that it costs 30 percent more to make sweaters in the U.K., the investment is regarded as an important safety valve since the U.S. restricts imports of Asian textiles but allows European manufacturers to ship unlimited numbers of garments.[53]

Because Taiwanese and Korean garment makers tend to be less flexible than their Hong Kong counterparts, their internationalization began somewhat later. By the early 1980s, however, three Taiwanese firms had established joint ventures in Panama to produce pullovers, jeans and slacks destined for the American market,[54] and others had invested in Macao and Malaysia.[55] In 1989, Taiwanese firms invested nearly $2 billion in Thailand, the Philippines, Indonesia and Malaysia, much of it in the textile and clothing industry.[56] As the data in Table 3.4 show, prior to the mid-1980s, Korean firms also had few overseas investments in textiles and clothing, but in 1986 the pace of internationalization picked up and 105 new foreign investments were approved in the three year period 1988-90. Thirty-three of the 35 investments in the Indonesian textile and clothing industry were made during this period, as were 23 of the 24 investments in Guatemala. Like their Hong Kong competitors, three Korean clothing firms have also located in Europe.

A number of consequences flow from this pattern of adjustment by the NIEs over the past 25 years. Perhaps the most important of these, for the purposes of this paper, has been the ability of the NIEs to create new barriers to entry for potential Third World newcomers. The effects of this process are evident from the data in Table 3.5, which clearly identifies three distinct periods. In the 1960s, as the NIEs began to export, the share of the top 15 clothing exporters in total world exports began to fall and the share of the NIEs within the top 15 rose dramatically. By 1973 Hong Kong, Korea, Taiwan and China had become major clothing exporters, accounting for 33.5 percent of the clothing exports of the top fifteen exporters. During the 1970s and early 1980s, the more restrictive MFA led to growing concentration of clothing exports among the top 15 exporters who accounted for 80 percent of world clothing exports by 1986. Over that period, the NIEs

TABLE 3.4

FOREIGN INVESTMENT OF KOREAN TEXTILE AND CLOTHING FIRMS AS OF MARCH 31, 1990

Country   Year of Investment Approval

Total	Value U.S.$ mil	1982	1983	1984	1985	1986	1987	1988	1989	1990
Dominican Rep. 14	10.3	1	2	-	-	3	4	5	-	-
Costa Rica 7	13.2	-	-	-	1	4	1	1	-	-
Guatemala 24	21.6	-	-	-	-	1	-	3	17	3
Other L. American(a) 13	22.9	-	-	-	-	1	1	3	4	3
Indonesia 35	39.4	-	-	-	-	-	2	7	16	10
Philippines 10	6.9	-	-	-	-	-	1	1	6	2
Sri Lanka(b) 7	14.4	1	-	-	-	-	1	-	3	1
Other Asia (c) 13	16.4	-	-	-	-	-	1	2	5	5
U.S. 10	18.2	-	-	1	-	1	3	1	3	1
Europe(d) 3	2.4	-	-	-	-	-	-	1	2	-
Other 2	2.2	-	-	-	-	-	-	-	-	-

Notes: (a) Includes Jamaica (3), Panama (4), Honduras (2) one of which was established in 1978, Colombia (1), Brazil (1) and Paraguay (1).
          (b) Includes one investment in 1978.
          (c) Includes Thailand (3), Bangladesh (1), Pakistan (1), Hong Kong (1), India (1), China (4), Malaysia (1) and Burma (1).
          (d) Includes Ireland (1), Turkey (2).

Source: Korea Federation of Textile Industries, March 31, 1990, SCS.

consolidated their position within the top 15 clothing exporters, their share of exports rising to 49.2 percent, and with only one new country, India, entering their ranks. Since 1986, the overall share of the top 15 exporters in world clothing exports has declined to 71 percent suggesting that a large number of

TABLE 3.5
TOP 15 WORLD EXPORTERS OF CLOTHING
(BILLION U.S. DOLLARS)

1963		1973		1982		1986		1989	
Italy	0.34	H.K.	1.39	H.K.	4.73	H.K.	8.39	H.K.	14.0
H.K.	0.24	Italy	1.30	Italy	4.41	Italy	7.57	Italy	9.4
France	0.20	France	1.04	Korea	3.86	Korea	5.48	Korea	9.1
Japan	0.20	Germany	0.90	Taiwan	2.90	Taiwan	4.23	China	6.1
Germany	0.15	Korea	0.75	Germany	2.52	Germany	4.20	Germany	5.6
U.K.	0.11	Taiwan	0.71	China	2.20	China	2.97	Taiwan	4.7
Benelux	0.10	Benelux	0.57	France	1.82	France	2.57	France	3.6
U.S.	0.09	U.K.	0.44	U.K.	1.47	U.K.	1.80	Turkey	2.8
Neth.	0.07	Neth.	0.41	U.S.	0.99	Portugal	1.48	Portugal	2.6
Switz.	0.04	Japan	0.37	Benelux	0.75	Turkey	1.20	U.K.	2.4
Austria	0.04	U.S.	0.29	Romania	0.71	Neth.	1.11	Thailand	2.3
Yugoslav.	0.02	Poland	0.28	Neth.	0.69	Benelux	1.05	U.S.	2.2
Portugal	0.02	Romania	0.25	Finland	0.65	U.S.	0.88	India	1.9
Canada	0.01	Finland	0.21	Portugal	0.65	India	0.79	Neth.	1.6
Taiwan	0.01	China	0.20	Yugoslavia	0.61	Japan	0.73	Greece	1.5

Share of top 15 in total world exports:

    84%   78%   73%   80%   71%

Share of LDCs in top 15:

    4.5%   33.5%   47.3%   49.2%   54.5%

Source: GATT—Textiles and Clothing, p. 43; GATT—International Trade 86-87 (Geneva: GATT, 1987) p. 18; GATT—International Trade 89-90 p. 66.

newcomers have begun to export. As the data on internationalization reveal, however, much of this output is a function of overseas investment and subcontracting relationships established with firms in the advanced industrial countries and more recently with firms in the NIEs. Within the group of 15 major clothing exporters, moreover, the share of the established NIEs, has risen and only Thailand from among the second tier NIEs has been able to enter the ranks of the world's major clothing exporters.

If the *Liz Claiborne-Fang Brothers* example can be generalized, increased international subcontracting may not benefit newcomers as much as it will the large Hong Kong, Taiwan and Korean firms that have become the principal interlocutors for the large OECD manufacturers and distributors seeking to subcontract. The case of Thailand is exemplary.

Ever since Thailand actively began to promote private investment during the 1960s, a large number of foreign companies have invested in the textile and clothing industry there. By the mid-1980s, most of the large integrated textile-clothing firms in Thailand were joint ventures with Japanese, followed by Taiwanese, and Korean partners.[57] American firms tended to license production or simply subcontract to local firms.[58] Much of this investment, particularly in the clothing industry, was export-oriented and destined for the U.S. market. In the summer of 1986, the surge in exports from Thailand led to a U.S. embargo on all clothing imports from that country.[59] While many of the larger Asian subcontractors could shift production elsewhere, the impact on employment and output in Thailand was impressive and more fragile independent producers were badly affected. The subsequent export recovery has strengthened the larger firms, most of which are joint ventures, at the expense of smaller, locally owned family firms. In addition, the emergence of independent Thai textile and clothing exporters has been handicapped by the high cost of imported yarn and the relatively poor quality of weaving and finishing operations. Dependence on imported fabrics for the garment industry is thus growing[60] and, along with it, reliance on the Asian NIE firms who supply these fabrics and manage the process of subcontracting.[61]

Over the next decade, changes in technology and in the mode of competition are likely to widen the gap between the existing NIEs and the second tier textile and clothing exporters, and to reinforce the competition among them. Simultaneously these changes will give rise to new contradictions in the process of adjustment within the NIEs themselves.

New innovations in sewing, for example, will emerge, and, like the overhead transport networks that speed the flow-through of garments between workstations, their diffusion is likely to be rapid. Although these technologies will remain accessible to all Third World producers, costs will deter some, and an inability to operate the new technologies efficiently will reduce their effectiveness in many other LDCs. Hence, only the larger NIE firms may, once again, be able to take advantage of these innovations rapidly.

Moreover, in an increasingly fashion and cost sensitive world not all Third World countries will be attractive candidates for subcontracting in the future. Although the MFA encourages the continued growth of international subcontracting, the integration of design, production and commercialization tends to favour those sites nearest to major consuming markets, and the use of designer labels creates yet another barrier to entry to independent producers from the less developed countries. The spread of computer aided design, inventory and management systems, moreover, enables larger firms in the OECD countries to analyze their cost structures, varying the combination of fibres, fabrics and colours used, and optimizing the composition of their collections to cater to the differing price and "creativity" elasticities of demand in different market segments. The production of any given article can thus be integrated into an overall optimizing strategy that changes in relation to the emergence of new efficient techniques, or in accordance with the changing characteristics of final markets, or of potential production sites. This increases the vulnerability of Third World subcontractors to changes in the advanced industrial countries.

While the major Asian NIEs are clearly efficient producers of high quality output and have the capacity to adjust within this sector quite flexibly, it must not be forgotten that this ability is the product of a long period of apprenticeship which would-be NIEs have not yet had. In addition, the integrated nature of their operations have enabled these first-tier NIEs to react rapidly to changes in technology and in the complex pattern of quotas that now govern international trade, using the MFA to both safeguard their position as dominant exporters and to keep their costs low. Even they, however, do not have the full range of technological capabilities required to *initiate* changes and become industry leaders themselves. At both the conceptualization and the commercialization ends of the production process, with rare exceptions, they remain dependent on their links to manufacturers and distributors in the advanced industrial countries.

ENDNOTES

Research for this paper was made possible, in part, by a grant from the Social Sciences and Humanities Research Council of Canada.

1. The distinction here is between firms that are competitors in their own right and those that are able to export because they are subcontractors in a network controlled by a principal at both the conceptual and marketing ends of the production process, and that enjoy this role only to the extent that labour costs are low enough to compensate for relatively less efficient production. The key question then is the extent to which subcontractors master all of the technological capabilities needed to become independent competitors. It is not intuitively obvious that such learning automatically or invariably occurs.

2. Howard Pack, *Productivity, Technology and Industrial Development: A Case Study in Textiles* (New York: Oxford University Press for the World Bank, 1987), p. 7.

3. Using weaving as our example, in the former case production methods differ depending upon the principle by which the weft is inserted into the warp, by shuttle, rapier, projectile or air jet. In the latter, the emphasis is on the labour/capital ratio that characterizes the production process.

4. Michael A. Amsalem, *Technology Choice in Developing Countries The Textile and Pulp and Paper Industries* (Cambridge, MA. The MIT Press, 1983); Barend de Vries and Willem Brakel, *Restructuring of Manufacturing Industry—The Experience of the Textile Industry in Pakistan, Philippines, Portugal, and Turkey,* World Bank Staff Working Papers Number 558 (Washington, DC: 1983); Sanjaya Lall, "Acquisition of Technological Capability Project World Bank India Sector Overview: Textiles" (Oxford, April 1984); Hasa Mfaume Mlawa, "The Acquisition of Technology, Technological Capability and Technical Change: A Study of the Textile Industry in Tanzania," (unpublished D. Phil. Thesis, University of Sussex, England, January 1983); David Morawetz, *Why the Emperor's New Clothes Are Not Made in Colombia: A Case Study in Latin American and East Asian Manufactured Exports* (New York: Oxford University Press, 1981); Lynn K. Mytelka, "Stimulating Effective Technology Transfer: The Case of Textiles in Africa," in N. Rosenberg and C. Frischtak (eds.), *International Technology Transfer* (New York: Praeger, 1985), pp. 77-127; L.K. Mytelka, "Ivorian industry at the crossroads," in Frances Stewart, Sanjaya Lall and Samuel Wangwe (eds.), *Alternative Development Strategies in Sub-Saharan Africa* (London: Macmillan, forthcoming); and Pack, *Productivity, Technology and Industrial Development....*

5. These data are from OECD, *National Accounts,* Volume 2, various years; EUROSTAT, *National Accounts Statistics,* various years; United Nations, *Yearbook of National Accounts Statistics,* various years; GATT, *Demand, Production and Trade in Textiles an Clothing,* Report by the Secretariat (Geneva: Gatt, Doc. No. COM.TEX/W/23 16 December 1990); and idem *Updating the 1984 GATT Secretariat Study "Textiles and Clothing in the World Economy"* (Geneva: Doc. No. MTN.GNG/NG4/W/8, 30 November 1987).

6. UNCTAD, Program of Co-operation among Developing Countries, Exporters of Textiles and Clothing, "The Multi-fibre Arrangement in Theory and Practice," Back-up Study on International Trade in Textiles and Clothing, Revised Draft, Karachi Workshop, July 21-26, 1984, p. 120.

7. L.K. Mytelka, "New Modes of Competition in the Textile and Clothing Industry: Some Consequences for Third World Exporters," in Jorge Niosi (ed.), *Technology and National Competitiveness* (Montreal: McGill-Queen's University Press, 1991), pp. 225-246.

8.   L.K. Mytelka, "In Search of a Partner: The State and the Textile Industry in France," in S. Cohen and P. Gourevitch (eds.), *France in a Troubled World Economy* (U.K.: Butterworth, 1982), pp. 132-150; L.K. Mytelka and Rianne Mahon, "Industry, the State and the New Protectionism: Textiles in Canada and France," *International Organization* 37/4 (Autumn 1983); G. Shepherd, "Textiles: New Ways of Surviving in an Old Industry," in G. Shepherd, F. Duchene and C. Saunders (eds.), *Public and Private Strategies for Change* (London: Frances Pinter, 1983), pp. 26-51.; and B. Toyne *et al.*, *The Global Textile Industry* (London: George Allen and Unwin, 1984).

9.   In the case of open-end spinning, for example, this meant restriction to coarser counts, and in knitting to synthetic fibres.

10. CGP (Commissariat General du Plan), *L'Enjeu du textile française: Le Marché mondial* (Paris: CGP, Commission "Prospective des échanges internationaux," Rapporteur—L.K. Mytelka, 1986), pp. 99-110.

11. V. Frobel, J. Heinrichs and O. Kreye, *The New International Division of Labour: Structural Unemployment in Industrialised Countries and Industrialization in Developing Countries* (Cambridge: Cambridge University Press, 1980); Pierre Dubois and Giusto Barisi, *Le Défi technologique dans l'industrie de l'habillement: Les Stratégies des entrepreneurs français et italiens* (Paris: CNRS, ATP Internationale—1981, 1982).

12. ITMF (International Textile Manufacturers Federation), *International Textile Machinery Shipment Statistics* (Zurich: ITMF, 1986).

13. ITMF, *International Production Cost Comparison Spinning/Weaving* (Zurich: ITMF, 1979, 1983, 1987).

14. In the United States, for example, *West Point Pepperell* took over *Cluett Peabody* in 1985 and *J.P. Stevens* in 1988. It was taken over in turn by *Farley* in 1988. *Farley* along with *Burlington* now dominate the U.S. textile industry. In the U.K. *Carrington Viyella* and *Vantona* merged and in 1986 were taken over by *Coats Patons*, which in turn took over *Tootal* in 1990. A similar pattern has emerged in France and Italy. Concentration is also occurring in the clothing industry. One of the most recent examples is the takeover of Germany's leading men's fashion company, *Hugo Boss*, by the Japanese group, *Leyton House*. Refer to Henri Loizeau, "L'Habillement allemand sied à ses concurrents," *L'Usine Nouvelle* No. 2251 (18 Janvier 1990), p. 41.

15. See L.K. Mytelka, "Stimulating Effective Technology Transfer," "Ivorian industry at the crossroads," and "New Modes of Competition."

16. K. Fukuda, "Technological Development Trends in Textile Machinery," *Digest of Japanese Industry and Technology*, No. 172 (1982), p. 11.

17. U. Hartmann, "Structural Adjustment: The West German Experience," CEPS/EPL Conference, Centre Borschette, Bruxelles, Decembre 9-10, 1985, pp. 11-12.

18. *Ibid.* p. 12.

19. Y. Kuramoto, "Technological Development in Weaving Machinery of Japan," *Digest of Japanese Industry and Technology*, No. 207 (1985), p. 13.

20. *L'Usine Nouvelle*, No. 18 (May 5, 1988), p. 56.

21. Interview, February 19, 1985.

22. Interview, May 30, 1985.

23. James Lardner, "Annals of Business: The Sweater Trade," *The New Yorker* Parts 1 and 2, January 11, 1987 and January 18, 1987.

24. *Financial Times*, April 28, 1988.

25. ITCB (International Textiles and Clothing Bureau), "Textiles and Clothing: Recent Developments in Trade, Technology, and Trade Policy," Agenda Item 1, Seoul Meeting September, 3-7, 1985, pp. 11-15.

26. Employment, however, declined dramatically. By way of illustration, the level of textile and clothing output in the EC in 1983 was only ten percent below that in 1973 (Index of 102.7 in textiles and 103.4 in clothing) but over the same period, employment in the textile industry fell by 43.4 percent and in clothing by 41.2 percent. Refer to GATT, *Demand, Production and Trade in Textile and Clothing*, p. 5.

27. *Ibid.*, p. 25.

28. ITMF, *International Production Cost Comparison*.

29. "Now the name of the game is style," *Financial Times* "Survey" April 28, 1988, p. 1.

30. *Ibid.*

31. Leigh Bruce, "The Bright New Worlds of Benetton," *International Management*, November 1987, p. 29.

32. James Heskett and Sergio Signorelli, "How Benetton has streamlined and branched out worldwide in casual clothing market," Condensed version of Harvard Business School case 9-685-014, *International Management* May 1985, pp. 79-82.

33. "Steilmann Fashions a Sharper Image," *Financial Times*, June 11, 1988.

34. CGP, *L'Enjeu du Textile*, pp. 58-68.

35. K. Hoffman and H. Rush, *Microelectronics and Clothing: The Impact of Technical change on a Global Industry* (Brighton: SPRU, University of Sussex, January 1985), pp. 4.4-4; F. Clauzel, "La robotization du prêt-à-porter," *Journal du Textile*, Octobre 8, 1985, pp. 42-47.

36. Interview, Juki, June 1990.

37. D. Michel, "Automation: Trois fois moins de temps pour faire une chemise," *L'Usine Nouvelle*, Supplément AU, No. 29 (18 juillet 1985).

38. M. Daniel, "Une expérience d'automation dans la chemise," Colloque CESTA/FIT, Paris, 20-22 juin 1985; Didier Gout, "Confection: L'arrivée des cellules flexibles," *L'Usine Nouvelle*, No. 222 (June 1989), pp. 44-45.

39. "Survey of the World Textile Industry," *Financial Times,* March 22, 1989, p. IV.

40. Fiorenza Belussi, *Benetton: Information Technology in Production and Distribution: A Case Study of the Innovative Potential of Traditional Sectors,* SPRU Occasional Paper Series, No. 25 (Brighton: University of Sussex, 1987).

41. *New York Times* September 9, 1990, p. 4.

42. J. Lardner, "Annals of Business," p. 45.

43. *Ibid.,* p. 58.

44. Many of the largest Hong Kong clothing manufacturers, for example, have a long association with the textile industry, dating back to pre-revolutionary Shanghai. S.C. Fang, father of Kenneth, Jeffrey and Vincent Fang, owners of *Fang Bros.,* ran spinning and weaving factories in Shanghai before fleeing to Hong Kong. See Lardner, "Annals of Business...." Francis Tien, father of James Tien, head of the *Manhattan Garments* group of Hong Kong, was another of the Shanghai entrepreneurs who brought expertise and equipment to Hong Kong's infant textile industry in the 1950s. See L. Goodstadt, "Textile house of the rising son," *South.* March 1985, p. 64. Similarly in Korea the effective manipulation of textile technology during the 1960s and 1970s was a product of decades of industrial growth—ten percent per year in the period 1928-40—and although much of the factory-based textile industry was Japanese owned prior to the 1930s, by 1939 almost 60 percent of the textile plants were owned by Koreans. See Martin Bell and Kurt Hoffman, *Industrial Development with Imported Technology: A Strategic Perspective on Policy,* SPRU (Brighton: University of Sussex, September 1981), p. 146.

45. Jang Jung-Soo, "Korea's Textile Industry: A Battle on Two Fronts," *Business Korea.* October 1984, p. 24.

46. Ashoka Mody and David Wheeler, "Towards a Vanishing Middle: Competition in the World Garment Industry," *World Development,* 15/10-11 (1987), pp. 1269-1284.

47. *Ibid.,* p. 1270.

48. *Korea Times.* November 5, 1990.

49. "Heavy S. Korea aid for textiles," *Financial Times.* November 28, 1989.

50. In the late 1980s, *Fang Brothers* opened six retail stores in prime malls in Miami, California, Texas and Georgia. See Lardner, "Annals of Business," p. 48. Like *Benetton, The GAP* and *The Limited* in the U.S., *Caroll* and *Manouchian* in France and *Next* in the U.K., the *"Florida Adams"* stores, inspired apparently by the appeal of the "Indiana Jones" movies, sell a line of basic co-ordinated sportswear articles differentiated only by "name". *Non-No Fashions,* established in 1971, is a pioneer in the development of the fashion industry in Korea. In 1985 they introduced their "Chatelaine" line and in 1987 opened a "Chatelaine" shop on Rodeo Drive in Beverly Hills. Interviews of textile and clothing manufacturers, Korea, May 1990.

51.   Interviews, 1990. *Chaebol* are the highly centralized conglomerates that have been at the forefront of the Korean "economic miracle."

52.   These data have been culled from a variety of sources including: *Business Week* August 26, 1985; Goodstadt, "Textile House," p. 84; ITGLWF, *Multinational Companies in the Textile, Garment and Leather Industries* (Brussels: International Textile, Garment and Leather Workers' Federation, 1984), pp.110-113; and United States International Trade Commission (USITC), "Emerging Textile Exporting Countries," Publication No. 1716 (Washington, D.C.: ITC, July 1985), p. 187.

53.   "Hong Kong's End Run Around U.S. Protectionism," *Business Week,* August 26, 1985.

54.   USITC, Emerging Textile Exporting Countries, p. 424.

55.   UNCTAD, *The Multi-fibre Arrangement,* Annex 5.32.

56.   Michael Bociurkiw, "Textile firm weaves a diverse tapestry," *Globe and Mail* November 12, 1990, p. B6; and C.E.P.I.I., *La Lettre du C.E.P.I.I.* (Paris: Centre d'Etudes Prospectives et d'Informations Internationales, Octobre 23, 1990), p. 3.

57.   USITC, "Emerging Textile Exporting Countries," p. 389.

58.   *Ibid.,* p. 390.

59.   In the case of Indonesia, whose apparel exports jumped from $4.8 million in 1977 to $154.1 million in 1983 and to $295.7 million in 1984 (*UN COM-TRADE Database*), much of it directed towards the U.S. market, tighter quotas over a larger number of MFA categories were negotiated bilaterally with the U.S. in 1985. See Steven Jones, "Textile Pact Eases Indonesia-U.S. Spat," *The Asian Wall Street Journal,* July 5-6, 1985, p. 1. The NIEs are not immune from this problem as illustrated by the imposition of voluntary export restraints on Korea by Japan in 1989 following a surge in clothing imports from that country.

60.   Raphael Chaponniere, "Scope and Outline for Asean Regional Co-operation in the Textiles and Textile Products Industry" draft report prepared for UNIDO (1985), p. 87.

61.   Similar difficulties affect other 'second tier' exporters such as Morocco. See Mytelka, "New Modes of Competition in the Textile and Clothing Industry".

	CHAPTER 4
Flexible Specialization: What's That Got to Do with the Price of Fish?	Barbara Neis

INTRODUCTION

There is general agreement among crisis theorists that capitalism was in crisis during the 1970s and is currently undergoing a process of restructuring.[1] However, they have offered divergent explanations for that crisis and arrive at different conclusions as to the significance of the current restructuring process for the future of capitalism and society as a whole. Michael Piore and Charles Sabel,[2] for example, adopt an institutionalist approach. They maintain that we are poised at a "Second Industrial Divide" which creates the possibility of restructuring capitalism away from the mass production of commodities by deskilled workers, towards "flexible specialization" involving the production of customized commodities in a community-based context that encourages innovation and limits competition. Rather than reducing workers to appendages of machines, as in the case of mass production, flexible specialization allows for a relationship between workers and technology similar to that which once existed between artisans and their tools.[3]

Others view the current intense interest in the informal economy and in more "flexible" labour supplies, forms of technology and strategies for managerial control, as nothing more than a new ideological package for the same old capitalism. They maintain, correctly, that this emphasis on flexibility is not new[4] and that, at the point of production, the "elasticity" of human labour, the adaptive capacity of workers and the scope for intensification have always been crucial to capital.[5] In this view, the search for greater workplace "flexibility" is often fused with managerial strategies for control that constrain and limit this search to forms of "flexibility" that do not threaten managerial control.[6] Moreover, the Japanese systems of management which Piore and Sabel identify with flexible specialization, are said to be integrally linked to weak welfare state structures that reinforce dependence on the corporations and strengthen sexist and racist divisions among workers.[7]

Alain Lipietz also adopts an institutionalist approach to the analysis of capitalist crisis and, like Piore and Sabel, identifies tendencies towards more flexible production within the current process of crisis and restructuring.[8] However, he offers a somewhat different explanation for the current crisis, one which is more systematically rooted in an understanding of the dynamics of accumulation and of the related tensions between flexibility and control. Lipietz's approach, and that of the Regulationists in general, also emphasizes historical context, providing more conceptual space for envisaging the emergence of diverse political and social arrangements within a particular regime of accumulation.[9]

This paper takes up the debate around Piore and Sabel's concept of "flexible specialization" within a broader context that identifies the 1970s crisis as one of Fordist regimes of accumulation.[10] It is based on a case study which analyses the crisis and restructuring of the North Atlantic and Newfoundland fishing industries in the 1970s and 1980s. In this instance the forces that may have eroded the process of Fordist accumulation are different from those identified by Lipietz and by Piore and Sabel.[11] By combining the historical specificity of a case study with the general conceptual categories associated with the regulation approach the paper seeks to enhance our general understanding of the current crisis.

The direction of crisis and restructuring in the fishery during the 1970s was from a Fordist, towards a more flexible or post-Fordist regime of accumulation. I will argue that the forces underlying this process were the outcome of ecological factors. These were mediated by changes in the regulation regime at the point of intersection between capitalist production and the fishery resource, and by changes in the relationship between domestic work and capitalist production at the final demand stage of the production-realization cycle. The combined impact of these changes was to deepen the conflict between responsiveness and control at the point of production within the fishery. This, in turn, undermined accumulation and contributed to changes in the regime and the mode of accumulation within the industry.

The study diverges from most crisis research by focusing on an industry that would generally be defined as marginal or peripheral to capitalism and that is not located within the industrial heartland. However, it is precisely the "peripheral" nature of the fishery that makes this case study valuable because the industry presents us with a situation in which the linkages between nature, production, and realization are relatively simple. An exploration of these linkages will reveal some hitherto neglected forces that may have contributed to the development of the crisis of Canada's version of the Fordist regime and that are playing an important role in the current round of restructuring.[12]

CRISIS IN THE FISHING INDUSTRY

The northwest Atlantic fishery expanded dramatically after World War II and, until 1977, the enormous fish stocks of this area were largely unregulated. An Atlantic Canadian household-based inshore fishery, in which the communities themselves regulated access within a three-mile limit, co-existed with a largely unregulated corporate trawler fleet fishing the Grand Banks alongside vessels from Spain, Portugal and France. From the 1950s the development of factory freezer trawlers (FFTs) in Britain, their subsequent adoption by the Soviet Union and other countries, and the rapid expansion of the infrastructure for frozen food marketing that characterized the rise of Fordism in North America and Europe dramatically altered the structure of this fishery. By 1965, fleets of FFTs from the Soviet Union and other Eastern bloc countries, Japan, Cuba, West Germany, and Britain created a "city of lights" in the northwest Atlantic.[13]

Total catches in the northwest Atlantic expanded dramatically after 1955, but peaked for foreign vessels in 1968 and for Newfoundland in 1969, after which they declined from almost 1.8 million metric tons to only .47 in 1977, a reduction of almost 74 percent.[14] Stock depletion had clearly undermined accumulation in the Atlantic Canadian fishery in 1968 and again in 1974. On both occasions, the federal and the provincial governments responded by pouring government money into the industry. Prior to 1974, most of this money went into financing local companies, constructing trawlers, and encouraging multinational food conglomerates to set up operations in Newfoundland. However, on each occasion the presence of the conglomerates thus attracted was shortlived as they were soon supplanted by regional firms.

The 1974 crisis resulted in increased state regulation of access to the resource and the rate at which it could be exploited. In 1977, in part because of increased interest in offshore minerals, Canada introduced an exclusive economic management zone that extended jurisdiction to 200 miles. Increased regulation of the resource, predictions of global food shortages,[15] massive stock recoveries and generous government subsidies combined to encourage expanded investment in the fishery.[16] This was further stimulated as companies competed to improve yields; to increase the range of species processed and products produced; and to assert control over a fishery being temporarily (as it turned out) restructured towards increased reliance on inshore and nearshore, owner-operated fisheries. This latter pattern also meant that this period of expansion saw the rapid unionization of inshore fishers, plant workers and trawler workers in Newfoundland and Labrador.[17]

In the early 1980s, the pace of accumulation in the Atlantic fishery declined again as high interest rates, heavy debts associated with high capital costs, and declining productivity undermined accumulation. On this occasion the hardest hit firms were larger, vertically-integrated trawler firms like Nickerson-National Sea, Fishery Products and the Lake Group. The symptoms of this crisis included a prolonged strike-lockout between fish processors and trawler workers, and between fish processors and inshore fishers in 1980. By August 1981,

> eighteen processing plants and trawler operations were closed down in Atlantic Canada, mainly those of National Sea and Nickerson's, throwing four thousand people out of work...The industry was in need of reorganization, and at risk were 129 trawlers, 45 processing plants, and a debt of over $300 million, held principally by the Bank of Nova Scotia (over $200 million), the Province of Nova Scotia (over $40 million), and the Province of Newfoundland ($30 million).[18]

In the fall of 1983, after a major task force investigation and months of negotiations, agreements to restructure the ownership of the major companies were signed.

I have elsewhere reviewed existing explanations for the crisis that occurred in the Atlantic fishery during the early 1980s.[19] This chapter develops an explanation of that crisis based on insights gained from the regulation approach and from labour process, ecological, and feminist research. This explanation attempts to account both for the displacement of Fordist regimes of accumulation within the North Atlantic fishery in the 1970s by a regime of accumulation based on more flexible technologies, more decentralized, community-based production and a reskilling of work, and for the threatened bankruptcy of those firms most closely wedded to Fordism in the early 1980s.

THE ANALYTICAL FRAMEWORK

The institutionalist approaches that seem to offer the best basis for an analysis of the trends observed in the North Atlantic fishery during the 1970s are Piore and Sabel's "flexible specialization" approach and Lipietz's Regulation approach. Despite significant differences in their explanations for the causes of the current capitalist crisis, both Lipietz[20] and Piore and Sabel[21] concur about the possibilities that confront capitalism as a result. Restructuring could, but will not necessarily, involve labour processes characterized by less separation between conception and execution and greater reliance on more flexible technologies producing a broader range of more specialized commodities. There are, however, some important shortcomings in both of these analytical frameworks and in the explanations they offer for the crisis in Fordism.

Piore and Sabel locate the origins of the crisis in the saturation of markets for mass produced goods. However, the notion of market saturation explains little, and the related assumption that capital stands in a passive relationship to final markets is problematic since, as has been noted by Braverman and others, the shaping of market demand is a multimillion dollar industry. If market saturation jeopardizes capitalist profitability, capital will clearly attempt to manipulate consumption demand so as to create new markets.[22]

Also, these advocates of a "flexible" future generally pay insufficient attention to the problem of capitalist control since they often discuss productivity, flexibility, and rigidity without linking these to the problems inherent in the production and realization of surplus value. But this constitutes the basis of capitalist production and ensures that the control of the labour process and the relationship between the reserve army of labour and capitalist profitability must remain central concerns of capital.[23] In contrast to Samuel Bowles, David Gordon and Thomas Weisskopf,[24] these authors see no contradiction between full employment and capitalism. Moreover, because of their neglect of the problem of control, Piore and Sabel collapse a wide variety of structures that involve varying degrees of workers' control into the single conceptual category of "flexible specialization."

The regulation approach's view—that the crisis is one of Fordist regimes of accumulation—provides a better basis for identifying those common features of Fordism that led to the crisis, while still capturing the diversity of forms that these processes can take in specific social formations.[25] Lipietz's recognition that Fordism must articulate with noncapitalist domains in society is a particularly important insight for an analysis of the fishery crisis. In short, Lipietz offers a less problematic explanation for the crisis of Fordism and a less flawed analysis of possible future directions for capitalist production than Piore and Sabel.

Lipietz attributes the crisis of Fordism primarily to a decline in productivity resulting from the fact that Fordist control, based on the separation of conception and execution, had reached its logical limits by having appropriated all relevant workers' knowledge. This declining productivity forced Fordist firms to substitute machines for workers, thereby driving up the organic composition of capital and undermining accumulation. However, this approach cannot account for the increased strength of labour during the period of crisis both in the fishery and elsewhere.[26]

Both approaches, like most other crisis theories, neglect the barriers to capital accumulation which nature imposes[27] and overlook the possibility that capitalist penetration of domestic production could play a role in the development of capitalist crisis. The rationale for including these domains in the analysis of capitalist crisis is both logical and empirical. Logically, the capitalist mode of production depends upon these domains and cannot operate independently of them. Empirically, an analysis of the crisis in the fishing industry suggests that ecological factors, and factors related to changes in the relationship between capitalist and household production, played key roles in precipitating a crisis to which those firms most closely wedded to Fordism were particularly vulnerable. However, in order to understand the relationship between accumulation and developments at these opposite ends of the production-realization cycle, it is necessary to conceptualize Fordism somewhat differently from both Lipietz and Piore and Sabel. The work of Craig R. Littler and Graeme Salaman[28] offers a useful basis for this reconceptualization.

Littler and Salaman view the strong pressures to shift from mass to batch production in Britain during the current crisis as a result of the basic contradiction within capitalism between human responsiveness (flexibility) and co-ordination and control. From this perspective, the crisis of Fordism is rooted in an essential tension in the capital/labour relation "between the need to regulate and dominate the production process versus the need to maximize the creativity and reliability of wage labour."[29] They identify three dimensions of the resulting struggle to regulate and dominate the production process: the employment relation dimension, the constraint dimension, and the job design dimension. The employment relation is governed by both internal and external labour markets and by associated welfare state structures. The constraint dimension refers to the degree to which conception is monopolized by management;[30] while the job design dimension refers to the degree to which job tasks are fragmented. Along each of these dimensions, there is a frontier of control,[31] the location of which is the outcome of class and gender struggle, regionalism, state policy and, the relationship of a particular industry to nature and markets. Thus, a regime of accumulation, like Fordism, that relies on tight managerial control over the constraint and the job design dimensions, and on relatively untrained workers, will sacrifice human responsiveness for greater control.

Following Littler and Salaman, the crisis of Fordism thus results from forces that deepened this fundamental contradiction between human responsiveness and control, undermining the profitability of firms wedded to this regime of accumulation, and enhancing the profitability of others. The forces that might cause such a deepening of this contradiction could be located at many points in the production-realization process. These would include the relationship of capitalist production to nature, and its relationship to the realm of consumption, for example, the household. In other words, regimes of accumulation need to be conceptualized as totalities that contain both capitalist and noncapitalist domains, and changes at any point in this totality may be identified as possible threats to accumulation, potentially undermining the existing regime of accumulation. Of course, as Jane Jenson suggests,[32] the way in which such changes will affect a regime of accumulation will depend on the institutional basis for that regime in a specific time and place, and the relationships between different social formations.

The analytical framework outlined above implies a somewhat different heuristic definition of Fordism which acknowledges more clearly than the regulation framework that the precise structure will vary between and within social formations. This definition includes not only the regulatory regime associated with Fordist production, but also the ecological basis for that regime and the regulatory regime that mediates its relationship with nature; and looks beyond the cash register to the relationship between Fordism and "consumption work." As such, it encourages us to examine the possibility that accumulation could be threatened by changes in these relationships.

The Fordist relationship between capitalism and nature was based on seeking out, at a global level, large, dependable supplies of relatively homogeneous raw materials such as oil and wheat. In other words, Fordism relied heavily on direct and indirect control of such natural resources by large multinational corporations and relatively little on knowledge about nature and on efforts to transform nature (although the degree varied, for example, between agriculture and fishing). This accounts, in part, for the jigsaw pattern of development and underdevelopment that occurred in countries such as Canada, whose economies were heavily dependent on resource extraction and export.

Large, dependable supplies of cheap, homogeneous raw materials and regulatory regimes and corporate structures that ensured their availability for economic exploitation facilitated the emergence of a Fordist labour process. In this process the benefits that could be derived from increased human responsiveness tended to be sacrificed for those which could be secured through greater control. While it is generally argued that the labour process was based on a high degree of job fragmentation and a severe separation of conception from execution, it was also community-based. Internal labour markets and community-based production provided a foundation for the mass markets that were an integral component of the postwar compromise between labour and capital. The creation of nationally based welfare state structures and the introduction of Keynesian macroeconomic policies also sustained the mass consumption that was integral to Fordism.

In addition, Fordism depended on the "consumption work" done in private households where mass produced commodities were assembled and transformed to fit the requirements of individual households and their members. This "consumption work" was structured by gendered, generational and marital relations and was not subject to the same constraints as capitalist production.[33] The flexibility of this "consumption work" (primarily women's) provided the bridge between mass produced, standardised commodities and individual needs. A mass market for household oriented flexible technologies embodied in such things as electric appliances, telephones and recipe books was, thus, constituted. Women used their kitchens, living rooms and dining rooms to provide the elegant and the mundane, and to accommodate the needs of children and husbands.

Starting from this broad, heuristic definition of Fordism, what could explain the crisis of accumulation, the associated pressures to move in the direction of more flexible technologies, the increased reliance on skilled labour and indeed, the increased power of labour, that seems to have emerged during the 1970s?[34] One possible explanation is that Fordism ran up against the barriers of nature as both ecological and political forces limited capital's access to cheap, homogeneous raw materials. This helped to undermine the profitability of technologies and labour processes and to increase the competitiveness of alternatives that were more flexible, less wasteful and more reliant on skilled workers.

In addition, at the opposite end of the production-realization cycle, as Fordist producers in search of new markets expanded into areas previously located in households, certain markets for mass produced goods were eroded. As this expansion supplanted the flexibility of household consumption work with the rigidities of work governed by the requirements of capitalist production, a broad range of goods and services formerly provided in the home through women's unpaid "consumption work" came to be provided by paid workers in specialized outlets.

As unpaid "consumption work" was displaced by capitalist production, specialized facilities and production processes were established which sought to provide the range of atmospheres and commodities to which household members had become accustomed in their own homes. These changes eroded the market for many mass produced commodities and created, in their place, niche markets for more specialized products. As a result markets as a whole became more segmented in the sense that more and more products now had to meet the specialized requirements of highly specific markets and were not readily saleable in others.

The combined impact of the changes in the relationship between capitalist production and nature and in the relationship between capitalist production and household consumption was to enhance the benefits which could be derived from a greater emphasis on human responsiveness in the labour process. This was, in turn, reflected in the increased competitiveness of batch production,[35] and in the increasing threat to Fordist accumulation regimes. The following case study of the crisis of the North Atlantic and Newfoundland fishing industries in the 1970s and 1980s provides a concrete illustration of these processes.

THE CASE STUDY

As has been argued elsewhere, Fordist regimes of accumulation took a variety of different forms[36] in that they were not all characterized by the same relationship to nature, the same degree of dependence on mass markets or by the same production relations. These differences reflected the influence of politics and political structures, of class struggle, of gender relations and, more broadly, of the historical context within which Fordism had developed in specific countries and regions. Thus the version of Fordism that developed in Newfoundland's fishery was quite different from that of Britain, Germany, Iceland or Norway.

This case study explores the collapse of a number of different regimes of accumulation in the North Atlantic fishery in the 1970s. The establishment of 200 mile limits and the related increase in the regulation of the fishery resource, combined with the increased segmentation of the markets for fish products caused by the expansion of the fast food industry in the United States, deepened the contradiction and altered the trade-offs between human responsiveness and control within various fishing industries. As a result, those most closely tied to Fordist regimes of accumulation were severely weakened when the urgent need for new labour processes initiated a period of crisis and restructuring in the North Atlantic fishery.

Following World War II, the rapid development of Fordist production in Western Europe and in the United States created the impetus for a dramatic expansion of the North Atlantic fishery. This brought fishing industries associated with several different regimes of accumulation into direct competition for the abundant and relatively homogeneous fish stocks of the north Atlantic. It also resulted in the rapid depletion of those stocks.

Cheap energy supplies, war reparations payments, the rapid development of the infrastructure necessary for home consumption of frozen food products, the existence of ample, suitable fish stocks, protein shortages in both Western and Eastern bloc countries, and the absence of regulations to limit the ecological impact of expanded production, provided the impetus for the construction of huge fleets of FFTs in the Soviet Union, Japan, West Germany and, to a lesser extent, in Britain. These fleets contributed to a dramatic increase in global fish production between 1955 and 1968. According to Food and Agriculture Organization statistics (which, it is generally accepted, underestimate catch rates), the total annual global catch increased by eight percent annually in the postwar period until it peaked at the 60 million ton level in 1974.[37]

During the 1950s, many of the FFTs fished off the coasts of Iceland and Norway. But stocks in these areas became depleted and, after Iceland and Norway introduced 12 mile limits, these fleets increasingly concentrated themselves off the coast of Atlantic Canada and the northeastern United States. Some sense of the scale of this invasion can be garnered from the fact that 1,076 Western European and Communist bloc fishing vessels fished off the

North American coast in the northwest Atlantic in 1974.[38]

The countries associated most closely with FFT technology had varying regimes of accumulation. Some, like those of Germany and Britain, were variants of Fordism. Others, such as that of the Soviet Union, could be defined as state socialist. However, despite the important differences between these regimes, it is possible to argue that FFT technology represented an extreme example of the sacrifice of human responsiveness for greater control. The result was a rigid technology with a highly exploitive and constrained relationship to the natural resource on which it depended, whose profitability depended heavily on mass markets for highly standardized products. It also entailed a strong separation of work from community and of conception from execution, and produced highly fragmented jobs embedded in rigid, standardized technologies.

FFTs were characterized by a highly destructive and wasteful relationship between production and nature. The need for homogeneity was such that even valuable species of fish were often discarded or converted into fish meal.[39] The technology combined automated vessel propulsion with highly mechanized harvesting and processing of fish to produce a mobile factory that could move from stock to stock, or follow fish migration routes. The profitable operation of FFTs absolutely required access to fish stocks that were dense and relatively homogeneous and thus suited to automated harvesting and processing. However, fish stocks of this kind were relatively rare and were concentrated in the roughly 15 percent of the world's oceans that are relatively shallow and nontropical. This is why the fishing efforts of FFTs were exclusively confined to areas such as the North Atlantic, which are characterized by large concentrations of a narrow range of fish species including cod, redfish and the herring family.[40]

FFTs could be operated year-round and with more continuity than other available technologies but this depended on the availability of workers willing to be separate from their communities for prolonged periods. This separation of work and community also meant that there was pressure to pay, feed and clothe workers between work periods since they could no longer be so easily sent home or laid off. Thus FFTs depended either on relatively high cost labour or on vulnerable labour, without trade union or citizenship rights.

Finally, in the capitalist economies, the profitable operation of the FFTs also depended upon the existence of mass markets and on corporate control over those markets. Such markets for fish, created in the early postwar period, were primarily located in the retail sector where mass produced, semi-processed, frozen fish products were marketed to housewives, small restaurant owners and firms offering food service to institutions. Control over these markets was based primarily on the relative cheapness of the mass produced commodities and on the use of advertising to create markets for certain brand name products. However, in all three markets consumers could, relatively easily, substitute alternative protein products or cheaper fish products for these mass produced products if prices were to increase substantially.

THE CRISIS OF FORDISM

By the late 1960s, the institutional and ecological basis for the FFTs had begun to disappear. The key factor in this process was fish stock depletion and the associated creation of a regulatory regime designed to conserve fish stocks. The profitable operation of FFTs had depended, in a fundamental sense, on the rupturing of relations between community and production. When fish stocks collapsed in the 1960s, the absence of a community base made the FFT fleets politically more vulnerable to exclusion from access to the resource.

The threat of global shortages of key raw materials and agricultural products in the 1970s contributed to a temporary shift in geopolitical power by strengthening raw material producing countries and regions in relation to the industrial heartland.[41] This, and the related development of a global economic crisis, led to increased government efforts to control resource development and resource rents in resource producing regions and nations. In Canada, this period was characterized by a more strident assertion of national sovereignty in the Arctic and off the Atlantic and Pacific coasts, and by more intense federal-provincial and interprovincial struggles over resource development and resource rents.[42]

The Canadian government's interest in resources was fuelled by the fiscal problems caused by a crisis in the manufacturing sector. Resource development and resource rents represented a relatively secure and legitimate realm for state intervention and for the enhancement of state revenues. Like many other nations Canada thus extended its jurisdiction to 200 miles in the 1970s and this, combined with increased energy costs and depleted stocks, destroyed the profitability of the FFT based technology.

The development of national regulatory regimes to encourage stock recovery and to limit access to fish stocks further deepened the contradiction and altered the optimal balance between human responsiveness and control within Fordist and state socialist regimes of accumulation, thus setting off a period of global restructuring of fisheries that is still in progress. Within capitalist fisheries, the decline of the FFTs has generally encouraged the expansion of national, shore-based fisheries, as in Atlantic Canada. Profits in those branches that had been most closely wedded to Fordism were especially threatened and in the 1970s an additional threat emerged as the rapid expansion of the fast food and food service industries eroded commodity markets for fish. The combined impact of these changes led to the near collapse of the big, vertically-integrated fish companies like Fishery Products and Nickerson-National Sea, whose operations were most closely wedded to Fordism.

PERIPHERAL PERMEABLE FORDISM

The Fordist revolution that had contributed to the development of FFTs had also encouraged the expansion of quite different fishing industries in Scandinavia, Iceland and Atlantic Canada. In contrast to those based on FFTs, these fisheries were more community-based and varied greatly in the extent to which they depended upon the mass production of a narrow range of semi-processed commodities destined for standardized markets. Historical, political, economic and ecological differences contributed to the emergence of such varied regimes of accumulation. The regime that emerged in the Newfoundland fishing industry after World War II relied heavily on American markets, developed a wasteful relationship to the resource, and was highly dependent on unskilled, untrained and vulnerable workers. This made it more vulnerable to crisis and to marginalization in the 1980s than the regimes that had emerged in Scandinavia and Iceland.

Canada's proximity to abundant fish resources, suited to mass production and to the large American market, as well as its commitment to resource development through various regional development packages encouraged the expansion of the Atlantic Canadian fishing industry, including that of Newfoundland, after World War II. By the 1960s a new accumulation regime had emerged in the fishery which reflected wider Canadian restructuring patterns and Newfoundland's peripheral location within Canada. This regime could be called "peripheral permeable Fordism."

Jenson has characterized the Canadian version of Fordism as "permeable Fordism." Its main feature was a strong "commitment to increased continental integration based on exporting resources and importing capital."[43] Unlike European Fordism, permeable Fordism relied less on the prospect of a strong labour movement, mobilized in political parties, achieving a compromise between capital and labour facilitated by state structures, than on "a privatized form of wage relations" in which the government effectively oversaw private bargaining between labour and capital.[44]

Permeable Fordism encouraged vulnerable and uneven development. It was based on a weak and belated commitment to full employment, reflected in the volatile and generally high levels of unemployment prevailing in Canada's resource-dependent regions. It also led to a complex network of federal-provincial relations, with provinces responsible for onshore resource management and for labour legislation and the federal government responsible for offshore resource management, regional development, and Keynesian welfare programs.

The regulatory regimes found in resource-dependent regions like Atlantic Canada could be described as peripheral permeable Fordist in that they embodied a Fordist relationship to nature and depended on external, American mass markets. But they emerged with more diverse production relations, weaker trade unions and a somewhat different politics from those found in the Canadian heartland. This was partly the result of regional income disparities and the assignment to the provinces of responsibility for labour legislation. The establishment of peripheral permeable Fordism within the Newfoundland fishery was strongly encouraged by a government resettlement plan that created reserves of labour in communities where life was commodified. The plan depended on federal and provincial subsidies, the dismantling of the institutional basis for the competing saltfish industry, legislation denying fishers the right to unionize, and the widening of access to unemployment insurance.[45]

Peripheral permeable Fordism was not based on mobile factory freezer technology, nor were production relations characterized by a high degree of separation of conception from execution or of job fragmentation. In fact, technology adapted from FFTs, and markets created by the fish stick revolution in the United States provided the basis for a different form of expanded production. The industry restructured from the household based production of saltfish to the mass production of semi-processed blocks of fish fillets. Fish harvested both by corporate-owned fresh fish trawlers and by small, artisanal inshore fishers was processed in onshore plants. Firms made use of freezing and filleting technologies developed for FFTs to produce fish blocks for the fish stick market. Such block products required little skilled labour (job fragmentation was not necessary), allowed companies to make full use of freezing technology, and did not require consistent size or quality of raw material.

Furthermore, they allowed management to streamline production.[46]

Block markets, however, were unstable because they were not controlled by Newfoundland firms. The fishstick boom expanded the supply of raw materials available to the growing U.S. food conglomerates by allowing firms to utilize abundant species, thus broadening sources of supply. The threat to profits implicit in the resulting instability of this market was reduced by low levels of mechanization and by partial reliance on the inshore and nearshore fisheries for labour and raw material. This allowed firms to transfer some of the risks to workers and fishers.

Similarly, combined reliance on both trawler and inshore technology, and the construction of plants in different regions of the island, helped to protect firms from the effects of seasonal and regional fluctuations in fish supplies resulting from the natural movement of stocks and the industry's exclusive reliance on nature for reproduction of this resource. Firms operating plants in different regions of Newfoundland, some of which were serviced by offshore trawlers, could fish and process different stocks and operate year-round. Other plants relied on fish harvested in owner-operated nearshore and inshore vessels so that their relationship to the natural processes lay somewhere between the passive relations of the household fishery with its stationary gear, and that of the FFTs, which were able to cut across regional and seasonal variations in the supplies of fish.

In contrast to FFTs, this type of production was community-based and entailed certain strengths and weaknesses as regards the ability to compete. While onshore processing limited the mobility of harvesting technology, it gave these firms access to more flexible supplies of labour so that management could recruit additional, temporary workers (primarily women and young people) during periods of peak demand for labour. These workers could then be sent home during periods when markets were depressed or when supplies of fish were in short supply.

Plants were often built in relatively isolated communities, giving firms a monopoly in the local markets for both labour and fish (fresh fish is highly perishable).[47] The decentralized structure of firms with plants located in several communities and regions enhanced this control. By owning several plants and relying on corporate trawlers and owner-operated enterprises, management increased its control over individual groups of workers and fishers. Multiplant ownership limited the ability of workers in single communities to strike for higher wages because vessels could be diverted to alternative plants, and companies could increase their reliance on fish derived from or processed in a different sector.[48]

Other important mechanisms of control included nepotistic, sectarian, and gendered hiring practices, varying degrees of corporate ownership of other businesses in the community, or the effective control of housing, electrical power, water supplies or municipal governments. These various mechanisms often contributed to the development of close ties between community and work that interfered with the development of industrial unionism. Such development was, at any rate, discouraged by existing labour legislation under which fishers and trawler workers did not have the right to unionize.[49]

At the same time, management exercised only limited control over the organization and content of work on the factory floor since control could not effectively be based on a high degree of separation between conception and execution or job fragmentation. There were only a few supervisors, training was limited and worker-controlled. Fathers introduced sons onto the shopfloor. Control was thus concentrated in the area of employment as workers paid for the privilege of nepotism and sex segregation with low wages, compulsory overtime, long workdays, and long work weeks. Management could normally rely on the pressures of a backlog of work and limits on the freedom to strike to maintain productivity. Then, as now, the threat of plant closure and the existence of large reserves of unemployed were additional mechanisms of control which were enhanced in communities that were totally dependent on this industry.

Family ownership limited the supplies of capital available to most of these firms, but this problem could be partially overcome because of the availability of considerable government subsidies provided through the federal government's regional development programs. Moreover, the structure of these firms and communities helped to ensure the availability of such subsidies since it encouraged the emergence of community-based class alliances in support of such subsidies whenever plant closures threatened. This leverage was particularly important given the firms' low degree of control over the resource and its markets.[50]

THE CRISIS OF PERIPHERAL PERMEABLE FORDISM

The crisis of global Fordism provided the basis for an expansion of this peripheral permeable Fordism. Firms responded to the increased regulation of access to fish by increasing their reliance on the more flexible, artisanal inshore fisheries and by diversifying into other species. One result was the rapid expansion of the inshore and nearshore fisheries and the substantial decentralization of production and control that characterized the industry during the 1970s.

However, as production expanded and became more decentralized, class relations within the industry changed and the frontiers of control shifted within both the harvesting and the processing sectors. Periodic labour shortages, associated with expanded production and technological reversals, led in some cases to a return to more labour intensive production methods.[51] Raw material shortages prompted an increased need for skilled labour. The effectiveness of community-based control mechanisms was undermined, and the position of workers and fishers was strengthened in relation to capital. The spread of industrial unionism was the result.

The single enterprise community structure of the industry contributed to the development of periodic labour shortages. In the past, the expanding population of most communities had provided management with ample reserves of labour, but this was no longer adequate to deal with the rapid fluctuations in prices, in supplies of fish, and hence, in the demand for labour that characterized the early 1970s.[52] Periodic labour shortages now came to play a crucial role in strengthening workers at strategic points in their drive for unionization and wage gains.

Isolation limited the size of the available labour reserves and, to a lesser extent, the supplies of fish available to individual plants. While these limitations could be partially overcome by improved transportation between communities and by increased reliance on more mobile forms of fishing technology, such as longliners and nearshore draggers, the existence of better roads and of more mobile fishing gear also meant that fishers could more easily deliver their catches to competing plants. The firms thus lost some of their control over markets for fish.

Resource depletion also threatened profits and strengthened workers and fishers by forcing management to reorganize production and rely more on skilled workers in order to reduce waste and produce higher quality products. Many companies introduced incentive systems with bonuses tied to both quantity of output and to yield (the percentage of the fish that ended up in fillets rather than waste). Some introduced individual workstations and some stopped using fish filleting machines.

Towards the end of the 1970s, the bargaining power of fishers and workers was further enhanced by changing market structures that increased the demand for key species, high quality raw materials and specialized products.[53] Although the traditional retail markets for frozen fillet packs and block products remained important in the late 1970s, they were smaller and more

unstable than in the past. Moreover, competition intensified as other countries, such as Korea and Argentina, responded to the stronger market demand
created by stock depletion by increasing their production of standardized commodities. Furthermore the transformation of U.S. chicken production reduced
prices and encouraged consumers to switch from fish to chicken[54] so that
prices for traditional standardized block and fillet products fell in the early
1980s. At this time, the majority of Atlantic Canada's frozen groundfish products were still in these categories despite efforts to diversify.[55]

The decline in the price of standardized fish products was exacerbated by
increasing market segmentation and the development of niche markets. Since
1960 the production and service of meals based on fish products had come to
be increasingly dominated by large capitalist firms using a Taylorist labour
process, which combined reliance on unskilled, replaceable workers with
automation and highly centralized control.[56] The rapid expansion of the food
service industries and the development of competing fast food chains eroded
the markets for standardized fish products and increased the demand for specialized products, often suited to the specific requirements of chains like
MacDonald's or Arthur Treacher's, but also to more elite food service establishments. These trends have been further strengthened as the fast food chains
have penetrated captive, institutional food markets as well.

The negative impact of these developments was particularly great in that
part of the Newfoundland fishing industry that had specialized in the mass production of standardized products.[57] The process of restructuring the industry
was especially costly and difficult because most of these firms were not yet
geared for the move to specialized products.[58] For them, the shift would
require either the adoption of more labour intensive forms of production or
the introduction of new technology and changes in the design and organization of fish processing. Changes in either direction threatened productivity in
fishplants and on board trawlers (which had already been undermined by stock
depletion), and necessitated the shift to more decentralized production, and
the processing of a broader range of species.

Batch production enhances and changes problems of managerial co-ordination and control.[59] Since the number of factors determining the level of
productivity is multiplied, it becomes more difficult for management to control
the pace and intensity of work. The need to meet the stringent and differing
requirements of individual market niches further adds to these problems and
tends to be costly in terms of both labour time and raw material. Furthermore,
if a shipment is rejected due to quality problems, its specialized nature makes
it difficult to redirect to an alternative buyer.[60] Thus, the transition from mass

production to batch production in the fishery produced a shift in the frontiers of control which favoured labour.

The reorganization of the labour process in response to changing market demand and more unstable supplies of raw material posed severe new problems of co-ordination and control, while increasing the labour time required for production (of more specialized packs) and for grading. The shift to batch production thus posed a profound threat to profits. This was particularly evident in the early 1980s, when Newfoundland companies had to compete with industries in Iceland, Denmark and the Faroe Islands which had moved to batch production several years earlier and which had never been as tightly tied to mass production.[61]

In general, then, in the 1970s global shortages of fish and the greater flexibility of the Newfoundland firms in comparison to the FFTs helped to protect the profitability of peripheral permeable Fordism. By 1980, however, these conditions had changed. The prices of standardized fish products declined substantially as a result of a scientific-technical revolution in the harvesting and processing of fish and other protein products, and a recovery of fish stocks within the new 200 mile regulatory regimes.[62] The decline primarily reflected a reduction in the labour time necessary to produce such products. Attempts to move to batch production, to increase yield and to process a broader range of species undermined productivity in the short term, however, and shifted frontiers of control in favour of fishers and workers. This set the stage for the threatened collapse of many of these Newfoundland firms in the early 1980s.

CONCLUSIONS AND CURRENT TRENDS

Anna Pollert has called "flexibility" the "song of the eighties."[63] As she suggests, it is not just management doing the singing. Policy analysts, dual labour market theorists and those analyzing the informal economy have also joined the choir. Flexibility is ideologically salient because it fits with the neo-conservative emphasis on the importance of free markets, on the so-called curative elements of "labour market flexibility" and on the costs of state intervention and union regulation of labour markets. It also fits with the notion that it is these factors, rather than global changes and the contradictions within capitalism, that are producing such severe "problems" and "distortions" in today's economies.

This chapter's analysis of the roots of the crisis in the fishing industry suggests that, despite the importance of the criticisms levelled by Pollert and others at the advocates of "flexibility," there is some validity to the notion that the crisis of the 1970s was rooted in rigidities. The crisis was reflected in new strategies of managerial control and revealed the greater resilience of processes based on more flexible technologies, as documented by Piore and Sabel.[64] While flexibility is not new, it is important to note that, during the crisis, the locus of flexibility shifted somewhat from the so-called "peripheral spheres" of raw material extraction, household consumption and craft production into the mass production industries.[65] However, to claim that the crisis was rooted in the contradiction between human responsiveness and control in Fordism is not the same as claiming that capitalism is now capable of restructuring, or likely to restructure in the direction of flexible specialization in the way envisaged by Piore and Sabel.

Natural barriers contributed to the crisis of Fordism in the fishery and these have continued to hamper efforts to establish a new, effective regime of accumulation, not only in the North Atlantic, but globally as well. In Atlantic Canada, the crisis of the early 1980s was resolved by a process of "restructuring" that involved substantial government aid and was largely confined to a consolidation of ownership and control over a vertically-integrated fishery in the hands of two companies, National Sea and Fishery Products International. Since then, these companies have been attempting to tighten their control over the industry's resources and work processes[66] and in this they have been encouraged by neoconservative federal policies. These include cutbacks in workers' and fishers' access to unemployment insurance, which threatens the survival of the inshore, artisanal fishery, as well as a refusal to reduce offshore fish quotas to levels that could ensure the recovery of inshore fish landings. The revival of the artisanal inshore fisheries and the increased reliance on skilled labour that had occurred in the 1970s represented a pattern of restructuring similar to that envisaged by Piore and Sabel's "flexible specialization." It is now clearly under attack.

ENDNOTES

An earlier version of this paper was presented to the Conference on Canadian Political Economy in the Era of Free Trade, Carleton University, Ottawa, April 6-8, 1990. The author would like to thank Peter Armitage, Fred Bienefeld, Wallace Clement, Jane Jenson and Martha MacDonald for helpful comments on earlier drafts. This paper is a revised summary of a more detailed discussion of crisis theory and the fisheries crisis in Barbara Neis, "From Codblock to Fishfood: The Crisis and Restructuring in the Newfoundland Fishing Industry: 1968-1986," Ph.D. dissertation, University of Toronto, 1988.

1.   See *Review of Radical Political Economics*, 18/1 and 2, 1986; Samuel Bowles, David Gordon and Thomas Weisskopf, *Beyond the Wasteland: A Democratic Alternative to Economic Decline* (Garden City, NY: Doubleday, 1983); Alain Lipietz, "New Tendencies in the International Division of Labor: Regimes of Accumulation and Modes of Regulation," in Allen J. Scott and Michael Storper (eds.), *Production, Work and Territory* (Boston: Allen Unwin, 1986), pp. 16-40; Michael Piore and Charles Sabel, *The Second Industrial Divide: Possibilities for Prosperity* (New York: Basic Books, 1984); and David Wolfe, "Capitalist Crisis and Marxist Theory," *Labour/Le Travail*, 17 (Spring 1986), pp. 225-254.

2.   Piore and Sabel, *The Second Industrial Divide.*

3.   For a similar though simpler argument see Larry Hirschhorn, *Beyond Mechanization: Work and Technology in a Postindustrial Age* (Cambridge, MA: MIT Press, 1986).

4.   On the contrary, monopoly capitalism has always included domains within which there was neither a rigid labour process nor an eight-hour day. Women and young people have acted as flexible supplies of labour for capital, while women's and children's work in the household, and reciprocal, noncapitalist community ties have, in some contexts, filled the gap between the wage, welfare state institutions and household needs. See Karen Brodkin Sacks, "Generations of Working Class Families," in Karen Brodkin Sacks and Dorothy Remy (eds.), *My Troubles are Going to Have Trouble with Me: Everyday Trials and Triumphs of Women Workers* (New Brunswick, NJ: Rutgers University Press, 1984), pp. 15-38.

5.   Theo Nichols, "The Sociology of Accidents and Social Production of Industrial Injury," in Geoff Esland, Graeme Salaman and Mary-Anne Speakman (eds.), *People and Work* (Edinburgh: The Open University Press, 1975); and Anna Pollert, "'Flexible' Patterns of Work and Ideology: The New-Right, Post

Industrialism and Dualist Analysis: An Exploration in the Dissemination of Ideas About the Nature of Employment in the 1980s," (Paper presented to The Annual Conference of the British Sociological Association, April 6-9, 1987).

6.   David F. Noble, *Forces of Production: A Social History of Industrial Automation* (New York: Alfred A. Knopf, 1984). Also refer to Pollert, "'Flexible' Patterns of Work and Ideology..."

7.   Robert Drago and Terry McDonough, "Capitalist Shopfloor Initiatives, Restructuring, and Organizing in the '80s," *Review of Radical Political Economics*, 16/4 (1984), pp. 52-71. Also see Leo Panitch, "Capitalist Restructuring and Labour Strategies," *Studies in Political Economy*, 25 (Autumn 1987), pp. 131-150.

8.   Refer to the following articles by Alan Lipietz: "The Globalization of the General Crisis of Fordism," SNID Occasional Paper No. 84-203, Program of Studies in National and International Development, Queen's University, Kingston, 1984; "New Tendencies in the International Division of Labor"; and "Reflections on a Tale: The Marxist Foundations of the Concepts of Regulation and Accumulation," *Studies in Political Economy*, 26 (Summer 1988), pp. 7-36.

9.   Jane Jenson,"'Different' but not 'exceptional': Canada's Permeable Fordism," in *Canadian Review of Sociology and Anthropology*, 26/1 (1989), p. 70.

10.   See Lipietz, "New Tendencies."

11.   Although it is not possible to generalize in any simple sense from the crisis in one industry to capital as a whole, case studies of this kind can help move the analysis of capitalist crisis and restructuring from abstract theorizing, ahistoricism and, often, economic determinism towards an analysis that locates broader economic forces and capitalist contradictions in their social, political and historical context. Refer to Pat Armstrong, *Labour Pains: Women's Work in Crisis* (Toronto: Women's Press, 1984); Bowles *et al.*, *Beyond the Wasteland*; D. Gordon, R. Edwards, and M. Reich, *Segmented Work, Divided Workers: The Historical Transformation of Labour in the United States* (Cambridge: University Press, 1982); Jenson, "'Different' but not 'exceptional'"; Michael A. Lebowitz, "The General and the Specific in Marx's Theory of Crisis," *Studies in Political Economy*, 7 (Winter 1982), pp. 5-26; and Lipietz, "New Tendencies."

12.   Jenson, "'Different' but not 'exceptional.'"

13.   Wm. Warner, *Distant Water: The Fate of the North Atlantic Fisherman* (Boston: Little Brown and Co., 1983).

14.   Peter Sinclair, *State Intervention in the Newfoundland Fisheries* (Aldershot: Gower Press, 1987).

15.   Martin Kenney, Linda Lobao, James Curry and W. Richard Goe, "Midwestern Agriculture in U.S. Fordism," *Sociologia Ruralis*, 29/2 (1989), pp. 131-147.

16.   After 1974, the emphasis in government policy shifted towards encouraging the expansion of the inshore and offshore fisheries and increased plant construction. From 1976-77 to 1980-81, government expenditures in the

Newfoundland fishery increased by more than 40 percent. During this period, the most extensive government subsidies went to support the expansion of the inshore and nearshore fisheries. Subsidies were provided for plant construction, expansion, infrastructure and vessel purchase. The federal government also subsidized the price of fish. Wm. Schrank, B. Skoda, N. Roy, E. Tsoa, "Canadian Government Financial Intervention in a Marine Fishery: The Case of Newfoundland, 1972/73-1980/81," in V. Konrad, L. Morin and R. Erb (eds.), *Resource Economics in Emerging Free Trade: Proceedings of a Maine/Canadian Trade Conference, January 9-10, 1986* (Orono, ME: University of Maine Press, 1986).

17.   The Newfoundland government introduced limited changes to labour laws legalizing the unionization of inshore fishers during the early 1970s.

18.   Wallace Clement, *The Struggle to Organize: Resistance in Canada's Fishery* (Toronto: McClelland and Stewart, 1986), p. 169.

19.   See Neis, "From Codblock to Fishfood," Chapter Two.

20.   Lipietz, "The Globalization of the General Crisis."

21.   Piore and Sabel, *The Second Industrial Divide.*

22.   H. Braverman, *Labour and Monopoly Capital* (New York: Monthly Review Press, 1974); and Stuart Ewin, *Captains of Consciousness: Advertising and the Social Roots of the Consumer Culture* (New York: McGraw-Hill, 1986).

23.   Lebowitz, "The General and the Specific."

24.   Bowles *et al.*, *Beyond the Wasteland.*

25.   Jenson, "'Different' but not 'exceptional.'"

26.   It is also possible that the increased organic composition of capital reflected not just more machines but the incompatibility between Fordist production regimes and pressures to diversify production so that, unable to adapt Fordist technology and production relations to the production of a wider variety of products, firms were forced to construct new production lines and new factories. This, in turn, would threaten accumulation by driving up the organic composition of capital and strengthening workers. See Bowles *et al.*, *Beyond the Wasteland.*

27.   Lebowitz, "The General and the Specific." An exception is the new journal *Capitalism, Socialism, Nature.*

28.   Craig R. Littler and Graeme Salaman, *Class At Work: The Design, Allocation and Control of Jobs* (London: Batsford Academic and Educational Ltd., 1984).

29.   *Ibid.* p. 90. This tension between "flexibility" and control is also rooted in capital's need to transform the forces of production and, as others have recognized, in the excess profits that are possible with early innovation. Phillipe Faucher and Chris DeBresson, "'L'école de la régulation' on Technological Change," (Paper presented to the conference on Canadian Political Economy in the Era of Free Trade, Ottawa, Carleton, April 6-8, 1990); and Raphael Kaplinsky, "Post-Fordist Industrial Restructuring: Policy Implications for an Industrially Advanced

Economy," *idem*. Transformation of the forces of production requires access to the creative powers and knowledge of workers. As is widely recognized, control can interfere with this access. Refer to Michael Duncan, "Microelectronics: Five Areas of Subordination," in Les Levidow and Bob Young (eds.), *Science, Technology and the Labour Process*, Marxist Studies, Vol. 1, Conference of Socialist Economists (London: Black Rose Press, 1981); Littler and Salaman, *Class at Work*; Leslie Nulty, "Case Studies of IAM Local Experience with the Introduction of New Technology," in Donald Kennedy *et al.* (eds.), *Labour and Technology: Union Response to Changing Environments* (University Park, PA.: Dept. of Labour Studies, Pennsylvania State University, 1982); James Rinehart, "Appropriating Workers' Knowledge: Quality Control Circles at a General Motors Plant," in *Studies in Political Economy*, 14 (Spring 1984), pp. 75-98; and Shostack, "High Tech, High Touch and Labour," *Social Policy* Winter 1983, p. 13.

30.   In contexts where management increases its knowledge of the production process, workers do not necessarily lose this knowledge, as implied in Braverman's 1974 analysis. See Stephen Wood and John Kelly, "Taylorism, Responsible Autonomy and Management Strategy," in Stephen Wood (ed.), *The Degradation of Work? Skill, Deskilling and the Labour Process* (London: Hutchinson, 1982), pp. 76-77.

31.   Craig Heron and Robert Storey, "On the Job in Canada," in Heron and Storey (eds.), *On the Job: Confronting the Labour Process in Canada* (Montreal: McGill-Queen's, 1986).

32.   Jenson, "'Different' but not 'exceptional.'"

33.   Marjorie Devault, "Mothers' Household Work," (Paper prepared for presentation at the Motherwork Workshop, Simone de Beauvoir Institute, Concordia University, Montreal, October 1985). Also refer to Devault, "Doing Housework: Feeding and Family Life," in Naomi Gerstel and Harriet Engel Gross (eds.), *Families and Work* (Philadelphia: Temple U. Press, 1987), and Jackie West, "The Political Economy of the Family in Capitalism: Women, Reproduction and Wage Labour," in Theo Nichols (ed.), *Capital and Labour: a Marxist Primer* (Glasgow: Fontana, 1980), pp. 174-189.

34.   Bowles *et al*, *Beyond the Wasteland*.

35.   Littler and Salaman, *Class at Work*.

36.   Jenson, "'Different' but not 'exceptional.'"

37.   Warner, *Distant Wate.*, pp. 86-87.

38.   *Ibid.*, p. 58.

39.   Vladil Lysenko, *A Crime Against the World* (London: Victor Gollancz, 1983).

40.   Warner, *Distant Water*.

41.   Piore and Sabel, *The Second Industrial Divide*; and J. Richards and L. Pratt, *Prairie Capitalism: Power and Influence in the New West* (Toronto:

McClelland and Stewart, 1979).

42. The land based character of the resource development that occurred in the post-war period meant that, in the offshore, questions of federal-provincial jurisdiction and international jurisdiction were, as yet, largely unresolved. Pat Marchak, "Uncommon Property," in Pat Marchak *et al.*, *Uncommon Property: The Fishing and Fish-Processing Industries in British Columbia* (Toronto: Methuen, 1987). Jenson argues that the crisis of permeable Fordism within Canada has been manifested primarily in struggles over federalism. See Jenson, "'Different' but not 'exceptional.'"

43. Jenson, "'Different' but not 'exceptional,'" p. 78.

44. *Ibid.*

45. Neis, "From Codblock to Fishfood," Appendix B.

46. During the 1950s and 1960s, more and more raw material ended up in block products. Thus, whereas in 1953, there were no frozen cod blocks produced in Newfoundland, by 1963 just over 31 percent of all cod landings ended up in blocks. Fillet products, which had utilized 14 percent of cod landings in 1953, had decreased to five percent in 1963. Other species of groundfish, including plaice, greysole, and redfish were processed exclusively into fillets until 1960 after which there was a dramatic increase in the percentage of these species packed in block. Only in the case of haddock did the ratio of block to fillet products remain roughly stable. See S.S. Mensinkai, *Plant Location and Plant Size in the Fish Processing Industry of Newfoundland,* Canadian Fisheries Reports, No. 11 (Ottawa: Department of Fisheries and Oceans, 1968), p. 71 and Table 2.12.

47. Gordon Inglis, *More than Just a Union: The Story of the NFFAWU* (St. John's: Jesperson Press, 1985); and Mensinkai, *Plant Location.*

48. Cyril Strong, *My Life as a Newfoundland Union Organizer* (St. John's: Committee on Canadian Labour History, 1987).

49. Neis, "From Codblock to Fishfood," Appendix B.

50. Newfoundland fish products competed with each other and with products from elsewhere in the markets. Lack of market control contributed to the development of periodic crises in the industry which these firms survived by driving down prices to primary producers, cutting back on production, layoffs and by pressuring the state for financial aid.

51. The labour process became more labour intensive as management in plants, such as Catalina, abandoned the use of cutting machines not suited for use with the species that were abundant or for use with the softer textured fish that were caught during longer trawler trips. This technological reversal contributed to the need for closer managerial control at the point of production, declining productivity in fishplants and shortages of skilled labour. Fishery Research Group, *The Social Impact of Technological Change in Newfoundland's Deepsea Fishery.* Labour Canada and the Institute of Social and Economic Research (St. John's: Memorial University, 1986).

52.   This occurred, for example, as a result of National Sea Products' rapid expansion of redfish production with the introduction of the midwater trawl and the decision to exploit previously under-utilized Gulf of St. Lawrence stocks. Gene Barrett, "Capital and the State in Atlantic Canada: The Structural Context of Fishery Policy Between 1939 and 1977," in Cynthia Lamson and Hanson (eds.), *Atlantic Fisheries and Coastal Communities: Fisheries Decision-making Case Studies* (Halifax: Dalhousie Ocean Studies Program, 1984), pp. 77-104.

53.   Peter Sinclair, *From Traps to Draggers: Domestic Commodity Production in Northwest Newfoundland 1850-198,* Social and Economic Studies, No. 31 (St. John's: Institute of Social and Economic Research, Memorial University, 1985).

54.   Bryant Fairley, "Looking for Solutions: Towards a Political Economy of Fishing in Newfoundland in the 1980s," (SNID Occasional Paper No. 85-101, Program of Studies in National and International Development, Queen's University, Kingston, 1985).

55.   In 1979, Canada supplied 24 percent of the groundfish flowing into the public food service segment, 35 percent of that in the captive food service segment, and 43 percent of the retail market. In the late 1970s, Canadian products were concentrated in the middle quality, price-sensitive niches in these market segments. Canada, Task Force on the Atlantic Fisheries, *Navigating Troubled Waters: A New Policy for the Atlantic Fisheries* (Ottawa: Ministry of Supply and Services, 1983), p. 134.

56.   Ester Reiter, "Out of the Frying Pan and into the Fryer—The Organization of Work in a Fast Food Outlet," (Ph.D. dissertation, Department of Sociology, University of Toronto, Toronto, 1985).

57.   Although some Newfoundland firms had increased their production of more specialized fish products in the late 1970s, the degree of diversification had remained limited. Peter Sinclair, "The State Goes Fishing: The Emergence of Public Ownership in the Newfoundland Fishing Industry," (ISER Research and Policy Papers. No. 1, Memorial University, St. John's, 1985).

58.   The production of specialized products needs high quality raw materials and an effective grading system. The best way to maximize the use of the raw material in this context is to allow for selective harvesting and dispersal of the raw material between enterprises geared to the processing of a few specialized products. The Newfoundland firms have only recently introduced a system of dockside grading, and corporate control over grading has resulted in conflict between trawler workers and the companies. Also, the vertically-integrated firms that dominate the industry, in which companies own both vessels and plants, are structurally less well suited to this dynamic than a system where fish is harvested and auctioned, such as exists in Denmark, or where a co-operative with a broad range of different production facilities can move raw material between enterprises.

59.   Littler and Salaman, *Class at Work.*

60.   The food service industry, for example, has a very low bone tolerance. If this requirement is not met the shipment will be rejected.

61.   Their earlier forays in this direction meant that these countries reaped the high profits made possible by the combination of early innovation and associated shortages of competing supplies. As companies elsewhere have increased their production of specialized products, such as Long John Silver fillets, profits have declined. Aldwin Boone and Robert Verge, "Fish Processing in Newfoundland and Labrador: The Present State of the Art and the Potential for Development: A Study in the Application of Industrial Engineering Techniques in the Fish Processing Sector of the Newfoundland Fishing Industry," Submitted to DFO, St. John's, December 1984.

62.   Fairley, "Looking for Solutions."

63.   Pollert, "'Flexible' Patterns."

64.   Piore and Sabel, *The Second Industrial Divide.*

65.   To some extent, this shift is the result of the increased capitalist competition that has been a feature of the current crisis. As Leo Panitch has suggested, capitalist competition, especially competition from countries such as Japan and Western Europe, has contributed to the crisis in key sectors of the American economy and thus in Canada as well, given the extent to which the Canadian economy is dominated by American multinationals and reliance on the American market. Declining monopoly control over markets has forced corporations to try to "organize production so that they can respond flexibly to an environment they don't and can't control monolithically. It is in this search for flexible responses that the new trends to 'outsourcing' and 'just-in-time' production processes find their rationale." See Panitch, "Capitalist Restructuring," p. 137. This is also a key factor underlying the search for flexible labour supplies, flexible technologies and changes in other dimensions of managerial control.

66.   Fishery Research Group, "The Social Impact;" Susan Williams and Barbara Neis, *Occupational Health in Newfoundland's Deepsea Fishery: Stress and Repetitive Strain Injuries Among Plantworkers* (St John's: Memorial University, Institute of Social and Economic Research, 1990); and Neis, "From Codblock to Fishfood."

Labour

CHAPTER 5

WHAT COMES NEXT? CANAdiAN EMPLOYMENT POLiCiES

GREGORY Albo

What has finally to be said, though, is that the major changes in work and production which are now happening and which are only weakly interpreted by the received ideas...are evidence as much of opportunity as of danger.... In the reality of labour saving, and in the availability of new skills and activities, we could, quite practically, enter a new world of human work. Sharing the political effort to make it like that is then in practice our first task.

Raymond Williams[1]

INTRODUCTION

In both intellectual and trade-union circles, there now appears to be a consensus that a dramatic transformation of work is occurring. The issue at hand,
as Raymond Williams observes, is evident: what should a socialist policy be for
the labour process and employment structures coming after Fordism? The
debate in Canada has tended to be narrowly focused. Indeed, much as industrial policy was central to disputes about the economic crisis of the 1970s,
training policy is invoked today as the means to overcome the traditional
weaknesses of Canadian manufacturing. In coping with the marked uncertainty resulting from technological change and intensified competition for world
markets, national training regimes have been identified as a decisive institutional variable demarcating stories of manufacturing success from the tales of
failure. Yet just as Canada fared poorly in comparisons with other states in
industrial policy, Canada does no better, and possibly worse, in training the
national labour force. A "new" solution to the old Canadian problem—the
weak manufacturing core of the economy—now seems to reside in upgrading
training.[2]

This debate needs to be placed in its wider setting. The Fordist model,
based on mass production technologies utilizing semi-skilled workers and dedicated machines, is being displaced by a regime of flexible automation, built
around the flexibility of new technologies and a core of polyvalent workers
that can adjust process and product as final demand alters. The precise contours of this new production regime lie somewhere between two organizational poles: a core of multi-skilled workers providing a functional flexibility within
the internal labour market of the firm, with a majority of peripheralized workers moving in a constant flow of dismissals and hirings in the external labour
market as product demand alters; or a broadly-based reskilling of the labour
force, tied to an extension of employment security that incorporates peripheral workers, so that flexible adjustment occurs via responsible autonomy for
workers within the labour process and without resort to unemployment
shocks.[3] Given the dangers and opportunities implicit in these widely divergent scenarios, the basic material interest of workers in training and employment policy are unlikely to converge with the interest of manufacturers in
maximizing labour flexibility to preserve market shares in the short run.

The narrow parameters of the contemporary training debate in Canada,
however, presuppose that the routes out of the crisis of Fordism are few, and
singularly dependent on market-responsive, high value-added manufacturing
within new industrial districts. This is, perhaps, best illustrated in the post-

Fordist future projected by the widely discussed Ontario Premier's Council Report:

> ...we cannot cling to low-wage, low value-added activities where we have no competitve advantages, but must move into the high value-added, high-wage goods and services wherein lie our best hopes for prosperity over the long term.... A critical determinant of whether we can make the transition will be the education, skills, ingenuity and adaptability of our workers. They must be prepared for work which will demand the sophisticated knowledge and talents that are the trademarks of a truly developed nation.[4]

Such a strategy may indeed be, in part, a precondition for high levels of manufacturing employment. Expanding manufacturing might also make a modest contribution to reducing unemployment. Yet the claims of the post-Fordists in Canada are much bolder: the creation of a supply of skilled labour will lead to the effective demand for the commodities produced and, ultimately, to good jobs and full employment for all. This reinvigorated form of Say's law—supply creates its own demand which Keynes rightly challenged, provides the rationale for deepening the income and skill polarization of the labour market while selling itself as the cure.

The return of stagflation in the 1990s indicates the overwhelming failure of neoliberal strategies to overcome the barriers to sustained accumulation which first presented themselves in the 1970s. We are still in the period "after Fordism." According to different national settings and political projects, alternate economic paths remain possible. In Canada, the pressures of international competition, especially from continental free trade, have intensified the reliance on defensive forms of flexibility of wage and cost competition. Only pockets of high-quality production have appeared. The historical shortcomings of training and employment policy have contributed to this tendency.

The crisis in the labour market, therefore, challenges the labour movement, and the Left more generally, to engage in a broader set of democratic struggles for the "requalification of work," based on "quality training" and the "right to work." The route to an offensive flexibility—reskilled workers producing high-quality, socially useful goods—requires the extension of solidarity to the jobless, via a concerted attack on working hours and efforts to shift income to the poor who have a higher propensity to consume domestically produced goods. The post-Fordist pursuit of international manufacturing competitiveness alone will result in the private gains of the few from new technologies at the expense of the possible democratic gains of the many.

THE ROAD TO DEFENSIVE FLEXIBILITY: THE HISTORY OF EMPLOYMENT POLICY

The dynamic relationship between technological change, work organization and skills has been neglected until recently.[5] In the standard economics or sociology literature, technology or organizations were seen to entail a certain type of labour process and thus a specific growth process. The wider context of the national form of economic adjustment and the narrower processes of skilling were either ignored or treated as static parameters. Yet these institutions, which set the terms of exchange between wages and skills in the labour market, play an important role in regulating the organization of the workplace and the pattern of accumulation.[6] In other words, a *social choice* is involved in the organization of the workplace, albeit a choice constrained by the social relations of capitalism.[7] The "technical capacities" of the national labour force is an important factor affecting these choices.

The processes of skills production are critical to industrial restructuring, not just because they allow for flexibility in responding to market shifts, but for the *kind* of flexibility they can create. Industrial restructuring by definition implies that old labour processes and accumulation regimes give way to a new order. The mass production processes of Fordism tended to rely on a sharp separation of conception and execution. This rigid differentiation of tasks produced a skill polarization: conception requiring specialist technical skills concentrated in design offices; skilled manufacturing, and trades jobs filled by apprenticeship or specialist training; and a mass of unskilled assembly jobs with limited specific training tied to a minute division of labour. In contrast, flexible automation tends to use reprogrammable technologies to reintegrate production and design. As a consequence, the labour process can be more flexible in responding to differentiated product demand. Flexible automation, moreover, requires skills that will make workers more flexible: multiskilling; general skills rather than specific ones; and analytic and problem-solving abilities rather than procedural capacities. Thus, for core workers at least, skills are likely to be crucial to a reorganized labour process, both to exploit the potential productivity of new technologies and to involve workers directly in improving productivity.[8] Nevertheless just as Fordism differed across countries, there is unlikely to be a uniform adaptation of the new forms of work organization under a regime of flexible automation.

National forms of labour adjustment will be crucial. The condition of workers in capitalist labour markets is not determined solely by qualifications and skills. These are only one dimension of the labour regime, which also includes wage-determination, work-time allocation, worker mobility, and the labour process. As the period of Fordism demonstrated, suppressing unemployment is central to workers' struggles to shape the form of economic adjustment. Thus the essential message of Göran Therborn's *Why Some Peoples Are More Unemployed Than Others* cannot be stressed enough: the roads to employment success for workers are littered with the debris of class struggles to restrict the use of unemployment shocks to achieve economic adjustment.[9]

Indeed, tight labour markets would appear to be crucial in determining whether an *offensive* strategy of flexibility can be adopted, whereby technological upgrading is combined with the extensions of workers' rights. The alternative is a strategy of *defensive* flexibility, with the pressures of international competition leading to a downward ratcheting of social rights and living standards. As Boyer has observed, these divergent tendencies demarcate the opportunity and the danger of flexible automation:

> On the one hand, there is the opportunity to mitigate some of the worst features of Fordism: less need for a hierarchy exercising authoritarian control, the possibility of doing away with tedious, dangerous, or purely repetitive jobs, opportunities of raising qualifications through general and adequate technical training.... But on the other hand not all companies or sectors are in a position to adopt this strategy: falling back on cheap, unskilled labour is a great temptation—and a very real danger, particularly as minimum wage levels are lowered.... Equally, it is not certain that computerization will undermine the historical division between manual labour and intellectual work. If some repetitive tasks can be abolished and others made potentially more varied and interesting, the rationalization and Taylorization of intellectual work itself may occur. To summarize, the present changes seem to be relatively open-ended: they are so diverse that they cannot be rigidly determined solely by what is technologically possible.[10]

The rationalization of industry can lead to a deepening of traditional mass production technologies with only isolated pockets of quality production, further de-skilling, and high unemployment. Alternatively, the restructuring of work with flexible technologies offers the opportunity to reconstruct core manufacturing sectors and establish the basis for entirely new forms of work relations. This is the choice with respect to employment policy.

THE POSTWAR ORDER:
WHAT HAPPENED TO EMPLOYMENT POLICY?

Canada's labour adjustment policies have a long history. The empirical trends are well known, but they bear repeating. First, flexibility has been provided by high unemployment levels. Unemployment tends to be the highest among the major capitalist countries and has been rising since the 1960s, with important spatial concentrations. Second, rapid labour force and employment growth have added to market flexibility. Extensive economic growth based on widening the labour stock was an important characteristic of postwar Fordism in Canada, fueling job growth in the low-wage service sector as well as precarious forms of employment. Third, training has depended, by and large, upon actions of firms and individual workers. Despite large inflows of skilled immigrant labour, skill shortages have been constant. Fourth, a fragmented collective bargaining system generated localized bargaining. Wage differentials tend to be large, and the non-unionized workforce has little employment security. Finally, labour market institutions are centred at the enterprise level, so adjustment has been largely conducted through the market.

Overall, macroeconomic policy is intended to provide an adequate level of demand; labour market expenditures are dominated by income security programs, based on the insurance principle and intended to cushion short-term spells of unemployment. These postwar trends underline the tendency to adopt defensive measures of adjustment. Current trends in labour market flexibility in Canada need to be assessed in relation to a long-term growth process that has been relatively extensive, relying on the expansion of output by rapid labour force growth and employment in low-wage, low-productivity sectors.

Contemporary debates about the inadequacies of Canadian training policy have a certain familiarity. Over the postwar period a new wave of reform issued from each significant shift in the labour market. Moreover, each labour market reform promised a new balance between market-based employment strategies and the failure of the market to supply either enough training or jobs.

A broader labour market "bargain" that would include national labour market institutions did not figure in the commitment to maintain high and stable levels of employment promised in the 1945 *White Paper on Employment and Income*. The reliance on market forms of economic adjustment was central to the document. Indeed, the underlying theme of the White Paper was dependent industrialization: employment levels in Canada would depend upon trade in raw materials and capital inflows, in particular as sources of effective demand. Market forces would dominate production and distribution, and no role for the state in stabilizing investment levels or in constraining the labour market was set out. The federal government would support employment levels by allowing fiscal deficits to run up during a recession, and by indirect measures of tax and budgetary policy. Employment goals were consequently modest, avoiding specific targets.

With employment policy playing only a marginal role in the postwar order in Canada, there was little incentive to modernize labour market institutions. Therefore, labour market policies barely changed for almost two decades after the war. The only major new policy of the period was a national unemployment insurance program in 1940. The insurance scheme also led to the consolidation of the National Employment Service (NES), designed to deliver the program and to play a minor information role by posting jobs.

Training, the other significant component of labour market policy, also was in place before 1945 and developed in response to war mobilization. The 1942 Vocational Training and Co-ordination Act grew out of existing programs of support for provincial vocational education institutions, enacted in 1937 and 1939 to train unemployed youth. The Act failed, however, to expand the levels of training and to build training institutions across the country.[11] As a result, industrial training remained especially reliant upon "poaching" skilled workers from other nations, a characteristic of dependent industrialization in Canada dating back to the National Policy.[12] Training policies did not figure prominently as either a positive means of adjustment or for the retraining of the unemployed. Low skill levels and loose labour markets were structurally imbedded in the truncated form of Fordism which dominated growth.

THE GREAT AUTOMATION SCARE AND THE MODERNIZATION OF LABOUR MARKET POLICY

The long cycle from 1956-66 of high unemployment, followed by an unprecedented economic recovery, began the process of modernization of Canadian labour market policies. In a debate which remarkably mirrors the current discussion of new technologies, the Great Automation Scare put training policies at the centre of employment policy. Taylorism, it should be recalled, involved not just the splintering of tasks, but the concerted application of technical advances to production. This tended to produce a triadic segmentation of the labour market, commonly observed in North America, of technical, semi-skilled and unskilled workers. Automation under Fordism further separated conception and execution, increasing the number of technical employees needed to maintain and oversee automated processes. These technical skills required more formal training, and could not be obtained from existing apprenticeship training. The emphasis on expanding training also found support from a slightly different concern. It was argued by many that the increase in unemployment in the early 1960s was structural, the result of a mismatch between the existing skills of workers and new job openings. Keynesians dismissed these training-centred accounts, seeing instead lack of effective demand as the basis of unemployment. Whatever the source of the problem identified, it nonetheless became accepted opinion in both camps that the tradeoff between unemployment and inflation could be improved through policies to enhance adjustment in the labour market. In particular, training policies could help dissolve skill bottlenecks, which developed during recoveries and slowed growth.

Two other factors also greatly favoured the expansion of training.[13] With Europe booming by the 1960s, there were fewer skilled workers available to stock the Canadian labour market and the number of youth entering the labour market was about to soar. A new training system thus had to be put in place quickly, and the federal government in 1960 patched together the Technical and Vocational Training Act (TVTA). Although the new act gathered disparate programs into one scheme, it changed little with respect to apprenticeships or training in industry. Industry was encouraged to expand training, but industry continued to prefer not to train, so the postwar failures of market-driven training structures were compounded. The significant departure, partially a result of the TVTA, was the explosion in capital expenditures and training allowances for both vocational high schools and community colleges targeted at youth. The infrastructure for a publicly based training system was established. Indeed, these institutional programs, in the absence of private training systems, quickly became the cornerstone of training policy until the 1980s. Training policy, however, remained only tenuously linked to industrial policy making.

The TVTA remained the major labour market policy through the early 1960s, but that was soon to change. With Fordism at its peak as the decade closed, the concept of "active labour market policies" spread across the capitalist bloc. Active policies meant a variety of measures to speed the pace of adjustment of the labour supply so that more employment could be purchased with lower levels of inflation. In Canada, this was the mandate given to the new Department of Manpower and Immigration in 1966. The administrative reorganization consolidated existing labour market programs. The two main innovations of the Department illustrate well the continuities with the previous policy of relying on the market for labour adjustment. The Manpower Mobility Program and the creation of local Canada Employment Centres had the objective of improving price signals through better information and the removal of barriers to mobility.

To some extent, the 1967 Adult Occupational Training Act, which replaced the TVTA, went against the policy norm of relying on market determination of occupational skill distribution. It increased the role of government in targeting training needs. The TVTA had left occupational selection up to individual trainees and course offerings up to colleges. Large skill gaps remained a problem, as did over-enrollment in some courses. To compensate for the combined failure of the market and passive state funding of training, the federal government began to purchase occupational spaces in provincial training institutions after making employment forecasts. The new approach also stressed retraining adult workers suffering job displacement due to technological change.[14] This shift in emphasis was partly a result of the impact of automation which helped spark the dramatic rise in working-class protest in the mid-1960s, notably wildcat railway and postal worker strikes over redundancies and automated processes. In other words, the new training policy responded to pressures for employment security, as technology changed and fears of job loss mounted.

The late 1960s, in many respects, represented the high point of labour market policies in Canada. Strong growth and steadily improving productivity kept employment strong and incomes growing, with unemployment only moderately increasing between cyclical peaks. In turn, the stability of Fordist production processes allowed skill needs to be met by amending the postwar training regime to include occupational targeting, while still relying on immigration to keep the labour market well stocked. Dependent industrialization and dependent skills formation could continue to march in tandem.

The decline of Fordism in the early 1970s shattered the job market. Unemployment levels spiralled upwards, as the rate of employment growth consistently failed to match labour force growth. Labour market policy initially shifted the supply-side focus to the demand side in an attempt to provide short-term employment for youth and the unemployed. The Canada Works Program provided community-based direct job creation and general training. Such programs, however, could not stop the surging unemployment. Each level of additional demand stimulation purchased fewer jobs, partly because of shifting capital-labour ratios and partly because of inflation. Indeed, without continuing economic growth, the structural contradictions between rapid growth in the labour supply, stability in the hours of work, and low levels of unemployment could no longer be contained. The labour market conditions which produced the extensive postwar growth now provided the basis for imposing forms of labour market flexibility which would overturn the employment security provided earlier.

While the labour movement and much of the Left held tenaciously to Keynesianism and the old growth model, notably in the Canadian Labour Congress (CLC) embrace of incomes policies, the Right began to forge a new agenda. It was already accepted in the main economic policy branches of the government that little could be done for the unemployed by 1975, when the Bank of Canada gave its official approval to monetarism. The new theories of unemployment suggested workers were voluntarily unemployed, either because they were searching for work or keeping their "reservation wages" too high. Labour market programs slowly began to fall in line with the new thinking, by targeting individual responses to market incentives. Unemployment insurance levels and requirements were tightened. Employment creation shifted from communities to wage subsidy incentives for businesses, as in the Employment Tax Credit Scheme of 1978-81. Similarily, the Canada Manpower Training Program began to shift from broad-based, formal skilling to narrow, on-the-job training to meet specific skill shortages. Basic skills funding was reduced.[15] In these years, the crisis was still largely seen as transitional, however, so the intent was to clear labour market imbalances by reintroducing some wage and skill flexibility, without assaulting the entire labour regime of Fordism.

THE REVENGE OF THE MARKET
AND THE COLLAPSE OF LABOUR MARKET POLICY

This narrow defensive flexibility was not to last. The deep recession of 1981-82 forcefully altered the political and economic landscape in Canada. Since 1982 government policy has single-mindedly pursued the rationalization of product and labour markets to secure export markets. Labour market policy has been central to this strategy, and in particular to forcing workers to bear the burden of adjustment. Downward wage pressure has been imposed, with real wage losses the pattern set for most of the 1980s. A series of government studies in the early 1980s generalized the need to extend flexibility to the entire labour market.

The influential *Dodge Report* asserted that governments could do little to effect the aggregate level of employment which was set by market forces. Policies, however, could improve flexibility by reducing disincentives to work, by eliminating job creation programs, and by relying less on institutional training and more on industrial training. Despite record volumes of unemployment from 1982-84, direct employment creation schemes were abandoned within federal labour market policy.[16]

There was one exception to the embrace of market-based employment strategy after the *Dodge Report*. The National Training Program of 1982 did attempt occupational targeting of the skill mix. Training expenditures would cover fewer programs, which explicitly meant less funds for basic skills development for the unemployed. Instead, high-quality, high-skills training in selected occupations, where skill shortages existed or which had received "national occupation" designation as critical skills, would be targeted. Training policies were, therefore, to be more selective and supply core worker skills, which the market was failing to provide, to meet the specific needs of industry.

The occupational targeting of such functionally specific skills was also the downfall of the National Training Program, however. Its skills projections were premised upon the success of Liberals' resource-based megaprojects. With the recession, these projects were scrapped, so industry did not spend training allocations, and the narrowly based high-quality skills soon became redundant.[17] The conclusion drawn by business groups in Canada, including small businesses which received few training benefits and large capitalists who wanted greater control over training, was simple: state-administered training schemes based on imaginary occupational projections were a waste of training funds; business itself should control training levels and content. This conclusion was wholly congruent with the more general shift to neoconservatism in federal policy making, and the offloading of social programs to provincial governments and the market.

The change in government in 1984 brought the Tories and the solidification of a labour market strategy for defensive flexibility. The Tories thoroughly embraced the New Right position that governments not only cannot, but also should not, create jobs. Expanding employment in community-based "third sectors," where useful services but not profitable private consumption goods might be provided, was a waste of productive wealth. Labour market policy should provide incentives for private employers to train; governments should not attempt to determine which skills were needed nor to control the delivery of training. This was the reasoning of the consultation paper on training introduced by the Tory government in 1984. It argued that institutional training in

Canada was too rigid, especially for the service sector, where job growth was strongest. The new employment strategy should build around the notion of work experience for youth and workers re-entering the labour market, and less on the development of specific or formal skills, especially skills associated with worker credentials in apprenticeship or technical training, which increased their leverage in the labour market.[18]

This thinking formed the basis of the Canadian Jobs Strategy (CJS), implemented in 1985 and is still the core of federal labour market policy. The basic premise of the CJS is that the private sector can best determine training needs, and it should control delivery as well. Funds are available to firms providing initial work experience with some minimal training component. In this employer-centred, non-institutional system, small and large businesses can supply training. The privatization of training under the CJS thus completes the return to market determination of skills training, and marks the abandonment of an employment policy with the objective of improving the condition of the unemployed.[19]

The wage subsidy scheme that takes up the bulk of labour market funds under the CJS has added to the polarization of skills in the labour market. Some workers still receive formal qualifications, although apprenticeships and technical degrees are becoming more restrictive, but short-term, job-specific nontransferable training is more common. This strategy has had the effect of providing individual firms with cheap labour, undermining worker qualifications, and depositing large numbers of workers in low-wage segments of the workforce.

The recently announced Labour Force Development Strategy (LFDS) of the federal government to some extent recognizes that the market-driven training strategy has failed. The quality training necessary to compete in many sectors is not being provided by existing institutional programs and business is not picking up the slack. Basic skills such as literacy and numerical proficiency, necessary for service-sector work, are also lacking.[20] Some form of joint business-labour regulation is proposed to replace strict reliance on wage subsidies to encourage training. At the same time, the LFDS strips the funds for increased training out of the unemployment insurance budget by stiffening eligibility requirements, and leaves intact the privatized training structure.

THE CONSOLIDATION OF DEFENSIVE ADJUSTMENT IN CANADA

The new federal labour market strategy illustrates how imbedded the logic of defensive adjustment is in employment and training policy. This labour force strategy repeats the long history of labour market policy. In this sense, the national form of economic adjustment in Canada of relatively extensive economic growth dependent upon expanding low-wage employment sectors continues. Raising the quality of training for core workers alone, as the new Labour Force Development Strategy proposes, is unlikely to break the reinforcing circle of low productivity, low-wage job growth and institutionally unstable, market-centred employment policies.

The deterioration in employment since the crisis of Fordism began has evoked a response exhibiting significant policy instability. This point is crucial. The Canadian case unequivocally demonstrates that, at least in the provision of training, an important parallel can be drawn between markets and states. Markets have proven to be, theoretically and historically, extremely inadequate providers of worker qualifications. States may also suffer from "institutional failure": repeated strategic shifts, and resulting institutional instability, can severely disrupt the provision of even those "goods" best provided by non-market mechanisms.[21] The lack of internal coherence in the state's labour market policy shifts have all contributed to the present inadequacies of labour market policy.[22] The result should not be unexpected. If national training structures are important to the choice of paths of economic adjustment, the history of employment policy seems to have cut off several roads.

Institutional failure, however, is only part of the story; political failures are also important. The instability of labour market policy is ultimately related to the inability of the labour movement to lessen worker competition and impose a strong political commitment to full employment. Without the power of a politicised labour movement to keep the labour market tight, and thus sustain pressure for offensive forms of flexible adjustment, a strategy of defensive flexibility, undermining further the labour market position of workers has been consolidated in Canada. The most visible sign of this neo-liberal project has been, of course, continental free trade: Canadian access to U.S. markets is to be assured, while state economic policies to build the national market are curtailed. Deregulating the labour market by overturning existing forms of employment security has also been important:. Trade union freedom of collective action has been restricted; wage flexibility has replaced productivity bargaining; collective agreements have been stripped of union security clauses; and training facilities have been privatized. Canada today represents a *locus classicus* case of defensive adjustment: labour market flexibility ensures that wage-earners bear the costs of the instability of international trade, budgetary restraints, and new production processes.[23]

TRAINING, JOBS, AND DEMOCRACY

> The elements of a "new culture" and "new way of life" which are being spread around under the American label, are still just tentative feelers.... What is today called "Americanism" is to a large extent an advance criticism of an old strata which will in fact be crushed by an eventual new order and which are already in the grips of a wave of social panic, dissolution and despair. It is an unconscious attempt at reaction on the part of those who are impotent to rebuild and who are emphasizing the negative aspects of the revolution. But it is not from the social groups "condemned" by the new order that reconstruction is to be expected, but from those on whom is imposed the burden of creating with their own suffering the material bases of the new order. It is they who "must" find for themselves an "original," and not Americanised, system of living, to turn into "freedom" what today is "necessity."
>
> A. Gramsci[24]

The disastrous social and economic consequences of defensive flexibility have led to a search for an alternative. Attempting to preserve old forms of industrial activity and methods only contributes to the vicious spiral of cost competition in output and labour markets. Canada, and especially Ontario, would lose any such battle with low-cost exporters in Mexico and the "union-free" states of the U.S. Positive forms of economic flexibility are required to cope with market uncertainty generated by continental rationalization. Upgrading the quality of goods production to compete in more specialized markets, whether it be the post-Fordist variants of flexible specialization or diversified quality production, is the recommended route.[25] Competition would occur on the basis of the quality of goods and not their production costs; high wages and good jobs could thereby be preserved. As one of the studies for the influential *Vision 2000* review of Ontario's colleges concluded:

> The key to international competitiveness involves the cumulative technological base of society, including the production skills and tacit knowledge of much of the workforce...Overall, the key to success in the emerging technological era appears to be a commitment to training and a willingness to empower workers with skills and greater autonomy.[26]

The rest follows: as the competitiveness of manufacturing improves, unemployment levels would be brought down, the crisis of Fordism ended, and a new world of liberated work entered.

With few alternatives seemingly available, and maintaining that industrial employment remains important, this position has been endorsed by much of the Left. It has had special resonance in regions that traditionally have had large industrial cores and now seek a supply-side strategy for the regeneration of the manufacturing base. As Robin Murray recently put it: "In the era of mass production the powerful locational pull was proximity to markets. Now it is technical labour and its associated infrastructure that has become the dominant factor in shaping the hierarchy of space."[27]

Industry has been centred in Ontario; it is here that the post-Fordist strategy has been taken up most vigorously. With federal economic policy under the Tories adopting market solutions, the Ontario state is the one government able to support a stripped-down industrial policy oriented to creating high-tech, export-based Canadian multinationals. In contrast to other provinces where training policies have been reduced to providing for temporary low-wage jobs, quality training policies in Ontario would support quality production. When compared to the neoliberal alternative, this reasoning has its attractions, but it also has its limits.

This "manufacturing matters" thesis oddly mirrors the "post-industrial society" thesis it so firmly rejects.[28] The latter suggests that new technologies and evolving economic structures mean good jobs will be found in information services and that full employment is obsolete because paid work should no longer be necessary to secure adequate income. The former proposes that resparking productivity in manufacturing, and especially further building up an export base, will be sufficient to re-establish high wages *and* a high volume of employment. Neither thesis has been of much help in addressing the jobs crisis, however.

On the one hand, there is little indication that income claims are becoming less attached to paid labour; if anything, welfare provisions are becoming more work-dependent and increasing pauperization the most visible sign of the employment crisis.[29] Indeed, *contra* the post-industrial utopians, levels of proletarianization have been increasing, manufacturing shares of employment remain significant, and, as the changing role of women strikingly illustrates, access to paid work is the *sine qua non* of democratic participation. On the other hand, manufacturing competitiveness alone is hardly enough to ensure high wages, which are a consequence of broader structural factors and social struggles. High-quality manufacturing can be even more competitive with low wages, as the Asian NICs are impressively demonstrating.[30] Moreover, the manufacturing-matters thesis tends to exhibit a simple fallacy of composition: employment gains at the firm level are extended to the economy as a whole. The aggregate employment impact, however, depends upon the rules for sharing out productivity increases and export revenues, as well as the various factors which determine the supply of labour.[31] The critical question, as Ajit Singh pointed out some time ago, is whether the manufacturing sector meets domestic needs and also earns enough foreign exchange to pay for required imports, *at socially acceptable levels of exchange rate, output and employment*.[32]

DEFENSIVE FLEXIBILITY OR REQUALIFICATION OF WORK: THE PROSPECT FOR NATIONAL SETTINGS

The conditions under which for high-quality production may be established are quite varied, therefore, and different national settings need to be examined closely.[33] In Canada and the U.S., a segmentation of the North American labour market has been occurring, as the weaknesses of centralized collective bargaining and high unemployment allow individual firms to externalize the costs of flexibility. The break with Taylorism, indeed, was made possible by the political defeat of workers' organizations through the 1970s and 1980s. Moreover, although reuniting conception and execution has offered real gains for some workers in terms of new skills and job enrichment, these gains have not been extended to all. The multiskilled, flexible core worker has gained additional security from companies which wish to protect their training investments; the peripheral worker has had more insecurity and less training. "Precarious" forms of employment have soared: part-time work, contracting out, fixed-term contracts, and serial redundancies have all increased.[34]

As well, individualized forms of training at the workplace often accompany the new techniques; consequently, individualized bargaining between the involved worker and management tends to develop. In turn, this process contributes to a further fragmentation of wage formation as wages become tied to individual productivity through bonus systems. It is more difficult to establish a wage pattern as a result, and particularly to generalize wage gains to peripheral workers. Yet, the *collective* negotiation of worker involvement in production remains crucial to blocking defensive flexibility at the firm level.[35]

Even if we grant that a regime of flexible automation allows a virtuous circle between the available supplies of labour (in terms of qualifications) and the demand for labour (in terms of job content and wages), it still does not follow that the aggregate level of employment will be sufficient to lower unemployment levels. As Phillimore has noted: "Paradoxically, the better use production makes of the quality of labour, the smaller the quantity required."[36] The reskilling of workers to exploit new technologies will alter the internal labour market of the firm, and to a degree the product strategy, but it will not directly alter the aggregate level of employment. Chris Freeman and his colleagues have posed the right questions:

> Historically speaking, over the past two centuries it is incontestable that the combined effect of these forces [of technological advance and growth in demand], together with the persistent reduction in working hours, has made it possible to generate millions of new jobs on a scale which more than offset the tendency of rising unemployment as a result of labour-saving technical change. The questions which must be asked, therefore, are: first, why has this process been periodically disrupted? Secondly, are there special features about the present trends in technology and in the economy which would permanently (or for a long time) prevent a return to another period of high growth in output and employment, as occurred after previous periods of deep structural change and recession?[37]

It is difficult, then, to isolate a strategy for the requalification of work for the manufacturing sector. Larger questions about the structure and organization of industry, the desired rate and quality of the growth model, and the quantity of labour supplied in terms of hours and numbers of workers are central to determining aggregate employment levels.[38]

An employment strategy that places a premium on labour is central to the way new technologies will be introduced, as there is no generalized logic of upskilling from flexible automation.[39] This is a simple point, but one that is consistently neglected by the post-Fordists. With large labour reserves, firms will not adopt an exclusive strategy of functional flexibility. Fluctuations in output may be met by a labour deployment strategy that utilizes various forms of precarious employment. Industrial restructuring would expand the qualifications for core workers, leaving a substantial portion of workers cut off from new skills because training investments would be lost through their periodic unemployment. A new training regime of itself will neither increase the job opportunities or skills of marginalized workers. Manufacturing certainly does matter, but not as its protagonists would suggest.[40]

In national settings with an unstable training regime and a slack labour market, like that of Canada, a strategy for an offensive flexibility must begin from the principle of extending solidarity to the jobless, through new measures for employment and reduction of work-time. Flexibility strategies do not of themselves lower unemployment, and yet low unemployment is the precondition for a modernization of industry that would make the labour process emerging after Fordism educationally intensive for all workers.

ALTERNATE PRINCIPLES
FOR SOCIALIST EMPLOYMENT POLICY

It is precisely because flexible automation is part of the creation of a "new order," in Gramsci's sense, that current struggles of the labour movement tend to raise more questions than answers. What political strategies and organizational forms can provide the basis for working-class unity in a setting of increasingly diverse forms of wage-labour and mass unemployment? How do we make this project *truly popular* and move beyond the equation of socialist politics with either Keynesianism or statism? What types of policies will fit with the diversity of social spaces yet combat uneven development? Is a production-centred politics adequate to accommodate the needs of the unemployed, women, or the environment? Are concrete solidarities across national boundaries necessary? And, finally can these diverse struggles be combined in an alternative socialist politics? These are perplexing questions, yet they must be addressed if the restructuring of work is to extend substantive worker autonomy over the labour process and equitably distribute paid work. Several principles for a progressive employment strategy can be elaborated, however.[41]

1) Macroeconomic balance remains important, but new forms of investment planning and collective bargaining norms are even more so.
If full employment remains a central objective, valuable lessons of the Fordist period must not be forgotten in the rush to embrace new times. A simple Keynesian reflation will be profoundly inadequate. Macroeconomic balance will have to entail new mechanisms of control to constrain and shape market forces: worker participation in popular planning at the firm and industry level; national planning agreements over investment flows; regional and local development boards; and public ownership of core sectors. The instability generated by the Free Trade Agreement and the recession of 1990-91 illustrates all too well that investment in new technologies cannot be generated by market forces alone.

Similarly, the lesson of Fordism that there must be consumers as well as producers means that free collective bargaining still has its place. But again, past bargaining practices, which were narrowly focused on wage struggles, are not enough: wage solidarity with the poorly paid takes precedence; equal pay for equal work is crucial; increased choice between leisure and wages is vital; and the quality of production and consumption itself can no longer be ignored. Moreover, in solidarity with the jobless, a bargaining norm of an "annual free time factor" must take precedence over annual wage improvements in sharing out productivity increases. The macroeconomic logic of Fordism is deepened while qualitatively transforming its contents from a focus on consuming goods to increasing free time.[42]

2) The right to work in practice will entail less work.
A tight labour market is central to a training policy aimed at upgrading the skills of all workers.[43] Macroeconomic expansion will not be sufficient to lower unemployment, and exporting more soon becomes a zero-sum game of dumping job losses on the countries of the South (one of the terrible consequences of 1980s growth). The right to work, therefore, must be directly linked to a "decline in work," measured by annual hours per worker. Recent experience suggests that growth rates would have to consistently approach levels of the postwar boom to lower unemployment. But this would be enormously costly to the natural environment, and also block redistributive efforts to shift output to the South by soaking up available investment funds. Moreover, the unemployment that goes unmeasured because workers have been discouraged or have shifted to part-time, or because of the lower participation rates of women would still not be remedied. Collective bargaining to reduce working hours so as to equitably distribute paid work, say to a maximum of 1500 hours per year with severe restrictions on overtime work, is unavoidable. Work solidarity between workers means increasing the purchasing power and working hours of the unemployed and marginalized relative to core workers.

The politics of time should not be limited to fixing standard hours. A whole range of measures to radically reshape and liberate the allocation of worktime are possible: flex hours, banked time, single seniority lists based on hours worked, sabbatical leaves, early retirement, and sharing domestic labour. The government might sign "solidarity contracts" with employers and unions to develop such schemes, financial aid being conditional on the expansion of employment, particularly for young people. The struggle for working-time flexibility merges the demand for jobs with the demands of other progressive forces that paid work accommodate the diversity of lived experiences, giving workers time when it is needed most.[44] The right to work raises the question of how we work.

3) Quality training must be for quality products within a slower, quality growth model.

It is surely correct for the labour movement to accept measures which overturn Taylorism, but the upgrading of training to increase worker involvement in production can mean many things. In employer-centered versions, it means multiskilling core workers and preserving the training investment by limiting mobility. Quality training from the standpoint of workers is quite different: long-term, broad skills rather than short-term, specific ones; transferable skills over firm-specific skills; theoretical as well as practical knowledge; and extension of worker autonomy over the labour process. Technical degrees and apprenticeships provide for a broader skills base, more satisfying work, and transferable, recognized skills. Thus formal qualifications, earned through institutional training or a mixture of formal training and on-the-job training, tend to allow workers more flexibility and control over their labour process.

The requalification of work requires that the broad skills of technical competency be extended to all workers. In Canada the failure of privatized training systems and the improbability of corporatist regulation makes the community college system the most appropriate place to expand workers' skills. In doing so, these institutions will have to internalize flexibility in program delivery while preserving common standards, increasing transferable skills, and extending opportunities for continual learning into working-class communities.[45]

Linking the demand for training to the quality of production connects what goes into the labour process with the use-values that come out. This is important. The requalification of work rejects the narrow management rights clauses of Fordism, and extends both the need and capacity of workers to control the introduction of new technologies and to discuss alternate product design. Indeed, a portion of liberated freetime should be dedicated to increasing worker participation in running the enterprises at which they work. Unions too could develop their own technology networks, popular plans for industry, and socially useful products. To put it more sharply, upward adjustment to quality products and skills can mean two things: producing extraordinary consumption items for a privileged stratum, or quality products for a mass market that also re-shapes the way we live (Porsches or rapid mass transit; opera houses or community theatre centres; antibiotics-saturated beef or organic grains).[46] To the extent workers recapture the skills and capacities of their own labour power, these visions become credible alternatives for democratic socialist planning.

4) The democratic principle of equal access to knowledge must extend training to all workers.

The struggle against a rigid division between conception and execution has long been a demand of the socialist movement, and a variety of programs and structures are necessary. Educational opportunities should be available in all regions and at all ages. Basic literacy and skills are fundamental to participation in society and at work, and a diversity of public and community programs should be supported. Similarly, access to training means flexibility in delivery and adequate training allowances so older workers and low-income earners are not excluded. It also means that an emphasis on continual learning at the firm does not exclude younger workers from gaining training or employment.

Equal access to knowledge also entails, of course, equality of opportunity for women, Aboriginal people, and racial minorities. "Skill" is a social construction which has often been used to exclude and reinforce elitism.[47] The requalification of work obliges, therefore, equality of opportunity and solidaristic recognition of differential skills.

5) Continual learning is a workers' educational and cultural demand.

The continual application of new techniques and innovations in production means that continual learning must be incorporated as a key element in the requalification of work. Older workers need skill upgrading; workers permanently displaced need retraining. Workers with specific skills or trades should have access to both formal and on-the-job training through flexible programs for upgrading during working hours. To better prepare for task and skill changes, unions need information about production plans well in advance of implementation. But other forms of training and learning, specific to the job or not, are a social right for all workers. Learning should be an ordinary part of life. Annual paid educational leaves that are universally available will allow training choices are not limited to the specific needs of the job.[48]

6) Democratic administration is essential to implementing labour market policy.

Insofar as the requalification of work contributes to expanding the capacity of workers collectively to shape their futures, substantive aspects of democracy are included. Representative forms of democracy for the bodies governing employment are important—indeed, they are critical if collective negotiation of worker involvement is to incorporate the unorganized and jobless.

Currently, training, except where it is part of collective agreements, occurs almost completely on the basis of employer voluntarism. There are a variety of proposals to expand training argue for either a bipartite or tripartite training board system, albeit with some extension to community groups, but ignore other aspects of employment policy.[49] Such corporatist structures have strong limitations in that they tend to be dominated by the most economically powerful producer groups, and thus institutionalize the inequalities of capitalist social relations. A wider, mandated representation allows women, racial minorities, and the jobless to have their interests represented as well.

Even the inclusion of community groups has limits, however, as there is no direct democratic participation of the workers themselves in the delegation of responsibility to the labour market boards. Indeed, it may be necessary to establish a statutory labour market system structured through local, democratically accountable bodies similar to school boards. If encompassed within a national labour market policy, the local boards would decentralize decision making, allowing local communities to be more broadly active in establishing production, employment and training priorities.[50]

It could be argued too that Work and Environment Boards incorporating environmental considerations into employment planning are needed. Such bodies could be divided into units concerned with workplace ecology, unemployment, training, domestic labour, employment equity and sustainable production. The proliferation of labour market policy bodies already requires administrative consolidation alongside decentralization of the delivery of the service. Through such publicly elected labour market boards, workers and their communities could be directly involved in the collective negotiation over the conditions of work, as well as the environmental conditions of production, with the providers of jobs and training.

The demands which make up this vision of requalified work read like a kind of socialist wish list in the Canada of today, an extension of social rights in a period of downward adjustment of the collective rights and status of workers.[51] But so it should be. For even if the best alternative to be hoped for in present political conditions is the bundling of a progressive qualification process with quality capitalist production, it is equally evident that this narrow, post-Fordist strategy is unlikely to succeed on its own terms. The future for workers and the jobless outside the core sector remains dismal and increasingly insecure. The election of an NDP government in Ontario did little to correct this, or to alter the necessity of building the political currents to support a progressive model of development. It is, therefore, inescapable that we stake out a broader collective project that seeks to expand creative capacities—particularly in redefining the nature of work and the allocation of time—and begins to forge new social alliances.

JOB COMPETITION OR WORK SOLIDARITY: EXPANDING POLITICAL VISIONS

When Fordism was making its historical appearance and vocational training institutions were springing up to ready workers for the new trades, the American educator John Dewey noted the critical democratic choice at hand:

> Those who believe in the continuous separate existence of what they are pleased to call the "lower classes" or the "labouring classes" would naturally rejoice to have schools in which these "classes" would be segregated. And some employers of labour would doubtless rejoice to have schools supported by public taxation supply them with additional food for their mills.
> Alternative forms of work and training, however, existed which acknowledged the interest of workers in advancing their skills:
> ..the development of such intelligent initiative, ingenuity and executive capacity as shall make workers as far as may be possible, the masters of their own industrial fate... The kind of vocational education in which I am interested is not one which will "adapt" workers to the existing regime; I am not sufficiently in love with the regime for that. It seems to me that the business of all who would not be educational time-servers is... to strive for a kind of vocational education which will alter the existing industrial system and ultimately transform it.[52]

Even more than in the past, the technologies embodied in flexible automation offer a vast potential to develop the intelligent initiative, ingenuity and executive capacity of workers. A small step in this direction will mean training and jobs. The danger in Canada in the post-FTA world is that the labour movement will focus its political efforts on shoring up the local manufacturing sector as the winds of continental adjustment and global competition howl.[53] Such a narrow, short-term strategy of bolstering regional capitals however, will inevitably fuel the competitive bargaining for manufacturing jobs between subnational states on both sides of the border. This competitive process is visible already in the Premier's Council's strategy in Ontario and the story could be repeated across the country. Without a broader, democratic vision of the future of work incorporating the jobless, new training policies tied to quality manufacturing for the new global economy will continue to reproduce the skill and income polarizations characteristic of the 1980s.

It is a startling paradox of Canadian history that just as the labour movement is finally finding is own way, after a century in the shadow of Gompers, it has become imperative that we find new mechanisms of solidarity and support that span the continent.[54] The internationalization of the struggle for work solidarity is necessary to put in place the kind of international order which will maximize national autonomy for alternate, ecologically sound development paths, and replace the present vicious circle of freer trade, intensified competition, followed by accelerated environmental and work degradation. Struggles around the requalification and democratization of work are more likely to contribute to this joint project than those seeking manufacturing competitiveness. They may, to quote Gramsci's words again: "turn into 'freedom' what today is 'necessity.'"

ENDNOTES

I would like to thank Jane Jenson and Rianne Mahon for their insightful, encouraging comments on an earlier draft of this paper.

1.   Raymond Williams, *Towards 2000* (London: Penguin, 1983), p. 101.

2.   The case for a joint worker-management interest in upgrading training for quality production has been forcefully presented in: L. Muszynski and D. Wolfe, "New Technology and Training: Lessons from Abroad," *Canadian Public Policy*, 15:3 (1989); W. Streeck, "Industrial Relations and Industrial Change: The Restructuring of the World Automobile Industry," *Economic and Industrial Democracy* (EID), 8:4 (1987); and a slew of government reports, most notably, Ontario Council of Regents, *Vision 2000: Quality and Opportunity* (Toronto: 1990) and Premier's Council of Ontario, *People and Skills in the New Global Economy* (Toronto: Queen's Printer, 1990).

3.   See: R. Mahon, "From Fordism to ?: New Technology, Labour Markets and Unions," *EID*, 8:1 (1987); H. Kern and M. Schumann, "Limits of the Division of Labour: New Production and Employment Concepts in West German Industry," *EID*, 8:2 (1987); and F. Wilkinson, "The Restructuring of Labour Markets," *Labour and Society*, 13:4 (1988).

4.   *People and Skills in the New Global Economy*, p. 1. It should be noted that training is not being put forward, as it was in the 1960s, as a solution to structural unemployment and skill bottlenecks. The argument now is even more convoluted: skilled workers will create the high-quality products in demand, and such demand, in turn, will employ these very same workers. As domestic markets are not likely to be deep enough, export-led industrialization is key, with foreign exchange earnings trickling down to non-manufacturing workers.

5.   R. Hyman and W. Streeck (eds.), *New Technology and Industrial Relations* (Oxford; Basil Blackwell, 1988); A. Sorge and M. Warner, *Comparative Factory Organization* (London: Gower, 1986); and M. Maurice, F. Sellier and J. Silvestre, *The Social Foundations of Industrial Power* (Cambridge: MIT Press, 1986).

6.   Or as Storper recently put it: "In reality, both 'firms' and 'industries' are being redefined, such that the notion of returns as strictly internal loses its meaning in any dynamic, historical sense. In sum, in functioning industrial systems, both the division of labour and technological innovations tend to be endogenously and dynamically reproduced and are, in turn, mutually reinforcing." See: "The Transition to Flexible Specialization in the U.S. Film Industry," *Cambridge Journal of Economics*, 13:2 (1989), p. 297.

7.   On the different factors shaping the skilling process see: S. Wood (ed.), *The Degradation of Work* (London: Hutchinson, 1982); E. Batstone *et al.*, *New Technology and the Process of Labour Regulation* (Oxford: Clarendon, 1987), Ch. 1; and R. Allen, "The Impact of Technical Change on Employment, Wages and the Distribution of Skills: A Historical Perspective," in C. Riddell (ed.), *Adjusting to Change: Labour Market Adjustment in Canada* (Toronto: University of Toronto Press, 1986). Especially fascinating on this issue, in relation to economic performance, is: T. Nichols, *The British Worker Question* (London: Routledge, 1986).

8.   Although differing in their assessment of flexible automation, several authors note the new skills profiles: R. Kaplinsky, "Industrial Restructuring: Some Questions for Education and Training," *IDS Bulletin*, 20:1 (1989); A. Phillimore, "Flexible Specialization, Work Organization and Skills," *New Technology, Work and Employment*, 4:2 (1989); and P. Mehaut, "New Firms' Training Policies and Changes in the Wage-Earning Relationship," *Labour and Society*, 13:4 (1988).

9.   Göran Therborn, *Why Some People Are More Unemployed Than Others* (London: Verso 1986), pp. 20-36. Also see: J. Grahl and P. Teague, "Labour Market Flexibility in West Germany, Britain and France," *West European Politics* (1990).

10. R. Boyer, *The Search for Labour Market Flexibility* (Oxford: Clarendon Press 1988), p. 260. This choice has been discussed with respect to Canadian trade unions in G. Albo, "The 'New Realism' and Canadian Workers," in A. Gagnon and J. Bickerton (eds.), *Canadian Politics* (Peterborough: Broadview Press 1990).

11.   The exception was wartime, when there was no choice but to train the domestic labour force.

12.   S. Dupré, *et al. Federalism and Policy Development* (Toronto: University of Toronto, 1973), pp. 14-5; and G. Laxer, *Open for Business* (Toronto: Oxford, 1990), p. 35. Canada compares interestingly to the U.S.: B. Elbaum, "Why Apprenticeship Persisted in Britain But Not in the United States," *Journal of Economic History*, 49:2 (1989).

13.   See: OECD, *A Medium Term Strategy for Employment and Manpower Policies* (Paris: OECD 1978), Ch. 2; and L Muszynski, "The Politics of Labour Market Policy," in B. Doern (ed.), *The Politics of Economic Policy* (Toronto: University of Toronto Press, 1985), pp. 260-3.

14.   S. Peitchinis, "The Development of Manpower and Economic Development: Is Co-ordination Possible?," *Relations Industrielles*, 22:1 (1967); and R. Phidd and B. Doern, *The Politics and Management of Canadian Economic Policy* (Toronto, 1978), pp. 374-9.

15.   B. Cullen, *Employment Strategy* (Ottawa: Supply and Services, 1976).

16.   Task Force on Labour Market Development, *Labour Market Development in the 1980s* (Ottawa: Supply and Services, 1981); Economic Council of Canada, *In Short Supply: Jobs and Skills in the 1980s* (Ottawa: Supply and Services, 1982); and *Canadian Labour Markets in the 1980s* (Kingston: Queen's Industrial Relations Centre, 1983).

17.   CEIAC, *The National Training Act* (Ottawa: Supply and Services, 1985), R. Abella, *Equality in Employment, Vol. 1* (Ottawa: Supply and Services, 1984), pp. 158-75; and Economic Council of Canada, *Strengthening Growth* (Ottawa: Supply and Services, 1985), pp. 41-2 and 103-4.

18.   CEIC, *Consultation Paper: Training* (Ottawa: Supply and Services, 1984); CEIC, *Canadian Jobs Strategy* (Ottawa: Supply and Services, 1985).

19.   Senate of Canada, *In Training: Only Work Works* (1987); and M. Prince and J. Rice, "The CJS: Supply-Side Social Policy," in *idem (*eds.), *How Ottawa Spends 1989-90* (Ottawa: Carleton University Press, 1989).

20.   CEIC, *Success in the Works* (Ottawa: S and S, 1990); and R. Mahon, "Adjusting to Win? The New Tory Training Initiative," in K. Graham (ed.), *How Ottawa Spends 1990-91* (Ottawa: Carleton University Press, 1990), pp. 16-9.

21.   Cf. Therborn, *Some Peoples*, p. 132.

22.   The current situation is discussed in: R. Mahon, "Towards a Highly Qualified Workforce: Improving the Terms of the Equity-Efficiency Tradeoff," in *Colleges and the Changing Economy* (Toronto: Ontario Council of Regents, 1989).

23.   See the range of country studies in: S. Rosenberg (ed.), *The State and the Labor Market* (New York: Plenum Press, 1989). Even if she fails to adequately recognize technological discontinuities, Anna Pollert's 'deconstruction' of flexibility needs to be accounted for (and most praisers of post-Fordism do not):

"The 'Flexible' Firm: Fixation or Fact?." *Work, Employment and Society*, 2:3 (1988); and C Smith, "Flexible Specialization, Automation and Mass Production," *Work, Employment and Society*, 3:2 (1989).

24. "Americanism and Fordism," *Selections from the Prison Notebooks* (New York: International Publishers. 1971), p. 317.

25. Piore and Sabel, *Industrial Divide*; A. Sorge and W. Streeck, "Industrial Relation and Technical Change," in Hyman and Streeck (eds.), *New Technology*; Muszynski and Wolfe, "New Technology"; and Premier's Council, *Competing in the New Global Economy, Vol.1* (Toronto: Queen's Printer 1988). These varied strategies are assessed very interestingly in: E. Schoenberger, "From Fordism to Flexible Accumulation: Technology, Competitive Strategies, and International Location," *Society and Space*, 6:3 (1988).

26. D. Wolfe, "New Technology and Education: A Challenge for the Colleges," in *Colleges and the Changing Economy* (Toronto: Ontario Council of Regents, 1989), p. 16.

27. "Regional Economic Policy in Europe in the 1990s in the Light of the Experience of the 1980s," (Paper prepared for Agenor, March 1990), 10. In contrast, see: N. Smith, "The Region is Dead! Long Live the Region!" *Political Geography Quarterly*, 7:2 (1988).

28. The following particularly applies to the Americans (Block versus Cohen and Zysman), but it also is characteristic of the Europeans (Gorz and Offe versus Streeck and Sorge on the continent). It used to also cover the British, but then "New Times" came along and the new realists decided manufacturing was the rage.

29. The 'green' argument on rupturing the link between paid employment and income is political nonsense but also socially unjust: it is premised on reducing the consumption levels of active workers to increase the consumption of (by choice) inactive individuals and not on the basis of more useful work for all or by spreading work. Individual contributions to total social labour are a *right* and *obligation*. Although wrong, the most interesting case for this work-income split to lower unemployment, tied to a reformulated incomes policy, has come from liberals such as James Meade and Ron Dore.

30. Guy Standing observes that because high-tech is already present in many low-wage countries, notably the Pacific Rim, the flexibility views are fanciful. See *Labour Market Analysis and Employment Planning* (World Employment Program Working Paper N. 23, 1988), p. 15.

31. See the essays (especially Robert Boyer) gathered in J. Kregel, E. Matzner and A. Roncaglia (eds.), *Barriers to Full Employment* (London: Macmillan, 1988).

32. A. Singh, "U.K. Industry and the World Economy: A Case of De-industrialization?" *Cambridge Journal of Economics*, 1:2 (1977).

33. Within the international literature, the work of Rianne Mahon has been excep-

tional in pointing to the importance of national settings and class struggles in shaping any flexible automation regime, in contrast to the often sweeping generalizations characteristic of much of the post-Fordist literature. See especially Mahon, "From Fordism to ?"

34. L. Poulin-Simon, "Labour Market Flexibility: A Canadian Perspective," in G. Laflamme *et. al* (eds.), *Flexibility and Labour Markets in Canada and the United States* (Geneva: ILO, 1989), pp. 66-8.

35. D. Leborgne and A. Lipietz, "New Technologies, New Modes of Regulation: Some Spatial Implication," *Society and Space*, 6:3 (1988), p. 269; and Mehaut, 'Training Policies.'

36. Phillimore, "Flexible Specialization," p. 87.

37. C. Freeman and L. Soete, "Introduction," in *idem* (eds.), *Technical Change and Full Employment* (Oxford: Basil Blackwell, 1987), p. 5. Also see: Wilkinson, "Restructuring of Labour Markets."

38. The empirical study by B. Rowthorn and A. Glyn, which follows up work by Therborn, also notes that low unemployment is only loosely correlated with economic growth, and while avoiding a collapse in industrial employment may be an important precondition for lowering unemployment, growth in service employment is crucial. But having noted this, they tell us nothing about new rules of co-ordination for employment policy, and simply invoke the alleged successes of the "corporatist countries." See: 'The Diversity of Unemployment Experience Since 1973,' in S. Marglin and J. Schor (eds.), *The Golden Age of Capitalism* (Oxford: Clarendon, 1990).

39. S. Wood, 'The Transformation of Work?' in *idem* (ed.), *The Transformation of Work?* (London: Unwin and Hyman, 1989), pp. 13-20.

40. As Sheila Rowbotham noted, "The awkward fact is that new forms of organizing production involve many workers who are not at all in control of their work... An anlysis which is to be the basis of an effective strategy has to alert us to several potentials in flexibility in terms of conditions and organizationsl responses." "PostFordism," *Z Magazine* (Sept. 1990), p. 35. It is these different potentials which has led A. Gorz, in his most recent book, to suggest bleakly that "it is a small core of privileged workers who are integrated into new-style enterprises at the expense of a mass of people who are marginalized and whose job security is destroyed...who are often reduced to competing for the privilege of selling personal services (including shoe-shining and house-cleaning) to those who retain a secure income." *Critique of Economic Reason* (London: Verso, 1990), pp. 70-1.

41. See the article by Robin Murray on this strategy: "Ownership, Control and the Market," *New Left Review*, 164 (1987), p. 96.

42. See the following: A. Lipietz. "An Alternative Design for the 21st Century," (mimeo); and R. Mahon, "From Solidaristic Wages to Solidaristic Work: A Post-Fordist Historic Compromise for Sweden?" *Economic and Industrial*

Democracy, 12:3 (1991). It is important that these bargaining principles become generalized, otherwise productivity gains from worker involvement are contained within the firm and serve to polarize workers. See the discussion by M. Aoki on quasi-rents: "A New Paradigm of Work Organization and Co-ordination?" in Marglin and Schor (eds.), *Golden Age*.

43. See: M. Rustin, *For a Pluralist Socialism* (London: Verso, 1985); C. Gill, *Work, Unemployment and New Technology* (Oxford: Polity, 1985), Ch. 7; and M. Wiedemeyer, "New Technology in West Germany: The Employment Debate," *New Technology, Work and Employment*, 4:1 (1989), pp. 63-4.

44. A. Gorz, *Paths to Paradise* (London: Pluto, 1985); M. Luxton, "Time for Myself: Women's Work and the 'Fight for Shorter Hours,'" in M. Luxton and H.J. Maroney (eds.), *Feminism and Political Economy* (Toronto: Metheun, 1987); and European Trade Union Institute, *Flexibility and Jobs: Myths and Realities* (Brussels: ETUI, 1985). The essays by Gauvin and Michon on France and Berg on Norway are interesting discussions of the political dynamic created by the struggle for the 6-hour day. See: Rosenberg (ed.), *State and the Labor Market*.

45. These views have had a slight echo in many recent government reports in Canadian, notably Ontario Council of Regents, *Vision 2000: Quality and Opportunity* (Toronto, 1990). Also see N. Jackson, "Working Knowledge: The Politics of Skills Training," *Our Times* 8:3 (1989).

46. These are, of course, part of the many issues raised by local experiences in Britain, and also discussed more recently. See M. Mackintosh and H. Wainwright (eds.), *A Taste of Power* (London: Verso, 1989); and N. Costello, J. Michie and S. Milne, *Beyond the Casino Economy* (London: Verso, 1989). On linking worktime reduction and popular planning, see the insightful comments of S. Gindin, "Time-Out: Reducing Worktime to Our Benefits," *Our Times* (March 1991).

47. On the dangers of unequal access under flexible automation see: J. Jenson, "The Talents of Women, the Skills of Men: Flexible Specialization and Women," in S. Wood (ed.), *The Transformation of Work?* (London: Unwin Hyman, 1989); and C. Cockburn, *Two-Track Training* (London: Macmillan, 1987).

48. Muszynski and Wolfe, "New Technology," pp. 250-1; and P. Osterman, *Employment Futures* (Oxford: Oxford University Press, 1988), pp. 159-60.

49. For a discussion of recent Canadian proposals for training boards and the effort to democratize training boards in Britain, see: R. Mahon, "Adjusting to Win?"; and C. Benn and J. Fairley (eds.), *Challenging the MSC* (London: Pluto, 1986).

50. M. Rustin, *Pluralist Socialism*, pp. 161-2; and L. Panitch, "Capitalist Restructuring and Labour Strategies," *Studies in Political Economy*, 24 (1987), p. 148.

51. "Modern methods of production have given us the possibility of ease and security for all; we have chosen, instead, to have overwork for some and starvation

for the others. Hitherto we have continued to be as energetic as we were before there were machines; in this we have been foolish, but there is no reason to go on being foolish forever." Bertrand Russell, *In Praise of Idleness* (London: Unwin, 1935), p. 25.

52.   J.Dewey, "An Undemocratic Proposal," in M. Lazerson and W. Grubb (eds.), *American Education and Vocationalism: A Documentary History 1870-1970* (New York: Teachers College Press, 1974), pp. 143-7.

53.   A striking illustration of this failure of vision on the Left is the widely endorsed 1990 CLC Convention Document N. 14, *A New Decade: Our Future*, which asserts the need for full employment, but makes no serious arguments on how to get there, except by driving up growth (which is irreconcilable with environmental claims). Indeed, the discussion of the future of work is slight, with not even a mention of work-time reduction! NDP economic documents are even more barren of forward-looking thinking. In contrast, see the stimulating paper produced by Sam Gindin and David Robertson, "Democracy and Productive Capacity: Notes Toward an Alternative to Competitiveness," (mimeo, 1990).

54.   For some discussions along these lines see: R. Mahon, "Post-Fordism, Canada and the FTA: Some Issues for the Left," in Daniel Drache and Maric Gertler (eds.), *The New Era of Global Competition: State Policy and Market Power* (Montreal: McGill-Queen's University Press, 1991); G. Albo, "Canada, Left-Nationalism and Younger Voices," *Studies in Political Economy*, 33 (1990); and, more generally, M. Davis, *Prisoners of the American Dream* (London: Verso, 1986), p. 301ff.

PART II

Politics: Identity and Solidarity

	CHAPTER 6
All the World's a Stage: Ideas, Spaces and Times in Canadian Political Economy	JANE JENSON

Post - Redin -

INTRODUCTION

One of the consequences of two decades of 'crisis' economics and 'crisis' politics has been the reconceptualization of some basic categories of political economy. Whereas in the 1960s and even the 1970s social theory was relatively content with methods which stressed the stability—or reproduction—of society and social relations, the last decade has seriously challenged such approaches. We need only recall opposition to structuralism and functionalism in sociology and political science, debates about theories of the state conducted among neo-Marxists and critiqued by neo-institutionalists, the post-structuralist assault against modernism, the crumbling of social-democratic thinking in the face of a new international and domestic order, and the emergence of post-modern, neo-Nietzschean approaches. Canadian political economy, having drawn heavily upon these traditions in the past, has also participated in this experience of re-thinking and re-conceptualization.

Three theoretical trajectories in particular have been central to the reconstruction and reconceptualization of social theory: feminism, neo-Marxism and neo-institutionalism. After examining some of the efforts made within these streams to think about ideas, space and time, this article proposes a lens for reading the recent Canadian experience of economic and political restructuring.

THREE THEORETICAL TRAJECTORIES

Feminists and feminist theorists have made important contributions to the ways we think about ideas and space and time. Since the late 1960s the women's movement has claimed the world must change, that long-standing forms of production, family, and gender relations cannot continue. Moreover, given the male-centredness of much past practice, feminists have demanded that science and politics change their standpoints dramatically. They have been critical, *first* of the gender blindness of traditional categories of social theory, *then* of gender biases in such theory which made it possible only to consider the experience of men, *then* of theory's failure to take experience and its meanings into account. These concerns have led feminists to challenge long-standing notions about identity and politics, about history, about difference. Indeed the goals and hopes of feminism for a more open and welcoming world, where pluralism is accepted and a variety of value choices are possible, are seen by many to hold the promise of a new foundation for theory and politics.

Their theoretical perspectives enabled feminists to establish at the heart of social theory a consideration of the oppressive character of existing gender relations and the liberating potential of altered ones. Several such efforts focused on the way in which gender is socially constructed at the level of "everyday life." One of the first insights of the women's movements—out of which feminist analyses grew—was that the ways that women and men "spoke" about each other, about families, and about society set crucial limits on their struggles. Feminists were quick to recognise that in order for their lives to be "made visible" women had to claim their voices and label their oppression. They had to compel others to take them and their ideas seriously. Thus, the "feminist turn" has involved thinking about the ways ideas powerfully organize our lives and define our interests.[1]

Feminism is also a politics of empowerment, and as such it draws attention to the possibilities and specificities of political action. Recent controversies within feminist theory—among black and white women and First and Third World women—have demonstrated, for example, the immense variability in gender consciousness, a variability which reveals that the concepts of feminine/feminist identity are not essentialist but are, rather, bounded by time and space. As Simone de Beauvoir told us so long ago, one is not born but becomes a woman, and, moreover, one becomes a woman of colour, a white woman, a bourgeois woman, a French woman.

This attention to historical specificity and the refusal of essentialism is not unique to feminism, of course. Marxism has experienced a similar turn, apparent in the attention paid to civil society, ideas and the specificities of time and place.[2] For those building on the work of Gramsci, ideas have become newly important precisely because they provide the "mental frameworks—the languages, the concepts, categories, imagery of thought, and the systems of representation—which different classes and social groups deploy in order to make sense of, define, figure out and render intelligible the way society works."[3] Consequently, analyses which sought to understand the seeming acceptance by the subordinate classes of social relations of domination in capitalist society through the mystifying or falsifying power of ideology have been replaced by ones which focus on the power relations which lie behind ideas as they become a material force. This reorientation has also involved a turn away from structuralism's concern with ideology's contribution to the reproduction of social relations towards a more political analysis of the processes by which new ideas arise. In this process, there has been a turn to history and to concrete analyses, and therefore to variation across time and space.[4]

A further and parallel source for attention to ideas has developed recently among political sociology's neo-institutionalists. The short shrift given to "ideas" within much of the early neo-institutionalist work followed in part from its starting point.[5] Criticizing both structural-functionalist and neo-Marxist perspectives on the state, those who advocated "bringing the state back in" in order to examine cross-national differences in policy outcomes were most interested in exploring variation in the role of institutions across space. In trying to account for policy differences, they emphasized the autonomy of the state from civil society and the independent role of policy decision makers, as well as rejecting neo-Marxist state theory as supposedly too abstract for comparative analysis.[6] Instead, they focused on state structures, in order to explore how politics and policies were jointly conditioned by institutional arrangements and social relationships.[7] In this process, however, the definition of interests was seldom problematized. Why actors did what they did, their ideas about utopias and goals, and their definitions of self were taken as given.

Nevertheless, as the crisis of the last decades took hold and some political actors set out to reshape the basic policy instruments of the postwar state's arsenal—especially economic and social policy—neo-institutionalism was increasingly forced to incorporate historical perspective.[8] Explanations for policy change over time became the goal.[9] Since state structures had rarely altered, the power of ideas emerged as a possible force underlying changes within regimes in the same country. Consequently, analysis turned towards understanding the linkages between policy paradigms and particular configurations of economic and political arrangements, which rise with such paradigms and die as they die.[10]

As this brief overview illustrates, these three diverse bodies of literature have contributed to a shift towards a consideration of identities, ideas and interest formation in recent social theory. These theoretical efforts have also meant new attention to the variety of actors shaping politics. They also reflect, therefore, a new and important focus on the variation of ideas and political practices in space and in time. Such reconsiderations inform this article, which proposes a way to think about ideas, space and time. In doing so it explores three major issues. I begin by suggesting that we need to pay greater analytic attention to representations of self and the politics of identity. Such a stress on identity politics leads immediately to a discussion of the structure/agency question. Consideration of that long-standing quandary of social theory has recently resulted in sustained attention to time and space. As soon as deterministic formulations are replaced by ones with greater attention to subjectivity, it becomes clear that only in specific places and times is it possible to observe the meeting of the general and particular, with politics being an historical construction of people making their own history albeit never under conditions of their own choosing. Finally, as we move through the present moment of turbulence towards the 21st century we must search for imaginative and alternative ways of struggling for the long-standing progressive goals of equality, respect for difference, and empowerment. The new attention in the present moment to ideas, time and space partakes of this creativity, as part of the search to understand and make the future.

THINKING ABOUT THE HERE AND NOW

Political practice for the last two decades has been very much influenced by a set of new actors who often reject the legitimacy of the view that the politics of production models social relations. They promote instead alternative definitions of political time and space. New social movements have claimed not only new identities but also have participated in the formulation of a critique of past practices in favour of several competing definitions of this particular moment.[11] An array of time-denoting labels provides the markers for swirling political debate as well as controversies within social theory. Time is of the essence in discussions of the "posts": post-structuralism, post-industrialism, post-capitalism, post-Marxism, post-modernism, post-Enlightenment, post-Fordism, and even New Times. With such labelling, the debates within social theory have put time on the agenda, just as many have also begun to make claims that a compression of space is occurring.[12] As so many people struggle to make sense of their own identities and to legitimate in the social and political world the identities they have created through individual and collective struggle, the spaces for and of politics proliferate. The notion that new actors have come into being, or that traditional ones face a new situation, involves alterations in understandings of space.[13]

Feminists, anti-racists, ecologists, and gays insist on creating new space for new politics in the family, the city, the environment, and the community. They reject the long-standing Left notion that the pre-eminent political spaces are the workplace, parliament, and nation. Moreover, geographical space contracts as social movements utilize advanced technologies and communications networks to create new ties around the globe, linking the new politics with those of Third World women, opponents of apartheid, Amazonian Indians, and peace and Green activists, East and West. New social movements create transnational networks while old social movements—like the labour movement—move to knit cross-border ties in a world of restructured regional blocs.

These approaches highlight the significance of the relations between time and space by drawing attention to the ways in which temporality and spatiality are crucial elements of historical processes. Yet the emergence of such politics now—at a moment of political and economic crisis and restructuring—also implies that the potential for political experimentation is not the same at all times. Some moments recreate stability in social relations while others generate more change. Moreover, this time-bound conceptualization of innovation itself suggests that notions of spatiality are neither fixed nor always equally fluid. Some moments may bring new representations of the political spaces while others hew to the familiar boundaries.

From this perspective, then, the relative stability of the recent past looks somewhat "miraculous". It was a particular historical moment in which, out of a range of possible identities and bases for consciousness, the version of politics which took root in many places was one that mobilized production-based identities. From this angle the present looks much less like the end of history and much more like the end of an epoch. But this analytic stance leads us to ask why the present is a moment in which identities are contested.

It is important to remember that "identity politics" is not a creation of the new social movements nor a hallmark of post-modernity. Politics is always, has always been, about identities. The mere existence of a "politics of identities" now may not serve as sufficient reason either to abandon social theoretical categories which acknowledge the continued influence of accumulation and production or to announce the end of the "politics of production". Nevertheless, production-based politics and production-based identities no longer mobilize as much, as easily, or as convincingly as they once did. Therefore, we must also understand why the position of a social group in the production process is *no longer* as likely to define its collective identity and why relations in production are no longer the pivotal representation around and in relation to which a variety of actors organize themselves. In other words, we still must explain the present, and the turbulence which has undone a previous consensus about space and time, identities and interests—that is, a consensus on the ordering principles of politics.

REGIMES AND CRISIS: THE POLITICS OF IDENTITY

There has been a persistent tension in social theory between structuralist and agency-centred explanations. Structuralist discussions are parsimonious, neat, law-like and forceful. Moreover, the notion that powerful laws are at work—those of capitalism or patriarchy, for example—is useful for generating and focusing anger and mobilizing opposition. Nevertheless, such forms of argumentation are limited, for all the usual reasons. They are general, and particular cases may not follow exactly the same trajectory. They may ultimately not be empowering: if structures bear down, how can victims resist?[14] Agency-centred arguments are more politically enticing, then, because they put the issue of strategy front and centre. Moreover, they are useful for understanding historical variety. The problem is that they are often messy, full of contingencies. Clearly, the constant rise and fall of these two forms of explanation means that each offers something which the other lacks. If the pendulum swings too far, a correction arises.

The analytic challenge is to stop veering from one to the other, by assuming history is open-ended even if real effects of institutionalized practices and structural constraints exist. History is a set of arrangements experienced by each actor as the constraints within which action occurs. Yet if actors are endowed with the ability to act strategically, then their actions must be seen as creative of the different histories which they live. Thus focusing on the politics of action is as important as structural analysis; neither can be abandoned.

In doing so, it is useful to remember that politics—whether or not it is being experienced in a moment of turbulence—is always identity politics. The implication of this conceptual starting point is that analysis must always take into account the constitution of actors. From this perspective, politics can be seen as a process in which actors create their constituencies by generating support for their preferred formulation of their own collective identity (and often that of their protagonists) and for the enumeration of interests which follows from that collective identity. This definition of politics depends upon an understanding of the dual aspects of representation. One type of representation involves actors' *representation of self* to others, via a collective identity. A second type, familiar from the language of liberal democracy, is the *representation of interests*. These two senses of the term representation are closely linked. Both involve power, namely the power to give meaning to social relations, and thereby to represent and dispute interests.[15]

But everything is not possible. Even if identities and the interests to which they give meaning are never other than subjective and relative, nevertheless specific conjunctures do give greater weight to some identities and interests, because of the form of social relations prevailing at that moment.[16] Thus, the argument also depends upon making an analytic separation between two worlds, the esoteric world of on-going structures and the exoteric realm of everyday life, or Marx's 'enchanted world'.[17] With this distinction the analysis acquires a double starting point, from which two different "stories" are produced. The first story starts with the long-standing observation, which forms the heart of social theory, that social relations continue through time, no matter whether participants comprehend the structures and social laws which set out major constraints on the ways that they construct their lives. This is the realm of esoteric knowledge. Such knowledge makes possible the theoretical demonstration that social relations form structures whose contradictions are temporarily regulated and thereby stabilized. Building on this observation, the movement of history can be described by providing a set of categories appropriate for identifying its patterns.

The starting point for the second story is the claim that only by acknowledging space for agency and the choices following from it can we understand how stable arrangements of social relations are constituted and sustained. Only in this way can social theorists account for and analyze the ways in which, despite the contradictory nature of social relations, an ensemble of institutional forms, networks, and explicit or implicit norms emerge, live and die. In this story lived experience is a process of learning which results in acceptance or modification of the usual ways of stabilizing contradictions. With this foray into the exoteric world it is possible to comprehend *how* and in *what ways* contradictory social relations are (temporarily) stabilized.

When both these stories are told, history becomes a dialectical process—the open-ended result of actors struggling to create their lives. It also makes it possible to imagine and pursue democracy, equality and the expansion of human dignity through the empowerment of people, because actors are simultaneously subjects of social structures which persist, regardless of whether the subjects perceive them, and acting subjects, carrying in their practices, and the meaning systems which motivate them, not just the possibilities of reproduction but also of social change and transformation.[18]

From this perspective, representation is as "real" as the intrinsic connections which are visible only once the informed analyst has removed the "obscurity."[19] Underpinning actors' strategies in the market, in the family, in bed, in the workplace, in school, etc. are the representations of social relations they make to themselves and to others.[20] The representations expressed via such strategies are never "false", although they may be—from the perspective of an analysis of the esoteric—incomplete.[21] Politics consists of struggles to sustain or change the power of such representations.[22] They form part of a dialectic; structural analysis is not substitutable for understanding representations, nor can representations be substituted for structures.

The terrain on which actors struggle over representation is the *universe of political discourse*, within which identities are socially constructed.[23] Because actors with a variety of collective identities co-exist in this universe, their practices and meaning systems jostle each other for attention and legitimacy. Politics becomes conflict about collective identities—about *who* has a right to make claims—as much as it is conflict among groups and organizations over disputed claims about who gets what, when, and how. But it is also struggle about *where* politics occurs. Both kinds of representation involve designating the spaces which actors understand to be "political." Whether issues are described as "public" or "private", "national", "global" or "local", "of the family" or "of the state" is a crucial element in actors' representations of self and interests.

Representation involves, among other things, naming oneself; only an actor with a name is recognizable to others. Successful contenders for political and ideological influence can recognize themselves when they have an identity and it is this identity which makes them recognizable to others. The specific actors named in any case depend upon relations of power—which are limited by structural relationships but not determined by them—because such relations organize the conflict over mutual recognition. Competition for representational power, in other words, constitutes a system of inclusion and exclusion, in which only certain collective identities are constituted. Nevertheless, competing meanings for the same social relation may continue to exist in the shadow world of the universe of political discourse, perpetuated by the practices of marginalized actors.[24] There are moments, moreover, when these alternatives are reasserted, making demands for the future, and bringing with them new definitions of legitimate actors and political spaces.

Thus, while politics always involves processes of representation and the social construction of collective identities, observation of history shows us that not all times are equally open to *innovation* in identities, their meaning systems, and political practice. At times a relative societal consensus about the names of the actors, their interests, and political spaces exists. Conflict takes place within the terms of an on-going representational regime. At other moments turbulence exists in the universe of political discourse. Not only distributional effects but also the very boundaries of politics and the right of some actors to make claims are challenged. Under such conditions alternative meaning systems and practices proliferate in the universe of political discourse. Such situations can be termed ones of *crisis*.[25]

The analytic stance adopted leads, then, to skepticism about system reproduction, and stresses its fragility. If stability and change are the focus, then the question changes: how can social relations take on stabilized forms, even though they are contradictory? Longish periods of economic and social stability do occur, during which a set of institutional forms, procedures and habits reproduce social relations. Indeed, one of the miracles of social life is that, despite the contradictions at the heart of social relations, there are historically observable moments when systems of social relations crystallize, stalling contradictions at least for a time, and creating a *model of development*. Nevertheless, since social relations are not experienced as structures by actors, we must still ask *how* it happens that such models continue through time. An

answer to this question requires a foray into the exoteric world of representational power as well.

A model of development is the particular achievement of each national
society. It is a combination of institutionalized social relations which are reproduced over time; thus it is composed of the practices and meanings which sustain structures. Throughout the history of capitalism situations have existed of
long-term stabilization of the allocation of social production between consumption and accumulation. The existence of such a *regime of accumulation*
implies a certain correspondence between transformation of the conditions of
production and reproduction of wage-labour, including between certain of the
modalities in which capitalism is articulated with other modes of production
within a national social formation.[26] A *social bloc* composed of a stable system of alliances, compromises and patterns of domination among social
groups provides a good match for the regime of accumulation. While the leading fraction of the capitalist class may "place its stamp" on the model of development, and is likely to be a dominant political force, its political position
depends upon its ability to participate in a project which can secure the consent of virtually all important groups in any social formation.[27] The unity and
opposition of the social relations in the regime of accumulation and social bloc
stamp out *places*, which mark a trajectory through time.[28]

A model of development, composed of places, whose reproduction over
time indicates that it is in regulation, does not occur magically. That it is stable
certainly does not explain its existence. Explanations for its constitution and
continuity must focus on the ways in which actors organize social relations
through the meanings which they give them, as well as through their practices. These are, of course, limited; not everything is possible.[29] Nevertheless,
patterns which in the eyes of observers constitute quite similar structures, can
be represented by actors in diverse, albeit coherent and meaningful ways.
Actors experience and represent a social relation as if it were the product of
their own strategy in playing a particular *part*. Moreover, since the strategy is
selected by each actor, albeit acting within the constraints of that part, the
result is a great deal of variation in possible representational *styles*.

In this discussion of structures, representations and levels of analysis, a
new metaphor has emerged. Gone is the image of the heavy weight of structures "bearing down" on actors, creating agentless structures. But neither is
this a world of Robinson Crusoe and Friday "choosing" to establish a hierarchically organized society in a world of structureless agents. The argument
here, in all its complexity, leads to the metaphor of history as theatre.

A play usually has a well-defined form (following the structure of a tragedy, for example) but each drama has its own roles and relationships, which constitute it, providing the material of that particular work. Thus, the surface difference of names and places can be "swept away" by the observer of the play who sees its structure in the form of the play. Nevertheless, it is not a play until it has been given particular material, until the content has been defined.[30] Therefore, within the structure of the play, parts are assigned by the author in compliance with the underlying form and according to limits which make it possible for each character to do some things and impossible to do others. Actors' parts are, in other words, constrained by the form (or structure) of the drama. At the same time, the assigned parts themselves serve as constraints on each actor performing the play. Lines must be said, entries and exits made according to the logic set out by the plot of the play. Yet the interpretation of each role, within such limits, belongs to the actors. The politics of the production may lead them to choose to redefine the historical time of a traditional play by presenting it in modern dress. They may choose to play dramatic roles with greater or lesser degrees of comedy or seriousness. They may adorn the set or leave it empty. There are, indeed, innumerable styles for playing a part, yet it always remains a role, limited by the author's material, in accordance with the underlying form of the drama.[31]

The interest of this metaphor lies in the reality that with constraints there is simultaneously a mutability and unpredictability due to the variations in styles so that an innovative and creative style of playing the parts can transform the play instead of simply reproducing it. The styles of any production may be "true" to the author's intentions, retaining a long-established interpretative style. Other styles may alter the play by changing the setting, the gestures, the movements of the actors, but nevertheless the play remains recognizable in its original form. There are also, however, certain productions in which the alterations in the style, the refusal to attach the same meanings as in the original, the shift in perspective due to the actors' stylistic strategy for their parts transform the play into another—with another message, another meaning.[32] These transformations may succeed—and a new work of art result—or they may fail and the audience will leave the theatre with the heavy sense of just having witnessed an artistic crisis.

One consequence of accepting this metaphor is that analysis must provide ways to conduct concrete investigations of historically developed sets of practices and meanings which provide the actual mechanisms of regulation.[33] Making a loose distinction between the realm of commodity and wage relations—the basic relations of production—and the domain of other social relations, we can label these regulatory mechanisms the *mode of regulation* and the *societal paradigm*.

Stabilization of a regime of accumulation depends, then, upon its being institutionalized as norms, habits, and laws in a mode of regulation which guarantees that its agents conform more or less to the schema of reproduction in their day-to-day behaviour and in their struggles within contradictory social relations. When a set of practices, and the meanings which accompany them, succeed in stabilizing a regime of accumulation, we can say a mode of regulation exists. Representations in this mode of regulation name the legitimate actors in the social relations of production, identify their interests, and locate the spaces of the "politics of production". A societal paradigm is similarly a shared set of interconnected norms, habits and laws which make sense of the many social relations beyond the realm of production.[34]

If a mode of regulation and societal paradigm's sets of interconnected premises come to be widely shared as the result of a social compromise, they are hegemonic, and there are socially limited ways of living social relations which exist as effective constraints. By designating how to play the parts, these norms and institutions allocate actors to their places in social relations. Divergences are minimal and confined to disputes internal to the representational system itself; they are insufficient to undermine the regime of accumulation and the social bloc. The constitution of an hegemonic mode of regulation and societal paradigm, within which only some collective identities are represented, is the product of politics in its broadest sense. We can catalogue any number of institutions—ranging from political parties, trade unions and other social movements to the various apparatuses of the state, churches, corporations, families, and scientific establishment—as the multiple sites of its constitution.[35]

IN SEARCH OF THE FUTURE

The conceptual apparatus elaborated here generates a particular reading of the current struggle over alternative futures for Canada. It is clear that the present is a moment of turbulence, one of economic and political restructuring. Hence there is turmoil in the universe of political discourse. This context of crisis exposes both the structuring effects of the past and the importance of struggles to create the future, including new representations of basic identities in production and beyond. Therefore, the analytic task undertaken here is to explore the contestation over who the actors most important for the post-Fordist future might be, as well as anticipating a shift in the spaces of politics as designated by them. Yet no actors are completely unconstrained. The structural arrangements of Fordism, and especially the spaces of accumulation, are being dramatically reshaped as the postwar model reaches it limits. All actors find themselves facing new conditions, to be sure, but never ones which are completely of their own making.

In undertaking this analysis at two levels it is important to understand the past. By analyzing the model of development which is in crisis, it becomes possible to understand the lines of cleavage along which it is crumbling, and thereby to see why certain conflicts over ideas about the future and its political spaces have come to the fore.

This section looks first at the mode of regulation and then at the societal paradigm to describe the ways in which contestation of identities and the interests associated with them shape current contestations over the country's future. Before doing so, however, the broad outlines of this story can be briefly summarized as follows. The postwar regime of accumulation entered a crisis in the 1970s, as the practices and meanings of the mode of regulation and societal paradigm no longer bounded underlying contradictions. The social bloc began to shift its strategy in light of adjustments taking place in both the domestic and global economy. The familiar places stamped out by the arrangements of postwar Fordism disappeared or took on new meaning, as various actors adjusted their styles. Indeed new actors began to appear. One result was to create unfamiliar conflicts in the struggle over economic and political restructuring, pitting social movements against business, bypassing traditional representational institutions, and bringing a neo-liberal discourse about the proper relationship between state and society. This discourse, even more than in the past, was differentiated by location, as Quebec and the rest of Canada further distanced themselves in designing their strategies for the future.

Canada's postwar model of development had come out of the crisis politics of the 1930s and restructuring during the war.[36] This particular model was similar in many ways to those constructed in other countries; the places structured by accumulation practices were not unique. Nevertheless, there were some particularities to the mode of regulation and societal paradigm. Political actors assumed roles different from those played by similar actors elsewhere. Especially relevant were differences in workplace, partisan and state politics.[37]

The postwar model of development included an expanded commitment to increased continental integration based on exporting resources and importing capital. The Canadian economy was permeated by international—or, more exactly, continental—effects. This reflected the composition of its social bloc, balanced towards the staples fraction.[38] In addition, the model did not depend on mobilization of the labour movement in partisan politics, with the state facilitating a compromise between capital and labour, but rather on governments overseeing the actions of firms and unions in private collective bargaining relations.[39] As elsewhere, the Canadian economy expanded dramatically after the war—an expansion based on mass production and consumption industries as well as on resource exports. Yet the regime of accumulation had three aspects which were somewhat different: reliance on relatively unprocessed natural resources as leading sectors; high rates of capital and goods imports; and a state that spent little on social programs and left labour-management relations to the arena of private collective bargaining. Nevertheless, the basic economic arrangements of both labour-management relations and state macro-economic policy followed the lines made familiar in other countries with comparable regimes of accumulation, which we usually label Fordist.

In the current turbulent moment of restructuring, some of the basic terms of the mode of regulation, which provided the everyday practices and meanings for the regime of accumulation, have come into dispute. Engaged in new struggles in the politics of production, trade unions in particular have begun to represent themselves and their interests in innovative ways, and to engage in political activities which have the potential to effectively limit some of the choices which capital and the state will be able to make about the future. Nevertheless, the struggle is a difficult one, as these unions also attempt to deal with the legacies of their Fordist past.

Armed with the collective bargaining rights won in wartime and postwar struggles, unions were able to increase their workplace power in the 1960s and early 1970s. In particular they could increase the wage bill to their benefit. Especially important in setting wage trends were unionized public employees. Therefore, as the Canadian economy entered into crisis and began to restructure, one strategy immediately pursued by both corporations and governments was to attack and attempt to dislodge this union power. Throughout the late 1970s and 1980s a series of hard-fought strikes, legislative interventions to end public-sector work stoppages, and assaults on collective bargaining rights reshaped labour-management relations into a form of "permanent exceptionalism".[40]

Faced with this offensive by employers—both private and public—and governments—both federal and provincial—against the terms of the postwar mode of regulation, the organized labour force responded in a variety of ways which have produced a new set of representations of self in their political styles. There has been a move away from "International" unionism towards Canadian organizations, often because of divergences among Canadian and American leaders over strategic reactions to corporate restructuring.[41] Political space has changed in a second way as well. In the 1980s both individual unions and the Canadian Labour Congress significantly broadened the domain of politics beyond the workplace. In the late 1970s the CLC devoted greater effort to partisan politics by supporting the NDP more actively. By the 1980s that strategy was supplemented by punctual participation in an innovative form of politics which combined social movement mobilization with some elements of traditional interest group lobbying. Individual unions too followed this route. Unions' participation in the opposition to the Macdonald Commission and in the Pro-Canada Network against the Free Trade Agreement reflects this innovation in representation of the unions' interests, their allies, and the spaces for doing politics.

A third change in representation may signal another innovative form for the future. Several provincial governments as well as the federal one have made overtures to unions to participate in new kinds of tripartite bodies to design programs for restructuring industry and re-locating Canadian production in the new global economy. Initiatives coming from the Ontario Premier's Council, the federal Advisory Council on Adjustment, etc., not only reflect government and corporate interpretations of and responses to restructuring, but also propose new spaces for political action. Unions involved in such consultations are in the midst of efforts to push such representations of the future in progressive directions. The outcome of this struggle remains, of course, uncertain.[42]

It is not yet possible to clearly identify an hegemonic project which could pull together a recast social bloc and stabilize a regime of accumulation around a mode of regulation granting adequate recognition to these actors mobilized in the politics of production. Competing alternatives exist precisely because a compromise which could consistently satisfy not only transnational but also domestic corporations, create jobs, and keep basic economic indicators healthy has yet to be discovered. Nevertheless any such redesigned project will be profoundly shaped by the move towards official integration of the North American economies via the NAFTA. Thus, the current challenge facing progressive forces is to discover a response to business and state initiatives which not only protects Canadian workers but also recognizes the thickening transnational ties.

If the terms of Canada's Fordist mode of regulation were different but nevertheless quite similar to those which existed elsewhere, the same can not be said for other arrangements. The compromise which institutionalized the societal paradigm, especially the politics of parties and the state, depended less on partisan politics than on federal-provincial negotiations. No class compromise was organized in the party system between Left and Right parties; its crucial representational and institutional underpinnings lay elsewhere, in a discourse of nation-building.

In countries where left parties, especially social democratic ones, had constructed and set out the rationale for programs of the welfare state, citizenship rights, based on the contribution of workers to the well-being of the whole economy and thus the nation, provided the discursive rationale for state actions. Their foundation in notions of citizenship rights and entitlements meant that many welfare states emphasized a universalistic identity that might be labelled "citizen-worker."

In Canada, by contrast, the collective identity providing the glue for this social construction was a national one, which stressed the commonality of all residents of a large and dispersed country.[43] Representations of Canada's strength stressed its natural resources more than its producers. In this way the traditional vision of Canada as a space "north of the 49th parallel" came to incorporate the notion that the whole country formed a single effective political unit. The federal government claimed responsibility for unifying that space politically, while trusting business to make the economy grow with minimal governmental oversight.[44]

The result of this construction was that by 1945 the universe of political discourse had come to be dominated by Canada's particular language of nation-building and national identity.[45] Individuals—as citizens, as consumers, as producers—gained discursive visibility. The representation of space in this dominant political discourse was of Canada as a single space having one labour market, universal standards for social programs, and a central government with responsibility for assuring the well-being of the whole.

A re-composition of citizenship had taken place, around a basic policy and discursive consensus sponsored by the Liberals, supported by the Tories, and claimed as a victory by the CCF. For the mainstream parties reforms were meant to meet national needs for social justice. Social spending was represented as part of the state's proposals for reconstructing the nation after the travails of wartime mobilization. Keynesian and social policies stressing redistribution via transfer payments, like unemployment insurance, social assistance and family allowances, tended to address Canadians as individuals more than as members of collectivities like classes, for example.

Moreover, because so much analysis of the Depression had focused on the economic and social liabilities of decentralized federal arrangements, federalism received much attention. Given the accumulation strategy of the social bloc as well as the wage relation being created, federalism was most implicated in the stabilization of the model of development, with the federal and provincial governments sharing responsibility for labour relations and social policy.

This societal paradigm contributed to the stabilization of the model of development for a number of decades, and accumulation proceeded. Nevertheless, by the mid-1960s cracks began to appear as they had in the mode of regulation. New styles emerged. In 1960 the province of Quebec, in the midst of the Quiet Revolution, moved to complete the welfare state by extending social services and organizing them through state institutions rather than religious ones. This modernization—which was initially simply an expression of conflict *within* the existing terms of the regulatory system—spread to other provinces and the federal government, so that by the late 1960s Canada had an extended welfare state. Yet, at the same time, contradictions began to intensify. The political discourse of federal-provincial conflict over competing national and provincial identities had been used to complete these state programs. In the process the provincial governments had gained not only the political space for independent action but also the material and discursive resources to compete with the federal government and among themselves. When the 1970s brought disputes over state spending and development strategies as part of the emerging crisis, federal-provincial institutions and the "national" identity were fully implicated. Cultural and regional conflicts about the future of the country heated up. Disputes over who had the right to be labelled a nation constituted a central theme within the language of politics. Canada's crisis became one over strategies for nationhood as well over economic development. Indeed the two were inseparable.

As the nation-building content of the postwar societal paradigm came to be challenged by province builders over the past two decades, the politics of identity became explicit. Provinces clearly have regained the power to shape representation. They used that power in the 1970s and 1980s to restructure economic relations in ways which often implied abandoning efforts to protect the borders of the domestic economy—a strategy which had existed since Macdonald's National Policy—and moving towards closer ties with the U.S. economy.[46] By 1985 the Macdonald Report provided the federal government and opinion leaders with the intellectual coherence and rationale for free trade. This project, as designed with the support of transnational business, the

Premiers of resource-exporting provinces and the federal Tories, is a continentalist and decentralizing alternative. By tightly linking the two economies and using the supposed constraints imposed by the new trading relationship as a rationale for restructuring production and downsizing state responsibility for the economy and social equity, a discourse now exists for English Canada's neo-liberalism. The language of competitiveness organizes not only the language of politics for discussing the economy, but increasingly that for constitutional matters as well.

Yet this language is not precisely the same in Quebec. Post-Fordism has brought even more regional diversity in strategic responses by key actors. In Quebec, support for free trade, promoted by politicians of both provincial parties and by the business community, was less rooted in a strict neo-liberalism of market forces.[47] Rather, it was based on a re-interpretation of the role of the Quebec state in guaranteeing the future of the province by continuing to promote a francophone business class. This strategy, to be sure, granted priority to the private sector in designing the province's move into the global environment and the response within Quebec to new competitive conditions. Yet the state retained an oversight responsibility which involved careful monitoring of the effects of trading arrangements and support for efforts of Québécois firms to compete. Quebec's tendency to more corporatist forms of decision-making was not abandoned.

In the context of the federal government's laissez-faire attitude to the fate of Canadian business after 1988, the strategy required mounting a claim that even more of the levers of economic development should be held in provincial hands. Thus, Quebec's pressure for a new constitutional division of power changed, as in the past, from the widely shared goal in that province of guaranteeing a space for an autonomous strategy to one of managing free trade.[48]

If a compromise between these two projects is found, the "national" project of a new social bloc and regime of accumulation would be one with quite different spatial boundaries. It would be continental in scope and regulated by the North American economy and new political institutions, whether the latter come in the form of new federal arrangements or not. Since there is, within both business and state projects for the future, a great deal of pressure for fundamentally altering political institutions, new spaces may be created by the political disintegration of Canada.

The inability of the brokerage parties to rise to the occasion and to proffer clearly delineated alternative projects for the future may have finally closed the federal party system as a space for innovation.[49] Nevertheless, new avenues for politics have opened and they give space to those who contest the fragmented representation of Canada as part of North America. A broad-based coalition of the popular sector insists upon using nation-building language to describe its alternative future. This discourse is sometimes favoured by the new actors whose identities and interests have consolidated in the constitutional and economic politics of the 1980s, with women, Aboriginal peoples and visible minorities in the forefront. The alternative they propose, however, remains underdeveloped and defensive; it cannot yet claim to be a clearly articulated paradigm for future social relations. While the labour movement participates in this coalition, moreover, the terms for describing the alternative are poorly linked to any real comprehension of the innovations in production relations described above.

Because of the existence of at least these two alternative visions of the future, intense conflict continues over whether the traditional discourses of equality—both individual and regional—and nation-building will characterize the era of free trade or whether the future we face is a more polarized, unequal society dominated by decisions made elsewhere. Popular forces seek to design an equitable, empowering future for themselves. Transnational business and its allies stress the limits imposed by global competition and claim it makes restructuring necessary, including cutbacks in universal entitlements, state spending for social programs, and redistribution. Neither group has yet developed a representation of the future which can mobilize sufficient consensus to function as an hegemonic economic and social project. Alternative visions name different actors, identify various interests, and locate politics in different spaces. The future remains open.

As the country moves into the 1990s, then, the terms "Canada" and "Canadians" remain hotly contested. Whether they will include commitments to social and economic equality and to greater empowerment of the currently weak or whether they will be new forms of the usual is uncertain. The result can only emerge out of the competition among alternative representations of future paradigms and possibilities for regulation, including new democratic practices. Only when this conflict is resolved will the next "Canadian identity" acquire meaning and practical content, as we move into our restructured future under the constraints imposed by the era of free trade but always with choices about how to shape our lives within it.

ENDNOTES

This is a revision of a paper presented to the Conference on Canadian Political Economy in the Era of Free Trade, Carleton University, April 1990. For helpful comments on earlier drafts I am, as usual, indebted to many people. Thanks to Grant Amyot, Cristina de Ferro, Peter A. Hall, Teresa Healy, Bob Jessop, Anne Larivière, Alain Lipietz, Rianne Mahon, Alain Noël, François Rocher, Jean Rousseau, Rob Ryan and, in particular, Cathy Blacklock and E. Fuat Keyman.

1. For one discussion of feminism's contribution to the politics of identity, including the variability of feminist consciousness, see Seyla Benhabib and Drucilla Cornell (eds.), *Feminism as Critique* (Minneapolis: University of Minnesota, 1987), Introduction.

2. Obviously, the question of "interests" has been thoroughly discussed for decades in the literature on class formation and class consciousness. Nevertheless, in recent decades the turn to structuralism downplayed that question, although the important work of E.P. Thompson on the making of the English working class should never be ignored. Moreover, with the move of many people previously working on these matters towards analytical (rational choice) Marxism, the subject of "interests" disappeared into the black hole of "rationality." Finally, while some power-resource theorists have addressed the question of interests explicitly [Gøsta Esping-Andersen, *Politics Against Markets: The Social Democratic Road to Power* (Princeton: Princeton UP, 1985), for example], their political economy assumptions make it impossible for them to escape from the notion that all interests arise from relations in production.

3. Stuart Hall, "The Problem of Ideology—Marxism without guarantees," in Betty Matthews (ed.), *Marx: A Hundred Years On* (London: Lawrence and Wishart, 1983), p. 59. The discussion of Gramscians here owes a great deal to Hall's article.

4. Of course the Gramscian influence within Marxism is not confined to concerns about class or work by men. Socialist feminists have often used a Gramscian framework *because* of the analytic place given to ideas, and to the power relations encoded in such ideas. See, for example, Anne Showstack Sasson (ed.), *Women and the State* (London: Hutchison, 1987).

5. Peter A. Hall's neoinstitutionalist work is an exception to this characterization. He has stressed the role of ideas in linking institutions and shaping conflict. See, for example, his "Patterns of Economic Power: An Organizational Approach" in Stephen Bornstein *et al.* (eds.), *The State in Capitalist Europe* (London: Allen and Unwin, 1984). For another early focus on ideas, from within a neo-institutional text, see Rosemary C.R. Taylor, "State Intervention in Postwar

Western European Health Care," in Bornstein *et al.*, *The State in Capitalist Europe.*

6.   For such criticisms and efforts see, *inter alia* David Held and Joel Krieger, "Theories of the State: Some Competing Claims," in Stephen Bornstein *et al.*, *The State in Capitalist Europe*; Peter B. Evans, Dietrich Rueschemeyer and Theda Skocpol (eds.), *Bringing the State Back In* (Cambridge: Cambridge UP, 1985); and Margaret Weir, Ann Orloff, and Theda Skocpol (eds.), *The Politics of Social Policy in the United States* (Princeton: Princeton UP, 1988). For a critique of the state-centric approach and its difficulties in addressing questions of agency, see E. Fuat Keyman, "The Structure/Agency Problem in Political Economy: Critical Comments on the State-Centric Model." (paper prepared for the Annual Meeting of the Canadian Political Science Association, Victoria, B.C., May 1990).

7.   See, for example, Weir *et al.*, *The Politics of Social Policy*, pp. 10-16.

8.   It is worth noting the extent to which the rise of neoliberalism, as the ideational system of the dominant classes has inspired both neoinstitutionalists' turn to "ideas" and neo-Marxism's. See both Peter D. Q. M. Hall's "Policy Paradigms, Social Learning and the State: The Case of Economic Policy-Making in Britain." (paper presented to the Seventh International Conference of Europeanists, Washington DC, March 1990); and Stuart Hall's "The Toad in the garden: Thatcherism among the theorists," in C. Nelson and L. Grossberg (eds.), *Marxism and the Interpretation of Culture* (Urbana: University of Illinois, 1988), pp. 49-50. The latter reflects a shift from Marxism's focus on the "false consciousness of the working class" to explaining ideational differences among the bourgeoisie.

9.   For this reading of the neoinstitutionalists I am inspired by P. Hall, "Policy Paradigms." While I agree with his diagnosis, ultimately I do not completely agree with his prescription.

10.   For the most interesting of these formulations see the collection considering the spread of Keynesianism as a theory for economists, as a set of state policies, and as a societal world view see Peter A. Hall (ed.), *The Political Power of Economic Ideas: Keynesianism Across Nations* (Princeton: Princeton UP, 1989). For an elaboration of such approaches see Neil Bradford, "A Neo-Institutional Approach to Politics." (paper presented at the Annual Meeting of the Canadian Political Science Association, Kingston, Ontario, June 1991).

11.   For an excellent recent discussion see David Harvey, *The Condition of Postmodernity* (Oxford: Blackwell, 1989). For more partial considerations see Warren Magnusson and Rob Walker, "De-Centring the State: Political Theory and Canadian Political Economy," *Studies in Political Economy,* 26 (Summer 1988) and Jane Jenson and Fuat Keyman, "Must we all be postmodern?," *Studies in Political Economy,* 31 (Spring 1990).

12.   See Harvey, *The Condition of Postmodernity*, Part III. For the argument that the emergence of such disputes over space and time marks a crisis similar to the

one at the end of the 19th century, see Edward W. Soja, *Postmodern Geographies: The Reassertion of Space in Critical Social Theory* (London: Verso, 1989), pp. 4-5.

13. It is interesting to note the emergence of a reconceptualization of space among Québécois political economists, well in advance of such manifestations among their anglophone Canadian colleagues. Limits to the category "nation" and a focus on the Quebec-Canada couplet led to rethinking the concept of "region" from within political economy. This shift is reviewed in William Coleman, "The Political Economy of Quebec," in Wallace Clement and Glen Williams (eds.), *The New Canadian Political Economy* (Montreal: McGill-Queen's, 1989). The original citation is to Gérard Boismenu *et al.*, *Espace régional et nation: Pour un nouveau débat sur le Québec* (Montreal: Boréal, 1983). There Daniel Salée provides an overview of the shift in the object of analysis, while Gilles Bourque attributes some of it to feminists' re-thinking of the concept "nation". (See p. 215, note 2).

14. For a discussion of the costs of such forms of analysis for the NCPE see Rianne Mahon in "Review Symposium: New Developments in Comparative Political Economy," *Canadian Journal of Sociology,* 14 (1989), p. 502.

15. Resolution of basic definitional questions about the identity of the central protagonists places broad limits on the definition of interests of actors and also makes such definitions historical rather than "objective". In these terms the emergence of a universalising class identity in advanced capitalist societies was—and remains—the result of struggle in concrete circumstances. Success for class institutions in particular times and places should be measured by their ability to shape a meaning system representing class-based collective identities and political interests as coterminous, and to develop strategies to impose their worldview, including their definition of interests, on others. Janine Brodie and Jane Jenson, *Crisis, Challenge and Change: Party and Class in Canada Revisited* (Ottawa: Carleton University Press, 1988), Chapter 1.

16. For a similar discussion see Bob Jessop, *The Capitalist State* (Oxford: Martin Robertson, 1982), pp. 255-58.

17. This section on the esoteric/exoteric distinction depends upon my reading of Ricardo Hausmann and Alain Lipietz, "Esoteric vs Exoteric Economic Laws: The Forgotten Dialectic," CEPREMAP Série Orange, No. 8021, 1980. The argument is incorporated in Alain Lipietz, *The Enchanted World: Inflation, Credit and the World Crisis* (London: Verso, 1985).

18. It is not simply sociology which has struggled with this matter, of course. Much of western philosophy turns on the question of the mix between action and determinism. Each version of the discussion depends upon its social setting for the terms of its debate. Thus in 17th century France, Pascal used the discourse of theological debate and conflict in his struggle to distinguish between the unilateralism of both the Calvinists (who, through the doctrine of predetermination assigned all responsibility for salvation or damnation to God, refusing any space

for individuals to save themselves) and the Molinists (who as humanists insisted on the effective power of free will). For Pascal, the correct representation was one which refused a unilateral reading of the situation and insisted instead on recognizing that man is "two subjects" or in "two conditions" simultaneously. It was this double optic both caused Pascal to worry so long and hard about *grace* and also allowed him to resolve controversy in a way which left space for both the role of God and the actions of Christians. See Pascal, *De l'Esprit géométrique: Ecrits sur la Grace et autres textes* (Paris: Flammarion, 1985).

19. On the distinction between intrinsic connections and appearance see Haussman and Lipietz, "Esoteric vs Exoteric," pp. 1-2; *passim*. For a similar discussion of "reality" see Hall, "Marxism without guarantees," pp. 67-69.

20. For a discussion of the importance of such strategies for entrepreneurship see Alain Lipietz, "Reflections on a Tale: The Marxist Foundations of the Concepts of Regulation and Accumulation," *Studies in Political Economy,* 26 (1988), pp. 29-30.

21. For an excellent discussion of a Marxist approach to ideology, which discards the notion of "falsity", see S. Hall, "Marxism without guarantees," 68ff. In discussing market discourse Hall acknowledges that it is a distortion by stating

     the falseness therefore arises, not from the fact that the market is an illusion, a trick, a sleight-of-hand, but only in the sense that it is an *inadequate* explanation of a process... The other 'lost' moments of the circuit are, however, unconscious, not in the Freudian sense because they have been repressed from consciousness, but in the sense of being invisible, given the concepts and categories we are using. (*Ibid.* pp. 73-74.)

22. The struggles of workers' movements to elaborate and disseminate an alternative to market theory is an obvious example here, and the one used in both S. Hall, "Marxism without guarantees" and Lipietz, "Reflections on a Tale." Nevertheless, another obvious example comes from the contemporary women's movement struggle—and success—in creating the category "women", an actor unencumbered by a familial or other adjectival designation. See Jane Jenson, "Changing Discourse, Changing Agenda: Political Rights and Reproductive Policies in France," in Mary F. Katzenstein and Carol M. Mueller, *The Women's Movements of the United States and Western Europe* (Philadelphia: Temple University Press, 1987). Another example comes from sexual politics. For an excellent discussion of strategic conflicts over gay identities see Stephen Epstein, "Gay Politics, Ethnic Identity: The Limits of Social Construction," *Socialist Review,* 93/94.

23. For a discussion of the universe of political discourse see Jane Jenson, "Gender and Reproduction: Or, babies and the state," *Studies in Political Economy,* 20 (1986).

24. This argument is elaborated in Jane Jenson, "Paradigms and Political Discourse," *Canadian Journal of Political Science,* 22/2 (june 1989).

For similar formulations of this point see S. Hall, "Marxism without guarantees," p. 71 on the multi-referential quality of the language through which social relations are constituted; and Lipietz, "Reflections on a Tale," pp. 15-16 on the importance of "naming."

25. The conceptual apparatus which follows has been developed in dialogue and, therefore, collaboration with Alain Lipietz. For a different use of these concepts see, *inter alia*, his "La Trame, la chaine, et la régulation: Un Outil pour les sciences sociales," CEPREMAP Série Orange No. 8816, 1988 and "Governing the Economy," in James Hollifield and George Ross (eds.), *In Search of the New France* (NY: Routledge, 1991).

26. Alain Lipietz, *Mirages and Miracles: The Crises of Global Fordism* (London: Verso, 1987), p. 32.

27. For a thorough discussion of the theoretical lineage of the concept of social bloc see Rianne Mahon, *Politics of Industrial Restructuring: Canadian Textiles* (Toronto: University of Toronto Press, 1984), p. 9ff. For the joint use of regime of accumulation and social bloc, with reference to postwar France, see Lipietz, "Governing the Economy."

28. For a discussion of such trajectories see Lipietz, "La Trame, la chaine et la régulation," p. 8ff.

29. The abandonment of one of the stories—the esoteric—ultimately limits Luc Boltanski's analysis of the constitution of the category *cadres*, in an approach which shares many of my preoccupations with representation. He criticises determinist forms of argumentation and raises Durkheim's question about group formation. In doing so he says

> the relation between technological (or economic) determinism and the symbolic phenomena whereby technical factors are reinterpreted linguistically as collective nouns, representations, emblems, or taxonomies is itself mediated through conflicts between social actors with various objective attributes of their own (partially shared, partially idiosyncratic) and through the strategies that these actors adopt, given their views of the issues and interests at stake." *The Making of a Class: Cadres in French Society* (Cambridge: Cambridge University Press, 1987), p. 29.

Nevertheless, in actually carrying out his analysis, Boltanski loses sight of constraining social structures and processes. George Ross, "Destroyed by the Dialectic: Politics, the decline of Marxism, and the new middle strata in France," *Theory and Society*, vol. 16 (1987). In a sense, for Boltanski, anything becomes possible.

30. Even the most basic laws of capitalism never operate in the abstract, just as no 'tragedy' exists without its story. The only 'reality' is one which already has—because of its history—a specificity to its model of development derived from the dialectical relationship of the esoteric and exoteric.

31. For another discussion of these concepts see Lipietz, "La Trame, la chaine et la régulation," p. 10.

32. If society is always social, always composed of social relations, despite linking separate and autonomous actors, it is impossible to imagine a moment or a place without a play which instructs actors playing their parts. Even in crisis, actors still follow a script, although the changes in style may be so dramatic as to—in effect—transform it.

33. Another way of phrasing this comes from Stuart Hall who, in describing his "politicized" view of ideology says:

> the theory of ideology helps us to analyze how a particular set of ideas comes to dominate the social thinking of a historical bloc, in Gramsci's sense; and, thus, helps to unite such a bloc from the inside, and maintain its dominance and leadership over society as a whole. It has especially to do with the concepts and the languages of practical thought which stabilize a particular form of power and domination: or which reconcile and accommodate the mass of the people to their subordinate place in the social formation. It has also to do with the processes by which new forms of consciousness, new conceptions of the world arise, which move the masses of other people into historical action against the prevailing system. (See "Marxism without guarantees," p. 59.)

34. Just as the effects of wage and commodity relations spill over and organise many areas of life in capitalist society, so too are other social relations crucial for giving specific content to the realm of production. We know that the boundary between production and reproduction, work and not work, factory and home is always ultimately a blurred one. So too is the boundary between mode of regulation and societal paradigm, but the distinction is nonetheless useful for purposes of analysis. The concept of the societal paradigm is elaborated in Jane Jenson, "Representations in Crisis: The Roots of Canada's Permeable Fordism," *Canadian Journal of Political Science,* 23/4 (December 1990), p. 665.

35. In contrast to much analysis coming from the regulation approach—including that of Alain Lipietz—I am not privileging the state as an institution of regulation. Others, which also reflect the penetration of liberal democratic notions into civil society, are of importance. Indeed, it is possible to conceive of liberal democratic norms as providing a kind of organising principle for regulating the mode of regulation and societal paradigm. See Gilles Breton and Carol Levasseur, "Etat, rapport salarial et compromis institutionnalisés," in Gérard Boismenu and Daniel Drache (eds.), *Politique et régulation: Modèle de développement et trajectoire canadienne* (Montreal: Méridien, 1990).

36. It is important to read the next paragraphs as being the result of such struggles. The patterns described did not simply fall from the sky but are the consequence

of intensely competitive politics of identity and interest in the interwar and war years. For a description of those struggles see Jenson, "The Roots of Canada's Permeable Fordism."

37. For the analysis which supports the generalizations in the next few paragraphs see Jane Jenson, "'Different' but not 'exceptional': Canada's Permeable Fordism," *Canadian Review of Sociology and Anthropology*, 26/1 (1989). That paper explores the consequences of the postwar model of development for the unfolding crisis of the last two decades in Canada.

38. Rianne Mahon, *The Politics of Industrial Restructuring*, p. 11ff..

39. Charlotte Yates, "From Plant to Politics: The Canadian U.A.W., 1936-1984," (PhD thesis, Political Science, Carleton University, 1988). Gérard Boismenu labels this "Fordisme à dominante privé" in his "L'Etat et la régulation du rapport salarial depuis 1945," in Boismenu and Drache (eds.), *Politique et régulation,* p. 159.

40. Leo Panitch and Donald Swartz, *The Assault on Trade Union Freedoms* (Toronto: Garamond, 1988).

41. Charlotte Yates, "The Internal Dynamics of Union Power: Explaining Canadian Autoworkers' Militancy in the 1980s," *Studies in Political Economy,* 31 (1990).

42. For a detailed analysis of training policies see Rianne Mahon, "Adjusting to Win?: The Tories' New Training Initiative," in K. Graham (ed.), *How Ottawa Spends 1990-1991* (Ottawa: Carleton University Press, 1991). For the background to such initiatives at the federal level see Rianne Mahon, "Canadian Labour in the Battle of the 1980s," *Studies in Political Economy,* 11 (1983) and in Ontario, beginning in the 1970s, Yates, "From Plant to Politics," Chapter 8.

43. Thus, even in Quebec the usual identity—that of French-Canadian—was one which stressed the national union. Only in the 1960s did the identity of Québécois emerge, to both announce and contribute to the crisis of Canada's permeable Fordism.

44. For a description of the wartime experience as a model for the postwar business state-relation, see W.D Coleman and Kim Richard Nossel, "The State, War and Business in Canada, 1939-1945," in W. Grant *et al.* (eds.), *Organising Business for War: Corporatist Economic Organization during the Second World War* (Providence: Berg Publishers, 1990).

45. For an elaboration of this argument see Jane Jenson, "Citizenship and Equity: Variations Across Time and Across Space," in Janet Hiebert (ed.), *Political Ethics: A Canadian Perspective*, Research Report of the Royal Commission on Electoral Reform and Party Financing (Toronto: Dundurn Press, 1992).

46. Keith Banting and Richard Simeon, *And No One Cheered: Federalism, Democracy and the Constitution Act* (Toronto: Methuen, 1988), p. 11.

47.   My interpretation of the situation in Quebec has been very much influenced by reading François Rocher, "Continental Strategy: Quebec in North America," in Alain-G Gagnon, *Quebec: State and Society Revisited* (Scarborough: Nelson, forthcoming).

48.   Gilles Breton and Jane Jenson, "After Free Trade and Meech Lake: Quoi de neuf?," *Studies in Political Economy*, 34 (Spring 1991), p. 206.

49.   For an analysis of the federal party system's failure to organise elections as moments of choice, even in 1988, see Harold Clarke, Jane Jenson, Larry LeDuc and Jon Pammett, *Absent Mandate: Interpreting Change in Canadian Elections* (Toronto: Gage, forthcoming), Chapter 1 and *passim*.

CHAPTER
7

The Political Foundations of State Regulation in Canada	Alain Noël Gérard Boismenu Lizette Jalbert

How entrenched is state regulation in Canada? Recent debates on the Free Trade Agreement, the constitution, neo-liberalism, and global competition have all raised the possibility of a dramatic erosion of the institutions, practices, and norms that constitute the Canadian pattern of state regulation. Comparative studies on the state suggest abrupt changes are rare. The institutional consequences of the conservative policies of the 1980s, for example, have often been exaggerated.[1] What then can be said about the evolution of Canadian state regulation? Will everything change radically? Or are certain aspects of what the state does well entrenched in Canadian political culture, social forces, and institutions?

This chapter uses historical and comparative material to assess the evolution of state regulation in Canada. We argue that state regulation is the institutional outcome of social and political conflicts and therefore its evolution cannot be predicted.[2] Much can, nevertheless, be said about the resilience of existing social arrangements, the challenges posed by new problems, the potential of old and new social forces, and the political context in which decisions will be made and implemented. Precisely because the future is made and cannot be predicted, we must be sensitive to the ways in which structure and agency interact to make history. The fact that debates, collective actions, and social and political conflicts will determine the outcome, however, does not mean everything is possible. Historical and comparative studies indicate state regulation evolves in specific ways, and we already have some ideas about the social forces, collective actors, institutions, and issues likely to be important. Much can therefore be said about potential changes.

Following a short theoretical presentation in the first part, the chapter discusses the evolution of state regulation from two standpoints. First, its historical development is reviewed to identify the social forces involved, the roots of change, and the nature of the institutions created. The aim is not to establish definitive causal relationships, but to clarify what is at stake in current conflicts. The next part adds a comparative dimension to specify the character of social conflicts and partisan politics in Canada. Whereas the historical section outlines the roots and relative stability of Canadian state regulation, the comparative one qualifies this picture of continuity by showing how the Canadian experience is specific but very close to that of countries like Britain and the United States. Together, the two sections suggest an evolution less dramatic than that proposed by some but nevertheless close to the American pattern. A centrist version of the liberal policy pattern typical of such countries continues to be the default option for Canada, the option that social and political inertia would perpetuate.

Class, Conflicts, and State Regulation

After the 1988 free trade debate, many noted how Canadian political economy had failed to provide an adequate perspective on the state. As Rianne Mahon put it, "the very vitality of the new Canadian political economy in the 1970s would have led one to expect something more than the defence of the very status quo of which the 1970s political economy had been so critical."[3] A common diagnostic was that political economists often ended up praising the status quo because they had little else to offer.[4] This could be true but more seemed at stake. John Myles noted how the prevailing nationalist problematic had restricted Canadian political economy to a "truncated range of questions."[5] Largely defined by its contribution to the "creation and re-creation of Canada as a rich dependency," the state has mostly been characterized by its limitations.[6] Linked either to class, elites, or institutions, these limitations appear to be the primary source of Canada's specificity and constituted the main object of inquiry. Canadian political economy has thus produced the image of a constrained state, which manages its dependency with difficulty and always remains on the verge of losing its integrity. Not surprisingly, discussions of the free trade agreements, the constitutional accords, and the rise of global competition have easily turned into laments for the nation.

There is no point denying the constraints that have shaped state regulation in Canada. Giving analytical priority to limits and "things that did not happen," however, tends to negate the transformations that have given rise to the modern Canadian state and to deny any efficacy to social and political conflicts.[7] This chapter shifts the perspective to examine what has been achieved over the years. The aim is not to replace the traditional pessimism of Canadian political economists by a simple-minded optimism, but to give more importance to the content and social roots of state regulation.

The concept of state regulation is used to describe the role played by the state in the creation and reproduction of the institutions, practices and norms that make stable capital accumulation possible over long periods. Conflicts in and around capital accumulation and the working of capitalist democracy constantly generate social innovations and, in turn, these innovations impose changes in the institutions that regulate capitalist society. Major institutions, however, are not changed easily, particularly those involving the state. Stable patterns of regulation predominate over long periods, until social and political conflicts redefine them. Consequently, new social arrangements require time to build. They also perpetuate many aspects of the institutions they are replacing.[8] State regulation can thus be understood as a succession of institutionalized social arrangements produced and reproduced by social conflicts.

This conflict can be understood either in pluralist or in class terms. Pluralist concepts have the advantage of corresponding closely to what constitutes common sense in a liberal democracy. They also seem particularly adequate in societies like Canada, where class politics often appears irrelevant. Pluralist accounts, however, portray groups and their actions rather than social relations, and little can be said about accumulation and regulation without reference to the wage relation. More than a growth process, capital accumulation is a social relation between capitalists and wage-earners. As such, it creates specific "structures within which actors, individual and collective, deliberate upon goals, perceive and evaluate alternatives, and select courses of actions."[9] Capitalists and wage-earners, for instance, do not face identical problems and they do not have the same choices. Whether or not the wage relation leads to the formation of class-based collective actors, whether these actors emerge as political parties, business organizations, trade unions or social movements, and whether they succeed in influencing policies, depends on numerous factors. Class structures nevertheless determine realms of possibility that are neither endless nor unassailable.

To pose the problem of agency in class terms is not to deny the relevance of collective identities unrelated to class. The concept of class is used to acknowledge a social relation central to capitalist societies, the wage relation. Identifying this relation does not make it the only or even primary social fact. In some instances, gender or other social relations may take on more importance, and state regulation evolves with social and political conflicts formed on the basis of all types of social relations.[10] Class conflicts nevertheless have a special importance because they distinguish many contemporary historical periods and political arrangements. Class formation, the process by which class cleavages give rise or fail to give rise to concrete collective actors, counts very much, for instance, in explaining transitions from prewar to postwar forms of regulation in the 1930s and 1940s. It is also essential to account for constrasts between the social-democratic, corporatist, and liberal social arrangements that characterize different societies.

In advanced capitalist countries, partisan and industrial relations organizations are major sites of class formation. The relevance of class in electoral politics and the type of organization developed for collective bargaining are thus determinant for state regulation.[11] Again, other factors matter and non-class definitions of politics may well prevail over class conflicts. A weak political expression of class cleavages, however, can also be understood as an outcome of class formation.[12]

State regulation has political foundations precisely because it is linked to the process of class formation. Canadian policies and institutions have not been purely contingent creations of brokerage politicians and autonomous bureaucrats. Major innovations reflected specific class conflicts and were embodied in a balance of power typical of similar liberal democracies. The rest of this chapter outlines this evolution and explains the legacy it created for this country.

THE POLITICAL FOUNDATIONS
OF STATE REGULATION IN CANADA

In Canada, the involvement of the state in regulation can be divided into five periods. In the first, from Confederation to the First World War, the state did not tax or spend very much, but it intervened very significantly. In his work on the rise of the capitalist economy, Karl Polanyi argues that laissez-faire had to be planned, imposed by a strong state: "the road to the free market was opened and kept open by an enormous increase in continuous, centrally organized and controlled interventionism."[13] Few countries confirm his analysis better than Canada. A new state was created in 1867 with the purpose of securing a national market and promoting the development of a modern capitalist economy. It financed the construction of a massive transportation infrastructure, encouraged immigration and the opening of new territories, and adopted a protectionist industrialization strategy. Convinced economic cycles were unavoidable and committed to non-intervention in social matters, governments relied mostly on market mechanisms to regulate the economy and on charitable organizations to provide for the dispossessed. They nevertheless had to take into consideration the rise of an organized and enfranchised working class. In the 1880s, Ontario trade unions organized a percentage of workers they would not reach again until the 1940s, and "both Liberals and Conservatives courted a growing working-class constituency increasingly aware of its own potential as a 'spoiler' in electoral battles."[14] "Factory acts, bureaus of labour statistics, arbitration measures, suffrage extension, employers' liability acts" and legislation affecting work, the family, and charitable and public institutions responded to this new situation.[15] In these years, state intervention involved regulation more than expenditures.

The year 1914 opened a second period that lasted until the beginning of the Second World War and marked the transition from regulatory to expenditure-based interventions. Faced with increased social and political pressures after 1918, governments reluctantly adopted welfare measures falling into four categories: minimum wage laws continued a tradition of regulatory interventions yielding to the labour movement; workers' compensation programs introduced a form of compulsory social insurance restricted to specific categories of the population; mothers' allowances committed provincial governments to spend on public assistance; and public pensions became the first program to depart "from traditional poor law practice of restricting help to indigents."[16] Only the last two measures involved spending. Although mothers' allowances restricted benefits to claimants who met strict conditions and accepted controls, they constituted the first departure from the traditional reliance on local charity and forced provincial government to spend much more than they had expected.[17] Public pensions too constituted a breakthrough because they introduced the idea of benefits as entitlements, as rights for all citizens. At the same time, they perpetuated old practices like means tests and minimal allowances.[18]

Further changes came with the third period, which lasted roughly from 1940 to 1960. The story of a "Keynesian welfare state" emerging out of the depression and war experiences has often been told and can easily be exaggerated. Reluctant, ad hoc, and decentralized, state regulation did not suddenly become avowed, systematic, and centralized. For one thing, in economic policy, the adoption of Keynesian ideas in 1944 had more to do with political marketing than with policy innovation and in the following years it proved ineffective and superficial.[19] As for welfare measures, the most ambitious proposals for reconstruction were rejected and change remained gradual and piecemeal.[20] Three fundamental innovations were nevertheless introduced. First, a governmental responsibility for the state of the economy was acknowledged; business cycles became a political matter.[21] Second, two major welfare state innovations, unemployment insurance and family allowances, confirmed the notion of social programs as universal or almost-universal rights and opened the door to demands for more programs of this type.[22] Third, the state explicitly recognized the conflictual and uneven nature of capitalist relations of production and created rules that, within certain limits, compelled employers to recognize trade unions and to engage in collective bargaining. Nevertheless, the state itself failed to grant collective bargaining rights to its employees, thus showing the limits of this third innovation.[23] The 1950s were years of gradual changes within the framework established by these postwar innovations.

From 1960 to the mid-1970s, union membership and strike activities increased significantly, in both the private and the public sector.[24] Partisan competition and federal-provincial conflicts also intensified and a series of policies completed and deepened the innovations of the previous period. Unemployment insurance, family allowances, assistance programs, and pension plans were all revised and expanded, health care and housing programs created, and the state's intervention in the economy increased. This multiplication of programs and interventions translated into a rise in the level of public expenditures sufficient to speak of a qualitative change.[25] A patchwork of relief, social insurance, and universal programs distributed uneasily between the federal government and the provinces, the modern Canadian welfare state nevertheless expressed an unprecedented commitment to income security.[26] The economic role of the state was also confirmed with the creation in 1963 of the Economic Council of Canada and with the adoption of new supply-oriented initiatives in Ottawa and in most provinces.[27] Finally, a high level of militancy allowed major collective bargaining gains in both the private and the public sector.[28]

A new period opened in the mid-1970s, marked by monetarist policies, welfare-state retrenchments, and working-class losses. The break with previous periods must not be exaggerated, however. Compared to their counterparts in the United States and the United Kingdom, the Progressive Conservatives did not bring a radical break with the past. They appealed to continuity, pursuing the monetarism, spending restrictions, and coercive industrial relations practices initiated by the Liberals in the mid-1970s. The trend toward higher unemployment levels continued, the welfare state eroded by "default rather than design," and trade unions remained in a mostly defensive position.[29] John Myles notes that, "What withered away, was not the welfare state, but wage pressure and demands from labour and popular groups for a bigger and better welfare state;" change "was a product of the seventies, not a neo-conservative revolution of the eighties."[30]

If this last period confirmed anything, it was the resilience rather than the fragility of the institutions inherited from the earlier years. Retreats at the margins did not prevent progress on new fronts, in the realm of equality rights, for example. To explain this resilience and these recent changes, we must consider the social and political roots of a century of reforms.

A full explanation of the long development of state regulation in Canada would require detailed historical studies explaining each decision to act, reform, or change. Alone, a broad historical perspective nevertheless allows three observations. First, patterns appear in the patchwork of laws, programs, and institutions that gradually constituted the Canadian welfare state. Second, these patterns are related to the general evolution of capitalism in Canada. Third, the historical development of successive patterns of capitalism and state regulation was largely paced and shaped by the process of class formation.

To some extent incremental, the evolution of state regulation has not been solely a regular addition of minor, apparently inconsequential undertakings. Periodically, at times of rapid change, the social and economic role of the state was redefined. New principles were accepted and allowed qualitative changes. Devoted at the outset to the establishment of capitalist institutions and infrastructures, the Canadian state progressively added various regulatory controls, aimed at policing market and social relationships. The post-1918 social upheavals then led to the acceptance of spending as a means of intervention, and minor expenditures were undertaken to mitigate market failures. The Great Depression and the Second World War confirmed and accelerated this trend, and the 1960s brought further interventions in a number of areas, leading to marked increases in the level of expenditures.

Roughly parallel to similar developments abroad, this evolution was not haphazard. Changes in state regulation were an integral component of a broader historical transformation that saw Canadian capitalism change from an extensive to a predominantly intensive pattern of accumulation, and from competitive to monopolistic forms of regulation.[31] The economic recovery that started in 1896 with the wheat boom "marked a turning point in Canadian manufacturing growth and development."[32] While traditional industries declined, new ones grew steadily. By the 1920s, the rise of industries producing electricity, pulp and paper, and non-ferrous minerals had confirmed Canada's transition to a modern, mass-production economy, less dependent on agricultural production and territorial expansion.[33] Such a transition raised social and political challenges that could not be met with modest, incremental reforms. It would take years, and the experiences of an unprecedently long depression and a world war, to reach a new, relatively stable social arrangement centered around a new conception of markets and state regulation. After 1945 the state accepted some responsibility for overseeing economic conditions, collective bargaining, and minimal universal programs. However weak, these commitments represented a shift of vision imposed by years of social debates around questions of equity and efficiency in a mass-production economy. A second wave of conflicts and reforms came in the 1960s to expand and deepen these three commitments.

The rise of the mass-production economy undermined liberal patterns of regulation and left a void eventually filled by new practices and institutions, forged in social and political conflicts. Of course, many ideas and decisions came from intellectuals, experts, and bureaucrats. In the end, political decisions are always made by politicians and civil servants and there is no point denying their influence. Decisions involving principles and leading to major social changes, however, only become possible when social movements mobilize around new or renewed demands.[34] The social origins of institutions explain their resilience. Erosion may occur but major principles guiding state intervention are seldom discarded.

The relevance of class relations was affirmed throughout the postwar period by a conjunction of trends and events that gave a meaning and a content to the regulation principles adopted after the war. Consider the three areas of innovation opened in the immediate postwar years: macroeconomic stabilization, collective bargaining, and universal welfare provision.

Public references to Keynes did not translate into effective discretionary stabilization policies. Canada consistently fought potential inflation with deflationary bouts. The relative weakness of organized labour and of the Left meant the state was free not to pursue Keynesian discretionary policies, and led to a secular increase in the levels of unemployment and under-employment. At the same time, the rise of public-sector spending associated with the development of the welfare state had a significant stabilization effect. The state's Keynesianism was thus a by-product, the result of changes indirectly related to macroeconomic policies.[35]

In collective bargaining, the balance sheet is difficult to read. Pessimists of all political stripes see working-class gains as limited, transitory and eroding; optimists speak of a resilient model which gradually widens the social gap between this country and the United States.[36] The coming years may alter the picture, but at this point the empirical evidence tends to support a moderately optimistic assessment. Union membership and density remained stable in Canada as they declined dramatically in the United States, the American trend toward concession bargaining did not cross the border, union militancy remained more vigorous in Canada than in the United States, Canadian wings of international unions became increasingly autonomous, and the Canadian labour movement as a whole kept a good deal of political clout.[37] Although it remains within the confines of the North American model of decentralized industrial relations, the collective bargaining regimes represent in Canada an enduring legacy of the postwar period.

The adoption of a few universal programs in the postwar years only inaugurated the development of a modern welfare state. In Canada as in other countries, the welfare state was largely a product of the 1960s and 1970s.[38] Numerous commitments undertaken in the 1960s only began to have an impact on public finances in the 1970s.[39] The outcome was a liberal version of the social security welfare state; the principles of universality and wage replacement were accepted but not taken seriously enough to obtain full employment or to reduce poverty significantly. Much of this development can be related to the secular rise of unemployment, itself associated with the openness of the Canadian economy; the roots of government spending would be less political than economic.[40] Apart from the fact that the secular rise of unemployment was itself a consequence of political decisions, this account appears inconsistent with the observed governmental priorities. Health and education, not housing and job creation, were the main sources of innovations during the period. The rise of the welfare state responded less to a general unemployment problem than to specific social and political demands for reforms.[41] Health care programs, for instance, emerged in the 1960s out of a protracted conflict between progressive forces (mostly trade unions and the CCF/NDP) and supporters of the status quo (especially the medical and business establishments and the Progressive Conservatives). Provincial initiatives, a strong labour movement, and a succession of minority governments in Ottawa tipped the balance toward change.[42] However limited, changes in labour market policies also resulted from "the greater leverage enjoyed by an expanding labour movement in the 1960s, in the context of minority governments in which the NDP also had greater leverage."[43] This long reform process created a specific institutional outcome. Ungenerous by international standards, the Canadian welfare state nevertheless entrenched important historical gains.

This chequered evolution in economic policy, industrial relations and welfare provision can be attributed to a state which committed itself episodically to intervention in new areas. The content of the different interventions was then gradually defined through pressures and conflicts. Thus, even though the "centralizing momentum" of the federal government was lost to growing provincial governments at the end of the 1950s, "the decade of the 1960s marked the high point of welfare state development in Canada."[44] The conventional viewpoint linking centralism and welfare provision cannot account for this crucial period because it lacks "a sense of the societal dynamics that underpin both the evolution of state policy and the character of federalism."[45] Designed and implemented by politicians and bureaucrats, Canadian state regulation was not born out of a bureaucratic vision. It emerged gradually, following the adoption, institutionalization, and definition of new principles guiding intervention. Class and political conflicts, often expressed in regional terms, were at the roots of these new commitments and progressively defined their meaning.

Of course, the outcome had limitations. By international standards, Canada obtained a limited welfare state, more comparable to the American model than to European equivalents.[46] The argument presented here is that the adoption of a "liberal" welfare state can best be explained by the character of social and political conflicts in Canada. For this discussion it is necessary to turn to the second, comparative, half of the argument.

A LIBERAL STATE

An outcome of concrete historical conflicts, Canadian state regulation developed at its own pace and institutionalized specific practices. Detailed historical accounts are thus necessary to explain fully the timing and the content of each aspect of state intervention. At the same time, this long process paralleled similar evolutions elsewhere. In every advanced capitalist country, the postwar period saw the creation of political arrangements that involved state responsibility for the economy, new industrial relations rules, and improved welfare programs.

The widespread and relatively simultaneous adoption of reforms in these areas was not haphazard. Politically, these changes addressed fundamental questions left unsolved at the outset of the Second World War, particularly questions related to the place of the organized working class in society and the role of the state in the economy.[47] Economically, they responded to the problems posed by the rise of an economy increasingly dominated by mass production and driven by mass consumption. Liberal institutions and practices were replaced or complemented by new forms of regulation such as countercyclical policies, collective bargaining, and universal welfare programs. Most of these new forms of regulation involved the state either creating the institutional framework or implementing specific policies.

In Canada, the postwar state has generally been understood as narrowly constrained by external and internal forces. Such an evaluation is correct but not sufficient. Over the period all countries experienced external influences and all reforms respected the logic of capitalism. There may be qualitative differences between Canada and other countries, but the criteria for establishing and evaluating these differences must be specified.

Comparisons of advanced capitalist countries help clarify these criteria. Within the framework set by liberal democratic institutions, an advanced capitalist economy, and the postwar context, countries differed along specific political and institutional dimensions. Comparative studies usually consider the strength of trade unions and leftist parties, the presence of corporatist arrangements, the participation of social-democratic parties in government, and the type of institutions. From this point of view, advanced capitalist countries are usually clustered in three, or four, models: a social-democratic group including the Nordic countries and sometimes Austria, a corporatist group centered on Germany, and a liberal group including France, Italy and the U.K., U.S. and Canada, with the latter three countries sometimes grouped into a fourth category.

Each of these clusters, constructed more or less inductively, is a variant of ideal-typical state regulation. A study of these four models cannot provide a full political account, but it indicates how the rules of the game may vary from one country to another. New problems and conflicts do not raise the same strategic dilemmas in every model. In the first cluster of countries, the social-democratic model is best exemplified by Sweden and Norway. It also characterizes fairly well the other Nordic countries and Austria. This model reflects the power exercised by strong trade unions and social-democratic parties. With a membership including a majority of the labour force and with fairly centralized structures, trade unions tend to negotiate at the national level and to enter into corporatist arrangements. Collective bargaining includes macro-economic considerations and generally allows for widespread improvements in real incomes that are non-inflationary. The absence of strong inflationary pressures makes a social-democratic commitment to full employment viable and, in turn, full employment becomes a counterpart to union wage moderation. The stability generated by this outcome contributes to a low level of strike activity. Unable to use low wages to gain competitive advantage, employers are compelled to increase productivity, improve the quality of their products, and invest in training. Generous welfare programs complete the picture. Because social-democratic parties combine their commitment to universal social programs with high levels of taxation, a generous welfare state does not lead, in this case, to important fiscal deficits.

A social-democratic hegemony thus produced, in this first cluster of countries, forms of state regulation conducive to full employment with stable prices and to economic growth and international competitiveness. Outlined very briefly here, this model involves more than social corporatism or high levels of government spending. Economic policies are rooted in institutionalized commitments to full employment, collective bargaining reflects various understandings of wage solidarity, and welfare programs embody principles such as universality and citizenship rights.[48] State regulation is not simply more important than elsewhere; it is different. Obviously, this model has limitations, some related to its own always fragile arrangement of policies, others common to all advanced capitalist countries in recent years.[49] For most of the postwar period, the model nevertheless constituted a remarkable political outcome, a combination of institutions, policies, practices that was largely successful and placed the countries which adopted it in a relatively advantageous position to develop new arrangements for the coming years.[50]

The second model combines corporatism with different patterns of partisan arrangements. Germany is the typical case, but Belgium and the

Netherlands also fit in this cluster. These countries share some of the characteristics described above, each one being qualified by liberal influences. Trade unions are important but not as strong as in the first model, corporatism is present but not as developed, and social-democrats are influential but not hegemonic. Left-wing parties alternate in power with conservative parties and tend to govern in coalition anchored at the centre by small liberal parties. Patterns of state regulation reflect this political balance. The state does not intervene nor tax as much as in the first cluster of countries, its commitment to full employment is not very strong, welfare programs are less generous, and corporatism does not prevent a moderate level of strike activity. The welfare state, in particular, differs from the social-democratic model and, as Esping-Andersen explains, it shows its conservative origins.[51] Social programs recognize status and occupational categories rather than universal rights, and they correct the effects of labour market forces without eliminating them. The welfare state thus maintains existing social divisions by attenuating their worst effects. The emphasis is on income security for various categories of the population rather than on full employment and solidarity.

Less inclusive than the first model, the corporatist pattern nevertheless favours broad social agreements to regulate both production and distribution. Unable to prevent the secular rise of unemployment, it provides stable foundations for steady economic growth with limited inflation. The model is also been conducive to industrial relations changes in the direction of increased worker involvement. More likely to engender practices and institutions compatible with high wages, and skilled production, this model places countries in a good position to evolve towards relatively progressive forms of flexible industrial relations. The limits of the model appear in the uncertainty that persists in the content of these new practices, the coherence of the emerging model, and the fate of the categories of the population excluded from the core industrial occupations.[52]

The last two clusters correspond more closely to a liberal conception of society. The first one, which best describes France and Italy, can be characterized as politically voluntarist and socially conflictual, the second is liberal and centrist. In France and Italy, the presence of a strong Communist party long prevented the Left from governing or even from participating in governmental coalitions. Right-of-centre parties thus dominated postwar political life and they created conservative versions of the institutional arrangements discussed above. In the 1980s, these arrangements proved well entrenched: in France, ten years of Socialist presidency were not sufficient to transform the main institutions and practices.[53]

As with the second model, the Italian and French welfare states are organized around the conservative notion of income security. Economic policies
also stress price stability over full employment, and international competitiveness is sought more through the maintenance of low wages than through
innovation, quality, and productivity. The historical weakness of the Left
makes corporatism impossible; industrial relations occur in a political arena
where conflicts are short but frequent, intense and often unresolved. The state
intervenes case-by-case to settle labour disputes and to impose minimal conditions on employers. This model corresponds late and rather poorly to the ideal
type of the postwar arrangement: a clear link between wage and productivity
increases is not established broadly until late in the 1960s. A limited welfare
state and superficial corporatist arrangements contribute to such an outcome
but the model always remains vulnerable to renewed assertions of liberal pressures and market forces.

The fourth model is both more liberal and less confrontational than the
third. Before the 1980s, politics in the U.S., U.K. and Canada was anchored
at the centre. Left-wing parties were either weak or, when strong enough,
committed to moderation; in return, conservatives avoided radical options.
Expressed in Keynesian language, economic and social policies remained fundamentally traditional and produced political-business cycles of the type predicted in 1944 by Kalecki.[54] The welfare state reflects this stop-and-go logic
and, on the basis of principles established at critical junctures, it has grown
incrementally, as a complement to the market more than as an expression of
social rights. More specifically, the liberal welfare state combines assistance
programs based on means tests, insurance programs complementing private
sector options, and a few universal entitlements measures. The state reinforces market outcomes by creating distinct categories of eligibility for assistance among the poor and by sustaining the private, individualized provision
of social protection for the majority of the population. Collective bargaining as
well remains in the hands of private, atomized actors. Relatively weak and
decentralized, trade unions work at the firm level or express political demands,
but have little capacity to threaten governments and to enforce compromises.
The overall co-ordination of industrial relations rests on informal but nevertheless effective patterns of diffusion and "coercive comparisons." Combined with
the limited interventions of the state, this type of industrial relations links the
rise of aggregate demand to the evolution of productivity, but it does so with
less success than in countries typical of the first two models. As in France and
Italy, economic cycles persist, strikes are frequent, and inflation and unemployment have a secular tendency to rise. In the 1980s, these difficulties

brought about the demise of the Keynesian discourse and opened the door to more conservative policies. Approaches of monetarist inspiration failed to change the economic and social situation very much in one direction or another, but they contributed to establishing a new political equilibrium to the right of the postwar consensus. Partly a result of the first-past-the-post electoral system, however, this new balance of power remained fragile.[55] Transition towards new forms of production and industrial relations practices makes a pessimistic scenario of low competitiveness and high income polarization likely, but a reaction to these trends is also possible. In this case, a political renewal could lead some societies to question the features of this fourth model.

These four models make it easier to assess the impact of factors like federalism and continentalism. Without denying the particular problems posed by continental pressures and by a federal structure, the starting point of a discussion of state regulation in Canada must be the country's adoption of the liberal model. The qualitative specificity of Canadian policies and institutions has to do with external and constitutional constraints, but it is primarily rooted in the long hegemony of centrist parties committed to a liberal vision of state regulation and in the relative weakness of trade unions and of the Left in Canada.

In recent years, much has changed in Canadian politics. Undoubtedly, a turn to the right has been made. In 1975, nine years before the Conservatives' election, the federal government started to implement economic policies inspired by monetarism. Welfare-state expansion gave way to reformulation, and a new industrial relations era marked by coercion began.[56] Changes were significant but even after 1984, they were not drastic. Economic policies affirmed more openly a long-held bias against lowering unemployment levels, welfare state expenditures reached a plateau and the status quo was basically maintained. In industrial relations state coercion did not translate into a union decline similar to that observed in the United States and in many European countries.

The most interesting, and often overlooked, dimension of the current situation appears when one compares Canada to the United States, with which it evolved for most of the postwar period. Economic policies responded to cycles that were continental as much as domestic; trade unionism, labour laws and collective bargaining were inspired by American models; and welfare programs grew at a pace similar to that of the United States. By the mid-1960s, the two countries' convergence, or more precisely Canada's alignment with American norms, seemed almost complete. Significant differences in the pace and meaning of reforms remained, but the two countries followed similar macroeconomic policies, raised public expenditures around 28 or 29 percent of their

GNP (compared to 33 to 38 percent in Europe), were laggards with respect to the number and scope of welfare programs, and had trade-union memberships slightly below 30 percent of the nonagricultural workforce.[57] Around this time, however, the two countries started to move apart, at least with respect to industrial relations and the welfare state. Canadian unions maintained membership while their American counterparts began a long decline, and the proportion of social expenditures in the Canadian GNP (22.3 percent in 1986) grew closer to the OECD (22.5 percent) than to the U.S. average (18.2 percent).[58] As the Canadian and American economies became more integrated, the two societies accentuated their political differences.

The comparative perspective outlined here gives good indications about the limits and possibilities of state regulation in Canada. Close to the United States within the fourth model, Canada has in recent years distanced itself from American trends. The differences are still modest and they may not last. Forecasts are difficult because the observed divergences remain poorly understood and explained. A few conclusions nevertheless seem possible. First, the 1980s turn to the right has not been as pronounced in Canada. It failed to shake the country's centrist consensus on most aspects of state regulation.[59] Ironically, the federal and relatively decentralized nature of Canada, often deplored by the Left, may well explain the moderation of Canadian conservatives. The impact of federalism on state regulation has been much debated. Many authors have concluded that decentralization has impeded the development of state regulation; others have identified provincial initiatives as a main source of policy innovation.[60] Keith Banting is probably right to conclude that "the intersection of federalism, regionalism, and ideology" has generated "a pattern of policy change similar to what one would expect in a unitary state from a large coalition government."[61] Federalism would thus have helped to anchor Canadian politics near the centre in the 1980s.

The role of international trade in this process of change appears more ambiguous. During the postwar period, in Canada as elsewhere, state intervention increased as trade relations opened; the two trends proved complementary rather than contradictory.[62] In recent years, however, economic integration has gone beyond liberalizing trade. Global financial markets and continental integration have started to change the rules of the game, and they could have adverse effects on specific regulation models. In Canada, the free trade agreements raise the most obvious questions in this respect. Many believe the agreements will drastically undermine the foundations of Canadian state regulation. Given the basic original similarities between the Canadian and American models, and given that recent years have demonstrated increasing institutional differences despite high levels of trade, the risks may have been exaggerated. The economic constraints associated with free trade are not totally unlike those most advanced capitalist countries will face in the years to come. In the end, it is the political response to these new constraints, and not the constraints themselves, that will determine the nature of state regulation in a given country.

CONCLUSIONS

What was achieved in Canada over the years? Canadian political economy's answer to that question has been ambivalent. Preoccupied with what went wrong in the country's historical development, political economists have rarely posed the question. They have often reduced state regulation to a question of continental integration and evaluated policies in terms of their contribution to the country's autonomy. Helpful with respect to past failures in economic development, this point of view has at times encouraged a rather uncritical acceptance of nationalist policies. It has also failed to provide a good perspective on Canada's welfare state. Recent debates around free trade, for instance, exaggerate Canada's superiority vis-à-vis the United States in welfare provision and entitlement and fail to take into account the social and political foundations of this country's institutions.

This chapter contributes to an ongoing effort to recast Canadian political economy in a perspective incorporating the institutional effects of class formation and comparative analyses. It suggests the political foundations of state regulation best analyzed from a historical perspective. The major political innovations affecting the development of Canadian state regulation came at times of social and political upheavals and corresponded to new problems created by the transformation of capitalism. Rooted in the process of class formation, the reforms had the limitations typical of countries characterized by a liberal, centrist social and political balance of power. A comparison with countries with similar political arrangements confirms and complements historical findings and shows both the limitations and the relative resilience of Canada's model of state regulation.

In the 1980s, countries of what we have called the fourth model have seen marked shifts to the right in partisan politics and public policies. Francis G. Castles explains this realignment by slower economic growth and poor policy effectiveness in the 1970s and by first-past-the-post electoral systems, which make abrupt political and policy changes more likely.[63] Canada has not experienced changes comparable to what happened in Britain and the United States. A broad consensus on the most visible institutions and practices has prevented or limited open attacks on the welfare state or trade unions, while the weakness of nationalist ideology and the logic of federalism have made challenges to this consensus difficult. State regulation has nevertheless evolved in the direction indicated by the United States and Britain.

The model of state regulation that will emerge out of the current evolution is difficult to foresee. Canada could gradually reproduce the neo-conservative transformation observed in Britain and the United States, or it could move closer to models typical of continental European states. The United States and Britain themselves could also alter their course and reassert their traditional centrism.

In the wake of the coming redefinition of the country, a new political dynamic may emerge that will redefine state regulation for the 1990s. Predictions on such matters are not possible. History and political science teach us, however, that class and political conflicts—including conflicts on constitutional and regional questions—will matter as much as economic and continental constraints and that continuity and moderate policies are likely to prevail.

ENDNOTES

The authors wish to thank Jane Jenson for her much appreciated comments on earlier drafts, and to acknowledge the financial support of SSHRCC and the Fonds FCAR.

The community of political economists also notes with great regret Lizette Jalbert's untimely death, in April 1992.

1.   John Myles, "Decline or Impasse? The Current State of the Welfare State," *Studies in Political Economy*, 26 (Summer 1988).

2.   For similar arguments see Bob Jessop *et al.*, *Thatcherism: A Tale of Two Nations* (Cambridge: Polity Press, 1988), p. 13 and Jenson, this volume.

3. Rianne Mahon, "Review Symposium: New Developments in Comparative Political Economy," *Canadian Journal of Sociology*, 14/4 (Fall 1989), p. 502 and Gilles Breton and Jane Jenson, "After Free Trade and Meech Lake: Quoi de neuf," *Studies in Political Economy*, 34 (Spring 1991).

4. Mahon, "Review Symposium"; Gregory Albo, "Canada, Left-Nationalism and Younger Voices," *Studies in Political Economy*, 33 (Autumn 1990), p. 171.

5. John Myles, "Introduction. Understanding Canada: Comparative Political Economy Perspectives," *Canadian Review of Sociology and Anthropology*, 26/1 (February 1989), p. 2.

6. Myles, "Introduction" and Jane Jenson, "Representations in Crisis: The Roots of Canada's Permeable Fordism," *Canadian Journal of Political Science*, vol. 23/4, (December 1990), pp. 657-58.

7. Myles, "Introduction," p. 4; Mahon, "Review Symposium," p. 502; Jenson, "Representations in Crisis," pp. 654-56.

8. Alain Noël, "Accumulation, Regulation, and Social Change: An Essay on French Political Economy," *International Organization*, 41/2 (Spring 1987); Gérard Boismenu, "L'Etat et la régulation du rapport salarial depuis 1945," in Gérard Boismenu and Daniel Drache (eds.), *Politique et régulation: modèle de développement et trajectoire canadienne*, (Montréal: Méridien, 1990); Peter A. Hall, *Governing the Economy: The Politics of State Intervention in Britain and France* (Cambridge: Polity Press, 1986).

9. Adam Przeworski, *Capitalism and Social Democracy* (Cambridge: Cambridge University Press, 1985), pp. 81 and 96.

10. Bob Jessop, "Regulation Theories in Retrospect and Prospect," *Economy and Society*, 19/2 (May 1990), p. 198 and Jenson, this volume.

11. Alain Noël, "Action collective, politique partisane et relations industrielles," in Boismenu and Drache (eds.), *Politique et régulation* (Montréal: Méridien, 1990).

12. Janine Brodie and Jane Jenson, *Crisis, Challenge, and Change: Party and Class in Canada Revisited* (Carleton: Carleton University Press, 1988), p. 3.

13. Karl Polanyi, *The Great Transformation: The Political and Economic Origins of Our Time* (Boston: Beacon Press, 1944), p. 140.

14. Gregory S. Kealey and Bryan D. Palmer, *Dreaming of What Might Be: The Knights of Labor in Ontario, 1880-1900* (Cambridge: Cambridge University Press, 1982), p. 65; Bryan D. Palmer, *Working-Class Experience: The Rise and Reconstitution of Canadian Labour, 1800-1980* (Toronto: Butterworth, 1983), p. 124.

15. Palmer, *Working-Class Experience*, p. 124; Allan Moscovitch and Glenn Drover, "Social Expenditures and the Welfare State: The Canadian Experience in Historical Perspective," in Allan Moscovitch and Jim Albert (eds.), *The Benevolent State: The Growth of Welfare in Canada* (Toronto: Garamond, 1987), p. 18.

16. Dennis Guest, *The Emergence of Social Security in Canada* (Vancouver: University of British Columbia Press, 1980), p. 76.

17. Guest, *The Emergence*, pp. 62-63; Keith G. Banting, *The Welfare State and Canadian Federalism*, second edition (Montréal: McGill-Queen's University Press, 1987), p. 61.

18. Guest, *The Emergence*, pp. 75-76; John Myles, *Old Age in the Welfare State: The Political Economy of Public Pensions* (Boston: Little, Brown, 1984), pp. 38-39.

19. Alain Noël, "L'après guerre au Canada: Politiques keynésiennes ou nouvelles formes de régulation?," in Gérard Boismenu and Gilles Dostaler (eds.), *La 'Théorie générale' et le keynésianisme* (Montréal: ACFAS, 1987); Robert M. Campbell, *Illusions: The Politics of the Keynesian Experience in Canada, 1945-1975* (Peterborough: Broadview Press, 1987).

20. Dennis Guest, "World War II and the Welfare State in Canada," in Moscovitch and Drover (eds.), *The Benevolent State*; Guest, *The Emergence*, pp. 142-44.

21. Alain Noël, "Jobs! Jobs! Jobs! The Political Management of Unemployment," in Alain-G. Gagnon and James P. Bickerton (eds.), *Canadian Politics: An Introduction to the Discipline* (Peterborough: Broadview Press, 1990), p. 457.

22. Guest, *The Emergence*, p. 143.

23. Leo Panitch and Donald Swartz, *The Assault on Trade Union Freedoms: From Consent to Coercion Revisited* (Toronto: Garamond, 1988), pp. 17-27.

24. Robert Lacroix, *Les Grèves au Canada: Causes et conséquences* (Montréal: Les Presses de l'Université de Montréal, 1987), pp. 59-78.

25. Moscovitch and Drover, "Social Expenditures and the Welfare State," pp. 30-31.

26. Ronald Manzer, *Public Policies and Political Development in Canada* (Toronto: University of Toronto Press, 1985), p. 51.

27. Campbell, *Grand Illusions*, pp. 145-48; Gérard Boismenu, "Keynésianisme et niveau provincial de l'Etat canadien," in Boismenu and Dostaler (eds.), *La 'Théorie générale' et le keynésianisme*, p. 126.

28. John R. Calvert, "The Divergent Paths of Canadian and American Labor," in Mike Davis and Michael Sprinker (eds.), *Reshaping the U.S. Left: Popular Struggles in the 1980s* (London: Verso, 1988); Judith Maxwell, *Challenges to Complacency* (Montreal: C.D. Howe Research Institute, 1976), pp. 72-129.

29. Gérard Boismenu, "L'Etat et la régulation du rapport salarial depuis 1945," and François Houle, "L'Etat et le social à l'heure du marché continental," in Boismenu and Drache (eds.), *Politique et régulation*; Noël, "Jobs! Jobs! Jobs!"; Ramesh Mishra, *The Welfare State in Capitalist Society: Policies of Retrenchment and Maintenance in Europe, North America and Australia* (Toronto: University of Toronto Press, 1990), p. 76; Alain Noël and Keith Gardner, "The Gainers Strike: Capitalist Offensive, Militancy, and the Politics of

Industrial Relations in Canada," *Studies in Political Economy*, 31 (Spring 1990).

30. Myles, "Decline or Impasse?," p. 77.

31. On these concepts, see Noël, "Accumulation, Regulation, and Social Change."

32. Morris Altman, "A Revision of Canadian Economic Growth: 1870-1910 (A Challenge to the Gradualist Interpretation)," *Canadian Journal of Economics*, 20/1 (February 1987), p. 104.

33. Altman, "A Revision," pp. 104-105; Kenneth Norrie and Douglas Owram, *A History of the Canadian Economy* (Toronto: Harcourt Brace Jovanovich, 1991), p. 442.

34. For a good discussion of the theoretical issues involved see: Michael Goldfield, "Worker Insurgency, Radical Organization, and New Deal Legislation," *American Political Science Review*, 83/4 (December 1989), and *idem*, "Explaining New Deal Labor Policy," *American Political Science Review*, 84/4 (December 1990).

35. Noël, "Jobs! Jobs! Jobs!"

36. For three variants of pessimism, see: Panitch and Swartz, *The Assault on Trade Union Freedoms*; Yonatan Reshef, "Union Decline: A View from Canada," *Journal of Labor Research*, 11/1 (Winter 1990); and Leo Troy, "Is the U.S. Unique in the Decline of Private Sector Unionism?," *Journal of Labor Research*, 11/2 (Spring 1990). Optimistic points of view are presented in: Calvert, "The Divergent Paths of Canadian and American Labor;" Sam Gindin, "Breaking Away: The Formation of the Canadian Auto Workers," *Studies in Political Economy*, 29 (Summer 1989); and David Kettler, James Struthers, and Christopher Huxley, "Unionization and Labour Regimes in Canada and the United States: Considerations for Comparative Research," *Labour/Le Travail*, 25 (Spring 1990).

37. Calvert, "The Divergent Paths"; Gindin, "Breaking Away"; Noël and Gardner, "The Gainers Strike"; and Holmes and Pradeep, this volume.

38. Göran Therborn and Joop Roebroek, "The Irreversible Welfare State: Its Recent Maturation, Its Encounter with the Economic Crisis, and Its Future Prospects," *International Journal of Health Services*, 16/3 (1986), p. 323; Myles, "Decline or Impasse?," p. 80.

39. David R. Cameron, "The Growth of Government Spending: The Canadian Experience in Comparative Perspective," in Keith Banting (ed.), *State and Society: Canada in Comparative Perspective*, Studies for the Royal Commission on the Economic Union and Development Prospects for Canada, vol. 31 (Toronto: University of Toronto Press, 1986), pp. 34-35.

40. Cameron, " The Growth," pp. 46-47.

41. Julia S. O'Connor, "Welfare Expenditure and Policy Orientation in Canada in Comparative Perspective," *Canadian Review of Sociology and Anthropology*, 26/1 (February 1989), pp. 134-41.

42. J. Harvey Perry, *A Fiscal History of Canada—The Postwar Years* (Toronto: Canadian Tax Foundation, 1989), pp. 627 and 641. The reform of education, the other area where expenditures increased rapidly, was apparently less controversial; and thus spending for education rose with economic growth and post-secondary enrollments. See Perry, "A Fiscal History," pp. 779-83 and William M. Chandler, "Canadian Socialism and Policy Impact: Contagion from the Left?," *Canadian Journal of Political Science*, 10/4 (December 1977), p. 777.

43. Leon Muszynski, "The Politics of Labour Market Policy," in G. Bruce Doern (ed.), *The Politics of Economic Policy*, Studies for the Royal Commission on the Economic Union and Development Prospects for Canada, vol. 40 (Toronto: University of Toronto Press, 1985), p. 299.

44. Ernie Lightman and Allan Irving, "Restructuring Canada's Welfare State," *Journal of Social Policy*, 20/1 (January 1991), pp. 70-71. The authors do not see a contradiction between these observations and their view that decentralization undermines the Canadian welfare state. See also Lizette Jalbert, "L'Etat interventionniste de providence canadien en perspective," *Cahiers du GRÉTSÉ*, 9 (Montréal: Université de Montréal, April 1992).

45. Richard Simeon and Ian Robinson, *State, Society, and the Development of Canadian Federalism*, Studies for the Royal Commission on the Economic Union and Development Prospects for Canada, vol. 71 (Toronto: University of Toronto Press, 1990), p. 193.

46. O'Connor, "Welfare Expenditure," p. 132.

47. Charles S. Maier, "Nineteen Forty-Five: Continuity or Rupture?," *Europa*, 5/2 (1982), p. 119.

48. Göran Therborn, *Why Some Peoples are More Unemployed than Others* (London: Verso, 1986); Gøsta Esping-Andersen, *The Three Worlds of Welfare Capitalism*, (Princeton: Princeton Univ. Press, 1990).

49. Jan Fagerberg, Ådne Cappelen, Lars Mjøset, and Rune Skarstein, "The Decline of Social-Democratic State Capitalism in Norway," *New Left Review*, 181 (May/June 1990); Paulette Kurzer, "Unemployment in Open Economies: The Impact of Trade, Finance and European Integration," *Comparative Political Studies*, 24/1 (April 1991).

50. Rianne Mahon, "From Fordism to ?: New Technology, Labour Markets and Unions," *Economic and Industrial Democracy*, 8/1 (February 1987); Jonas Pontusson, "The Politics of New Technology and Job Redesign: A Comparison of Volvo and British Leyland," *Economic and Industrial Democracy*, 11/3 (August 1990).

51. Esping-Andersen, *The Three Worlds of Welfare Capitalism*.

52. Mahon, "From Fordism to ?"; Wolfgang Streeck, "Neo-Corporatist Industrial Relations and the Economic Crisis in West Germany," in John Goldthorpe (ed.), *Order and Conflict in Contemporary Capitalism* (Oxford: Clarendon, 1984) ;

Christopher S. Allen, "Trade Unions, Worker Participation, and Flexibility: Linking the Micro to the Macro," *Comparative Politics*, 22/3 (April 1990).

53. Bruno Théret, "Néo-libéralisme, inégalités sociales et politiques fiscales de droite et de gauche dans la France des années 1980," *Revue Française de Science Politique*, 41/3 (June 1991); Alain Lipietz, *L'Audace ou l'enlisement: Sur les Politiques économiques de la gauche* (Paris: La Découverte, 1984).

54. David R. Cameron, "The Politics and Economics of the Business Cycle," in Thomas Ferguson and Joel Rogers (eds.), *The Political Economy: Readings in the Politics and Economics of American Public Policy* (New York: M.E. Sharpe, 1984).

55. Francis G. Castles, "The Dynamics of Policy Change: What Happened to the English-Speaking Nations in the 1980s," *European Journal of Political Research*, 18/5 (September 1990); Lizette Jalbert and Laurent Lepage (eds.), *Néo-conservatisme et restructuration de l'Etat* (Sillery: Presses de l'Université du Québec).

56. Noël, "Jobs! Jobs! Jobs!;" François Houle, "Economic Renewal and Social Policy;" and Greg Albo, "The 'New Realism' and Canadian Workers," in Gagnon and Bickerton (eds.), *Canadian Politics: An Introduction to the Discipline*; and Gérard Boismenu, "La Vraisemblance de la problématique de la régulation pour saisir la réalité canadienne: étude des indicateurs économiques en moyenne période," *Cahiers du GRÉTSÉ*, 1 (Montréal: Université de Montréal, June 1989).

57. Boismenu, "L'Etat et la régulation du rapport salarial;" Robert T. Kudrle and Theodore R. Marmor, "The Development of Welfare States in North America," in Peter Flora and Arnold J. Heidenheimer (eds.), *The Development of Welfare States in Europe and America* (New Brunswick: Transaction Books, 1981); Christopher Huxley, David Kettler, and James Struthers, "Is Canada's Experience 'Especially Instructive'?," in Seymour Martin Lipset (ed.), *Unions in Transition* (San Francisco: ICS Press, 1986).

58. Jalbert, "L'Etat interventionniste de providence canadien;" OCDE, *OCDE en chiffres: statistiques sur les pays membres 1989*, Supplément à l'Observateur de l'OCDE, no. 158 (June-July 1989), pp. 16-17.

59. Myles, "Decline or Impasse?;" André Blais, Donald E. Blake, and Stéphane Dion, "The Public/Private Sector Cleavage in North America: The Political Behavior and Attitudes of Public Sector Employees," *Comparative Political Studies*, 23/3 (October 1990), p. 397.

60. Lightman and Irving, "Restructuring Canada's Welfare State;" Daniel Latouche, *Canada and Quebec, Past and Future: An Essay*, Studies for the Royal Commission on the Economic Union and Development Prospects for Canada, vol. 70 (Toronto: University of Toronto Press, 1986), p. 116.

61. Keith Banting, "Political Meaning and Social Reform," in Katherine E. Swinton and Carol J. Rogerson (eds.), *Competing Constitutional Visions: The Meech Lake Accord*, (Toronto: Carswell, 1988), p. 172.

62.   Cameron, "The Growth of Government Spending;" Robert O. Keohane, "The World Political Economy and the Crisis of Embedded Liberalism," in Goldthorpe (ed.), *Order and Conflict in Contemporary Capitalism.*

63.   Castles, "The Dynamics of Policy Change."

	CHAPTER **8**
LABOUR MOVEMENT STRATEGIES **IN THE ERA OF FREE TRADE:** **THE UNEVEN TRANSFORMATION** **of INDUSTRIAL RELATIONS** **IN THE NORTH AMERICAN** **AUTOMOBILE INDUSTRY**	**JOHN HOLMES** **PRADEEP KUMAR**

INTRODUCTION

Paradoxically, in recent years while the economies of the United States and Canada have become even more interdependent with the signing of the Free Trade Agreement (FTA) and the accompanying trend towards the harmonization of economic and social policies and institutions, a "continental divide" has emerged in the goals, priorities and strategies of the two labour movements and, hence, in collective bargaining approaches and outcomes in the two countries. In 1984 the degree of divergence was underscored when the Canadian section of the United Automobile Workers (UAW) struck the Canadian subsidiary of General Motors in open defiance of the parent union's collective bargaining agenda. As a result of the strike the Canadians won a collective agreement which diverged from the American one in several fundamental ways. This event also precipitated the formation of an autonomous union, the Canadian Auto Workers (CAW), which has espoused a philosophy of social unionism and shown remarkable strength and dynamism in the period since the split.

The automobile industry presents an interesting case. The postwar period saw the development of an integrated and uniform industrial relations system within the North American auto industry. The industry was dominated by the Big Three—General Motors (GM), Ford and Chrysler—which emphasized cross-border uniformity in their industrial relations policies and practices. This uniformity was reinforced by the fact that autoworkers in both countries were represented by the UAW and by the fact that the Canadian public policy framework for private-sector labour relations was modeled on the American Wagner Act of 1935. Furthermore, during the extensive restructuring of the industry that occurred in the 1980s, the companies sought to introduce similar management methods in both their Canadian and American auto plants as part of the effort to reorganize and restructure production, work and industrial relations. The responses of the Canadian and American labour movements to these efforts, however, were quite distinct, with the result that there has been a growing divergence in collective bargaining strategies and outcomes between the two countries over the last decade.

The objective of this chapter is to outline the background to of this divergence and then to focus on two key matters that illustrate the difference between the social unionist orientation of the CAW and the enterprise unionist of the UAW. These matters are: first, the different reaction of the Canadian and American sections of the UAW to management's demands for contract concessions and a new wage-setting formula in the early 1980s; and, second, the different strategies adopted by the UAW and CAW in the latter half of the decade with respect to the introduction of Japanese-inspired co-operative forms of work organization and industrial relations.

PATTERN COLLECTIVE BARGAINING:
THE FORDIST LABOUR RELATIONS SYSTEM
IN THE AUTOMOBILE INDUSTRY[1]

Perhaps the single most important element of the Fordist model of industrialization in the postwar North American auto industry was the development of a stable labour relations system which was peculiar to the United States and Canada and governed collective bargaining and labour-management relations in the industry from the Second World War through to the early 1980s.[2] Its establishment was linked to the rise in the late 1930s and early 1940s of the industrial union, the UAW. The UAW organized virtually all North American workers in the vehicle-assembly sector and in the automakers' "captive" component plants, as well as a substantial majority of workers in the independent parts sector (IPS). This enabled the union to establish uniform pattern contracts in the industry.

The model for postwar labour contracts was set by the 1948 collective agreement between GM and the UAW in the United States (replicated in Canada in 1953). The three key elements were: the determination of wages through formula-like *wage rules* in multi-year national contracts; a *connective bargaining* structure defining the relationship, or connection, between national and plant-level bargaining, which led to a centrally imposed uniformity in wages and general contract provisions; and a so-called *job-control focus* which linked workers' rights to narrowly and strictly defined job classifications and provided for the contractual resolution of disagreements and grievances arising over matters covered by the contract.[3] The pattern set by the 1948 GM agreements quickly spread to other companies in the auto industry (and ultimately to other industries) and was to last for over 30 years.

The expiration of contracts with each of the major automakers was timed to occur in the same year. As contract renewal time approached, the union would select a target company (the company from which it thought, based on strategic and market considerations, it could wrest the best initial contract) for bargaining. Once agreement had been reached with that company, with or without a strike, the other automakers quickly settled for almost identical contracts, thereby establishing a uniform pattern among companies. During the 1960s and 1970s the U.S. contracts were always settled prior to the Canadian contracts. Thus, *de facto*, the American contracts established the pattern for the Canadian contracts.

The following are brief summaries of the three main elements which became such integral features of these postwar Fordist pattern contracts.

Wage rules

Annual wage increases, which were negotiated in multi-year national collective agreements with each company, consisted of two components: a cost-of-living adjustment (COLA) designed to protect real wages against price inflation and an annual improvement factor (AIF), linked explicitly to expected long-term rates of growth.[4] Once set, the national contract wage increases could not be modified in local bargaining. With only very minor exceptions, this formula was used to set wage increases among the major automakers and parts producers from 1948 to 1979. Monitoring by both companies and union ensured convergence towards identical wage rates between plants for each job classification.

These methods "took wages out of competition" by effectively eliminating variations in wage rates between companies and between plants within the same company.[5] Following the signing of the Auto Pact in 1965 the UAW pressed hard for, and in 1973 achieved, nominal wage parity between Canadian and American autoworkers.[6] The integration of collective bargaining between the two countries was further underscored by the fact that from 1968-81 there was simply one international collective agreement between the UAW and Chrysler, which covered all Chrysler workers whether they worked in the United States or Canada.

Connective bargaining

Connective bargaining defined the relationship between national and local bargaining in the industry. Through collective bargaining at the national level the union set the general wage increases and formulated the general principles and rules. Each union local negotiated the detailed job classifications and seniority provisions for the plants it represented and administered the collective agreement. The national office of the union, in pursuit of inter-plant uniformity, played an active role in plant-level bargaining and contract administration, requiring that local agreements receive its approval. This connected system of national and local bargaining between companies and the union effectively separated work-rule bargaining from wage determination and meant—particularly in a period of general growth and expanding markets such as existed in the 1950s and 1960s—that there was little pressure on unions at the local level to agree to the relaxation of work-rules in order to save jobs.

Job-control focus

The term 'job-control focus' refers to the very formalized and detailed nature of the collective agreements which linked workers' rights and obligations to a set of highly articulated and sharply delineated jobs and tasks. Central to this system was an elaborate job classification scheme that formed the core of each collective agreement and was built around narrowly defined jobs. These, in turn, were grouped into career ladders such that the mastery of one task ideally prepared the worker for a slightly more demanding one. Workers moved up the job ladder according to seniority and, similarly, during downturns, layoffs were in reverse order of seniority. Pay was determined by attaching a wage rate to the specific job being performed rather than to the qualifications or characteristics of the workers undertaking it. The job-control focus provided the union with a significant degree of control over the internal labour market and was the primary source of union power on the shopfloor. While the system made it relatively easy to lay off and rehire workers, it made it extremely difficult for management to redeploy workers within a plant: in other words, it resulted in a flexible external labour market but a very rigid internal one.

The day-to-day operation of this system was left to management discretion. There was an explicit agreement that it was the job of management to organize and direct work, the employees' obligation to follow instructions, and the unions' to ensure that management carried out its function in accordance with the literal interpretation and administration of the rules contained in the local contract.

Thus, from the late 1940s until the late 1970s there was a well-functioning labour relations system within the North American auto industry that was consistent with the general Fordist model of production within which it was embedded and that provided benefits to both workers and employers. In this sense, it was a central element of the hegemonic structure of postwar Fordism.

During the 1980s, however, North American capital increasingly came under pressure to reorganize and restructure production. In the automobile industry there were two main sources of such pressure. First, the industry was forced to adjust to a significant shift in competitive conditions occasioned by the increasing exposure of the domestic market to intense international competition, in particular by the rise of Japan as a major producer and exporter of automobiles. The new competition, which initially took the form of increasing import penetration of the North American market by vehicles built in Japan, was later driven by direct investment in North American based assembly and component production facilities, which have come to be known as "transplants." Second, North American automakers experienced significant erosion in their competitive position due to escalating production costs. Throughout the 1950s and 1960s the annual increases in base wage-rates had been financed out of sustained increases in labour productivity. This stagnated, however, in the early 1970s and for over a decade showed no signs of recovery. Coupled with the contractual annual real wage increases, which had become an entrenched feature of postwar pattern bargaining, the poor productivity performance led to rapidly escalating unit production costs, further weakening the international competitiveness of North American automakers.[7]

It was this unprecedented sea-change in trade, investment flows and international labour cost competitiveness that both forced and shaped the restructuring of the North American auto industry during the 1980s. In an effort to become competitive with the Japanese, North American automakers first attempted simply to cut costs. Eventually they were forced into far-reaching changes in both product and process technologies. The 1980s, therefore, witnessed a wave of new investment in both the construction of "greenfield" plants and in the modernization of existing Big Three facilities. Much of this investment was tied to the introduction of advanced forms of automation and the reorganization of work and production both within individual plants and across the wider production system.[8]

At the heart of the restructuring lay the need to lower production costs and increase productivity: this placed heavy demands on the auto industrial relations system. After an initial phase of concession bargaining at the beginning of the 1980s—during which management simply sought a reduction in nominal wages, deferment of scheduled COLA increases, and roll-backs on benefits such as holiday entitlements—pressure mounted to restructure the whole compensation system and, particularly, to reorganize work and construct a more co-operative shopfloor and plant-level relationship between labour and management. Kochan, Katz and McKersie suggest that during the 1980s the traditional Fordist labour relations system was transformed to produce a "new industrial relations system" that, in the auto industry at least, was fashioned around lump-sum payments instead of regular annual increases in base wage rates; profit-sharing schemes; and, the redesign and broadening of jobs to allow management more control and flexibility in the deployment of the workforce.[9] As part of this transformation the union was pressed to abandon the adversarial job-control system in favour of a new high-trust or co-operative relationship built around variants of the team concept. While the traditional system assumed that workers had no personal responsibility for efficiency or productivity, in the new system workers are expected to participate in groups in order to pool and apply their knowledge and tacit skills to improve productivity and quality.

The memorandum of understanding (and subsequent collective agreement) signed by the UAW with GM for the new greenfield Saturn production facility in Springhill, Tennessee covered virtually all of these elements.[10] Many other plants, particularly in the United States, embodied at least some of these practices by the end of the decade. Taken as a package these new work and industrial relations practices constitute what is referred to by GM as "World Class Contracts" (Table 8.1) and by Chrysler as "Modern Operating Agreements." It is to the differential responses of the Canadian and American labour movements to these developments that we now turn.

FROM CONCESSION BARGAINING
TO NEW WAGE RULES: INITIAL DIVERGENCE, 1979-84

A comparison of auto industry labour contracts negotiated in both the United States and Canada since 1979 reveals a growing divergence in the content of agreements between the two countries.[11] The first signs of divergence appeared in the unions' response to management's demand for concessions on wages and benefits during the early 1980s when company restructuring strategies were firmly centred on cost-cutting. The 1984 round of contract negotiations saw the establishment of a new pattern contract in the United States that changed the traditional rules for wage formation in the industry. This led to further divergence. Although these events are now reasonably well known in the literature, it is useful briefly to review and contextualize them in order to provide a backdrop to the later analysis of the divergence between Canadian and American auto unions' responses to work reorganization and co-operative industrial relations.[12]

A self-conscious choice of different strategic directions by the two sections of the union clearly underlay the divergence in outcomes. In the United States the leadership of the UAW was confronted with huge losses of jobs and of union membership because of a series of plant closings and large numbers of workers on temporary or permanent layoff. It thus made employment security its number one bargaining priority and agreed to trade off concessions on wage increases and work-rules and actively to promote a more "co-operative" relationship with management. In Canada, however, the union experienced far fewer layoffs and plant closings and had been aggressively organizing to bolster its membership. It rejected concession bargaining, continued to press for long-term income security through improved wage and benefit settlements using the traditional formulae, and resisted (or at least did not embrace wholeheartedly) management's efforts to transform the traditional shopfloor relationships between workers, their union representatives, and management.[13]

The 1979 negotiations between Chrysler and the UAW marked the beginning of the "era of concession bargaining" in the auto industry. Canadian Chrysler workers, covered by the same collective agreement as American Chrysler workers, accepted the 1979 package of concessions in the interest of preserving trans-border uniformity in contracts. When Chrysler (followed by GM and Ford) demanded and won further concessions in the United States, however, the Canadian leadership, backed by the mandate provided by the UAW Canadian Council's official rejection of concession bargaining, refused either to reopen contracts or to recommend further concessions to its membership.

In hindsight, it is plain that the 1982 round of contract negotiations with Chrysler was a milestone in the development of the distinct path that Canadian autoworkers later decided to pursue, independent of the union in the United States.[14] In 1982, Canadian autoworkers not only rejected the concessions made by the union in the United States, but after a five-week strike against Chrysler Canada won a wage increase that for the first time established the pattern for the United States as well. The Chrysler strike demonstrated to Canadian autoworkers that not only could they win a difficult strike on their own, but also that their leadership's analysis "... that management's strategy of restructuring through concessions was not the *only* one available" was sound and viable.[15]

In the 1984 round of collective bargaining, the UAW formally surrendered the traditional wage-setting formula of AIF plus COLA in favour of annual lump-sum payments and continued profit sharing. In contrast to the old AIF increases, these lump sums were not to be folded into the base rate.[16] The Canadians in 1984 rejected the new pattern for wage determination set in the United States and instead concentrated their bargaining on re-establishing the traditional contract model through the restoration of wage increases determined by COLA and AIF and the maintenance of wage uniformity between companies and plants. They continued to reject on principle the concept of profit sharing. After a twelve-and-a-half day strike in late October 1984 the Canadians obtained a contract on their terms. This contract, however, was only won after an intense struggle which pitted the Canadian wing of the UAW not only against GM but also against the leadership of the UAW. The strain within the UAW proved too great and in 1985 the Canadian region left the International UAW to form the autonomous CAW. Although management again placed the elimination of the AIF high on its bargaining agenda in both the 1987 and 1990 contract negotiations in Canada, the CAW again successfully bargained to retain annual increases in base rates as opposed to accepting lump-sum payments and profit sharing.

The divergence in wage-setting rules has resulted in sizable differences in both base wage rates (Table 8.2) and total earnings received within the same company between Canada and the United States.[17] In general, Canadian workers finished the 1980s significantly ahead (in nominal terms) of their American counterparts with regard to both base wage rates and total compensation.[18]

The choice of different strategic directions followed by the two sections of the union during the first half of the 1980s must be understood in light of two key contextual factors. The first is the geographically uneven development of the North American auto industry which produced an absolute and relative expansion of the industry in Canada during the 1980s and, thus, placed the Canadian wing of the union in a far stronger bargaining position than its American counterpart. The second factor is the fundamental differences in political ideology between the Canadian and American sections of the union with regard to concessions specifically and the future strategic trajectory of the labour movement more generally.

The performance indicators of output, employment, plant capacity utilization rates, and trade under the Auto Pact all reveal that although the North American auto industry as a whole experienced considerable difficulties, the Canadian portion of the industry fared much better than its American counterpart during the 1980s.[19] While the industry in the United States failed to regain the levels of employment and production attained in the late 1970s, the industry in Canada not only staged a rapid recovery from the deep recession at the beginning of the decade but continued to prosper throughout the 1980s. Although Canada's share of the total North American market for vehicles remained at around nine percent, its share of total North American vehicle production and industry employment both rose to about 15 percent.

By far the most significant factor underlying the stronger performance of the industry in Canada during the 1980s was the real labour cost advantage enjoyed by the Big Three in Canada. This advantage, which by the mid-1980s was of the order of 30 percent, was related to the lower value of the Canadian dollar against the U.S. dollar and the lower cost of employee benefits, particularly the health insurance costs subsidized in Canada through universal medical care (Table 8.3). Taking into account that productivity and efficiency in Canadian assembly plants were generally equal or greater than the plants in the United States, these labour cost savings were both substantial and significant.[20]

The differences in ideology and political culture between the labour movements in Canada and the United States also shaped the strategic choice of the union in the two countries. While these differences had relatively inconsequential effects on bargaining outcomes during the 1960s, when employment and real wages were rising steadily on both sides of the border, they suddenly assumed a new significance in the recessionary climate of the early 1980s. For example, the Canadian UAW's opposition to management's demands for concessions was part of the general campaign by the Canadian labour movement against concession bargaining and was very much shaped by its particular understanding of the fundamental nature and purpose of trade unionism. The Canadians feared that irreparable damage would be done to the longer term commitment of the rank and file of the union if they followed the lead of the UAW leadership in the United States and granted uncritical support to concessions. "The fight *against* concessions was therefore a fight *for* the continued health of the trade union movement."[21] The debate about concessions that occurred at a special 1981 meeting of the Canadian Council of the UAW and led to the adoption of an official anti-concessions position by the union, and later at the Canadian Labour Congress convention in 1982, focused on:

> ...why [concessions] were disastrous for working people; why they would not bring job security to workers; how they would divert attention from real alternatives; how they would fragment workers; why accepting them would be to argue that unions had bargained "too well" in the past and should, therefore, forever be weakened; and why in general acquiescence to their logic would eventually destroy the lifeblood of unions. [22]

The Council's "no concessions" resolutions prohibited union locals in Canada from deviating from the wage scales and work practices specified in the Master Agreement.

In summary, autoworkers in Canada had considerable bargaining strength during the first half of the 1980s due to the significant real labour cost advantage enjoyed by Canadian plants. The advantage was so large that it enabled the Canadians to resist the cost-cutting concessions on wages and benefits that had been accepted by the union in the United States, without seriously jeopardizing the competitiveness of the Canadian segment of the industry.

THE QUEST FOR "COMPETITIVENESS": UNION RESPONSES TO DEMANDS FOR WORK REORGANIZATION AND CO-OPERATIVE INDUSTRIAL RELATIONS

Midway through the 1980s competitive conditions again shifted within the North American auto industry, forcing automakers to reassess their restructuring strategies. In turn, the continued restructuring of the industry posed a new set of strategic choices for the UAW and CAW. Once again the choices that each union made were quite distinct. The new competitive environment arose out of the wave of greenfield transplant assembly and parts plants built in the United States by Japanese automakers and the collapse of unionization in the American independent parts sector. Both developments significantly threatened the competitive position of the Big Three. The corporate strategy therefore shifted from restructuring based on cost-cutting through wage and benefit concessions, labour shedding, and the introduction of advanced automation, to the development of a strategy designed to increase productivity through the reorganization of work and the development of more co-operative industrial relations.[23]

The transplants and new competitive standards

When the Big Three and the UAW pressured the Japanese in the early 1980s to build cars in North America, both management and labour assumed that this would quickly lead to a levelling of the playing field for automakers vying for the North American market. Forced to pay UAW wages and accept Big Three work practices, the Japanese automakers would lose the cost advantage that they had enjoyed by producing in Japan. By the end of the 1980s, the major Japanese automakers (and the Korean firm Hyundai) had opened or had under development 13 vehicle-assembly plants and three engine plants in the United States and Canada.[24] With only a few exceptions, however, the Asian automakers built their vehicle-assembly plants in the Upper South and the rural small towns of the U.S. Midwest, and Ontario and Quebec. They hired mostly young workers with little previous industrial experience. In addition to the investment in assembly and engine plants, over 300 new Japanese-owned or Japanese/U.S. joint-venture parts plants were built in North America during the 1980s. The vast majority of these plants are located in the United States. Virtually all have been built on greenfield sites, and only one is unionized.[25]

Two particular aspects of the transplants have had a significant impact on competitive conditions within the industry: their lower compensation costs related to their young and inexperienced workforce and the transplants' new standards of productivity and product quality for North American vehicle assembly plants.[26] For example, the average age of workers at Honda Marysville (Ohio) which began operations in 1983 is still only 30. By comparison the average age of Ford's American labour force is in the mid-40s. Even though most of the non-union transplant assembly plants pay base wage rates close to UAW rates (Table 8.4) they enjoy a tremendous savings in benefit costs, especially for pension and medical insurance premiums, because of the younger labour force. Greenfield parts manufacturers enjoy similar cost advantages to greenfield assemblers as well as paying significantly lower wage rates than the unionized portion of the components industry. It has been estimated that transplant suppliers in the United States may have labour costs that are almost 40 percent below those for the parts industry as a whole.[27] These cost advantages have absolutely nothing to do with greater productivity, a more skilled labour force, or better technology. They are simply a function of building a new plant and using a young non-union labour force. The rapid growth during the 1980s of non-union plants (both Japanese and American-owned) contributed to the collapse of the pattern bargaining structure in the U.S. parts sector (IPS) and seriously eroded the cost advantage enjoyed by Canadian plants vis-à-vis those in the United States.[28]

Perhaps an even more far-reaching consequence of the development of the transplant sector was the establishment of new productivity and product quality standards in the North American auto industry. The most dramatic and important example of this impact is the extraordinary success of the production model developed in the first of the transplants, NUMMI, a plant located in the San Francisco Bay Area of California and operated under Toyota management by a Toyota/GM joint-venture company. In just two years, NUMMI went from an "interesting experiment" to the "success story" of the auto industry. By the end of 1986 NUMMI had become both the standard and the model for the North American auto industry, especially for GM. The significance of NUMMI stems from the direct comparison that is made to the former GM-Fremont plant that had stood on the same site. With essentially the same plant, technology, workers, wage rates, union, and union leaders, NUMMI organized a production system that far exceeded in productivity and product quality not only the former GM-Fremont plant but also every other GM assembly plant in the United States. NUMMI demonstrated that Japanese auto production management practices were transferable to North America and that American workers could achieve levels of productivity and quality that even compared favourably with the Toyota Takaoka plant in Japan.[29]

Although there were obviously other factors at play, the key to NUMMI's success was viewed as the fostering of union-management co-operation achieved through the development and implementation of the "team concept" approach to the reorganization of work and production. NUMMI had an extraordinarily powerful demonstration effect and was the inspiration for the major push by the Big Three (and by General Motors in particular) in the latter half of the decade to reorganize work, introduce new forms of team organization, and develop more co-operative industrial relations practices.[30]

Again, the UAW and CAW responses to this strategy have diverged markedly. Although discernible in the earlier differences over concession bargaining and wage-setting, it is with regard to the issue of co-operative industrial relations that the contrast between the UAW's shift towards co-operative enterprise unionism and the CAW's continued recognition of the adversarial relationship between capital and labour and commitment to social unionism becomes plain.

ENTERPRISE UNIONISM AND SOCIAL UNIONISM: THE UAW AND CAW DIVERGE

Beginning as early as the 1982 round of contract negotiations, management on both sides of the border pressed for and achieved the development of plant-level labour-management committees which would have the power to negotiate changes in local (and even national) agreements in order to preserve or increase the number of jobs at a plant. In the United States, the 1982 and 1984 contracts permitted the formation of such committees to negotiate mid-contract changes in job classifications and work rules but *only* when plants either were faced with losing work to outsourcing or had the chance to secure significant new investment. The role of such committees, however, was considerably extended and strengthened in the now famous Attachment C to the 1987 Ford and GM collective agreements in the United States. Under Attachment C, local labour-management committees became more permanent entities under the umbrella of national joint labour-management committees and were made responsible for considering how to enhance quality and competitiveness. Language in the 1987 Master Agreements also made explicit the UAW International leadership's commitment to assist management in reducing work-rule restrictions. In return for its willingness and commitment to help the

Big Three improve "competitiveness" the UAW leadership won what it claimed were stronger employment security guarantees for UAW members.[31]

In contrast to the stance adopted by the leadership of the International UAW, the Canadian Region and subsequently the CAW rejected the idea that labour should unconditionally join management in focusing its attention on how to make the North American automakers more competitive in return for job guarantees. The Canadians argued that it was impossible for the automakers to provide job guarantees, and, more importantly, that plant level accommodation with management through joint committees on competitiveness would only facilitate corporate efforts to subject locals to "whipsawing". This would seriously undermine solidaristic contract bargaining by "indoctrinating workers into the game of competing with other workers."[32] The CAW argued that the NUMMI and GM Saturn agreements negotiated by the UAW in the U.S. and held up by management as the models for a new "World Class Contracts," established "new structures which management will use to undermine the union itself." Together with profit sharing, which they also steadfastly resisted, the CAW viewed such contracts as moving towards a form of plant-level or enterprise unionism that, if adopted, would subordinate worker concerns and interests to managerial goals.

Before examining in more detail the different stances adopted by the unions in the two countries, let us first examine the precise nature of the changes being sought. Virtually all of the changes are designed to make the plant more competitive by removing rigidities within the internal labour market in order to increase the flexibility with which management can schedule and assign work and hence enhance its ability to organize work in a more efficient and less costly manner. These changes include:

- the broadening of the content of individual jobs and the concomitant reduction in the number of job classifications;

- restrictions on seniority and transfer rights to reduce *worker initiated* mobility within the internal labour market;

- changing methods of work relief time;

- increasing plant utilization through increasing the number of straight hours worked and increasing managerial control over the scheduling of overtime;

- new rules to reduce absenteeism; and

- more informal shopfloor dispute resolution mechanisms to reduce the number of formal grievances.

Attention here is chiefly focused on practices following from ideas such as the team concept, jointness, employee involvement, the operating or natural work unit, and quality network.[33] As a CAW statement on work reorganization states, no matter what label is used when these practices are introduced,

> ...the [management] selling point is both the stick and the carrot: the threat of competitiveness and the promise of a new "partnership" between workers and management, a partnership allegedly leading to greater worker control, greater security, and more enjoyable work.[34]

As noted earlier, the stimulus for management's drive to introduce the team concept throughout the GM system was the success of NUMMI. The organization of teams at NUMMI was facilitated by having only one production and two skilled-trades job classifications and by reducing the importance of seniority in allocating workers to jobs. Workers' rights to transfer to another team were based not on seniority but on production needs and the tasks that a worker had mastered. The emphasis was on worker flexibility rather than task specialization and on the increased involvement of workers in the production process. Team leaders, who were hourly employees and union members, were

> ...carefully selected and trained by management to play a genuine leadership role, co-ordinating work, checking parts and equipment, problem-solving, doing some repair work, filling in for absent members, keeping records, leading team meetings, looking for ways to encourage quality and productivity, and encouraging members to provide input.[35]

Thus, team leaders performed many of the duties of traditional first-line supervisors except they had no responsibility for dismissals. Teams at NUMMI usually consisted of four members and one leader. Three or four teams constituted a group and the group leader was the first line of management, although again the group leader's role was seen to be one of co-ordination and facilitation. Union co-ordinators (who were also full-time workers) were elected to solve labour-management problems on the shopfloor and keep the number of formal grievances to an absolute minimum.

The productivity superiority of NUMMI-style team forms of work organization over the single-job organization of work in more traditional assembly plants lies in the following:

> ...when workers are organized in teams or groups, managers usually gain a greater ability to move people around (as "job-control unionism" begins to break down), thus keeping everyone busy all the time.

> When several workers and a team leader all know the tasks compos-
> ing each job, management gets more information and can more eas-
> ily regularize work standards across jobs and push for the steady and
> uniform raising of these standards. And when workers can be pulled
> together in a group responsible for one part of production and the
> quality of its output, peer pressure can often be shifted away from
> traditional shopfloor "slow down, you'll work us out of a job" con-
> sciousness to a new emphasis on collective productivity and quality
> of output. There is no doubt that the current effort by auto industry
> managers to introduce teams is a form of speedup.[36]

Although initially cautious, by 1985 the top UAW leadership was implicitly endorsing the team concept as a strategy to help the United States auto industry regain its competitive edge. The International Executive Board of the UAW signed a team concept agreement with GM-Saturn in July 1985. During 1986 and 1987 the UAW-Chrysler Department actively worked with Chrysler to spread a standard version of the team concept through a half dozen of Chrysler's U.S. plants. In 1987 the UAW explicitly endorsed the team concept in the national union contracts signed with Ford and GM, and the International headquarters instructed local bargaining committees that, since the implementation of the team concept was necessary to restore the competitiveness of the American automobile industry, if they did not agree to incorporate it into their local contracts, they would put their plant at risk for closing.[37] By March 1988 some form of the team concept had been formally agreed to in the United States in at least 17 GM assembly plants and a number of GM captive parts plants, in six Chrysler and two Ford plants, and in all the Japanese transplants and joint-ventures.[38] By the end of the decade, top management in the Big Three and many of their plant managers believed in the necessity to move as quickly as possible to the introduction of team forms of work organization in all their plants. Given the position adopted by the UAW leadership, the formal agreement to change built into local agreements, and the union's weak bargaining position, an emboldened management often sought to push through these changes in work organization with little negotiation or consultation at the shopfloor level. As a consequence, the results in some plants have been far removed from those found at NUMMI.[39]

Two common strategies have been used by the automakers to implement the team concept in American plants. First, it has been incorporated from the outset in greenfield plants such as GM's Orion and Fairfax assembly plants. Second, by whipsawing or threatening to close an existing plant or move work to another plant they have pressured the union local into agreeing to changes in the work rules contained within the local contract. The team concept itself tends to foster an ideological atmosphere which stresses competition between plants and workers' responsibility for winning work away from other plants. It involves a shift toward enterprise unionism where the union views itself as a partner of management.

Initially, and notwithstanding considerable management pressure, the leadership of the CAW steadfastly refused officially to endorse or contractually to agree to the adoption of the team concept in established Canadian plants. It argued that the plants already ranked among the highest in North America with respect to both quality and productivity and hence were more competitive than American plants. The UAW-Canada's initial stance on this issue was reinforced by the success that the Canadian wing of the union had enjoyed in rejecting concessions in the early 1980s. There was a sense that the union need not change and therefore should avoid entering into new programs that could threaten its traditional role and its independence from management.[40] Over time, however, the Canadian leadership's position with respect to workplace reorganization evolved. It would be misleading to say that there has been no sign of change in work practices in the Canadian auto industry.

In fact, in the period since the split with the UAW, on the shopfloor of a number of plants the CAW accepted some of the changes in work organization seen in the United States, including job classification consolidation and variants of team work.[41] However, while work practices in Canada have changed, they have done so without either the introduction of pay-for-knowledge wage structures or a significant erosion of seniority rights with respect to job allocations, and with little job rotation.[42] Where these changes have taken place in Canada, they have been introduced under similar circumstances to those where they first took root in the United States: as part of concessions exacted from plants threatened with closure (GM-Ste Therese); to secure substantial new investment (Chrysler-Bramalea, Ford-Windsor); or as part of the bargain for automatic union recognition in a greenfield plant (CAMI).[43]

In the latter half of the 1980s the CAW initiated an internal debate which culminated in the adoption of a position paper on the reorganization of work at a special 1989 Council meeting of the CAW.[44] The statement went to great pains to point out that the union "... supports efforts to involve and empower workers, to increase worker dignity, to produce quality products with pride, to make jobs more rewarding and workplaces more democratic." At the same time, it reiterated the CAW's resistance to the ideological messages that it saw in the new management programs, threatening the union's traditional identity and independence from management. Therefore, the union rejected management's discourse of "competitiveness" and the notion that management and labour now have common rather than adversarial interests.

While opposed to direct participation in management decision making, the CAW has favoured active participation with management at the strategic policy level. For example, the CAW was an active participant in the Federal Task Force on the Auto Industry, and in the Auto Industry Human Resources study conducted by the federal Department of Manpower and Immigration. Recognizing the pressures on local leaders for flexibility and co-operation in traditional plants, the CAW's national office remained neutral with respect to employee involvement at the workplace level, leaving the decision about whether to enter into new programs with management to the local leaders. It agreed to the inclusion of very few formal provisions for jointness within the collective agreements and did not encourage or recommend formal participation in team concepts and related new approaches. Yet the union leadership did not overtly resist management initiatives in these areas. Thus, informal incremental changes in work rules and industrial relations practices have been negotiated on the shopfloor in some Canadian plants. By contrast, in the U.S. changes have been more formally agreed to by both the national and/or local union leadership and incorporated into the collective agreements which management has then used to push through changes on the shopfloor with little consultation with workers.[45] The difference in the approaches of the UAW and CAW to the question of jointness is further demonstrated by the different forms of educational programs provided by the two unions. Since the 1982 contract the UAW has entered into *joint* training programs with each of the Big Three, programs which stress cultural as well as technical training. By contrast, the CAW through its Paid Educational Leave program offers *independent* educationals aimed at developing a cadre of social unionists to safeguard and promote the objectives of the union.

In summary, because of the intense competitive threat posed by Japanese imports and transplants, pressure from the national office on local unions to accommodate management initiatives, and the lack of any real debate within the union about which changes the locals should accept and which they should resist, there has been a relatively rapid (although still uneven) reorganization of the workplace in the United States auto industry largely on management's terms and quite often pushed through with very little shopfloor consultation. On the other hand, although the union in Canada probably does not have the power (even if it wished to exercise it) completely to block the plant-by-plant adoption of new work practices, workplace reorganization in Canada has been much more gradual and piecemeal in its introduction and more limited in its extent than in the United States. To the degree to which such practices

have been introduced they have been adopted within, and without threatening, the traditional adversarial collective bargaining structure. Where changes
have occurred they have been negotiated and bargained at the shopfloor level
rather than as part of the formal local collective agreement which may well
make them more stable and enduring than the changes in the United States.

CONCLUSIONS

Collective bargaining in the United States auto industry during the 1980s
has significantly modified the Fordist postwar labour relations system. In sharp
contrast to the uniformity in wages and working conditions achieved through
pattern bargaining, the 1980s have witnessed the development of significant
variations in both wages and working practices between companies and
plants. Management in its search for competitiveness has magnified the divi-
sive effects of intensified international competition by engineering and exploiting competition between different segments of the North American industry
by pitting newer, more secure plants against older, more vulnerable ones; captive parts plants against independent suppliers; Canadian plants against those
in the United States. If this process continues to run unchecked, the remaining
ties of solidaristic contract bargaining will finally be severed as union locals
become increasingly preoccupied with how to ensure the competitiveness of
their own individual plant. The end result could well be a fundamental transformation of the union and a new labour relations system in which unregulated
competition becomes an institutionalized feature.

In the Canadian auto industry the postwar industrial relations system has
been more resiliant. Of particular significance is the CAW's insistence on
maintaining the traditional role of the union and its adversarial relationship
with management and bargaining workplace change at the shopfloor level.
There is, however, growing evidence that the uniformity produced by that system is beginning to crumble, despite CAW insistence that it continues to place
a very high priority on maintaining uniformity in wages and work practices
within the Canadian auto industry.

As Sam Gindin notes, the real significance of the developments in the
United States is that the union leadership during the 1980s accepted a strategic change in the direction of collective bargaining and their own role in it.[46]
Changes in wage setting and work rules, which were initially interpreted as
temporary setbacks, are now presented to the membership as innovative
breakthroughs and victories.[47] The Canadians, however, have always viewed

the concessions made in the early 1980s as a *temporary* setback to collective bargaining and have explicitly and resolutely rejected the American strategy. Thus, throughout the 1980s there was an increasing divergence in both the bargaining strategies and the content of auto industry collective agreements between the United States and Canada. The divergence is attributed to both the geographically uneven economic context produced by restructuring in the auto industry and the distinct ideological and political culture of Canadian unions. The increasing confidence in the CAW which grew out of the anti-concessions campaign in the early 1980s, the victory in the 1982 Chrysler strike and the seccession from the UAW, and the greater level of accountability of the leadership to the rank and file in the Canadian union as compared with the UAW in the United States have also been important factors shaping the CAW's response to the challenge posed by work reorganization.[48]

In the 1990s industrial relations in the North American auto industry are characterized by a growing managerial emphasis on flexibility and competition, and an increasing diversity in wage and work practices between companies and plants and between the United States and Canada. As the Japanese transplant sector continues to expand and overcapacity continues to grow, the pressure exerted by management under the ideological banner of competitiveness is likely to become more intense. The incorporation of Mexico into a NAFTA will make the situation that much more difficult from labour's point of view.

To date, neither the UAW nor the CAW has discovered how to respond effectively to management's demands for flexibility and co-operation without leaving themselves open to whipsawing and the weakening of union solidarity. While the UAW leadership in the United States still shows little sign of developing any kind of effective counter-strategy, the CAW in Canada has taken a bold and innovative step with its statement on work reorganization. The statement clearly recognizes that the present restructuring of the auto industry, and the contradictions that it produces, *potentially* offer opportunities to the labour movement as well as threats. The central issues for the union are how to make new structures such as joint committees serve labour's interests as well as management's and how to incorporate new work practices in forms which would represent progressive gains for workers. There is an enormous amount at stake: can the auto and other industrial unions create a progressive response to the present restructuring or will they slide inexorably down the slippery slope towards company unionism and unregulated competition by uncritically embracing management's quest for competitiveness at all costs?

ENDNOTES

This paper draws, in part, on research conducted as part of a project funded by the Donner Canadian Foundation and the Ontario Ministry of Labour. The project is one element of a larger research program in the School of Policy Studies at Queen's University on "The Changing Canada-United States Relationship." The authors are solely responsible for the content and views expressed in the paper. We acknowledge the useful criticisms of the original paper furnished by Rianne Mahon and Leo Panitch.

1.   This section, with very minor modifications, is taken from John Holmes. "New production technologies, labour and the North American auto industry" in G.J.R. Linge and G.A. van der Knaap (eds.), *Labour, Environment and Industrial Change* (London: Routledge, 1989), pp. 87-106.

2.   One of the major differences between the collective bargaining system in North America and other Fordist countries such as Australia, Britain and other West European OECD countries is the decentralized and localized nature of bargaining in the former. For a fuller discussion of this point see R. Boyer, "Wage/Labour relations, growth and crisis: a hidden dialectic," in R. Boyer (ed.), *The Search for Labour Market Flexibility* (Oxford: Clarendon Press, 1988), pp. 3-25; G. Clark, "Restructuring the U.S. Economy: The NLRB, the Saturn Project, and Economic Justice," *Economic Geography*, 62/4, (1986); and W. Lewchuk, *American Technology and the British Vehicle Industry* (Cambridge: Cambridge University Press, 1987). A. Woodiwiss, *Rights vs. Conspiracy: A Sociological Essay on the History of Labor Law in the United States* (NY: Berg, 1990) provides an analysis of the historical development of collective labour law in North America.

3.   H.C. Katz, *Shifting Gears: Changing Labor Relations in the U.S. Automobile Industry* (Cambridge: MIT Press, 1985).

4.   During the late 1960s and 1970s the AIF was usually set at three percent.

5.   T.A. Kochan, "Adaptability of the U.S. industrial relations system," *Science,* 240 (April 15, 1988), p. 285.

6.   Nominal wage parity refers to wage rates that are equal when measured in national currencies.

7.   J. Holmes "The crisis of Fordism and the restructuring of the Canadian auto industry" in J. Holmes and C. Leys (eds.), *Frontyard/Backyard: The Americas in the Global Crisis* (Toronto: Between the Lines Press, 1987).

8.   For a description and analysis of these technologies see J. Holmes, "Technical change and the restructuring of the North American automobile industry," in K. Chapman and G. Humphrys (eds.), *Technical Change and Industrial Policy*

(Oxford: Basil Blackwell, 1987). There is a complex debate over whether this restructuring of labour processes and the broader production system in the auto industry represents simply the extension of Fordist methods (that is, neo-Fordism) or a more complete transformation to some flexible post-Fordist model of industrialization. Our own view is that the present auto production system is probably best characterized as one of "flexible mass production" or "diversified quality production." See A. Sorge and W. Streeck, "Industrial relations and technological change: The case for an extended perspective," in R. Hyman and W. Streeck (eds.), *New Technology and Industrial Relations* (Oxford: Basil Blackwell, 1988).

9.   T.A. Kochan, H.C. Katz and R.B. McKersie, *The Transformation of American Industrial Relations* (NY: Basic Books, 1986).

10. H.C. Katz, "Recent developments in U.S. auto labour relations," in S. Tolliday and J. Zeitlin (eds.), *The Automobile Industry and Its Workers: Between Fordism and Flexibility* (Oxford: Polity Press, 1986).

11. For a detailed analysis of these contracts see J. Holmes and A. Rusonik, "The break-up of an international labour union: uneven development in the North American auto industry and the schism in the UAW," *Environment and Planning A*, vol. 23, 1991.

12. S. Gindin, "Breaking Away: The Formation of the Canadian Auto Workers," *Studies in Political Economy*, #29 (Summer 1989); C. Yates, "The Internal Dynamics of Union Power: Explaining Canadian Autoworkers' Militancy in the 1980s," *Studies in Political Economy*, 31 (Spring 1990); Holmes and Rusonik, "The Break-up of an International Labour Union."

13. The emphasis placed on wages and benefits by the Canadians is also explained by three other income-related factors. First, there is more protection in Canada afforded against the consequences of layoff by government legislation and programs such as unemployment insurance and laws governing plant closing and severance pay. Second, higher rates of inflation in Canada as compared with the United States meant that wage restraint of the kind accepted by the American union would have had a more serious impact on real wages in Canada. Third, there is still a much larger differential in the U.S. than in Canada between auto industry wages and the average manufacturing wage which means that American autoworkers could afford to make significant concessions on earnings and yet still earn substantially more than the average industrial worker. Gindin, "Breaking Away," p. 85.

14. Gindin, "Breaking Away."

15. Yates, "The Internal Dynamics of Union Power," p. 100. The 1982 Chrysler Canada strike also provided a dramatic example of how the integration of the North American automobile industry which had begun with the Auto Pact and was further cemented by technological change and the development of just-in-time production methods provided Canadian autoworkers with a powerful lever. It demonstrated that strike action by a relatively small number of workers could cripple auto production throughout North America.

16.   In the United States wages were frozen and profit sharing introduced, first by Chrysler in 1980 and then by Ford and GM in 1982. However, on these occasions the traditional Fordist wage rules of AIF and COLA were viewed as being temporarily suspended rather than superseded. The 1984 UAW-GM contract established a new pattern for setting wage increases in the United States auto industry, a pattern that was quickly incorporated into contracts with Ford and Chrysler and renewed in both the 1987 and 1990 contracts.

17.   This is just one aspect of the break-up of the uniform pattern of wages. For a more detailed analysis of these variations in compensation see J. Holmes, "From uniformity to diversity: changing patterns of wages and work practices in the North American automobile industry," in J. Morris and P. Blyton (eds.), *A Flexible Future?* (Berlin: De Gruyter, 1991). Other aspects of wage determination have also made an appearance. For example, two-tier pay systems, and pay-for-knowledge payment systems in which wages are determined by the characteristics of the worker rather than the job were introduced into a number of American plants during the 1980s. The GM Saturn contract, for instance, provides for base wage rates which represent 80 percent of normal GM base rates with the other 20 percent being potentially awarded as productivity and profit-related bonuses.

18.   Estimates are that over the period 1982-89 Canadian assembly-line workers in General Motors earned $13,360 (in current dollars) more than their American counterparts, Chrysler Canada workers earned $8,255 more, and Ford Canada assembly workers earned $1,713 more. Even when allowance is made for the higher rate of inflation in Canada as compared to the United States, Canadian workers still enjoyed higher real wages at GM and Chrysler; American workers at Ford were better off than Canadians. For these estimates see H.C. Katz and N. Meltz, "Profit sharing and workers' earnings: the United States vs. Canada," unpublished paper, Centre for Industrial Relations, University of Toronto, 1990, p. 9.

19.   J. Holmes, "The globalization of production and Canada's mature industries: The case of the auto industry," in D. Drache and M. Gertler (eds.), *The New Era of Global Competition: State Policy and Market Power* (Montreal: McGill-Queen's Press, 1991).

20.   H.C. Katz and N. Meltz, "Changing work practices and productivity in the auto industry: a U.S.-Canada comparison," *Proceedings of the 26th Conference of the CIRA* (Quebec: Université Laval, 1989).

21.   Gindin, "Breaking Away," p. 81.

22.   Gindin, "Breaking Away," p. 73.

23.   This switch in strategy is perhaps most evident in the case of GM where management was confronted by the stark contrast between, on the one hand, the production engineering and management problems they had encountered with the "automation solution" in the extraordinarily expensive showcases of advanced robotics and automation such as the Orion and Hamtramck assembly

plants that GM had built in the early 1980s, and, on the other hand, by the astounding productivity and quality record of the NUMMI (GM/Toyota) plant in California, whose success was clearly not a function of using advanced technology.

24. Holmes, "The globalization of production and Canada's mature industries," Table 2.

25. A. Mair, R. Florida and M. Kenney, "The new geography of automobile production: Japanese transplants in North America," *Economic Geography* 64/4 (1988).

26. C. Howes, "The Future is Now and It's All Going Wrong: Automotive Restructuring and the Cost of Maturity," (Conference on Labour Market Segmentation, University of Notre Dame, 1988).

27. S. Herzenberg, "Whither social unionism? Labor-management relations in the U.S. and Canadian auto industries" (mimeograph, U.S. Bureau of Labor, Washington D.C., 1990).

28. Union coverage in the American IPS dropped from well over 50 percent in 1975 to less than a quarter by the late 1980s and by 1988 all but a handful of the 25 largest independent parts firms had at least one non-union plant and no major auto-parts segment was entirely organized. By contrast, union coverage in the Canadian parts sector has remained at over 70 percent, few of the major parts suppliers have succeeded in establishing non-union plants and a relatively uniform wage and benefit pattern between the major suppliers has been maintained. Coupled with a steadily appreciating Canadian dollar during the late 1980s, this has created serious problems for the Canadian parts industry.

29. J. Womack, D. Jones and D. Roos, *The Machine That Changed the World* (NY: Rawson Associates, 1990), p. 83.

30. Similarly, Diamond-Star and the Mazda plant at Flat Rock, Michigan became the demonstration sites for Chrysler and Ford respectively.

31. For example, the 1987 contracts guaranteed a fixed number of skilled and non-skilled jobs in each bargaining unit. During the life of the 1987 contract it became apparent that there was a massive loophole in the contract which still allowed companies to close plants in order to adjust volumes to market conditions. This led to considerable unrest within the rank and file, particularly in the case of GM and Chrysler when in 1989 the companies even idled plants which had embraced the new work rules. This became a major issue in the 1990 contract renewal talks.

32. Whipsawing involves management playing-off one plant against another in a competition to secure new work or protect existing jobs. It is precisely the existence of the decentralized and localized organization of collective bargaining in North America that, once the institutional mechanisms that were built into pattern bargaining began to break down, has facilitated whipsawing during the 1980s.

33. For descriptions of such practices see S. Wood, "Between Fordism and flexibili-
     ty?: the case of the U.S. automobile industry," in R. Hyman and W. Streeck
     (eds.), *New Technology and Industrial Relations* (Oxford: Basil Blackwell,
     1988), pp. 101-127; M. Parker and J. Slaughter, *Choosing Sides: The UAW
     and the Team Concept*, (Boston: South End Press, 1988); and B. Dankbaar,
     "Technical change and industrial relations: theoretical reflections on changes in
     the automobile industry," *Economic and Industrial Democracy*, 10 (1989).

34. Canadian Auto Workers, "Drawing lines on the team concept: the CAW state-
     ment on the reorganization of work," *Our Times*, December 1989, p. 22.

35. L. Turner, *Are Labor-Management Partnerships for Competitiveness
     Possible in America: The U.S. Auto Industry Examined,* BRIE Working Paper
     #36, University of California, Berkeley, 1988, p. 9.

36. Turner, *Are Labor-Management Partnerships for Competitiveness Possible
     in America*, p. 2. Note that the team concept as it has been developed in the
     United States is distinct from the notion of "team work" in Japan and has little
     to do with union-promoted concepts of "skilled group work" seen in Germany
     or Sweden.

37. It should also be noted that although wholeheartedly endorsed by the
     International leadership, jointness has not been completely accepted by the rank
     and file in the UAW-U.S., as evidenced by the challenge mounted to the
     International leadership by the dissident New Directions movement. See M.
     Massing, "Detroit's strange bedfellows," *New York Times Magazine*, February
     7, 1988 and various issues of *Labor Notes*. Given the union leadership's
     endorsement of team work and jointness, the New Directions movement is
     forced to adopt a strongly defensive position with respect to new work practices
     which, in general, it rejects outright. Because of the different position taken by
     the Canadian leadership, the CAW has taken a more proactive position which
     does not reject new work practices outright but rather seeks to shape them to
     reflect labour's interests rather than simply the interests of management.

38. Parker and Slaughter, *Choosing Sides*, p. 6.

39. C. Brown and M. Reich, "When does union-management co-operation work? A
     look at NUMMI and GM-Van Nuys," *California Management Review*, 31(4),
     1989 and Turner, *Are Labor-Management Partnerships for Competitiveness
     Possible*.

40. This point has caused much concern and apprehension to the Canadian union
     over the introduction of programs designed to reorganize the workplace and
     foster jointness. The CAW has argued that "...the new management agenda is a
     sophisticated drive to combine ideological pressures on working people with
     new structures in the workplace to dramatically change both the way workers
     think and the way unions respond. More specifically, the objective is to replace
     worker solidarity with total identification with the goals of the company," CAW,
     "Drawing lines on the team concept," p. 23.

41.   Holmes, "From uniformity to diversity."

42.   A similar situation in some American plants (for example, General Motors' Lansing and Lordstown assembly plants) again serves to emphasize the astounding degree of diversity that has developed at the plant level. See Turner, *Are Labor-Management Partnerships for Competitiveness Possible.*

43.   For details see Holmes, "From uniformity to diversity."

44.   CAW, "Drawing lines on the team concept." This move is reminiscent of the development of the "No Concessions" campaign of the early 1980s which also attempted to develop an alternative proactive stance rather than simply a defensive reaction to management demands. It should also be noted that the unanimous adoption of the Statement by the Special Council meeting masked some deep divisions within the union over the issue—the Quebec Council has a much less critical view of developments in the U.S.

45.   See the interview with Bob White in P. Kumar and D. Ryan (eds.), *The Canadian Union Movement in the 1980s: Perspectives From Union Leaders,* Research and Current Issues Series No. 53 (Kingston: Industrial Relations Centre, Queen's University, 1988) and the CAW's statement on the reorganization of work in *Our Times,* December 1989, for a further elaboration of the CAW's position on jointness.

46.   Gindin, "Breaking Away."

47.   For example, whereas a few years ago the charge of "being in bed with management" would have been the kiss of death for local union officials, in 1990 the advertisements for the new GM Saturn car show a UAW member saying "Imagine! Labor in bed with management...it was all worth it."

48.   Yates, "The internal dynamics of union power."

TABLE 8.1

KEY ELEMENTS OF A "WORLD CLASS" LOCAL LABOUR AGREEMENT, GM CANADA

- Joint statement and agreement on commitments and responsibilities

- Reduced number of job classes
    - Skilled: 2-9 Classifications
    - Nonskilled: 1-2 Classifications

- Provision for Work Team (or Work Group) concept

- Flexibility in skilled trades utilization
    - Right to access
    - Right to perform incidental work

- Increase management rights and flexibility re: Overtime requirements

- Simplified seniority group definition

- Improved layoff and recall provisions
    - Limited employee movement at layoff and recall
    - Priority to fill jobs by qualified employees

- Reduction in transfer activity
    - Between departments and shifts
    - Stress maintenance of cost and quality advantages associated with stability

- Reduce restrictive work practices

- Joint union/management commitment
    - Quality
    - Training
    - Operational effectiveness

- Separate progressive discipline procedures for absenteeism and all other shop rules

- Provision for living agreement concept

Source: GM, Canada Memorandum, 1987

Table 8.2

Production Assembler Base Wage Rates, 1975-89

[Base Wage Rates ($ National Currencies)—Assembler 4th Quarter (December) of Each Year]

	United States			Canada		
	GM	Ford	Chrysler	GM	Ford	Chrysler
1975	5.43	5.43	5.39	5.43	5.43	5.39
1976	6.88	6.88	6.84	6.88	6.88	6.84
1977	7.09	7.09	7.08	7.09	7.09	7.08
1978	7.30	7.305	7.29	7.30	7.30	7.29
1979	9.08	9.085	7.53	9.08	9.08	9.07
1980	9.35	9.36	7.75	9.35	9.35	9.07
1981	9.63	9.64	9.07	9.63	9.63	9.07
1982	9.63	9.64	9.07	9.63	9.63	9.34
1983	9.63	9.64	9.34	9.63	9.63	9.62
1984	12.82	12.825	9.62	12.82	12.82	9.62
1985	12.82	12.825	9.62	13.02	13.02	13.01
1986	12.82	12.825	12.81	13.22	13.22	13.21
1987	14.01	14.02	13.19	14.86	14.86	14.85
1988	14.01	14.02	14.00	15.85	15.85	15.84
1989	14.01	14.02	14.00	16.10	16.10	16.09

Source: UAW and CAW Research Departments.

TABLE 8.3
LABOUR COST COMPARISON FOR AUTO INDUSTRY
CANADA VS. UNITED STATES

[AVERAGE LABOUR COST FOR CALENDAR YEAR 1986]

	Canada Cdn$	U.S. U.S.$	Nominal Difference $
Base Pay	13.55	13.35	(0.20)
All Payroll Related Costs	18.92	17.99	(0.93)
Total Benefits	3.79	6.02	2.23
Total Labour Cost/Hour (Nominal)	22.71	24.01	1.30
Exchange	(6.37)		
Total Labour Cost/Hour In U.S. Funds	16.34	24.01	7.67

Source: Internal Memorandum, Big Three Automaker

TABLE 8.4
WAGE-BENEFIT COMPARISON,
NORTH AMERICAN VEHICLE PRODUCERS, 1989

Automaker	1A	1B	2	3	4	5	6
GM CAN.	16.10	1.72	none	none	none	—	—
FORD CAN.	16.10	1.72	none	none	none	—	—
CHRYSLER CAN.	16.09	1.72	none	none	none	—	—
GM U.S.	14.01	1.50	3% QE	50	600	14	35,462
FORD U.S.	14.02	1.50	3% QE	1060	500	13	37,434
CHRYSLER U.S.	14.00	1.50	3% QE	0	500	15	35,371
NUMMI	15.31	1.50	3% QE	none	none	15	36,031
MAZDA	13.63	1.50	none	none	1500	15	32,970
DIAMOND-STAR	11.95	1.50	none	none	none	14	28,038
HONDA	14.55	none	none	1601	1820	17	33,685
TOYOTA	14.23	none	none	none	none	14	29,598
SUBARU-ISUZU	13.94	none	none	none	none	13	28,995
NISSAN	13.95	none	*	**	none	13	32,579

* $1.55/hr paid every 6 months   ** 10.5% of 6 month bonus

1A. Base Wage Rate (Production/Assembler) $/hour (June 1990)
1B. COLA $/hour (June 1990)
 2. Average Bonus (QE = Qualified Earnings) 1989
 3. Profit Sharing 1989
 4. Attendance Award 1989
 5. Paid Holidays/Year
 6. Production Worker Average Pay 1989—assumes 2080 straight hours plus all bonusus and profit sharing as calculated by *Automotive News* from company information

Source: *Automotive News* July 2, 1990 and Table 3

FUTURE CONDITIONAL: WARS OF POSITION IN THE QUEBEC LABOUR MOVEMENT	CARLA Lipsig-Mummé

INTRODUCTION:
THE TWO WAVES OF ECONOMIC RESTRUCTURING

The decade stretching from the middle of the 1970s to the middle of the 1980s marked a watershed for union movements in most high wage economies and neither the Canadian nor the Quebec union movements are exceptions in this regard. The convergence of long-range changes in the international and domestic division of labour, the series of short, sharp shocks which resulted from the stagflation of the 1970s, and the election of conservative governments combined, in Canada as elsewhere, to provoke a first wave of economic restructuring and to end the postwar deal which had defined the parameters of union growth and action for a generation—the ancien régime, if you will. In the new, harsher environment, few national union movements were able to reposition themselves rapidly enough to imprint a union agenda on the new order taking shape. By the early 1980s most were facing a state in fiscal crisis which was either under assault or already captured by the political forces of the New Right. These forces were in alliance with fractions of capital whose dynamism in restructuring employment and the work process was forcing unions on to the defensive at the point of production as well as in the political arena. And in these countries, union movements found themselves losing members. Increasingly they found it difficult to protect working conditions and job security; they found it harder to organize the fragmenting working class; they found it impossible to resist the erosion of the full-time job. They were becoming, in short, the defensive spokesmen for a shrinking labour aristocracy. Alternative social agendas, or *projets de société*, were put on the backburner as the unions struggled simply to maintain the *status quo*.

It is no exaggeration to say that during this first stage of economic and social restructuring, the problem of the restructuring of work and employment moved to centre stage as the cause of union crisis, while the issue of labour's political strategy reentered from the wings as a possible solution.

How did union movements in developed countries face the failure of traditional strategies catalyzed by the first wave of international economic restructuring? Four responses crystallized. First, in countries such as Austria, Australia and the Nordic countries, union peak organizations sought to create or to intensify macro-corporatist relationships, in order to extend their influence over economic management. They chose, in other words, to magnify the control of the political over the economic, or to shift the resolution of private economic problems to the public, political arena. La Fédération des travailleurs et travailleuses du Québec (FTQ) represented an odd variant of this response in the 1970s, as it sought to create a preferential relationship with the Parti Québécois just before its election in 1976 and during its first term in office. Strategically it tried to pursue its double objective—of ensuring its lead over the Confédération des syndicats nationaux (CSN), and of influencing social and industrial policy—without moving into a traditional labourist relationship to the Parti Québécois.

Second, following political or economic defeat of national and symbolic significance, peak union organizations in countries such as the United States, Great Britain and France retreated into fragmentation, depoliticization, and *recentrage*, leaving the task of strategic defense to their national affiliates or even to ad hoc regional groupings. One result was the weakening of the peak council's organizational and political authority. Another was the breakdown of coherent national policy towards the capital offensive, so that division and contradiction came to characterize union response.

Third, in the face of the new environment and lacking or eschewing the corporatist option, some peak councils turned towards structural change and/or new alliances. Centrals like the Canadian Labour Congress allowed or encouraged affiliates to create or reinforce new sites of union authority, and new alliances with popular movements, the better to mobilize a flexible and co-ordinated response to increasing managerial militancy and anti-union policies of the state. The emphasis on structure and alliances seemed to indicate, during this first wave of economic restructuring, that the peak council sought to move from tactical towards strategic responses by broadening and diversifying its actions.

We may call the fourth pattern of national union response strategic paralysis: some union centrals simply continued doing what they had always done, regardless of the fact that it no longer worked. The Centrale de l'enseignement du Québec (CEQ) and the Confédération des syndicats nationaux (CSN) in Quebec fell into this category in the late 1970s. These centrals paid a heavy price in terms of internal cohesion, external influence, and ability to reposition when the second wave of economic restructuring broke.

The gathering of the second wave of economic and social transformation during the middle years of the 1980s struck union movements already destabilized by the end of the ancien régime in industrial relations. It built on and deepened major changes triggered by the first wave: deindustrialization and the mushroom growth of underregulated service sector jobs, the acceptance within union ranks of managerial strategies to marginalize unions on the shopfloor, the generalized deregulation of the labour market. In addition, labour suffered growing polarization between, on the one hand, the unionized and non-unionized populations, and on the other between the three groups within the ranks of the organized: the primary and secondary workers; the public sector employees; and the private sector service workers.

The second wave of economic restructuring also introduced two new elements which were to be of crucial importance to the union movements across the high-wage economies: trade liberalization and the formation of regional trading blocs; and the concomitant weakening of the real sovereignty of national states. In accelerating the integration of continental or pan-continental labour and product markets between unequal national partners, the trading blocs contributed to the reemergence of metropolis-hinterland economic relations within regions. This, in turn, placed cruel pressure on the junior trading partners, whose declining ability to regulate basic economic or social priorities effectively led to a widespread 'legitimation crisis.' In North America, for example, as continental economic integration proceeds, the national states of the junior economic partners exercise ever less real control over their economic and social life. The locus of decision-making is migrating to the metropolis. How realistic is it for unions to continue to target the Canadian state as the arena for defending gains and extending social and economic democracy?

In each of the three regional trading blocs, union movements have been forced to reexamine structure, affiliation, alliances and strategic targets, in the light of these developments.[1] In the first phase, national union movements in the high-wage countries were grappling with basically the same global economic changes everywhere, and they articulated four types of response, as discussed above. In the second phase, a process of differentiation became evident. Within each trading bloc the situation of the union movement in the dominant economy begins to diverge from that of unions in the weaker, more reactive economies. For example, at the same time as workers—organized or not—in the several countries grouped within the North American trading bloc are being made to compete with each other for manufacturing jobs, the need for effective, cross-border union alliances is greater than ever. Together the two major changes associated with the second wave of economic restructuring—the emergence of regional trading blocs and the weakening of the national state—have converged to pressure national union movements to take stock of their alliances, their structures and their arenas of intervention.

The Quebec labour movement has found it particularly difficult to adjust to the emerging political and economic realities of the second wave of economic restructuring, and this, in itself, is surprising. The strategic paralysis which has characterized the movement as a whole (if not all its components) over the recent years is unexpected, because Quebec labour had shown itself to be capable of enormous, rapid, comprehensive strategic repositioning from the mid1950s through the 1970s.

This chapter asks two questions: First, why has Quebec labour (which, in making the union movement the voice of a class and a generation during the 1960s and 1970s, articulated the boldest vision of unionism as a socializing and individually emancipating force that North America had seen since World War II) been unable to develop a viable and comprehensive strategy for survival and assertion *as a working class movement* in the emerging social order of the 1990s? I will be arguing that this failure is the fruit of a disastrous merger between elements of the unions' political tradition that were lost from sight or underestimated during the 1960s and 1970s. Among these, the moral legitimation of union pluralism and raiding, the historic failure to intervene effectively in electoral politics, internal divisions and divided loyalties, and schizophrenia towards the state, bulk large. At many critical historical junctures in Quebec life, national or Québécois identity and organizational loyalty have taken primacy over—or been equated to—class identity, and at these same junctures the Quebec union movement has hesitated and then retreated from taking leadership in the nationalist movement.[2] That hesitation has historic roots and is a principal source of strategic paralysis, both of which will be discussed below. Leadership of the nationalist coalition would have permitted the unions to imbue nationalism, which has been Quebec's chief source of internal cohesion from time immemorial, with a working class agenda. In 1988, for example, a working class nationalist agenda, distinguishing itself from the entrepreneurial nationalism of Québec Inc., would have opposed the Free Trade Agreement more effectively, and felt free to construct alliances with unions and community organizations elsewhere on the continent.[3] In the spring of 1990, too, when it was again possible for the union movement to take the leadership of renascent *indépendantisme*, the centrals hesitated, played with the idea of a labour manifesto, and ended by hitching their star to the conservative nationalism of Lucien Bouchard. This hesitancy remains to be explained.

The second question this chapter addresses is future strategies. Given the reemergence and fusion of exhausted and dangerous political traditions, given the refusal of all the three centrals since the failure of constitutional negotiations to advance a working class program, given, in short, the denial of politics, to what sources of renewal, re-enforcement and autonomy can Quebec labour look in the coming era of continental economic integration?

THE ROOTS OF STRATEGIC PARALYSIS

We in Canada have come to take for granted that Quebec is in most important ways a separate society. The union movement is assumed, by extension, to be separate from the Canadian labour movement as well, representing an isolated, internally cohesive and doubly exploited francophone working class. Historically, however, Quebec labour has not been free of the influence of labour ideologies which competed in Europe and the rest of North America, nor has it been homogeneous. Instead Quebec labour, before the Quiet Revolution, was a terrain on which three opposing views of the relation of unions to the state struggled for control: the Gomperism of North American craft unions; the corporatist anti-electoralism of confessional unionism, and the particular brand of labour social democracy which arose in the American CIO and which we may call Reutherism. Post-1960, the two American traditions merged within the FTQ. The social corporatism which had characterized the Confédération des travailleurs catholiques du Canada (CTCC) and the Corporation des instituteurs catholiques (CIC) during the Duplessis era merged with, and was transformed by, Marxist syndicalism, with which it shared the denial of the importance of direct union influence over the state. In relation to this last point, it is perhaps ironic that the most conservative of trade union centrals was to become host and staging ground for the most revolutionary trade union vision.[4] But this mosaic of competing ideologies, playing out their competition and transformation against the backdrop of the disintegration of the once tightly integrated and cohesive Catholic order, is in some ways symbolic and in some ways revealing of the interplay of institutional and ideological forces which have made the modernization of Quebec labour and society so complex.

Until the late 1950s the cohesion of Quebec was ensured by a dense network of social, linguistic and politically separate institutions presided over by the Catholic Church, its dependent bourgeoisie, and a pre-modern nationalist provincial state.[5] Within that network, the confessional unions associated with the CTCC (whose modern name is the Confédération des syndicats nationaux) and with the CIC (modern name: Centrale de l'enseignement du Québec) and community organizations, or *groupes populaires,* were seen, and saw themselves, as sharing the same vocation, as being part of the same social movement and sharing the same wellsprings in the European corporatism of the pre-World War II years.

As I have argued elsewhere, in the interwar years the tension between autonomy and integration in rapidly industrializing, externally dependent Quebec, had led to the division of the labour movement initially into two competing union peak organizations; divided along religious lines, as well as in their analysis of power relations in society, their interpretation of the parameters of unionism's role, and, finally, over the nature and objectives of union political action.[6] The Trades and Labour Congress (TLC) regrouped Quebec affiliates of craft unions which formed the American Federation of Labour: early branch-plant unionism in the Gomperist mold. In Quebec as in the United States they did not refuse all political action, but viewed it as a defensive necessity occasionally brought about by the union's weakness at the bargaining table. Political action was therefore seen to be instrumental, sporadic, defensive and non-partisan.[7] And although in the U.S. Gomperism would come to take on a jingoistic nationalism, in Quebec and English Canada the TLC was staunchly, if disingenuously, internationalist.

The Confédération des travailleurs catholiques du Canada (the CTCC, who would change its name to the CSN by dropping the Catholic designation in 1964), was founded under the Church's aegis in 1921, explicitly to counter the 'bolshevik' influence that the Church supposed the Trades and Labour Congress represented.[8] As the first, early modern, confederation of industrial unions in Canada, the CTCC grew rapidly during the 1920s when craft unions everywhere in North America were declining.[9] Its social corporatist ideology meant limiting the union to defensive negotiations in order to ensure that workers received 'decent' family wages; it meant that women's work outside the home was an indicator of individual, family and societal failure. Above all, unions were to be *sectoral* interest groups, charged with the defense of only one area of workers' lives within the larger web of confessional social institutions.

The social corporatism which reduced unions to sectoral and defensive representatives of workers also meant recognizing the legitimacy of private profit, the primacy of employers' rights, and the moral responsibilities of the state, which was seen to be a powerful, potentially friendly protector. The political operationalization of this vision of the union's role was quite different from the abstention or instrumental alliances that alternated in the TLC's behaviour, as well as from the range of political strategies followed by nonconfessional union movements in the 1920s and 1930s in Europe and North America. But it had much in common with the political behaviour of Catholic unions in Belgium, France and Portugal at the time. One of the most important elements of commonality was the socialization of union members into the vision of the union as a social movement operating—in conjunction with a network of community organizations like Jeunesse ouvrière catholique and Jeunesse étudiante catholique—within the larger societal movement to recatholicize capitalist society. This equation of the union with an evangelical social movement has undergone many transmutations in terms of its vision of the just society (its *projet de société*), but it remains a constant thread in the modern practice of the postconfessional centrals, the CSN and the CEQ. As these centrals radicalized their program in the late 1960s, it provided them with both the organizational tradition and internal structures to mobilize their members in a new, anticapitalist struggle.

From its inception in 1921 the CTCC had indulged in a modest statism: it believed the state had a role to play in protecting the vulnerable and it lobbied for legislation leading to the establishment of minimum conditions for all workers.[10] But if social corporatism allowed for lobbying and exerting moral pressure on policy makers, it emphatically excluded the definition of opposing class interests, the articulation of an autonomous union political agenda and alliance with a political party. Unions, as sectoral defense organizations under the tutelage of the Church, were not meant to advance a class-based vision of the just society or to engage in political struggles to control the state. In this formulation, unions could petition the state for needed protection, but were not to organize active, collective, opposition to it. They might act as the conscience of the state, might encourage it to respond to their needs by shaming it morally, but it was outside their domain to negotiate with it from a position of strength.

During the interwar years, the confessional reading of the state's responsibilities and the limits to union political action crystallized within the CTCC as a three-part political *modus operandi*. On the one hand, a mistrust of the state and of electoral politics ('L'Etat, c'est sale et salissant') was translated into the belief that the union could only defend its members properly if it remained institutionally independent of all electoral political organizations, whether in office or in opposition. (The CTCC's, and then the CSN's, constitution explicitly forbids affiliation to a political party.) On the other hand, a subservient and essentially cap-in-hand attitude towards the power-brokers of state social policy, was consonant with the hierarchical vision of society advanced by social corporatism. But though the union had a limited, collective bargaining and moral arbiter role to play in defending the interests of its members, its participation in a larger confessional social movement justified and lessened the negative effects of these sectoral constraints.

The truly fundamental ideological transformations the CTCC undertook as it evolved from a corporatist and confessional to a Marxist-syndicalist postconfessional organization in the 1960s and 1970s have been discussed elsewhere.[11] But what is striking is that while the radicalization of the CSN led to the scrapping of the second (or corporatist) part of the CTCC's political tradition, both the first part and a portion of the third have remained extraordinarily tenacious. For example, during the Free Trade election in 1988 the CSN's Executive argued passionately and successfully against those of its own members who proposed a temporary, non-structural alliance with the NDP to defeat free trade. The reasons given were redolent of the language of the CTCC in the late 1920s: It is not a union's role to dictate to its members how to vote, we are only here to bargain collectively, to venture into politics would be to intervene in the sphere of our members' private choices, and the moment we support a party, we surrender our autonomy. As a corollary, this continued refusal to seek direct political influence over state policy permits the CSN to continue to employ a 'purer-than-thou' approach to the government, an orientation which was the final component of the CTCC's original political tradition in its social corporatist period.

The Church was also instrumental in the 1930s in founding the Corporation des instituteurs catholiques (CIC), a professional corporation of teachers which would become the CEQ. Caught between its legal status and the professional identity of its members on the one hand, and the need to take trade union action to protect that professional status on the other, the CIC began behaving like a union sporadically in the 1940s, but did not emerge in public consciousness as a union central until the mid-1960s.[12]

By the late 1940s the two streams of Gomperist, branch plant unionism (incarnated in the Trades and Labour Congress) and the corporatism of the confessional unions (CTCC and CIC) were joined by a current of social democratic unionism associated with the Canadian Congress of Labour (CCL). Drawing their strength from heavy industry and textiles, by the mid-1950s its Quebec affiliates had established a reputation for unparalleled militancy and introduced social democratic options for union political action to the province.[13] In 1954-55 they advocated the founding of a labour party, thereby clearly drawing the lines between their orientation to labour in politics and that of their confessional and Gomperist rivals.

It is not too fanciful to suggest that during the 1920s and 1930s the competition between the TLC and CTCC reflected the Catholic offensive against both the American mode of industrialization and worker response to capitalist class relations. From this time on, union pluralism—the legitimation of raiding and the development of loyalty to a particular union central rather than to the union movement as a whole—became an unquestioned norm in Quebec labour practice. It might also be added that during the 1940s and the 1950s the arrival of the CCL introduced to Quebec the sort of social-democratic unionism that had long been prevalent in the North European economies and had taken the leadership in the U.S. and English Canada from the mid-1930s onwards. North American social democratic unionism remained a rallying place, until the Cold War, for the numerous forms of revolutionary unionism which had been forced to the margins by the hegemony of Gomperism. It is also important to stress, however, that the time span between social democratic unionism's introduction in Quebec and the purging of revolutionary members in the U.S. by its parent organization was very short indeed: the five years following the end of World War II. During the Cold War U.S. union social democracy underwent what I have called its 'Reutherization'. A continued belief in the necessity for effective, sophisticated, union political influence in electoral politics and social policy formation was combined with the purging of revolutionary elements who might question the capitalist basis of that policy. As well there was a conscious choice not to found a labour party, but to limit unionism's political presence to a sectoral pressure group within a larger, more heterogeneous progressive party. The political weakness of the AFL-CIO today is the logical result of that component of Reutherism which refused to allow the labour movement to attempt to transform the Democratic Party into a labour party in the 1950s, and is partly responsible for the failure of labour to obtain labour law reform in the U.S. today.

During *la grande noirceur* of the Duplessis 1950s, the TLC and the CCL affiliates merged to form the Fédération des travailleurs du Québec (FTQ). Gomperism and social democracy jockeyed for position for the first decade, but it had become clear by the beginning of the 1960s that the FTQ would give priority to the development of effective political influence over government social and labour policy. The confessional centrals (soon to be renamed the CSN and the CEQ), on the other hand, were pushed painfully away from corporatism by the brutality of Duplessiste labour relations in a series of watershed strikes. They moved towards a sporadic, tactical rapprochement with the unions that would found the FTQ.[14] The CSN in particular, would go on to play a pivotal role in the modernizing coalition which would lead the Quiet Revolution. But in the late 1950s the worker-priest—at once community activist, father-figure, and union director—typified the difficult transition and permitted the deconfessionalizing unions to retain their link to the deconfessionalizing community organizations with whom they shared past tradition and world views.

In the late 1950s and early 1960s, the late-breaking wave of society-wide modernization which swept Quebec dislodged the Church and secularized most of the institutions of community life.[15] During the heady years of the Quiet Revolution which followed (1960-1966), the Church withdrew from its overt role in most areas of civil society (except for education), ceding to the provincial state the task of modernization and the role of arbiter of newly secular civil society.

The Quebec economy was entering its second decade of unbroken growth. In large measure, American investment had stimulated this growth, which had two pertinent results. First, the Quebec state was given the financial margin to accomplish the modernization which had been delayed since the Second World War, and was now taking on all the allure of a national *projet de société*. Second, foreign investment remained so central to growth in all three economic sectors that sooner or later any policy of modernization would have to come to terms with the problem of external economic dependence.[16] 'Progressive statism', in combination with a moderate and diffuse nationalism, defined the mainstream mode of modernization in the 1960s.

The growth of the state triggered important shifts in the composition of the labour force. Between 1961 and 1969, direct and indirect employment by the state grew by 35 percent.[17] This tertiarization of the labour force had a massive impact on the unions. Roughly 175,000 new unionists from the public and parapublic sectors entered the ranks of organized labour between 1960 and 1970, coming to represent over one-third of all union members. They did not, however, spread their affiliation evenly, with the largest group going to the CSN. The CEQ multiplied its membership five-fold between 1959 and 1967, reflecting both the nationalization of education and the beginning of its move to broaden out into an industrial confederation of all workers in the education industry.

The FTQ fared less well during the Quiet Revolution. Tarred with the brush of American domination, on the defensive because of its subordination to the CLC, it did not have the structural freedom, the financial resources or the authentically Québécois social identity to operate as a central in its own right and in the eyes of the working class.[18] Although it had been the largest of the centrals at the beginning of the decade, by the end the CSN was almost its equal in membership. The FTQ gained only 10,000 new members during the 1960s, and most of these were blue-collar workers in the sub-central levels of government.[19]

Thus we may speak about a process of union modernization during the Quiet Revolution, effected within the context of an all-embracing national project. Yet the union centrals, and in particular the CEQ and the CSN, could not fail to recognize that the expansion of the state made the politicization of union industrial policy unavoidable. As strike after strike pitted the centrals against the Liberal government, the unions found themselves torn between collaboration in the national project and rejection of its implications for the new working class.

In a very real way the national question paralyzed the unions' political intervention during the Quiet Revolution.[20] The seductive progressive nationalism of the Liberals had made it easy for the government to foster competition among the unions, and to make the prospect of opposition not only difficult but somehow disloyal. But in 1966 the Liberals were defeated and the Quiet Revolution ground to a halt. Under the less than benign auspices of their conservative successors, neo-nationalism split into three streams. In the radicalizing days between 1968 and 1972, one current continued the orientation of the Quiet Revolution Liberals: federalist, moderately nationalist, and committed to welfare-capitalist modernization. A second current, equally we fare capitalist but with a minority voice of social democrats within, was more concerned with cultural sovereignty than with the hard problems of external economic dependence *vis-à-vis* the U.S. This was the core of the Parti Québécois. The third current, brought home to Quebec by the international student upheavals of 1968, was an eclectic mix of Marxist theories of under-development, national liberation, and distrust of state power—whoever was exercising it. This last was developed in a host of 'groupuscules' associated with Marxism-Leninism or with several of the Trotskyisms, and took full form within the unions as a new amalgam best termed Marxist syndicalism. It found a sympathetic hearing within the postconfessional CSN and CEQ, and in the years after 1968 would influence—and destabilize—organizational practices and structures.[21] The FTQ leadership, on the other hand, very rapidly con-tained the factional influence of the groupuscules on central procedures, col-lective bargaining decisions and leadership, but was prepared, for a brief few years, to borrow its language and its analysis of social power to mobilize mem-bers.[22] Taking root in the *groupes populaires* and the student movement as well as the union movement, Marxist syndicalism was at once a class, ethnic, and generational statement. As articulated in the unions, it was based on a certain number of postulates.[23] First, Quebec was defined as an externally dependent economic colony dominated by American capitalist interests. It was repeatedly described in the language of the political economy of underdevel-opment, and was likened to a hinterland of the American metropolis. Capitalism spoke English, but it was the English both of the U.S. and of its Canadian lackeys. Francophones were thus doubly exploited: as workers, and as a dispossessed nation. Second, the union movement came to see itself as the authentic and *leading* political representative of all the interests of the francophone working class, and national liberation was equated with class struggle. Whether this was as vanguard or as spokesperson would become a source of unceasing internal strife within the CSN and the CEQ in the 1970s. But it is at once an odd modernization of the sense of mission which had char-acterized Catholic labour ideology in its social corporatist heyday, and pro-vides an excuse for self-righteous raiding of other, less progressive unions. Third, other, more issue-specific groups, like the *groupes populaires* operat-ing in the domains of debt-counselling, tenants' rights, consumers' rights, housing co-ops, media watch, adult education, women's rights, and food co-ops, were meant to position themselves under the unions' wing. Fourth, the unions came to see themselves as a substitute for a revolutionary party, regrouping the broad coalition of community forces and challenging the power of the state through mass education, mass mobilization and extraparliamentary confrontation. State power might be challenged from *outside* the bourgeois system, by putting a quarter of a million demonstrators on Parliament Hill for example, but unions were neither to compromise themselves by attempting to lobby within the system, nor to corrupt their mission by consenting to share in governance.

Strong dreams, these, and worthy of the maximalist days of post-1968. The problem was that although the union centrals (who shared the Marxist syndicalist strategy with varying degrees of commitment) were able to act as a prism for the cultural challenge to capitalist society that young workers and students were mounting everywhere in these years, and were able to mobilize noteworthy and truly enormous street confrontations with the state between 1968 and 1972, mass mobilization neither produced transformative results in collective bargaining nor permitted the long-term political implementation of the unions' own agenda for social change. At best, during their syndicalist phase, the unions were able to block or modify offensive legislation, to introduce equity issues into collective bargaining, to ameliorate legislation concerning women's work, or to up the stakes sufficiently in a private sector industrial conflict so that the state stepped in. But the unions' own visions of an alternative society never came near to being seriously implemented. For syndicalism, in its modern or historic guises, never developed the strategies to move beyond mass mobilization to the realization of a union agenda. It had been conceived in the language of insurrection, and both the language and tactics were well suited to the all-out confrontations of 1968-1972. We can understand its adoption—but how to explain its longevity and institutionalization by Quebec labour throughout the 1970s and 1980s, when it had become clear that neither the state nor capitalism could be seriously destabilized from without?

Thus we arrive at the watershed year of 1972, when Marxist syndicalism reached its apogee, and the first of the modern critical junctures in Quebec labour's political realignment began.

CRITICAL HISTORICAL JUNCTURES: FROM THE FIRST TO THE SECOND WAVE OF ECONOMIC RESTRUCTURING

There are times in the lives of trade unions, as there are in most social movements, when the decisions that need to be taken are heavy with consequence, heavier than they would ordinarily be. These critical historical junctures[24] make or break the union, determine its orientations for the middle distance, decide how much faith members will continue to invest in it, determine its future alliances and its agenda. Unions can sometimes provoke a critical juncture, but they are rarely in control of its outcome. More often, capital or the state orchestrates these watersheds.

Once within a critical historical juncture, unions are rarely able to react strategically, if strategy entails a co-ordinated response over an extended period to a problem or series of problems the union recognizes as of major importance. More often, unions respond defensively and tactically, like urban guerillas protecting their base while inflicting as much damage as possible on an enemy they do not believe they can defeat.

The period of 1972 to 1976 was one such critical juncture for the Quebec labour movement. In Quebec, the first wave of economic restructuring ended two decades of growth and rapid modernization and combined the emergence of stubbornly high rates of unemployment with stalled economic growth and the refinement of a flexible, effective government strategy for containing the impact of union gains in the public sector on private sector collective bargaining. Coming after a decade of heady economic and social modernization which the society as a whole had experienced as a kind of nationalist Prague spring, the economic developments associated with the crisis of the early 1970s both produced a revolution of rising but blocked expectations which pushed the union movement to test the limits of what syndicalism could achieve, and prepared the terrain for the ascent of the Parti Québécois.

From the middle of the Quiet Revolution until the early 1970s a succession of provincial governments had defined the public sector as the pivot of economic growth, and its wage settlements came to be the barometer by which the private sector measured what it would have to concede. At the same time, successive provincial governments refined a standardized wage policy for the public and parapublic sectors, and erected an imposing network of bureaucratic structures to handle negotiations with the unions concerned.

The government's standardized wage policy in the public sector stimulated a parallel movement towards centralization within the public sector unions. In 1971 the three principal centrals—the CSN, the CEQ and the FTQ—formed a Common Front to bargain with the government. The Common Front—which continued to function until the PQ decentralized negotiations in an effort to destroy interunion solidarity after 1981—quickly became a *de facto* alternative structure to the union centrals themselves, pushing a wedge between private sector and public sector workers organized into the same central. In the FTQ, only ten percent of whose membership was involved in the

Common Front, the linking of that ten percent to other public sector unions affiliated to rival centrals did not pose a serious organizational problem. Since 100 percent of the CEQ's membership was employed in the public sector, the problem did not arise there either. In the CSN, however, where approximately 40 percent of members were employed in the public sector, the tension between the needs of the private sector workers (who were organizationally fragmented) and those of the public sector workers (whose involvement in the Common Front absorbed more and more of the CSN's energies and resources) exploded during 1972. The catalyst was a strike.

In the spring of 1972, Common Front negotiations with the Liberal government broke down. The 210,000 members of the Common Front were drawn from all three union centrals as well as a number of independent unions. In a very real way these workers typified the new Québécois working class—secular, anticapitalist, antiauthoritarian, nationalist and individualistic, with feminists playing an emerging, important role.[25]

Following the breakdown of talks, the Common Front workers walked out, ignoring injunctions.[26] Although no real prior planning had been undertaken, the strike quickly came to be seen as a general strike, and was joined, spontaneously, by a surprising array of private sector and even federal employees. In its brief existence—several days—the general strike triggered such actions as the capture of radio stations in several small cities and the broadcasting of union news, the closing of roads to outlying communities, and the closing of major Quebec ports by the longshoremen. Economic life was paralyzed without incurring, it seems, the hostility of the public. But since this was North America, this spontaneous brush fire of worker rebellion stimulated unreal hopes: syndicalist dreams of the worker uprising which would topple the state in one convulsive heave. As one of its chief organizers observed in the mid-1980s, comparing the confrontation with the Liberals in 1972 with the PQ attack on the public sector unions in 1982: "We were completely unprepared then [in 1972]. Taken by surprise. We did not understand the enormity of what we had before us and had made no preparation."[27]

During its first week the Common Front general strike was broken by back-to-work legislation introduced by the Liberals and supported by the Parti Québécois. Soon thereafter, the presidents of the CSN, FTQ, and CEQ—Marcel Pepin, Louis Laberge and Yvon Charbonneau—were sent to jail for contempt of court in leading an 'illegal' strike.[28] It would be hard to overestimate the impact of the Common Front strike of 1972 on subsequent union strategies. In the light of its failure, the centrals drew two different conclusions. The CSN and the CEQ, watching the supposedly pro-union PQ, which touted its *préjugé favorable aux travailleurs* while supporting antiunion legislation, concluded that any alliance with a mainstream political party, no matter how deep the shared commitment to independence, could not but lead to the loss of union autonomy and radicalism. The denial of politics, or, as it is fetchingly called in Quebec, trade union autonomy, continued to dominate strategies for these two centrals.

The CSN paid the highest of prices for its continued attachment to a strategy whose limits had been reached during the Common Front strike. Immediately following the breaking of the strike in 1972, it suffered the secession of approximately 60,000 of its members—approximately one-fourth of its total membership.[29] Some 30,000 of the secessionists, grouped in the stagnant manufacturing industries such as textiles, footwear and clothing, left in protest over what they saw as their poor-relation status within the CSN, which they perceived to be increasingly dominated by its public sector components. They also broke away because they could not recognize themselves in the central's increasingly Marxist discourse.[30] They then went on to form the Confédération des syndicats démocratiques (CSD), which continues to exist to this day, never having grown—a kind of pariah in the union community. Its political abstentionism, conceived in opposition to the syndicalism of its parent CSN, verges on the absolute.

Another 30,000 members seceded from the CSN in 1972 and 1973, but this time to form the independent Syndicat des fonctionnaires de la province du Québec.[31] In the ten years following 1972, the CSN would lose the majority of its white collar and professional public sector employees, as well as almost all its manufacturing sector, to become a peak organization overwhelmingly representing blue-collar public employees, mainly in the health sector. The disquieting growth of independent unions in Quebec—now between 25 and 30 percent of the total—springs from this time and from the hemorrhaging of the CSN.

The CEQ, on the other hand, followed the same logic and arrived at the same conclusions as the CSN, but did not suffer secession and division. Throughout the 1970s it continued a maximalist discourse, and institutionalized its schizophrenia towards politics and the state. It denounced, on the one hand, any collaboration with the bourgeois state in the form of joint or consultative committees, and was unsparing in its formal criticism of one of its vice-presidents, Guy Chevrette, when he was elected to the National Assembly for the PQ. On the other hand, the vast majority of CEQ members voted PQ. Many worked for the PQ in its electoral campaign and ran for office within the party.[32]

The fragmentation of the CSN triggered a return to raiding with the FTQ.[33] The FTQ, however, had drawn quite different lessons from the failure of the 1972 Common Front strike than had the CSN and the CEQ. To some degree, it returned to its own strategic tradition, from which it had been lured between 1968 and 1972.

It will be remembered that the industrial unions which merged into the FTQ in 1957 had pushed for the idea of a labour party as late as 1955. In other words they had remained within the trajectory of classical social democracy for a number of years after the CIO in the U.S. had rejected the idea of forming a labour party in favour of operating as a pressure group within the Democratic Party—what I have called Reutherism. The march of the Parti Québécois towards office, however, coupled with the emergence of Jean Gérin-Lajoie of the Steelworkers as an articulate and powerful spokesman for its interests within FTQ ranks, the continued marginality of the NDP in Quebec and the failure of Marxist syndicalism in 1972, combined to lead the FTQ towards Reutherism. This seemed to be an excellent way of creating a preferential relationship with the PQ that would bring it the benefits the CSN had earlier enjoyed from the Liberals, without seeming to make the PQ over into a labour party, a transformation the FTQ feared would endanger the nationalist and popular coalition meant to bring the PQ to office. From 1973 on the FTQ sought to develop increasingly close links to the Parti Québécois, but never sought structural influence or control.

For the FTQ the 1972 Common Front strike, coupled with the damage the CSN inflicted on it immediately thereafter through raiding and the Cliche Commission, revealed the dangers of inter-union collaboration and the romantic limits of Marxist syndicalism. Links to the PQ seemed to offer the FTQ the possibility of legislative protection against raiding and an opportunity for bettering labour legislation in areas such as health and safety and minimum wages. The FTQ tradition of social unionism was not hostile to the state because it *was* the state. In the wake of 1972, the union returned to this tradition, to distinguishing between friendly and unfriendly governments. It, of course, preferred to do business with a friendly party in power, more so if that party felt beholden to the FTQ.

The links the FTQ developed to the PQ during the 1973-76 period were to be crucial in orienting labour's political action for the following fifteen years. They began and remained non-structural, but FTQ members (like CSN and CEQ members) voted massively for the PQ, staffed its political machine, and financed its campaigns. In developing links with the PQ before it formed the government in 1976, the FTQ hoped to reinforce the national movement, to win an inside track *vis-à-vis* its union rivals, and to establish a channel of influence. But it did not seek to transform the PQ into a labour party. It assumed that it could combine fervent participation in a nationalist party whose objectives were defined by its bourgeois leadership, with the pursuit of social democratic goals. The FTQ's political schizophrenia was, therefore, of a different sort than the CSN's and CEQ's: it was content to imagine a labour party where only the PQ existed.

The FTQ gained much from its inside relationship to the PQ over its nine years in office, particularly through Labour Code reform. It did not, however, gain political power. The FTQ was to learn in the 1980s, as the economic crisis settled in and the second wave of restructuring shook the Quebec state, that the PQ entertained no sense of responsibility to the union movement. The FTQ's nationalist commitment and its social democracy were on a collision course.

From the critical historical juncture of the 1972-1976 years to the watershed of the second economic restructuring (1982-83), the Quebec union movement began to return to its historic separation into two streams. The formerly Catholic centrals, the CSN and the CEQ, remained syndicalist long after syndicalism had failed. The FTQ returned to Reutherism. In adapting Reutherism to the Quebec context, the FTQ thought it possible to combine labourism with bourgeois nationalism without seeming to control the political party that was its vehicle. In many ways, the failure to turn the PQ into a labour party before it formed the government must be laid at the door of the FTQ.

In 1982, after six years in power, after losing the referendum, the PQ awoke to the second wave of economic restructuring. Typically, for a party which assumed the state represented the whole of civil society, it responded first neither to unemployment nor to deindustrialization but to the crisis of its own deficit.

The PQ proposed to its 350,000 employees that they voluntarily accept wage cuts of up to 19.6 percent. Not surprisingly, the unions refused, thus entering into the next critical historical juncture from which they would emerge profoundly transformed. The PQ, with its *préjugé favorable aux travailleurs*, launched a campaign of *salissage*, presenting its employees as selfish fat cats whose good conditions were being maintained at the expense of recession-ridden private sector workers. It played the health sector off against education, the CSN against the CEQ. Late in 1982, by special legislation, the public sector lost its right to strike. In March, 1983, the teachers of the CEQ and the CSN, lacking the support of the CSN's health workers who remembered earlier betrayals, and unable to stir the FTQ which had few enough public sector members to be able to make excuses for the PQ, went back to work rather than split apart. Thus ended the Common Fronts and the dream of a radically transformative unionism.

The legislation that forced teachers back to work, Law 111, provided for the loss of three years' seniority for each day on illegal strike, made it illegal to resign or use other pressure tactics for three years after the law was passed, threatened decertification of rebellious unions, and made it illegal for teachers to appeal to the Quebec Charter of Rights against the law. In Quebec's National Assembly, no one spoke for the unions.

It might be argued that syndicalism should have been declared dead after 1972, that only the FTQ had the sense to cut its losses and work for small reformist gains. But what good had its preferential arrangement with the PQ done for its public sector members?

It might also be argued that the strength of revolutionary romanticism was so great within those formerly Catholic centrals, the CSN and the CEQ, that even a decade of stagnation could not convince them to look at politics as a possible way out of their *cul-de-sac*. Some voice in the National Assembly, speaking out against union busting, might have helped in 1983, but they had always declined to elect labour politicians.

Finally, it might be argued that when in the early 1970s the unions decided—by omission or by commission—to allow the avowedly bourgeois but then progressive nationalist PQ to take leadership of Quebec's national project, they were entering booby-trapped terrain. For both the FTQ in its way and the CSN and the CEQ in theirs allowed the PQ to enter into competition with them for the militant commitment of their members. Bourgeois nationalism, rather than working class social democracy, became—or remained?—the lodestone. Both the party and the unions saw themselves as the sole representatives of the population. Failing to act on those parts of their *projet de société* which were clearly different from the PQ's, refusing to enter into competition with the PQ for the definition of nationalism, actively encouraging or passively allowing their members to commit themselves first to the party, the unions were ill-protected when the PQ turned on them in the early 1980s during the second wave of economic restructuring. They were vulnerable in reaction to the state, and paralyzed in relation to the rapidly changing economic environment.

Instead, the unequivocal defeat of 1982-83, with the destruction of interunion collaboration in its last stronghold, the public sector, coupled as it was with a fiscal crisis, a tidal wave of deindustrialization and the expansion of underregulated privatization, forced these centrals to reexamine their strategies. Because both collectively and individually the centrals found themselves unable to move beyond certain of the strategic traditions that had historically bound their interaction as well as their reaction to both state and capital, the result was the disintegration of Quebec labour as a movement. Failing to realign *as a movement* after 1983, each of the centrals withdrew into itself to pursue separate and increasingly competitive organizational goals. They would not emerge to find some terrain for unity until the Meech crisis of 1990 brought them together, this time under the aegis of conservative indépendantisme.

Wars of Position

The years following the destruction of the Common Front by the Parti Québécois were bleak ones for the Quebec labour movement, marked by failure, helplessness, turning against each other and turning inwards. In retrospect, however, under all that stagnation a profound political realignment was occurring throughout Quebec society. If the years 1972-1982 had been a time of transition, the years between 1982 and 1987 mark the emergence of a new social order in Quebec.

The first evidence of this was political. As the PQ's 1982 budget had indicated, the party had resolved the tension between its historical penchant for welfare capitalism and the fiscal crisis of the early 1980s by adopting New Right fiscal policy and cutting back on the social safety network of which it had rightly been proud. Following the confrontation with the unions in 1982-83, prominent social democrats within the PQ withdrew or were pushed to the margins of the party, beginning with René Levesque. Independence, too, was moved to the sideline, to become an issue rarely discussed in depth and never with passion. By the time Jacques Parizeau emerged as the obvious and inevitable leader, the PQ had shifted not only its politics but its class base: it had all but completed its campaign to be considered a credible contender with the Liberal Party for spokesperson of the class it now defined as the dynamic leader of modern Quebec. Francophone entrepreneurs (rather than the francophone working class) the owners of the much vaunted small and medium sized businesses (known as the PME), were identified by the PQ as the vanguard, and it tailored its policies to their aspirations.

The PQ's exit right forced not only its social democrats but the whole generation of unaligned leftists out into the political cold. Ironically, the traditional refusal of labour politics by the CEQ and the CSN had left progressives with only the PQ to vote for since the early 1970s. In 1985, however, remembering the PQ's extraordinary attack in 1982, the CSN recommended negative voting to defeat péquiste candidates, even if this meant support for the Liberals, who, after all, had not gone union-busting for a relatively long time. The CEQ leadership, on the other hand, tried tentatively to move its membership towards some form of pro-active involvement in politics *as unionists*— rather than as individuals—but backed off in the face of widespread apathy.[34]

Like the CSN and the CEQ, the FTQ chose not to support the PQ in the 1985 provincial election, but did not break its ties to the party. Nor did its leadership seriously question the friendliness of the PQ to labour, although it chose to express it discreetly until 1987.

In this political vacuum for Quebec progressives, the NDP made surprising political gains within the CEQ and the FTQ if not within the CSN. While the party had never previously gained more than a toehold in the province, during the middle years of the 1980s it succeeded in attracting not just a larger membership, but credibility among unions and *groupes populaires* which had previously ignored it. The decline of nationalism and the rightward turn of the PQ, the election of the provincial Liberals and the federal Tories, all played a role. But the agile and flexible behind-the-scenes leadership of the Quebec NDP by Michel Agnaieff (the CEQ's Director-General), coupled with a rare openness on the part of the federal party, combined to make the NDP, briefly, a place where Québécois social democrats and other progressives could recognize their own aspirations.

Within the union movement, after 1983, the three centrals went their separate ways. The FTQ, least damaged by the confrontation with the PQ, less prone to existential anguish and crises of militancy, with a leadership more adept at channelling and containing membership questioning rather than responding to it, zeroed in on deindustrialization and plant closures in the private sector, focusing attention away from the PQ and its attack on the public sector. Even before the critical juncture of 1982-83, the FTQ had begun to formulate the innovative organizing strategies and the hybrid corporatism that would prepare it well for the emerging social order of the later 1980s. In organizing it created the Comcor, an interunion co-ordinating committee whose success is indicated by the FTQ's 35 percent growth between 1983 and 1989.[35] The new members were largely drawn from the private service sector. The FTQ's hybrid corporatism sprang from the belief that both direct and indirect state investment and active collaboration with the business community would be needed to create or save jobs in the declining manufacturing industries. But in order to obtain this funding and to weld unions, employers and the state into an effective job-creation mechanism, the ordinary conflicts of interest which divided the actors would have to be shelved. This meso-corporatism was focused into two distinct strategies. On the one hand was the Solidarity Fund, a contribution scheme for workers (and others) protected by government-sponsored tax breaks, whose twin goals of job creation and pension contribution to its participants were realized through its risk capital investments in Quebec PME, some of which have been non-union. On the other hand, job creation or retention was also pursued innovatively through 'neighbourhood corporatism', the creation of community-based, FTQ-CSN action committees with active participation from local employers in the dying industrial quarters of Montreal's southeast and southwest, whose objectives were to mobilize the citizens and to force the diverse levels of government to invest in neighbourhood economic regeneration.

The CSN and the CEQ, on the other hand, turned inward and against each other between 1983 and 1990. There was no Common Front in 1985 in the public sector negotiations, nor in 1989. Worse, legislative changes in the structure of public sector negotiations (made by a government that did not have a labour party to fight it) weakened the ability of the centrals to co-ordinate even their own affiliates at the bargaining table. As once the conservative government had used centralizing wage policy to push the unions onto the defensive, now the Liberals were using decentralization to destroy solidarity—where the unions had not already destroyed it themselves. Among militants, there was widespread recognition that the vision was gone, a vision which had set these two centrals apart from other North American unions by their willingness to name and act on the reality of class conflict, by the creativity of its militancy, and by the sense of community it had engendered.[36]

In a difficult period of soul-searching between 1983 and 1985, the CEQ first set itself to exploring the crisis in its members' commitment to militant trade unionism, as if a failure of militancy and of idealism rather than the bankruptcy of union negotiating strategy vis-à-vis the state had been responsible for the central's defeat in 1983. Then the CEQ set itself on the path of organizational survival and expansion. This was a three-pronged process. First, it sought to expand its representation beyond the education sector, to become a central for all public sector workers. To do so, it set out to affiliate certain key independent unions and to absorb chunks of the CSN through raiding. Its success in these areas has been ambivalent. While it grew at the rate of 13 and 11 percent in 1986 and 1987 respectively,[37] many of the independent unions it signed service contracts with have not gone on to become full affiliates.[38]

The second part of the CEQ's expansion strategy was to place renewed emphasis on professionalism, in order to give its members something to hang on to when collective bargaining failed to bring victories. It may be noted that this professionalization of union values has already begun to stir some tensions and contradictions among the teachers, the educational professionals and the support staff who have formed the backbone of the CEQ's industrial and federated structure for more than twenty years. In addition, the thousands of health sector workers who affiliated to or signed service agreements with the CEQ since 1988 do not all define themselves in professional terms, although professionalism is a source of tension and competition amongst them.

The final element in the CEQ's strategic repositioning concerns politics. In the wake of the 1983 débâcle the CEQ leadership toyed gingerly with the idea of labourist politics, and then pulled back, protecting itself by recommending only negative voting in the 1985 provincial and the 1988 federal elections. The members who now say they prefer the stock market pages of *La Presse* to its international pages are not perceived to be open to political action. After all, look what their heart-and-soul commitment to the PQ got them. And yet— how to break the tightening circle around public sector collective bargaining without politics?

The CSN had the hardest time in seeking a strategic realignment. Its needs were more complex and divergent. During the 1980s it sought strategy that would allow it to mediate the increasingly conflicting needs of its public and private sector unions, its low- and high-paid members, to protect itself against raiding, and to remain faithful to the solidaristic wage policy that had been its signature and its pride since the 1970s. Structural change became a strategic last resort for the CSN, and the leadership had difficulty selling it to the different groups of members. But new organizing, or the reorganization of light manufacturing, was an unexpected success. The central grew by 25 percent between 1983 and 1989—less than the other two centrals, but still respectable.[39]

That new organizing brought out the real divergence of ideology, vision and priorities between the CSN's public and private sector workers, and between both and the CSN's leadership. Until 1990 the private sector, hit as hard as was the FTQ by plant closures, technological layoffs, punitive disinvestment, deindustrialization and Free Trade, pushed the Executive towards what the latter traditionally considered to be class collaboration: quality circles, Japanese style management, productivity bargaining, participation in tripartite consultative committees on health and safety and other issues. From the other side the giant Fédération des affaires sociales, representing almost 40 percent of the CSN's total membership, has developed a tradition of rejecting as collaborationism any settlement that CSN negotiators gain for it in negotiation with the state. A case in point is the 1989 public sector negotiations, which the Liberal government easily aborted by passing Bill 160. This bill refined the effectively paralysing elements first brought forward in Bill 111 in 1983. The FAS, representing in the main blue-collar and semi-professional health sector worker, blamed its negotiators for their *mollesse* as they had in the past, for their unwillingness to call upon a supposedly untapped well of rank-and-file militancy which, had it been called up, would in some undefined way have been able to bring the state to its knees and to a fair contract settlement.[40] FAS' attitude towards collective bargaining in a political situation in which the unions have no political cards to play expresses unreconstructed syndicalism, of the sort that despises labourist electoralism but condemns the limited settlements that are possible without political clout. Politics, for this wing of the CSN, is unmediated class warfare—to be won outside of Parliament, not inside it.[41]

Not surprisingly, the CSN's Executive has responded unevenly to these conflicting pressures. Bound by its nonpartisan tradition, which dates from its corporatist and confessional origins, during the 1988 Free Trade election it went to considerable lengths to defeat the forces within its own ranks (grouped around the Conseil central de Montréal) which argued for a tactical alliance with the NDP in order to defeat the Conservatives. In light of the fact that the individuals comprising the Executive were unanimously opposed to Free Trade and that the CSN had repeatedly acknowledged that Free Trade would cause massive job loss in Quebec, one can only wonder at the strength of the tradition of political abstention.

But if the CSN leadership continued to feel electoral power to be unimportant until as recently as 1990, it had begun to undertake a difficult re-evaluation of its industrial strategy at the end of 1989. In CSN tradition, the President prepares a *rapport moral* for each biennial Congress, in which he or she offers a prescriptive evaluation of where the central is coming from and where it should be going. In preparation for the 1990 Congress Gérald Larose developed the idea of a *nouveau partenariat*, or 'new partnership', which represented a real about face on consultation, and signalled the end of even a formal commitment to militancy. Combining elements of the corporatist strategies put forward by Piore and Sabel concerning the union's role in regaining international competitiveness for national capital in the high wage countries, with ideas drawn from the AFL-CIO's "The Changing Situation of the Worker and his Union," Larose's 'new partnership' sketched out the need for new union linkages which would develop sectoral and regional coalitions between unions in the U.S., Quebec and English Canada.

ENTREPRENEURIAL NATIONALISM AND TRADE UNION NEO-CORPORATISM

Had the failure of Meech Lake not occurred, the three Quebec union centrals would probably have continued on the course sketched out above, with the FTQ innovating in meso-corporatism and instrumental alliances with employers and the state, the CSN approaching the FTQ's ideological position over the increasingly bitter opposition of its blue-collar public sector, and the CEQ deploying professionalism as a lure to create a public sector central at the expense of the CSN and through the affiliation of the independent unions who had in the main been affiliated to the CSN at some time in the past.

It is by now commonplace to point out that as late as February, 1990, independence was not on the agenda for any of the union centrals. The author's personal experience in working with President Larose of the CSN on his *rapport moral* is testimony to that: by the end of February there still was no mention of the national question in any of the document's many drafts. But two brief months later, by the beginning of May, the CSN in Congress would unequivocally endorse independence for the first time in its history.

As the national question erupted on every union's agenda in the spring of 1990, there were some trade unionists who tried to give nationalism a working class definition, to capture the movement for the Left. Shortly after the Laurier-Ste-Marie federal by-election was announced, members of the FTQ and the CEQ's leadership explored the possibility of developing a labour manifesto for independence, and choosing a candidate who would openly adhere to that manifesto. They approached the CSN, whom they assumed would agree, and to their surprise found that the CSN proposed to run one of its own staffers, Gilles Duceppe. In the discussions which straggled forward at the end of June and the beginning of July, the CSN did an end-run around the other centrals, and concluded a deal with the newly-formed conservative Bloc Québécois, so that Duceppe became its candidate. He won, handily, and history began to repeat itself. Once again the unions hesitated, then retreated before the appropriation of the national question by the working class. Once again, they hoped that labour-friendly candidates would influence social policy even though they had not set up the structure or the discipline of responsibility to the union movement. Once again, they chose to subordinate themselves to a political formation which did not share their world view, in the hopes of playing an influential role within a broad-based coalition for independence. Such had been their strategy when the PQ was in the ascendant in the early 1970s, such was their strategy again in 1990 *vis-à-vis* the Bloc Québécois. Only this time the *indépendantiste* grouping was under the leadership of an avowed conservative, who shared not even a minimal social vision with the unions. This time the three Quebec centrals had hitched their star to entrepreneurial nationalism.

In the year after the death of Meech, the political and industrial implications of this strategy began to crystallize. In the private sector, subordination to conservative *indépendantisme* led the CSN and the FTQ to sign a six-year, no strike agreement to encourage foreign investment in basic industry, led the Steelworkers of the FTQ, in concert with business spokespeople, to call upon the provincial government to short-circuit the environmental review of the Great Whale project since the project will create many thousands of jobs. In the public sector, it led the CSN and the CEQ to accept a government-imposed freeze on wage increases and unilaterally prolonged collective agreements, in the name of protecting the national project. It has led, in short, to a convergence of the three union centrals over a new form of corporatism. The union representatives on the Bélanger-Campeau Commission were articulate as defenders of the national project, but they were notably silent as defenders of the other interests of working people.

But will union neo-corporatism in the interest of entrepreneurial nationalism be sufficient to protect the unions and their members in the Free Trade era? Will the unions be able to reappropriate their voice of critic and defender of the vulnerable—which they have now voluntarily silenced—if independence is won? If the present political scenario results in independence for Quebec, how will the unions after independence bargain, strike, influence, oppose the political forces now dominating their coalition? Will it be possible for them to play their necessary role without being excoriated as underminers of the new nation? Within the union movement, there are those, like Gérald Larose, who argue that a labour party is necessary, but it will only be possible to found one after independence. There are others who hoped for a pan-Canadian labour party under the NDP, but no longer think it possible. There are still others, however, who fear that the renewed subordination of labour to the interests of capital in the name of neo-nationalism will, once again, sap the power of this extraordinarily vital movement to play a leading role in Quebec, and Canadian, social development.

ENDNOTES

The author gratefully acknowledges the financial aid of the Social Sciences and Humanities Research Council of Canada in carrying out some of the research for this paper.

1.   Peter Lange et al., Unions, Change and Crisis: French and Italian Union Strategy and the Political Economy: 1945-1980 (London: George Allen and Unwin, 1982); Peter Gourevitch et al., Unions and Economic Crisis: Britain, Sweden and Germany (London; Allen and Unwin, 1984); Stephen J. Silvia, "The Prospect of a Unified European Union Movement as a Result of 1992," (March, 1990); and Matthew Sanger, "Free Trade and Workers' Rights: The European Social Charter," (April 1991).

2.   Carla Lipsig-Mummé, "The Web of Dependence," in A. Gagnon (ed.), Quebec: State and Society (Toronto: Methuen, 1984).

3.   "Entrevue avec Monique Simard," Possibles, 15/1, (Winter 1991), p. 66.

4.   Ibid,. p. 67.

5.   See, for example, Marcel Rioux, Un peuple dans le siècle (Montreal: Boréal 1990), pp. 43-56; Hubert Guindon, "The Social Evolution of Quebec Reconsidered," Canadian Journal of Economics and Political Science, 26 (November 1960), pp. 553-6; and E. Corbett, Quebec Confronts Canada (Baltimore: Johns Hopkins, 1967).

6.   Carla Lipsig-Mummé, "Quebec Unions and the State: Conflict and Dependence," Studies in Political Economy, 3 (Spring 1980).

7.   Louis Maheu, "Problème social et naissance du syndicalisme catholique," in F. Harvey (ed.), Aspects historiques du mouvement ouvrier au Québec (Montreal: Boréal, 1973).

8.   Jacques Rouillard, Le syndicalisme catholique de 1900 à 1930 (Quebec: Les Presses de l'Université Laval, 1979).

9.   Canadian and U.S. labour historians commonly overlook the fact that the CTCC founded the first modern confederation of industrial unions that survived in this century in North America.

10.   L-M Tremblay, Le syndicalisme québécois: idéologies de la CSN et de la FTQ (Montreal: Les Presses de l'Université de Montréal, 1972).

11.   Rouillard, Le syndicalisme catholique...; Leo Roback, "Les formes historiques de la politization du syndicalisme au Québec," in G. Dion et al., La politization des relations du travail au Québec (Quebec: PUL, 1973), p. 17.

12. A corporation is a professional body in which membership is made obligatory by legislation if the professional wishes to practice.

13. Roback, "Les formes historiques...," p. 18.

14. *Ibid.*

15. J-L Roy, *La marche des Québécois: le temps des ruptures, 1945-1960* (Montreal: LEMEAC. 1976).

16. See, for example, S. Milner and H. Milner, *The Decolonization of Quebec* (Toronto: McLelland, 1973); Confédération des syndicats nationaux, *Ne comptons que sur nos propres moyens* (1971); K. McRoberts and D. Postgate, *Quebec: Social Change and Political Crisis* (Toronto, 1976).

17. B. Roy Lemoine, "The Modern Industrial State: Liberator or Exploiter?" *Our Generation,* 8/4, p.73; Roch Denis, *Lutte de classes et question nationale au Québec* (Montreal: Les Presses socialistes internationales, 1979), p. 179ff.

18. Paul Bernard, *Structures et pouvoirs de la FTQ* (Ottawa: Queen's Printer, 1969).

19. Carla Lipsig-Mummé, *La modernization du syndicalisme au Québec, 1960-1990* (forthcoming).

20. Louis LeBorgne, *La C.S.N. et la question nationale* (Montreal: Ed. Albert St-Martin, 1976).

21. Within the CSN the Marxist-Leninist presence redefined the relation between union staffers and union elected representatives to make staffers into the vanguard. Concretely this led to negotiation for staffer self-management and a reduction of the power of the elected over central policy and strategy.

22. See, for example FTQ, *L'Etat rouage de notre exploitation* (1971).

23. Marcel Pépin, *Lettre aux militants* (1969).

24. The phrase comes from Dr. Stephen Frenkel, University of New South Wales.

25. D. Ethier *et al.*, *Les travailleurs contre l'Etat bourgeois* (Montreal: L'Aurore, 1975), pp. 65-69.

26. *Ibid.* pp. 82-85.

27. Michel Agnaieff, who had co-ordinated inter-central action; interview with author, 1972.

28. At least one of the union presidents, Yvon Charbonneau, expected a second general strike to break out to protest their incarceration.

29. The CSN did not regain its 1972 membership levels until more than a decade later. See Lipsig-Mummé, *La modernization.*

30. The centrals all published orientation documents during 1971-1972, presenting a Marxist analysis of dependence and class and national domination.

31. At the Plenary of the CSN's biennial Congress at Quebec, in June 1972, the president of the SFPQ (Provincial Civil Service Union) expressed his belief that skilled workers could get a better deal for themselves if they broke away from a central like the CSN.

32. An internal CEQ study, carried out in the late 1980s, showed that between 1970 and 1983 fully 1/8 of the CEQ's then membership of approximately 100,000 had held elected office in the PQ.

33. After the defeat of the 1972 Common Front strike, the CSN sought to compensate for its losses by raiding the FTQ, particularly in construction and in hotels and restaurants. Among other tactics, the CSN called for a government inquiry into corruption in FTQ construction unions.

34. After holding a special General Council on the forthcoming election, the CEQ hired a hall in Montreal's Place des Arts and invited the education spokespersons for all parties to participate in a forum. It was poorly attended and the leadership of the CEQ read this as a warning to back off labourist politics.

35. Lipsig-Mummé et al., *Union Portraits* (forthcoming).

36. J-M. Piotte chronicles the destruction of the sense of movement in a remarkably poignant book, *La communauté perdue* (Montreal: VLB, 1987).

37. Lipsig-Mummé, *Union portraits*.

38. *Ibid.*

39. *Ibid.*

40. They presented a candidate to run against First Vice-President Monique Simard in the 1990 CSN elections, as a result of their criticism of the 1989 contract negotiations in the public sector which she led.

41. Lipsig-Mummé, "Les deux militantismes," *La Presse*, May 11, 1990.

		CHAPTER
		10
===		===
POST-FORDIST POLITICS, SOCIAL DEMOCRACY, LABOUR AND THE LEFT IN EUROPE		GEORGE ROSS

INTRODUCTION

Despite occasional important innovations such as the European Monetary System (EMS) in 1978, the momentum of European economic integration ground to a halt at the same time as the Fordist postwar boom. By the later 1970s the European Community (EC) appeared completely stymied by complex budgetary disputes, its byzantine Common Agricultural Policy and the increasing propensity of member states facing recession to subvert trade with non-tariff barriers. The Europessimism of the early 1980s gave way, however, to greater enthusiasm in consequence of the move towards "1992".

The 1992 project was first broached in the European Commission's June, 1985 White Paper on Completing the Internal Market.[1] The primary goal was described as "the welding together of the ... individual markets of the Member States into one single market" by "the removal of the physical...technical...and fiscal barriers" to trade.[2] This language, its elaboration in the list of 222 detailed provisions and the complex timetable for implementation of the White Paper and the Single European Act of 1986 (which modified the 1957 Treaty of Rome so as to facilitate the process) reflected a belief that despite decades of effort the European Common Market had not become sufficiently open. Based on explicit recognition that national economic areas in Europe were too small to be independently viable, the EC thus sought to make the Community into a coherent regional economic bloc with resolutely open circulation of capital, goods and people.

Buoyed up by the promises that 1992 would bring renewed economic growth, Europeans began to refer to themselves as the world's leading market with 320 million consumers, producing one-quarter of the world's economic turnover, world leader or near leader in agricultural exports, industry and finance and capital markets. In anticipation of the changes a wave of new mergers, acquisitions, consolidations, strategic alliances and direct foreign investment (including from the U.S. and Japan) began, along with corporate restructuring, accelerated introduction of new technologies and wide application of new employer strategies. Companies throughout Europe began to standardize their products. Henceforth they would try to cover the whole market, rationalize, "become European," and in the process benefit from large new economies of scale.[3] New competition in public procurement was set to break down once-protected markets in public transport, telecommunications, and other state services.

The heart of the 1992 project was a process of market deregulation, neoliberal to the core. Its origins were in the 1980s philosophy which claimed that the free market is a better way of allocating social resources than any form of conscious state action, however democratic its provenance. Despite this, however, Jacques Delors, President of the EC Commission and the major individual political actor promoting the project, rarely let an opportunity go by to announce that the *real* purpose of 1992 was to re-establish the conditions for a "European model of society." Continental Europe ought quite rightfully to be seen as perhaps the most important global bastion of a "humanized" capitalism, he noted, and 1992 was supposed to generate the dynamic mixed economy, tied to a humane scheme of industrial relations and an extensive welfare state to sustain it. The neo-liberalism was thus proposed as a way to re-establish conditions which would allow conscious social choices to attenuate the market's harshness.

There is a puzzle to be untangled here, then, and it is one which deepens when we recognize that it was French *Socialist* politicians who devised the crucial political maneuvers which led to the 1992 process, meaning that the changes were actually promoted from the left of centre. Finally, much of the European labour movement seemed favourably disposed, even though the labour market deregulatory dimensions of movements to "complete the European market" were patent.

This chapter explores these multiple puzzles. We are convinced that hidden in them there are fundamental issues about the future of the Left and labour in Europe. First we will argue that behind the Socialist leadership lies a reconfiguration of social democracy to confront post-Fordist conditions of accumulation. European labour's favorable disposition towards completing the internal market had a rather different meaning, we will contend, one which flows from a dramatic relocation of labour movements in the emerging European political economy. Thirdly, these changes in the positions of social democracy and labour place what we call the "Left of the Left," the traditional gadfly of official Left and labor organizations, in an entirely new position.

SOCIAL DEMOCRACY AND THE NEW EUROPE

A mere three decades ago widespread agreement existed in European societies about the underlying developmental logic of market-oriented social orders. "Fordism," defined loosely as a stage of capitalism in which mass production and consumption predominated and which implied specific structures of interest representation in politics and at workplace level, looked eternal. In postwar Europe full labour citizenship and major parts of what one could only call a social-democratic agenda were often equated with optimal success for capitalist economies. "Macro"-level analyses held that economic growth and reformist redistribution were compatible.[4] At the "micro" or workplace level, it was claimed that an institutionalized web of rules had made it possible to resolve peacefully the endemic conflict over rights, authority and distribution in the capitalist firm.[5]

At the base of this "old synthesis" was the postwar economic boom. Governments intervened in the economy along Keynesian lines to stabilize growth at high levels of employment and developed welfare state institutions to redistribute some of the fruits of growth. In addition, after 1945 employers, unions and workers reached settlements—which varied greatly both in national forms and timing—in which employers exchanged relatively high wages and employment security for predictability, labour discipline and tolerance of productivity-enhancing investment. Such postwar settlements existed at national, industrial and firm levels. They were sustained by Keynesian welfare states and encouraged by the international trade, monetary and institutional arrangements established largely because of American initiatives.

Many of these policy innovations had long been essential parts of unions' and social democratic parties' programmatic agendas. As long as all of these elements meshed together harmoniously, European economies experienced unprecedented prosperity. Fine-tuning the broader social-democratic agenda—expansion of social citizenship, state regulatory and redistributive activities and agreements between capital and labour at a variety of levels—became the centre of social and political debate. Thus the ideology and political culture of most European societies took on a distinctly social democratic and workerist tinge.

Signs of difficulty, often in the form of renewed industrial conflict, began to appear well before the first oil shock of 1973-74, but chronic problems emerged in the latter half of the 1970s.[6] Stagflation, defined as rising unemployment accompanied by inflation and declining growth, was common in an increasingly uncertain international trade and monetary context. Keynesian demand management and other forms of intervention began to produce perverse effects, leading economists and governments to question past policies and experiment with new ones. Employers began to seek new workplace strategies. More to our point, social democratic parties began to confront new electoral and policy troubles while their organized labour allies faced new challenges in the labour market market and political arenas.[7]

By the 1980s a double reconfiguration of the dominant locus of economic regulation was underway, away from the national to the international or supranational level on the one hand, and to the subnational level on the other. A decline in the role of states relative to markets constituted an important corollary of this. The first change meant that the partial insulation from the international market upon which postwar methods depended, and on which national firms, unions, and governments relied, ceased to exist. While transnational flows undermined the capacity of states to manage the economies within their borders, subsidiaries of global firms and networks of smaller firms geared to international markets spurred the growth and autonomy of regional and local economies. Hence the second shift. These changes have different implications for the different institutions organized at the national level and have been particularly threatening to the traditional agenda of social democracy.

POST-FORDIST SOCIAL DEMOCRACY

Traditionally, social democracy, always the preponderant force on the Left in Europe, proposed a politics of redistribution. Social democrats sought to transfer income, wealth, welfare and authority from the better off and the powerful to the less well off and the weakest and from capital to labour. Though its strength varied, social-democratic egalitarianism was neither wildly radical nor particularly anti-capitalist, especially once the immediate post-1945 years had passed. Social democrats employed Keynesian policies to produce growth and near full employment, welfare state programs, and active state intervention *within a certain type of capitalist order*. They made their peace with the expansionist, mass production and consumption-oriented corporate economy which dynamized the postwar boom by acknowledging the inevitability of an economy that combined an open market humanized and democratized by reformist programs. Social-democratic reformism in effect assumed the possibility of a positive-sum relationship among capital, labour and the state, often taking neo-corporatist forms which left ample room for profits, steadily increasing productivity, and redistribution of the fruits of steady economic growth.

François Mitterrand and Jacques Delors have arguably been the most important Socialist politicians in Europe in the last decade. Ideologically, they are the kind of Socialists who predominate in the leaderships of most important European Socialist parties. They are also in the vanguard of a basic and profound shift in the focus of social-democratic politics in Europe.[8] The 1980s prodded elites of all political persuasions, including Socialist, away from earlier beliefs that important economic flows could be effectively regulated nationally. It thus became conventional wisdom that national governments could do little to maintain employment and living standards other than to promote the competitiveness of national industries in the international arena. Within Europe, however, even this came to be viewed as beyond the capacity of existing national states.

Post-Fordist social democracy is much less redistributional than its postwar predecessors, since social democrats now read international economic constraints as precluding ambitious domestic reform plans. The new domestic political game is seen as much more zero-sum than Fordist social democratic politics ever was. Getting beyond deadlock, the new Socialists claim, will involve success in the national mission to promote international economic advance. Only if the mission succeeds will it then become possible to engage in further redistribution.

Here lies the beginning of the answer to the first of the puzzles. The post-Fordist Socialist vanguard, leaders like Mitterrand and Delors in particular, concluded that the most propitious context for any such success was a regional European economic bloc which could only be constructed on neo-liberal grounds.

The new Socialists are more managerial and technocratic than their predecessors. Their major political claim, which deserves to be taken seriously, is that capitalism will be better co-ordinated and more rational if central political tasks are taken away from capitalists and given to technically and politically skilled state managers. This form of social democracy is resolutely "modernist" in an economic sense, promising above all to produce the kind of state-of-the-art, "international best practice" national capitalism which these Socialists contend capitalists themselves cannot usually create on their own.

This social democracy is also much less workerist in outlook than the post-war version. Economic and social changes in Europe have led to a relative "post-industrialization" of occupational structures, such that it has become increasingly difficult to see blue-collar industrial workers as an expanding vanguard of social change. Responding in part to the decline and fragmentation of the working class, therefore, post-Fordist Socialism is relatively uncommitted to class-analytical visions of the political world. It is also much less beholden to union movements, and rather more willing than its predecessor to allow unemployment to rise.[9] But within this broad context, the new Socialists also advocate preserving as much as (international) economic constraints will allow of the national system of social services. The new social democracy is not, therefore, a complete capitulation to neo-liberalism. Indeed, one of its more positive sides is its enthusiasm for promoting solidarity through new co-operative workplace schemes and sharing costs across different social strata, all justified in a rhetoric of humanistic national unity.

Finally, the new social democracy has embraced a repertory of political strategies and tactics that are qualitatively more electoralist in a modern sense—incessant polling and "political marketing," carefully targeted advertising, calculated uses of television, stress upon personalities over issues and the like. Here the claim of those, usually policy intellectuals specializing in electoral high tech, who promote such new approaches is that they are a direct and necessary response to a decline in collective and party identification and the consequent individualization of electorates. However much this may have been true at the outset, reliance on political technology will almost certainly help make it become truer.

SOCIAL DEMOCRACY AND 1992

This remodelled definition of social democracy has predominated in recent Left enthusiasm for deepening the European Community. In the lead were the French and Spanish Socialists, who were both in power, and the German SPD, which was not but whose wealth and power conferred international influence, particularly over smaller European social-democratic parties and the Socialist International. The British Labour Party brought up the rear, as the British tended to do more generally on matters European, but it also became increasingly pro-European, partly as an anti-Thatcher strategem and partly because of its own conversion to new visions of social democracy. There are smaller battalions as well, the most notable being the Italian ex-Communist Party, the Party of the Democratic Left, which has slowly but surely been using pro-Europeanism to bring about new rapprochements with the leading European social-democratic parties.[10] The recent turn towards the EC by the Swedish Social Democrats, accompanied by most of the other symptoms of the coming of a new post-Fordist Socialism, ought to be seen as the most spectacular indicator of a trend.

The European Left strongly favored the 1992 process, despite its deregulatory nature. Socialist approval came with caveats, however. The new Socialists believed that market deregulation should be accompanied by European-level *dirigiste* policies, in particular regional policies to help out less developed areas in Europe. Quite as important, they insisted that deregulation should be accompanied by explicit efforts to construct a European social space. "Social Europe" was the label for an EC that would preserve adequate social programs—workplace health and safety, unemployment compensation, health care, pensions, equal pay for work of equal value, protection for the disabled, anti-poverty programs—and introduce them to areas where they did not exist. Advocates of Social Europe also sought to confirm existing national industrial relations systems that would protect workers' rights to bargain collectively and participate in certain workplace decisions and to extend such protection throughout Europe.

What is striking in all this is that the bulk of the official European Left, which had always claimed to critique and at least partially oppose national and

European capitalism, no longer did so with reference to the European level. Indeed, the Left, in this instance, had become a prime mover. There were, of course, a few European Left groups that did not completely share in this consensus. The Greens were divided rather strongly at the European level and they were reasonably well represented in the rather weak European Parliament. Though there is no intrinsic barrier to a mild "greening" of Socialist policies and electoral appeals, the post-Fordist Socialists have not yet figured out how to cope with environmental matters, leaving the Greens to exploit the issues. And then there is a small group of hard-nosed Communists—French, Portuguese, some Greeks and Spanish—who raised much stronger objections. However, they represented divided and declining parties and were unable to agree among themselves on a response to the new Europe.

There is thus a strong congruence between support for "Europe" and the post-Fordist conversion experience of much of the social-democratic Left. This official Left believed in 1992 primarily because it hoped that a Single European Market would bring increased economic growth, enhance the restructuring of European capital and renew European international competitiveness. Socialists saw this Europe-wide strategy, rather than any particular combination of domestic policies, as the real remedy for persistent unemployment. Their major caveat, expressed by Jacques Delors himself, was that the Europe which came out of 1992 must also preserve the "European model of society." They rejected hard-nosed neo-liberalism in favor of an active state working hand-in-hand with the private sector (at national and European levels) and preserving social programs and humane labour relations more or less intact. The European model of society thus translated into an amalgam of the Single Market, the welfare state and "social Europe."

1992 AND EUROPEAN LABOUR

A second puzzle involves the support for 1992 among European labour organizations. The great lesson which capital and most European governments derived from the profound economic crises emerging out of the oil shocks and stagflation of the 1970s and the recession of the early 1980s was that labour markets had been overly rigid in the boom years. In the period after the war, unions and workers had won victories in many places that consolidated union power on the shopfloor, increased union strength in collective bargaining at sectoral and national levels and exacted employer tolerance for higher wages, usually in exchange for union help in introducing productivity-enhancing production techniques. But by the mid-1980s elites in Europe, including many Socialists, began to argue that these victories had outlived their usefulness and had become important factors in the relative decline of European competitiveness. They became increasingly ready to challenge, and where possible to dismantle, important parts of earlier workplace agreements between labour and capital. Rigidities, they argued, had to be removed in the interests of new "flexibility." In most places, whether through aggressive actions on the part of capital or government policy or both, extensive measures were indeed taken towards introducing such flexibility. As a result the labour market situation had already changed considerably by the late 1980s.

RESTRUCTURING AND DEREGULATING

There have been a number of different approaches to deregulating the labour market in the interests of flexibility, including quite a bit of deliberate, and often spectacular, union-busting. Sometimes, as in the 1980 Fiat strike in Italy, the private sector has been the primary force behind such actions.[11] Quite as often, however, governments, whether Left or Right-leaning, have taken the lead. Socialist governments in Spain have been unusually vigorous in facing down unions.[12] While the French Socialists have been somewhat more discreet, they moved in similar directions. Their efforts to dismantle union power in the vast nationalized Renault empire since 1984 undermine existing patterns in French labour relations.[13] Thatcher's efforts to break union power through changed labour legislation and large events like the Miners' Strike partook of the same general dynamic.[14]

Rising unemployment since the mid-1970s, moreover, has itself contributed to deregulating labour markets. Explicit governmental policies to increase flexibility in hiring and firing regulations by softening rules about work time have worked in similar directions, expanding the often female part-time and flex-time labour force which has traditionally been more difficult to unionize.[15] Neo-Japanese approaches to workplace organization—quality circles, work teams, newly sophisticated efforts to create workplace co-operation and loyalties transcending the capital-labour divide—have become widespread among European employers.

Perhaps most importantly, there has been a slow but sure shift of industrial relations activities from national and industrial-sector levels downwards towards the firm itself. This decentralization of industrial relations, carried out in the name of flexibility and decentralized responsibility, has made the enterprise, as opposed to the industrial sector or the national government, the most important locus for labour movement activity.

In the Fordist period and before, while firm-level union activity was an essential component of labour action, unions had almost always sought to aggregate their rank-and-file resources to create sectoral- and national-level identities. Decentralization exercises a powerful new centrifugal effect on unions, making it much more difficult for labour organizations beyond firm and enterprise level to promote co-operation, whether between regions, private and public-sectors or workers in different industrial areas. Unions are thus under intense pressure to localize their efforts, if only to avoid being removed altogether from the firm by aggressive new strategies on capital's part. To the degree to which they respond to such pressure, they do so at the relative expense of high-level, and "class-oriented" mobilization.[16] As a result, class identities are undermined, while simultaneously union capacities to put pressure on a national level are weakened.

These changes—to which we might add occupational "post-industrialization"—have tended to weaken European unions substantially in their national contexts, decreasing membership, mobilizational strength, and bargaining power, and diminishing their capacities to make earlier postwar deals stick. In some places, for instance France, Italy, Spain and, to a lesser extent, Great Britain, this process has been dramatic. The major exception to such trends has been the West German union movement, which has benefited from the strongly competitive position of German capital within the EC, a strong legal position and the relative solidity of its somewhat corporatistic institutional arrangements at firm-level which include a favourable structure of bargaining.[17]

For labour, the deepening of the EC has thus been part of a larger economic and organizational logic, a general context of restructuring and Europeanizing of national capital begun long before the 1990s. Unions have characterized the major dangers in the moves toward greater integration as "social dumping." The single market, unions feared, would encourage capital to relocate its operations throughout the European 12 in search of cheap labour, nonconstraining industrial relations settings, and low social overhead costs in much the same way that U.S. corporations relocated to the South and Southwest of the United States during the postwar boom. The possibility also existed that member governments would pursue "low-ball bidding" on social policy and labour overhead costs to attract the newly mobile companies—and here, too, the American example was pertinent. Labour thus concluded that integration might encourage a downward spiral in social programs, industrial protection and the legal status of unions in Europe more generally.

INTERNATIONALIZING LABOUR?

What makes social dumping conceivable is the Europeanization of capital, predating but intensified by the 1992 reforms, combined with the creation of a relatively open European market within which capital could pursue a truly continental logic. Given such a setting, whose outlines had been clear even before the Single Market Act, one would have thought that unions would have tried mightily to develop Europe-wide organizations and bargaining techniques to match capital in strength and scope.[18]

Attempts to develop European-wide union co-operation and collective bargaining in specific industrial sectors have been in the works since the 1960s. There are a number of sectoral International Trade Secretariats within the International Confederation of Free Trade Unions (ICFTU) and there are 13 Industry Committees within the European Trade Union Confederation (ETUC), which is the ICFTU's European regional organization. There have also been some efforts to promote bargaining on a European scale in multinational firms, that is, firm-level rather than sectoral-level activities.

The bottom line thus far, however, is that unions have made very little progress towards European-level bargaining. With capital strong, unions considerably weakened on the national level (excepting, as always, the German unions), and cross-national collaborative union action embryonic, the balance of forces necessary to promote serious European-wide collective bargaining does not exist. With unions having difficulty acting together, employers have had little incentive to deal with disorganized and enfeebled unions. And while there are a few union-employer consultative arrangements in a number of French multinationals, even these partake more of trendy French paternalistic modernism than anything like real collective bargaining.[19]

There are two additional reasons for such a relatively gloomy assessment. First, most unions allocated the bulk of their resources where they were most likely to have an immediate effect, namely their own national market and political arenas. This approach, favoured even by the still-strong German unions, might be a rational strategy in the short run, since it allowed labour to apply its limited muscle where it could achieve maximum return.[20] It also clearly reflected the relative parochialism of most union bases concerning the changing economic situation. Moreover, the EC's movement forward had been the product more of hard bargaining between national governments than the effects of supranationality. Therefore nationally focused and credible labour efforts to shape national governmental positions still paid off on European matters more than weak transnational efforts.[21] The second reason, which was equally compelling, was that the general direction of changes in industrial relations bargaining was away from the sectoral and national levels down towards the firm itself, as we have noted. Post-Fordist restructuring decentralized bargaining away from larger arenas, including transnational ones, drawing trade union attention along with it.

National union movements were organizationally tied on the European level, however. Almost all union confederations in the member states belong to the European Trade Union Confederation.[22] ETUC is based in Brussels, has been largely funded by the wealthy German unions, and has for some time tried to promote transnational union goals in Europe. Furthermore, unions are represented on the Economic and Social Affairs Commission of the Community, a largely consultative official body which has some lobbying and public relations capacities.

From the beginning of his Commission Presidency, Delors pushed ETUC and the UNICE, the European-level employer association, to talk through a number of issues. Delors' stated purpose was less to reach bargained contracts than to develop common habits of discussion and to begin a dialogue that might lead somewhere in the future. There was something of a hidden agenda here as well, since Delors had clearly tried to use these talks as a way of getting ETUC and UNICE endorsement for his own policies. The results of these talks were far from spectacular. The "partners" together supported a vague list of Community macroeconomic policy aims, basically backing up Delors' good intentions on investment, price stability, and regional policies. But on substantive areas touching on capital-labour relations, in particular those concerning new technologies, the participants reached no substantial agreements and made little progress. Employers sought maximum freedom and flexibility while unions wanted contractually sanctified protection. As a consequence, nothing much happened.

Perhaps the most critical matter which this so-called "social dialogue" and similar forums failed to settle is the long-standing issue of writing a European company law. This would be a statute stipulating the rights and duties of companies who wished to register themselves legally on the EC level.[23] Unions persistently demanded a clause consecrating union rights of participation at firm level, even if different national union movements advanced different conceptions of such matters, leading to very complex proposals.[24] Nevertheless, employers did not feel compelled to give up much of anything to the ETUC, either on the company law or in social dialogue, and that discussion stalemated.[25] Rather more importantly, the employers' position was that as little as possible should be legislated, agreed or conceded on the European level.[26]

SOCIAL EUROPE?

The most important 1992 matter for labour was to draw up a European Charter of Fundamental Social Rights, intended as the major documentary contribution to "Social Europe." A qualified majority of the Council of Ministers adopted a version of this document at the EC Summit in Strasbourg in autumn 1989.[27] The ETUC sought a Social Charter which erected some barriers to social dumping and "sunbelt" strategies. It thus wanted a much more vigorous regional development policy, participatory rights for workers in firms everywhere (the company law issue), guaranteed social security for full- and part-time workers, equal workplace and wage treatment for men and women, stricter health and safety standards, and serious job training and retraining programs. ETUC also wanted the Social Charter to incorporate International Labour Organization (ILO) international labour standards in an official way.

Jacques Delors himself seemed to support such things.[28] Delors thus initiated a process of "social dialogue" with UNICE and ETUC. UNICE agreed in principle to a Charter, as long as it was not legally enforceable, a position which the Community's Economic and Social Commission supported. The EC Commission then produced a draft (for the Madrid Summit of June 1989) full of high-sounding principles but containing few enforcement mechanisms; it left the regulation of collective bargaining completely to member states and implementation of its principles to clause-by-clause approval of an Action Program by the Council of Ministers. The Action Program, produced by the Commission late in 1989, was generally weak. It could have some teeth, as on narrower questions of health and safety, protection for the disabled, equality between the sexes at work and vocational training, where existing EC treaty stipulations facilitated new regulations from EC level. But where this was not the case little progress was possible.

The Social Charter and Action Program sidestepped most of the key issues that had been discussed earlier.[29] The German DGB thus denounced it as a "wish list" and "cheap talk"; Socialist Members of the European Parliament reacted to it with considerable anger.[30] The story in brief was that the European Commission started out with some good will, but trimmed its sails in response to business hostility and opposition from member governments—the British in particular—with whom the Commission had simultaneously to deal about the important issue of monetary union.[31]

The larger puzzle of labour and the Community has an ironic final twist. Labour has had few successes and has shown very little power at European level. This record is a very good indicator of labour's present weakness in Europe, German union strength notwithstanding. The basic structures of union weakness are decentralization and fragmentation in bargaining, declining organizational strength, plus the general propensities of national union movements to apply their resources in the national arenas where they are likely to be most effective. These also mean that the weakened unions were not likely to place much future hope in European-level reforms or campaigns. On top of this, different national union movements had real conflicts of interest about important European matters.[32] Still, most of European labour strongly supported the 1992 process.

If this support is difficult to understand, one ought to reflect again on the political colour of the Brussels leadership. The European Commission under Delors may be the best any union movement could have hoped for at the time. Given the genuine miseries of the recent European past—low growth, high unemployment, and industrial decline—it was not surprising to find labour buying into the promises that 1992 would bring renewed European economic growth.

The irony within the irony, of course, is that this quite realistic calculation itself created a second-order strategic situation. The Delors people, who faced strong opposition to virtually everything they did, had every reason to try to bargain for union and labour support for their policies without giving very much in return. The end result is that weak unions moaned and groaned endlessly about not getting enough, but accepted what little they had gotten.

1992 AND THE LEFT: DEEPER MEANINGS

That the 1992 process was a turning point for European labour and the European Left is further underlined by movement towards European Monetary Union (EMU), bringing a common currency, a European Central Bank and extensive new supranational controls over national economic policies.[33] The EC Intergovernmental Conference on Political Integration held in Rome in

December 1990 began a turn towards common European security and defense policies to go along with an increasingly important Community role in foreign policy.[34] Europe in the 1990s will be a complex of interacting processes that together will undoubtedly create pressure for genuine federal arrangements.

The most significant thing for the Left in all this is the reformulation of social democracy. Socialists have subordinated the domestic redistributive goals of earlier forms of social democracy to a new quest for competitiveness: international position has definitively assumed priority over national Keynesianism. Given such priorities, promotion of general European international competitiveness might allow new payoffs to flow to specific national societies, thence to be redistributed. If social democracy remains committed to the maximum amount of social decency and social protection consistent with its broader economic policy and managerial ends, it should be clear that both the new social democracy and the new Europe are elite businesses. Political technocrats and policy intellectuals now *are* the official Left virtually everywhere. One consequence is that class-analytical and class-oriented political arguments and appeals are on their way out.[35] In part this is a response to the decline and fragmentation of a working class, which, formerly a *national* entity, is being "denationalized." The labour force of post-Fordist capitalism tends simultaneously towards transnationality and localization. It is wrong to claim, of course, that the repertory of issues which the labour movement has promoted for more than a century is no longer important. But labour, fragmented between the international and the local and having suffered major defeats in the class struggle, is becoming a less central and formidable social actor than it was during the postwar boom period.

The existing logic of capitalist restructuring will almost certainly further erode unions' national-level bargaining power. It is virtually certain that European labour will be unable to establish itself on a EC basis in anything remotely resembling the "neo-corporatist" forms it achieved in national political economies after 1945. Even if labour can find its way towards transnational co-operation on European levels, it will be immensely weakened by the time it reaches this destination. Furthermore, it must simultaneously seek out a path allowing it to confront the localization—of bargaining, of organization, of loyalties—created by capitalist innovations in technology and strategy.

There is a definite dynamic at work here. The less class-oriented and more managerially technocratic social democracy becomes, the more organized labour is likely to be weakened, since this social democracy will neither be a reliable policy ally for labour nor a viable vehicle for the pro-labour and class analytical political discourse which earlier social democracy promoted. Conversely, the weaker organized labour is, the more European social democracy is likely to move in the directions that we have outlined. Old-line productivist, labour-centered social democracy seems finished, then. Europe, which has always been its strongest bastion, now looks to be its last.

Specific projections about restructuring deepen this particular gloom. According to the *Cecchini Report*, 1992 would bring considerable new short-run unemployment as firms rationalized and deregulation took effect. Moreover, when—and if—the new job growth promised for 1992 actually appeared, it would occur not in older sectors or regions where unions were strong—most of which had already been hurt by restructuring—but in new sectors and geographical settings. The steel industry and automobile production would certainly survive, but in dramatically streamlined, high-technologized forms employing far fewer blue-collar workers. Services of all kinds—banking, insurance, retailing, marketing—would expand. Finally, despite persistent EC Commission efforts to underplay the possibilities of social dumping, even EC experts admitted that there would be a problem, particularly in labour-intensive economic activities.

Thus while all boats might rise on the tide of the Single Market, labour's boat would have to navigate some very rough seas before reaching port. The correlation between these kinds of problems and the slow and substantial rise of racist intolerance, usually directed against non-Europeans, is also clear.[36] Where there was a combination of rising economic insecurity, disappointments with unions and the political Left, and a proximity of immigrants, there was also likely to be a renaissance of racism.

TO THE LEFT OF THE LEFT?

Traditional social democracy, both because of its substantial resource base and the discourses it purveyed, always produced a "Left on its Left." For decades the bulk of the activists and intellectuals who agitated and practised in this political space took official social democracy's redistributive and transformative rhetoric much more seriously than did most social democrats themselves. This had the effect, over time, of structuring the specific patterns of a radicalism which was more thoroughgoing than official party leaders and functionaries were or could be. The Left of the Left was thus itself preponderantly class analytical, workerist, productivist and socialist-utopian. Moreover, it was considerably more angular and impatient in formulating such notions than the "revisionists and bureaucrats" it sought to move and, if possible, replace. The complex histories of Communism, Trotskyism and revolutionary Third Worldism in the twentieth century should demonstrate the issues here. Quite as important, this particular Left of the Left was consistently significant in prodding the official Left in directions that it would otherwise not have contemplated.

Capital-led restructuring and the consequent changes in social democratic outlooks and the position of labour create a radically new situation. Will post-Fordist social democracy produce a new Left on its Left?[37] There is no lack of tasks for such a formation to embrace. Technocratic wisdom to the contrary, there is nothing inevitable about unemployment, bad and undemocratic educational systems, environmental destruction, deteriorating public services or extreme inequalities of income, wealth and condition.[38] Furthermore post-Fordism creates a long list of issues concerning workplace democracy and representation that should be faced.[39]

It is probably safe to assume, on the basis of historical record, that a new Left of the Left will indeed emerge. The essential questions to be explored concern its likely shape. Here three profound changes must be noted at the outset. First, the earlier Left of the Left was revolutionary and socialist utopian in its outlooks. The collapse of the Soviet model in the 1980s, coming on the back of the many failures of Third Worldist socialism and the anti-Marxist conversion experience of large numbers of progressive intellectuals makes it a virtual certainty that notions of socialist revolution and socialist utopianism *will not* play much of a role in constituting a new Left of the Left. Second, labour strength obliged left radicals to adopt labour's discourses, even to criticize them. The relative decline of organized labour, perhaps the central factor in explaining the rise of post-Fordist social democracy, will be fundamental in shaping the outlines of a new European Left of the Left. Relative labour weakness undermines the earlier obligation to adopt a discourse of workerism. Thirdly, and partially connected, there is a genuine "crisis of Marxism" among intellectuals and labour organizations which will take years to overcome, should this occur at all.

In this context, over the last two decades the various transitions of labour and socialism have opened political space on the Left into which an array of new collective actors, the famous "New Social Movements," has plunged. In fact, there is really little "new" about these movements—they are easily assimilated to much in the history of social protest in capitalist society. As the protest vehicles of both the rising new middle strata and the socially marginalized in advanced capitalist societies which exploded onto the scene at precisely the point where the weight and salience of labour and workerism were in steep decline, they are nonetheless extremely important. They personify a new Left of the Left context, in other words, in which non-labour protest has emerged from behind labour's shadow to stake out its own progressive territory.

Left politics will thus include environmentalism, strategically sophisticated feminism, militant consumerism, and, quite as important, local and regional movements sparked by the geographical changes associated with capitalist restructuring. Labour itself, with its own specific set of important issues, has a very large place to assume in this new universe of movements, provided it can reconfigure its own outlooks and strategic calculus.

The relative prominence of such movements presents opportunities and problems. In many ways they have sketched alternative models to the bureaucratic organizational structures of conventional Left politics and significantly altered the definition of "the political" in advanced industrial societies. Yet their political valence is neither necessarily, nor universally progressive. Moroever, whatever their success in mobilizing committed people in relatively spontaneous, informally structured, non-hierarchical political activities, the movements have been unable to elaborate the organizational, ideological, and decision-making structures necessary for long-term, modulated, strategic action, with the exception of some Green parties.

People may indeed feel empowered when they mobilize in new movements. And they may cherish the memories of such feelings enough to want to reproduce them in future mobilizations. If specific movements are, however, unable to produce appropriate policy responses from elites, then specific mobilizations may have relatively short lives. Moreover, to the degree to which the movement really has few mechanisms—connections to a party, lobbying organizations, etc.—to make "them" respond in desirable ways, the elites retain immense freedom to respond in terms of their own interests.[40]

With the decline of earlier forms of official social democracy, constructed around a relatively coherent class-oriented picture of the social world which unified variegated social movements the new setting is quite disordered. It is conceivable that this disorder will become the principle of a new Left of the Left politics, constituted by decentralized mobilizations and actions of varying intensity both from social protest movements and labour. The lack of unifying concepts and hierarchies of purpose in this "disorderly" version of Left politics would mean that elite responses to such mobilizations and protests will largely escape non-elite control. Elites will have to respond to movement-originated "inputs from below," to be sure. The definition of actual policies of response to such "inputs" will remain an elite matter.

In this model, moreover, even the most rebellious among the different groups we have mentioned will face constant temptation to formalize their organizations and become pressure groups, for the simple reason that mobilization is very difficult to sustain over time without clear payoffs in terms of influence and policy. To the degree to which this occurs, it will play into the most likely reformulation of official politics in the new Europe which will combine technocratic elitism with a modernized interest group pluralism. Such interest group pluralism is solidly biased in favour of groups defending the interests of privilege in Europe, especially those of business. Given its centrality in national and EC economic missions and the mobility of its organizational resources, business will be able to choose among a greatly increased number of points of influential access (local and regional, national and international). Most other interests—including those on the Left of the Left—will be much less endowed with resources, less central, and less mobile (i.e. more localized) than capital. And it goes without saying that post-Fordist social democrats fishing for votes will strongly encourage movements to follow such trajectories.

The first problem that a transforming Left will thus face both nationally and internationally in the new Europe is to ensure that its mobilizations translate into genuine empowerment. The undercutting of mass mobilization and the obscurity of complex coalition politics are typical traps in such a situation. The opposite problem in such decentralized group mobilization is, of course, that movement groups, perceiving the relative absence of any satisfactory policy outlets for their energies, will instead accentuate differences between themselves and others which will make even occasional collaboration ever more difficult.

Some will be pleased that the class-oriented productivist politics of the "old Left" is in terminal trouble in modern Europe, others less so. Yet if the older Left had clear notions about how to connect mobilizations of discontent with policy changes, it is important now to recognize that given the relative decline of labour, the old model is less and less adequate to the task. What kind of Left will ultimately emerge from the new situation is difficult to project. Still, the raw materials of Left of the Left opposition to the new Europe, at both national and European levels, can only come from some form of new politics built out of the mobilization of movements, including the labour movement. At present, however, there exists little propensity to unify disparate movement efforts, notwithstanding talk about "radical democracy." That much work is needed to find the proper way is clear. For the moment, Europe is fortunate in possessing a "European model of society" which post-Fordist social democracy and the architects of "Europe" seek to defend. Things could be worse—as they indeed are elsewhere.

ENDNOTES

This chapter was written in 1991, before the next step in the move towards "Europe," the Maastrict Treaty of December 1992.

1.   The author of the White Paper was Lord Cockfield, then EC Commissioner for Competition. This is interesting because despite Prime Minister Thatcher's later accusations that Cockfield had "gone native" in Brussels, Cockfield was a devoted neo-liberal and this devotion shone through the White Paper.

2.   *Completing the Internal Market*, White Paper from the Commission of the European Communities to the European Council (Milan, 28-29 June 1985), COM(85) 310 final, pp. 8-9.

3.   See Francis Cripps and Terry War, *Europe in the World Economy* (Paris: Commissariat Général du Plan, 1987); Paolo Geurrieri and Pier Carlo Padoan, *The Political Economy of European Integration* (London: Harvester-Wheatsheaf, 1989).

4.   Perhaps the most interesting source reviewing this period is Steven Marglin and Juliet Schor (eds.), *The Golden Age of Capitalism: Reinterpreting the Postwar Period* (Oxford: Clarendon Press, 1990).

5.   Later theoreticians of neo-corporatism refined this vision to claim that tripartite collaboration between strongly organized labour unions, employers and an interventionist modern state could simultaneously produce economic health and distributive justice. Many of the essays in Suzanne Berger (ed.), *Organizing Interests in Western Europe* (Cambridge: Cambridge University Press, 1981), advance this claim.

6.   See Colin Crouch and Alessandro Pizzorno (eds.), *The Resurgence of Class Conflict in Western Europe Since 1968* (New York: Holmes and Meier, 1978), 2 vols.

7.   On such matters see Peter Lange, George Ross and Maurizio Vaniccelli, *French and Italian Unions in the Political Economy: 1945-1980* (London: Allen and Unwin, 1982), and Peter Gourevietch, Andrew Martin, George Ross *et al.*, *Unions and Economic Crisis: The Swedish, West German and British Cases* (London: Allen and Unwin, 1984).

8.   This shift took root almost everywhere in Europe by the 1980s. The political histories of Socialism in France and Spain crystallize this shift most graphically, however. See, for France, George Ross, Stanley Hoffmann and Sylvia Malzacher (eds.), *The Mitterrand Experiment* (Cambridge: Polity Press, 1987).

9.   Here we are speaking not absolutely, but in terms of changed trade-off calculations. Post-Fordist Socialists were more concerned with stimulating competitiveness than promoting full employment. Seeking growth and hoping that growth would diminish unemployment, their priority was not on the task of diminishing unemployment *per se*.

10. For the PCI-PDS, earlier Eurocommunism has been replaced by talk of a "Euroleft," a grand alliance of social democrats and ex-Communists. Thus the PDS no longer participates in the Communist group in the European Parliament in order to constitute itself alone in a special group, the better to seduce the Socialists.

11. See Richard M. Locke, "The Resurgence of the Local Union: Industrial Restructuring and Industrial Relations in Italy," *Politics and Society*, 18:3, 1990.

12. See Richard Gillespie, *The Spanish Socialist Party* (New York: Oxford UP, 1989); Augusto Lopez-Claros, "The Search for Efficiency in the Adjustment Process: Spain in the 1980s," *IMF Occasional Papers* (IMF: Washington D.C., 1988); Robert Fishman, *Working Class Organization and the Return to Democracy in Spain* (Ithaca: Cornell UP, 1990); Lynne Wozniak, "Economic Adjustment and Social Movements in Spain," *Kellogg Institute Working Papers* (Kellogg Institute: Notre Dame University, 1991).

13. See François Stankiewicz (ed.), *Les Stratégies d'entreprises face aux ressources humaines* (Paris: Economica, 1988); Ross, Hoffmann and Malzacher, *The Mitterrand Experiment*.

14. Leonard Rico, "The New Industrial Relations," *Industrial and Labour Relations Review*, October, 1987; Peter Jenkins, *Mrs. Thatcher's Revolution: The Ending of the Socialist Era* (Cambridge, MA: Harvard UP, 1989).

15. In general, see Robert Boyer (ed.), *La Flexibilité du travail en Europe* (Paris: La Découverte, 1986). On women's labour market participation and related matters see Jane Jenson et al., *The Feminization of the Labour Force* (New York: Polity-Oxford, 1987).

16. Guido Baglioni and Colin Crouch, *European Industrial Relations* (Beverly Hills: Sage, 1990) provides an up-to-date overview.

17. See Wolfgang Streeck, "Neo-Corporatist Industrial Relations and Economic Crisis in West Germany," in John Goldthorpe (ed.), *Order and Conflict in Contemporary Capitalism* (Oxford: Clarendon, 1984), and *idem,* "Industrial Relations in Germany, 1980-1987," *Labour*, 2 (Winter 1988).

18. For a pre-1992 overview see Barbara Barnouin, *The European Labour Movement and European Integration* (London: Frances Pinter, 1986) and

Georges Spyropouloos (ed.), *Trade Unions in a Changing Europe* (Maastricht: Presses Universitaires Européennes, 1989).

19. See Stephen Sylvia, "The Prospect of a Unified European Union Movement as a Result of 1992," paper prepared for the Seventh Conference of Europeanists, Washington, DC, 1990, and Michael Baun, "Europe 1992 and Trade Union Politics: Towards a European 'Industrial Relations Space'," (paper prepared for the Seventh Conference of Europeanists, Washington, DC, 1990. See also Herbert Northrop, Duncan Campbell and Betty Slowinski, "Multinational Union-Management Consultation in Europe: Resurgence in the 1980s?", *International Labour Review*, November-December 1988.

20. Wolfgang Streeck, "More Uncertainties: West German Unions Facing 1992," (paper prepared for the Seventh Conference of Europeanists, Washington D.C., March, 1990).

21. This is the conclusion of most careful observers of Europe. Supranationality—the determination of national actions from above—has not been absent. The Commission has played an important role and the European Court of Justice has played an even greater one. But movement forward has usually been determined by hard bargaining to solve particular problems, like the budget, agricultural policy, exchange rate policy, etc., among nations.

22. ETUC still excludes the French CGT and the Spanish Workers' Commissions, both of which have remained members of the Communist WFTU.

23. Michael Hutsebaut, "The Social Dimension of the Market, Second Part: Workers' Rights in European Companies," *Info 26* (Brussels: ETUC, 1988).

24. The Germans and Dutch want co-determination (even if they disagree about its forms) in which workers sit on company boards. The French and others want "works councils," separate bodies with consultative and other rights, while the British prefer "collectively bargained" solutions in which specific forms of workers' representation are not prescribed in advance, but European companies would be obliged to bargain around such matters. The company law proposal of 1989 would have allowed companies to choose from a menu including all three options, depending upon the actual place where the company was headquartered.

25. Paul Teague, "European Community Labour Market Harmonization," *Journal of Public Policy*, 9:1, 1989.

26. The employers' position on European-wide collective bargaining as well as the Social Charter is stated strongly by Zygmunt Tyszkiewicz, Secretary-General of UNICE, "European Social Policy—Striking the Right Balance," *European Affairs*, Winter 1989.

27. EC decisions on essential matters may have to be made by unanimity or by a qualified majority (in which a certain number of votes is enough for passage, with each country allotted votes in accordance with its importance), depending upon which parts of the Treaty the decisions are meant to modify. Qualified

majority voting is a recent phenomenon coinciding with the Single Market Act modifications to the 1957 Rome Treaty. Thus matters which refer directly to the Single Market Act can be decided by qualified majority.

28.   Indeed, his daughter, Martine Aubry (then a high civil servant), produced a document for the French government *Pour Une Europe Sociale* (Paris: Documentation Française, 1988) which underlined the message. See also Patrick Venturini, *1992: The European Social Dimension* (Brussels: European Commission, 1988) for a preliminary outline of the Social Charter by its principal author.

29.   See *Social Europe*, 2, 1990 for the Action Program.

30.   The European Parliament is relatively powerless except to talk publicly about Commission actions. Europarliamentary protest against the weakness of the Social Charter and Action Program was led, ironically, by the French President of the Socialist Group in Strasbourg, Jean-Pierre Cot, a member of the same French political party as Jacques Delors.

31.   The best review of the Charter and Action Program is written from the point of view of British unions, by Lord Wedderburn, *The Social Charter: European Company and Employment Rights* (London: The Institute for Employment Rights, 1990).

32.   It is not at all clear, for example, that unions in Mediterranean Europe would have that much to gain from really strong efforts to prevent capitalist "sunbelt strategies." Such strategies might result in a strengthening of southern European economies.

33.   Events in Central Europe increase the level of uncertainty. German unification, of course, enhanced German power within the EC, in part because of the inclusion in the EC of the ex-GDR. The new Germany's need for the EC as a place to hide its new international centrality, which led Chancellor Kohl towards greater commitment to Europeanism, may eventually have to be balanced against a Germany seeking to reassert its national interests. Pending membership applications to the EC from a number of EFTA countries (Austria, Sweden and Norway, to begin with) further complicate the immediate future.

The prevalent *political* balance in the EC could change as EC membership and the European environment changes. The EC has historically been overdetermined by two often-overlapping coalitions between social-democratic and Christian-Democratic forces and the French and German governments. What will new German power do to the delicate balance between French political leadership and German economic predominance which has so dominated recent EC history? The incorporation of EFTA countries will not change EC political coalitions appreciably but any eventual "association" of Eastern European countries may have a greater effect, depending upon their political evolution. Movement in the East towards full-blown economically liberal societies could upset the existing but delicate European political balance that rests in favour of the "European Model of Society."

34. In rapid order, beginning in Summer 1989, the EC began to co-ordinate food and financial aid to Poland and Hungary, established the European Bank for Reconstruction and Development to finance Eastern European redevelopment projects, got deeply involved in the Gulf War and decided to grant the Soviet Union a substantial amount of economic help, all the while initiating a quiet, behind-the-scenes discussion of defense matters.

35. In important ways this is a function of dramatic changes in the ways progressive Left intellectuals have come to see the social world in recent years. We have written about this for France, albeit somewhat polemically, in "Intellectuals Against the Left: The Case of France," in Ralph Miliband and Leo Panitch (eds.), *The Socialist Register, 1990* (London: Merlin Press, 1990).

36. France has been a most spectacular scene of such things in the last few years, even if racist intolerance is prominent in many other European settings. In France, Le Pen's Front National has clearly drawn much support from former supporters of the Left who have concluded in the 1980s that the Left's long-standing promises of economic security and reform were hollow.

37. Post-Fordist social democracy's technocratic definitions of reality which seek to portray constraints as insuperable will undoubtedly constitute a formidable barrier to mobilization at both the national and supranational level in Europe. Moreover, post-Fordist social-democratic technocrats have a bureaucratic allergy to democratic mobilization—they are incapable, it seems, of anything more than a modernized *noblesse oblige* which will prove profoundly uninviting to groundswells from below.

38. Patrick Camiller's sober assessment of the European situation in "Beyond 1992: The Left and Europe," *New Left Review*, 175, 1989 elaborates on these issues. See also *Marxism Today*, April, 1989, for a "New Times" vision of Europe which has a very different understanding of post-Fordism than the one suggested here.

39. Here we want to note our rejection of notions like Piore and Sabel's "yeoman democratic" response to "flexible specialization which are unconnected with underlying logics and therefore utopian "

40. Thus elites may respond by policy which speaks to elite and not movement needs, they may stimulate countermobilization, they may wait and see if the movement has staying power, or they may simply not respond at all.

PART
III

SPATIAL HORIZONS:
RECONFIGURING
THE MAP

|| CHAPTER
|| 11

GREENING THE NEW
CANADIAN POLITICAL ECONOMY

|| GLEN
|| WILLIAMS

The 1990s has been heralded as the decade of the environment for the advanced capitalist countries. Are the practitioners of the new Canadian political economy prepared? The exploration of environmental issues requires an analytical framework that can incorporate geographic space, production and trade, technology, and the organization of social power. Despite possessing such a framework, there has been remarkably little written within the Canadian political economy tradition that directly addresses the degradation of our environment.[1] With our strong record of aggressive intellectual trailblazing in other spheres of Canada's national political life, what accounts for our environmental blind spot? And how might Canadian political economy now begin to bring environmental issues into sharper focus?

This article can only reflect in a preliminary fashion on these questions. It seeks, however, to scout the terrain for future serious discussion and investigation of the environment by those working in the political economy tradition. As the result of the vast area to be covered, our considerations do not always fit together into a neat package with regular and predictable dimensions. This is because three separate sites must be incorporated into our survey if we are to record the principal features of this subject's vast topography. These include: the national specificity of Canadian popular discourse as it relates to the environment and the limitations of that popular discourse as revealed in mainstream political commentary and debate; the inadequate treatment of the environment within the new Canadian political economy; and, finally, an exploration of some ways in which the new Canadian political economy might creatively employ its unique method so as to expand productively the academic and public horizons of contemporary environmental debates.

CYCLONES AND ECO-HOSTILITY

Canada was developed as a resource hinterland for more advanced economic centres: France, Great Britain and the United States. Waves of super-exploitation of the natural resources, found in abundance on such a large land mass, have attended this form of economic development. Harold Innis left us with the arresting image of the cyclonic development of Canada's fur, fish, timber, wheat, pulp and paper, and mineral resource staples.[2] As the result of the unmediated application of advanced technologies to the natural ecosystem of Canada's geographic regions, these cyclones, without exception, left in their wake massive social and ecological destruction. Indeed, it was the despoliation by overexploitation of one resource product that often led directly to the search for a replacement resource staple to begin the cycle again.[3]

In understanding the expression of environmentalism within contemporary Canadian political discourse, the historic attitude of Canadians to this process of cyclonic development is key. Rather than objecting to the devastation of their natural environment by foreign economic enterprises, Canadians have typically identified their interests more closely with these foreign developers than with the preservation of their own environment. Native peoples have often stood as courageous exceptions to this rule, but the environmental insights of their civilizations were routed in the wake of the first continental cyclone, the fur trade.[4] Here, as elsewhere in the world, the European conquest societies scorned indigenous paradigms of appropriate technology and development that were at odds with their own "scientific" models of commodity-based production, and with their notion of "progress," premised upon dominance of the natural world.[5] Pioneer immigrants were committed to making over the land after first a European, and then an American, model, and owed their livelihoods to that process of transformation. Twentieth century urbanization created a majority settled in southern cities, who rarely encountered the environmental havoc that resulted from the resource development cyclones, and could continue to take comfort in the myth of an infinitely expansive unspoiled northern frontier. Those who actually lived on this frontier frequently found themselves to be in conflict with expressions of an urban conservationist ethic, as they directly depended on the employment booms the cyclones created. Contemporary examples of the struggle between native, conservationist, and resource exploitation perspectives can be drawn from the debates about logging in the Queen Charlotte Islands and the Carmanah Valley in British Columbia.

With these economic forces and attendant attitudes at work, it is scarcely surprising that much of Canada has suffered severe environmental damage as a consequence of promoting the export of Canadian resources to more highly industrialized centres. And these resource export industries have typically been owned or financed by investors in these same foreign centres. Clear cutting of vast stands of timber has led to soil erosion, water pollution and destruction of wildlife habitat from coast to coast. Until relatively recently, most governments and large companies paid only slight attention to forest management; existing harvest levels cannot be sustained in the majority of provinces. Waste from wood processing plants adds greatly to the pollution burden. Fish stocks on both coasts have been seriously depleted through the combined effects of the application of intensive harvesting techniques and water pollution. Fish in many of the largest interior lakes are edible only in small quantities because of chemical poisons. Imprudent agricultural techniques have resulted in massive soil erosion and added to the burden of water pollution. Perhaps the most vivid example of this process was the prairie dust bowl of the 1930s which affected fully one-quarter of Canada's arable land. Mines and mine smelters have rendered their surrounding local ecosystems moonscapes. Oil, natural gas, and the chemical industries associated with their development have spread their own witches' brew of toxic wastes to several provinces. Even the generation of "clean" hydro-electric power for export has torn up unimaginably large tracts of wilderness. For example, the water reservoirs created by Quebec's James Bay development have covered an area half the size of Lake Ontario. Quebec Hydro's plans for James Bay II call for an almost 50 percent increase in the land already flooded in the north of the province.

All of this is not to say that Canada has paid a higher price in ecological damage than have the foreign (mainly U.S.) centres that consume its resource exports. Industrial *and* resource producing regions of North America each burn in their own special rooms of a common environmental hell. Canadian staples production, as Innis observed, is a source of "disturbances not only within Canada but without."[6] Whether one considers Canada or the United States, the genius of the North American capitalist economy is eco-hostile in the sense that it is antithetical to a rational, social planning for production and consumption which provides for the maintenance of harmonious relations with the natural environment. The economic growth underpinning fordist mass consumption has been largely predicated on the inefficient squandering of materials and labour,[7] the massive subsidization of wasteful military production, and the reproduction of all of this on the base of a predatory economic international order led by the United States. Following the prevailing economic view, nature can be privately requisitioned, virtually without any limits. There is little sense that natural resources exist in systemic relationship with each other.[8] At its heart, the process of market allocation in North America (and, increasingly, elsewhere) elevates the automobile to absolute dictator of a Marx Brothers musical-comedy "Freedonia."[9] Here, the insatiable and toxic requirements of a system of individual car ownership define the terms of an upside down "sustainable development"—finding, pumping, and burning enough non-renewable fossil fuels to organize transportation, housing, employment, industry and recreation around its use!

Although we will see that Canada's territorial specificity has been key to the development of contemporary popular Canadian thinking on environmental issues, it is important to set out from the beginning the shallowness of the "nationalist" critique that has been generated through this process and its extreme distance from a more ecologically informed position. Put simply, in so far as popular Canadian national sentiment has been mobilized on environmental matters, we will see that it has typically taken on a very narrow *territorial* manifestation closely related to expressions of national *political* sovereignty. This territorial and political focus is curious and merits scrutiny because it would seem obvious that relations between production and the environment are actually played out on a mainly *economic* stage.

A very brief sketch of the some of the most relevant features of the Canadian social formation will prove helpful in establishing the context here. Most serious analysis of the post-1945 Canadian economy has demonstrated that in both the resource and industrial sectors, Canada has been organized as a *region* within a Fordist U.S. economy that held out the promise of an end-less flow of jobs and consumer goodies.[10] While retaining formal political sovereignty, there has been a widespread Canadian acceptance of U.S. leadership in continental economic development as well as foreign and defence policy. Consequently, for both the Canadian elites and mass, economic nationalism has rarely meant more than a desire to use the Canadian state system to gain some measure of greater control over the pace, extent, and benefits of continental economic integration. Nevertheless, while ceding economic leadership to the Americans, Canadians strongly manifest a desire to maintain distinctive territorial and socio-cultural boundaries between Canada and the United States.[11]

Accordingly, it is not surprising that the grand issues surrounding Canada's role within an eco-hostile U.S. economy have seldom energized our public debates over environmental issues. The degradation of Canada's environment through resource mismanagement by and for mainly U.S. economic interests acting to serve mainly U.S. markets has rarely been perceived by most Canadians as a "national" problem. This is not to say that the environment has been at the margins of national political controversy during the last decade—far from it. However, popular discourse around this issue has been carried on in a peculiarly Canadian manner. In large measure the environmental crisis reached domestic public consciousness during the 1980s through the avenue of Canada-U.S. inter-state relations. It centred around questions of *territory*, specifically the violation of Canada's territorial boundaries by American polluters. Thus, it was not based in, nor did it give rise to, a more fundamental critique of the eco-hostile character of North American production, and did not put into question the essentially disharmonious relationship of that form of production with the natural environment. As with many other topics in Canadian political life, space has taken precedence here over other mediums like race or class in organizing and channelling social conflict.[12]

ENVIRONMENTALISM AS THE POLITICS OF REGION

A succession of Canada-U.S. environmental conflicts rooted in the protection of Canada's territorial integrity have given the Canadian public a very regionally singular vision of the meaning of protecting their environment.[13] The transit of hazardous materials, with the attendant risk of spill and contamination, through coastal or other border areas has long been a sensitive issue. For example, the transport of Alaska oil through the Northwest Passage has sparked various attempts by Canada to demonstrate its sovereignty over this area and the shipping of oil by tanker from Alaska to the U.S. Northwest causes continuing concern. Irrigation issues, notably the Garrison Diversion Unit in the U.S. state of North Dakota, led to more than two decades of wrangling between the two countries. In its originally planned form, this project, which diverts Missouri River water into the dry North Dakota farmlands, would have led to contamination of the Hudson's Bay drainage system through Manitoba. Finally, in very recent years, Canadian governments have begun to express worries about the safe operation of nuclear power plants within bordering U.S. states. External Affairs has made representations about at least three such plants in Ohio, Michigan and Washington and Canadian environmental groups have identified 49 suspect U.S. plants that they feel pose a danger to Canadians.[14]

The most visible Canada-U.S. conflict over the environment in the 1980s, and the one which by itself forged many basic contemporary Canadian attitudes toward environmental matters, was unquestionably that of acid rain. Indeed, when Canadians were asked in the months preceding the 1988 "free trade" election to identify the most important issue to stress in bilateral talks, 45 percent chose acid rain, only 30 percent free trade and a further 21 percent saw these two issues as being equally important.[15] Moreover, 71 percent believed that the Canadian government had made little or no progress in getting the U.S. government to take action on acid rain and 57 percent felt that the Canadian government was not doing all it could to reach an agreement.[16] Indeed, almost two-fifths of Canadians felt that continued pressure through diplomatic and political channels was not enough and wanted to "look for some means of retaliation" against the U.S..[17]

The other major transborder environmental controversy of the 1980s was the very grave pollution of the Great Lakes-St. Lawrence River drainage system. Approximately one-third of the Canadian population lives in communities strung along these waters shared with the Americans. Although most readers will be generally familiar with both the acid rain and Great Lakes water quality cases, some space will now be given over here to a brief recapitulation of the political development of these issues. Through such an examination, we will be prepared at a later point to see how one might apply the insights of the new Canadian political economy to these cases in a manner which might transcend the severely constricted limits of popular discourse and public policy.

ACID RAIN

Canada-U.S. negotiations on acid rain actually began in the late 1970s and were prompted by scientific studies which pointed to the serious consequences of sulphur dioxide and nitrogen oxides emissions on forests, lakes and rivers. It at first appeared that progress on this problem could be made quickly. A memorandum of intent on transboundary air pollution was signed in 1980 pledging both governments to negotiate a formal agreement and in June 1981 these negotiations got underway. Canada had a particularly strong motive in pursuing these talks, as half the acid rain that falls on its territory is the result of U.S. polluters while only one-tenth of acid rain in the U.S. can be traced to Canadian sources. However, two important factors intervened to weaken the American resolve: (1) the oil crisis and the desire to move towards energy self-sufficiency through the use of U.S. coal; and (2) the assumption of U.S. executive power by the Reagan administration, which listened only to the lobby of the Appalachian coal-producing and the Midwest coal-consuming states on this issue.

After the U.S. withdrew from the talks in 1982, the contrasting positions of the two countries became ever more sharply defined. Canada argued that the U.S. was evading both its bilateral and international treaty obligations.[18] In an effort to harden a U.S. public opinion already worried about the effect of acid rain on the north-eastern states, Canadian provincial and federal governments began intensive lobbying of both the President and the Congress, intervened before U.S. regulatory agencies and courts, and launched a public relations campaign to educate American voters on the issue. The U.S. coal lobby counter-attacked by suggesting that the Canadians were doing little themselves to meet the 50 percent target reduction (by 1990) that they wanted to impose on the Americans; that the Canadian concern for placing controls on U.S. coal plants was motivated by the desire of provincial utility companies to export hydro and nuclear power; and, finally, that Canada's lobbying efforts were an interference in U.S. domestic affairs.

Stung by U.S. charges of inaction, the provinces and federal government agreed in 1984 to co-operate in reducing Canadian emissions by 50 percent by 1994. That year, 1984, also marked the coming to power in Ottawa of the Mulroney Conservatives who were determined to pursue a far less confrontational style in Canada-U.S. relations. Hostage to this orientation, and to the greater priority given to successful negotiation of a free trade agreement, the Canadian federal government subsequently spiked many of its foreign policy guns on this issue. For its part, a grateful Reagan administration stuffed cotton batting in its ears to mute the *pro forma* Canadian acid rain chorus. From time to time, it even showed itself willing to help the Ottawa Tories by offering symbolic concessions as evidence to Canadian public opinion that Mulroney's patience would eventually pay dividends. So transparent did this "phoney war" become that one U.S. Congressman from Minnesota was actually driven to accuse Mulroney of retarding American efforts to deal with acid rain. "Each time the Prime Minister of Canada sidles up to President Reagan on acid rain, he confuses the American public and diminishes the effective pressure from Congress," he argued.[19]

The 'sidling up' began at the 1985 summit between the two leaders, where it was decided to commission a report on acid rain by two special Envoys, a former Reagan cabinet member and a former Ontario Premier. In 1986, Reagan agreed to endorse the envoys' report which called for the expenditure of five billion dollars on research and demonstration projects on reduced acid coal firing. In 1987, Reagan suggested in a speech before the Canadian House of Commons that he would "consider" a bilateral accord on acid rain. Less than one month later, the head of the U.S. Environmental Protection Agency conceded that Reagan was only kidding: that such an accord would not include a controls program. Without question, the most burlesque of these staged events was the flying visit of then Vice-President Bush to Ottawa in January of 1987 and his subsequent appearance before the television cameras looking like a chastened schoolboy. Bush had been dispatched at an awkward stage of the free trade negotiations to shore up Mulroney's credentials as a Canadian nationalist by receiving a four hour "earful" from the Prime Minister on U.S. inaction on acid rain.

To his credit, Bush demonstrated much more readiness to move on this issue than his predecessor. In June of 1989, he announced a plan to cut acid rain producing emissions by one-half by the end of this century. However, his plan subsequently received mixed reviews both because the ensuing U.S. Clean Air Act falls somewhat short of his announced targets and because the Act actually allows for increased emissions from a number of Ohio Valley generating stations over the next few years. As well, the signing in early 1991 of a largely symbolic Canada-U.S. acid rain "Accord" does little to push forward a resolution of this issue. The Accord merely commits each country to enforce its already existing acid rain legislation and sets up no enforcement mechanism. Significantly, there is little immediate prospect of an acid rain treaty between Canada and the U.S. because it would require two-thirds majority support in Congress and would legally bind American behaviour.[20]

GREAT LAKES WATER

The conduct of bilateral relations in respect to curbing Great Lakes pollution is a model of square dealing in comparison with the posing, posturing, and foot dragging that has stalled progress on the control of acid rain. Three important agreements between Canada and the U.S. to reduce transborder pollution of the Lakes have been signed during the last two decades. In contrast to the acid rain situation, this progress has been the direct result of the polluters being for the most part themselves located on the Lakes and therefore unable to escape the consequences of their pollution.[21]

Pollution problems on parts of the Great Lakes were already severe at the end of the nineteenth century with an annual average of 85 typhoid deaths from using them as a source for drinking water. The deterioration of Great Lakes water quality led to the signing of the 1909 Canada-U.S. Boundary Waters Treaty and the establishment of the binational International Joint Commission (IJC). The IJC report of 1918 judged the Great Lake waters as "unsightly, malodorous, and absolutely unfit for domestic purposes."[22] In spite of the IJC's yeoman efforts in subsequent years to exhort both countries to take water conservation seriously, widespread pollution continued virtually unchecked. By the 1950s, over seven billion litres of waste were being discharged daily into the Great Lakes and in the 1960s the Cuyahoga River at Cleveland was so loaded with petroleum, chemicals and floating debris that it periodically burst into flames.[23] Nearly 1400 chemicals have been detected in the Lakes' ecosystem with 362 of these being synthetic chemicals and 24 of these known to be hazardous to humans.[24]

By the late 1960s, visual evidence of the pollution of the Great Lakes had reached such alarming levels (making credible warnings that the shallowest of the Lakes, Erie, was dying) that the public pressure necessary to force governments to implement some of the IJC's recommendations for a cleanup, began to mount. After extensive consultations and negotiations between the three provincial, eight state, and two federal jurisdictions concerned, Canada and the U.S. in 1972, 1978 and 1987 signed the Great Lakes Water Quality Agreements. All levels of government have subsequently spent close to 20 billion dollars on sewage treatment with over 200 communities in the Great Lakes Basin adding new or upgrading existing treatment plants. Phosphorous from detergents and agricultural runoff has been significantly reduced.

With demonstrable success in reducing visible pollutants, concern during the 1980s shifted to the control of the typically invisible but potentially far more dangerous pollution from toxic chemicals. In 1985, the IJC identified 42 "areas of concern" in the Basin (41 where toxic chemical contamination was present): 25 in the U.S., 12 in Canada, and five shared. This figure may actually be quite conservative: a citizens' group in Toronto catalogued 328 danger sites.[25] The 1987 Great Lakes Water Quality Agreement sets out specific timetables for cleaning up the 42 sites identified by the IJC.

Perhaps the hottest of the toxic "hot spots" is the Niagara River which drains the four upper Lakes into Lake Ontario. More than four million Canadians and one million Americans draw their drinking water from Lake Ontario. In 1986, Environment Canada reported that toxic chemicals originating in the Niagara have been discovered as far downstream as Quebec City. Yet a 1984 report of the Niagara River Toxics Committee (Ontario, New York, Canada, the United States) showed that 1400 kilograms of pollutants considered dangerous by the U.S. Environmental Protection Agency were pouring *daily* into the river. Ninety percent of this flow came from only ten sites (only one in Canada).[26] These include the notorious Hyde Park and Love Canal sites of Hooker/Occidental Chemicals. In February of 1987, Ontario, New York and the two federal governments signed a declaration of intent to lower toxic chemical discharge into the Niagara by 50 percent before 1996.

POLITICAL ECONOMY AND THE ENVIRONMENT

The significance of the acid rain and Great Lakes water cases to the formation of contemporary environmental consciousness in Canada can scarcely be overstated. Millions of Canadians first learned something of the environmental havoc that has been inflicted on their country through the terrifyingly personalized stories of their poisoned drinking water and dead northern lakes. Through the pronouncements of their media and political leadership, Canadians were told that Canada's genuine attempts to control these problems were being frustrated through an inconsiderate and arrogant American truculence. A national sentiment of moral superiority, epitomized in federal government distributed red and white "Stop Acid Rain" buttons, was aroused in a popular movement to protect Canadian territory from a hostile 'invasion' of U.S. pollutants. In this manner, any deeper questioning of the fundamentally eco-hostile basis of North American production on both sides of the border was passed over.

One of the new Canadian political economy's proudest claims is that it seeks as a primary goal to "know how societies are, and can be, transformed... frequently this means challenging conventional wisdom and ideological structures in the popular, academic, and political domains."[27] Regrettably, when it comes to being environmentally sensitive, the new Canadian political economy has more often reflected than challenged the conventional wisdom of popular discourse. If we turn our attention specifically to the just reviewed acid rain and Great Lakes water pollution cases, the picture is even bleaker. In spite of their centrality to the evolution of public environmental consciousness in Canada during the last decade, with the notable exception of a path-breaking 1982 chapter by Stephen Clarkson, the new Canadian political economy was virtually silent on these two issues.[28]

What accounts for this failure? A superficial answer to this question, focusing on the personal circumstances of the practitioners of the new Canadian political economy, could be constructed: after all, many of them have enjoyed relatively privileged access to the consumer bells and whistles delivered by an eco-hostile economy built on the radically inefficient squandering of materials and labour. It is also true that sometimes their view of the environmental movement was coloured by solidarity with the struggles of native and non-native fur harvesters against maudlin animal rights activists waving the banner of ecology.[29]

Beyond the personal, however, greater insight into the new Canadian political economy's failure to grasp the mantle of the environment can come through a consideration of the dependency and class theoretical frameworks that energized it from the 1970s until the late 1980s. These variants of neo-Marxist analysis stressed distribution—spatial and social—over the process or objectives of *production* as related to the social construction of nature. The issue that animated the dependency era was Canada's loss of economic potential due to American dominance. Class analysis, on the other hand, documented the social power of capital in relation to the working class. Most often, then, those engaged in political economy analysis have been preoccupied with a fairer social and/or spatial distribution of Fordism's bounty. Their critique of capitalism stopped somewhere short of an evaluation of the environmental degradation which ensued from using certain products or bringing them to market. Consequently, through its failure to give a central place to the structural threat posed to our natural environment by the eco-hostile character of continental production, the new Canadian political economy developed an obstructed view of the environment, one which was paralleled within mainstream political discourse. Just as Canada-U.S. environmental issues have most frequently become visible to the general public in a territorial dimension, so in the new Canadian political economy the environment has typically only been made visible in light of spatial or social exploitation.

Since we are unable to turn to a political economy literature on acid rain and Great Lakes water pollution to illustrate these points, we will choose instead as proxies some of the most important studies that have been produced by the new Canadian political economy on resources. My discussion of these works is not meant to highlight the shortcomings of the individual authors examined. On the contrary, these texts are worthy of consideration because they are such outstanding and influential contributions. Nor is my argument meant to apply only to the resource scholars, although the very direct relevance of environmental concerns for their subject matter is obvious.[30] I merely wish to demonstrate that while these works are animated by clear challenges to the spatial and/or social order of continental capitalism, its ecological order is only marginally contested.

One of the first important statements of the new Canadian political economy on resources, *Prairie Capitalism* by John Richards and Larry Pratt, is also one of the weakest on the environment. This book is driven by the question of state capacity to bring about a definitive break from the staple economy's structural deficiencies and concludes that "within the traditions and norms of North American capitalism, the choice of a staple-led strategy of development may well be the most rational course..."[31] The implications for the environment on how oil and natural gas are produced and consumed "within the traditions and norms of North American capitalism" are left unexplored. This need not have been the case. The book begins with the intriguing but undeveloped observation that "oil and gas are resources whose peculiar physical properties virtually compel intervention by the state in order to prevent a chaotic pattern of destructive competition" in the context of a discussion of environmental problems caused by flaring of natural gas during the 1920s.[32]

Wallace Clement's landmark companion studies on Canadian mining and fishing bridge the preoccupations of the dependency and class schools by documenting, respectively, spatial and social inequality. Somewhat less attention is given in *The Struggle to Organize* to the staples character of the fishery in its continental context. Instead, attention is focused on the class relations that underlie the organizational formation of the fishery.[33] *Hardrock Mining* differs in that it provides a more balanced discussion of class and regional power. Nevertheless, both books treat the environment as an add-on; its degradation is seen a function of unequal power relations rather than a integral feature of the system of production. *Hardrock Mining*, for example, includes a discussion of environmental damage at the end of a chapter on occupational health and safety. There, pollution is portrayed as a function of capital's control of the production process rather as any inherent attribute of production for Fordist mass consumption.

> Safety and the protection of health are inextricably bound to class interests. They are part of the power to define the work process and organization of work. The priorities of management and workers differ fundamentally... Outside the workplace management passes on to the community part of the cost of production in the form of pollution and environmental damage. The state in most instances sanctions and legitimizes the right of capital to control the workplace and pollute the environment.[34]

Political economy's most comprehensive examination of post-World War II Canadian resource production can be found in the outstanding archival study, *A Staple State*, by Melissa Clark-Jones. Her work charts the role of the Canadian federal state in facilitating and fostering "continental resource capitalism" in the mining, forest, and energy sectors. Challenging the value of the continentalist accumulation regime for Canada, she argues that it has resulted in a "declining emphasis on both maintenance of large-scale employment and the manufacturing condition..."[35] While the spatial order of the economy is contested, its ecological order is barely mentioned. There is a special incongruity here. Clark-Jones exhaustively documents how Canadian resources fed the machinery of the Cold War; machinery which, by definition, is at the heart of the eco-hostile American production system. Like Clement, however, Clark-Jones does no more than add the environment on to her critique of corporate capitalist power. "Macro decisions involving the use of technology and labour remain in the hands of monopolistic corporations," she notes, "while the taxpayer subsidizes such enterprise without gaining the control that could protect his or her job or community from the social fall-out of unemployment, pollution, and depletion of resources."[36]

With an examination of 1970s and early 1980s forestry in British Columbia, Patricia Marchak's *Green Gold* also documents the effects of social and spatial power inequalities. And while her study does not often stray outside these familiar confines, she displays greater sensitivity than any of the other authors surveyed here to the underlying complexities of integrating environmental issues into a political economy analysis. Consider, for example, the way in which her conclusion points far beyond remedies which apply only social or spatial justice to the ills carried by continental capitalism.

> We are at a stage of historical development where mass production techniques and energy-intensive industries are transparently problematic. These are the technologies of the multinational corporations. When such corporations argue their case in terms of competitive demands they are pursuing policies that steadily decrease the earth's resources, pollute the environment, and destroy the habitat of the earth's creatures. These are real dangers over and above the economic problems that they pose.[37]

Marchak even introduces the—for some—heretical notion that the organized working class can be part of the problem, rather than simply the agent of its solution. In reference to the Queen Charlotte Islands logging dispute she writes,

> while the union observes that large companies are more responsible caretakers of the resource than small companies (for the reason that they have a longer time-planning horizon), it is still true that large companies have been in control for much of the industry's history and the forest has been overcut, reforestation has not kept pace with requirements for a renewable resource, and responsible ecologists are strongly convinced that fish and wildlife resources have been severely damaged by poor logging practices... The point here is not to argue the case for or against this particular wilderness area, but to illustrate the structural situation in which a labour union is obliged to defend a vested interest in logging forested areas.[38]

PRODUCTION AND DISTRIBUTION REVISITED

In the recently published, provocatively titled *Environmentalism and the Future of Progressive Politics*, Trent University's Robert Paehlke posits a fundamental disjunction between environmentalism and Left analysis and politics. Indeed, he elevates environmentalism to the status of a political ideology distinct from conservatism, liberalism and socialism. "There is no necessary relationship between one's position on environmental issues and one's position on distributional issues," Paehlke claims. Furthermore, environmental ideology "is something more than a matter of the economic self-interest of the poor, the rich, or the middle classes, and ideological categories understood exclusively in distributional terms can no longer account for the whole ideological world."[39]

We noted earlier that the dependency and class theoretical frameworks employed by the new Canadian political economy during the 1970s and 1980s focused on *distribution* at the expense of addressing the ecological consequences of *production*. Does this confirm, as Paehlke argues, that a progressive political economy is fundamentally limited or flawed when it confronts the environment? On the contrary, just because we have so far failed to incorporate an environmental dynamic in a thoroughgoing manner, one cannot conclude that our method is inherently flawed. After all, the environment cannot somehow stand outside of society. Resources are socially and politically constructed and determined "in the sense that their value is related to the technologies used to exploit them and the existence of people to consume them."[40] Indeed, Paehlke himself admits that environmental policy tools have a distinct class character: "left, right, or centrist."[41] For example, when discussing the transition to a "soft energy path" (SEP) relying primarily on renewable sources of fuel, Paehlke observes that

> SEP sources, at present levels of demand, may well produce considerable environmental and economic stresses of their own. For example, there may be competition between biomass for fuel and for food. If an SEP is pursued in a free market, the rich may drive alcohol-fuelled cars while the poor go hungry.[42]

Further, in reference to allowing workers to capture direct benefits from engineering waste and planned obsolescence out of production, Paehlke observes that

> an interesting, though perhaps extreme, extension of the logic of time off for enhanced productivity would involve linking reductions in work time to product durability. Here the threat to the logic of the capitalist workplace is most apparent. Products deliberately designed, within the bounds of production costs, for durability and/or reparability would drastically cut into profits. Despite its compelling environmental logic, therefore, this proposal may be beyond the system's capability for adaptation.[43]

It would seem that production and distribution are not, after all, distant, separate galaxies in the ecological universe! Issues of production are also issues of distribution in the sense that they reflect the fearsome power of capital to organize the production process and to determine the varying rhythms and qualities of life accessible to different social strata. The new Canadian political economy is well positioned to bridge the production/distribution divide as it relates to the environment. We have already developed a sophisticated understanding of spatial and social inequalities that can be carried directly to an environmental analysis. It would now be appropriate to bring several of these understandings into play in order to show how the method of the new Canadian political economy might be employed to analyze environmental issues.

Earlier sections of this paper, it will be recalled, traced an outline of Canadian popular discourse on environmental issues through recounting the development of two focal debates around acid rain and Great Lakes water pollution. How could the insights of political economy help us transcend the limited horizons of popular discourse and public policy in these two cases? The following discussion represents one attempt to point us in the direction of what can be done with a creative application of the intellectual tools that we already possess. It is meant to be illustrative, reflecting nothing more than my own cut on Canadian political economy. It by no means exhausts the ways in which the new Canadian political economy could tackle either these specific cases or, more generally, the environment as a research category.

SUMMARY AND DISCUSSION

Although, as we have seen, Canada's national specificity has been central to the development of popular Canadian discourse on environmental issues, the "nationalist" critique that has been generated though this process has proceeded more from a territorial than an *ecological* base. Where continental environmental issues are perceived as purely economic (e.g. mega-project resource development) the chances of mobilization by Canadian environmental forces have been lower than where these issues are presented in a more classically territorial dimension (e.g. acid rain). This has led to an oversimplification and obfuscation of the integral and complementary roles that Canadian regions play within U.S. resource production and/or manufacturing. Acid rain and Great Lakes water pollution are not produced by "nations" but by a single eco-hostile economic system organized "in different spatial structures, particular bundles of functions within the overall relations of production."[44] In fact, northern North America's pollution problems are spatially specific to the regional organization of a single continental economy and solutions can only emerge within the complex network of federal, provincial/state and local political structures that mediate social conflict within this economy.

Accordingly, the acid rain and Great Lakes water cases force us to reconsider the appropriateness of employing conventional concepts like national state sovereignty in the analysis of such questions. Anthony Giddens tells us that

> sovereignty simultaneously provides an ordering principle for what is 'internal' to states and what is 'external' to them... A sovereign state

> is a political organization that has the capacity, within a delimited territory or territories, to make laws and effectively sanction their upkeep...[45]

However, to view the conduct of Canada-U.S. environmental relations as being driven by the expression of the "national" interests of two sovereign states is an oversimplification. Rather, as we witnessed in the acid rain case, the expression of "national" positions may actually reflect the domestic political ascendancy of elite or popular interests of some regions in Canada or the U.S. over others. "National" positions may even be the product of cross-border alliances between Canadian and U.S. interests and regions. We may be able to think more clearly about these interactions by discounting fixed notions of state sovereignty through adopting an *inter-federal* rather than an *international* relations perspective.

Federal systems in liberal democracies provide multiple points of institutional access for elite and popular interests. An attempt can always be made to compensate for political losses at one of the levels of a federal system by playing off one jurisdiction against another. This feature of the federal structure does not in itself favour the environmental lobby because business groups have historically been the most adept at employing it.[46] However, in an *inter-federal* system, environmental groups can increase both their legitimacy and effectiveness in their own domestic political arena by finding a means to enlist the support of national or regional governments of the other federation. For example, in 1981 the New York Public Interest Research Group caused a considerable Canadian outcry after showing that U.S. federal and state officials had been aware for years of the toxic chemical dumping of 27 million litres daily into the Niagara River and had deliberately kept this information from their Canadian counterparts.[47] By the same token, through allying itself with American environmental groups, Canadian governments have been able to increase the legitimacy and effectiveness of their representations within the U.S. political system.

The free trade debate of the late 1980s has led some observers to conclude that Canada may be destined in the not too distant future to be absorbed within the American Union. There is little to suggest that the relatively few representatives within the U.S. Congress and Senate that the Canadian provinces would gain through annexation would be enough to change the balance of American political power on environmental issues like acid rain or Great Lakes pollution. Nor is it likely that in a political system characterized by logrolling and lack of party discipline that the "Canadian" representatives would continue to speak as one on the environment. The present *intra-*

federal system, predicated on the spatial division of political sovereignty in northern North America, provides remarkably effective mechanisms for the *formulation and articulation* of a Canadian regional interest on environmental (and other) policy matters. It also provides the possibility of treaties and/or the creation of binational institutions (e.g. the IJC) to protect, on the basis of rough equality, the interests of less than one-tenth of the combined population of the two countries. Consider as an illustration the strong desire of Quebec residents, as evidenced in opinion polls, to control transborder acid rain.[48] It seems reasonable to suppose that the province has more to gain on this question from the collective lobby of a Canadian federation than anything Quebec on its own could mount either as a single state in an expanded American Union or as a hold-out independent nation outside an even larger United States which had absorbed the other Canadian provinces.

Finally, we must also conclude that while the inter-federal system may hold certain advantages for the *political* expression of environmental issues, its divided jurisdictional base places severe *administrative* constraints on the ability to deliver effective environmental controls. The last two biennial reports of the International Joint Commission have pointed to the failure of governments on both sides of the border to be able to develop and implement plans to meet the objectives set out in the Great Lakes Water Quality Agreements. For example, the IJC noted in its Third Biennial Report (1986) that

> while governments deserve praise for support of the ecosystem concept, there are mixed results in its actual implementation under the Agreement. In governmental programs, the traditional separation of responsibilities and authorities between and among international, federal, state, provincial, and local Great Lakes entities is often at odds with the pursuit of an integrated approach. All levels of government tend to react rather than anticipate and are not accustomed to acting in a unified manner for continuing and co-ordinated management.[49]

To put it more simply, in the context of an eco-hostile U.S. economy, the inter-federal system has been generating environmental light without significant amounts of heat. In late 1989, as a result of a two year joint study, the Canadian Institute for Research on Public Policy and the U.S. Conservation Foundation concluded that the Great Lakes were in an "environmental crisis" despite decades of promises to clean them up. Toxins present in Great Lakes water may be responsible for human birth defects, tumours, nerve and brain damage and may lead to "subtle alterations" in thinking and behaviour.[50]

CONCLUSIONS

Employing the method of political economy, as we have just done, to build several propositions about environmental issues delivers some rich and intriguing results. The environment is much more than simply a new subject to "add on" to an analysis already completely determined by relations of class and/or space. If Canadian political economy is to come to terms with the environmental revolution, it must do so in a far more inclusive and fundamental manner. At this point most of us recognize that race and gender, along with their dynamics of racism and patriarchy, must be fully incorporated into political economy research as categories with independent explanatory power.[51] This is a necessary condition for continuing to give intellectual leadership to academic research on Canada and in so doing play a direct role in shaping the popular discourse on politics in this country.

The environment or ecology, with its dynamic to be discovered in the problematic of the maintenance of harmonious relations between human production and nature, is a third category that we must now move toward the centre of our work. As we learned from our overview of the acid rain and Great Lakes water pollution cases, the eco-hostile basis of continental capitalism has not at all been well articulated in public debates or public policies on environmental matters. And, as ecological issues achieve greater salience in the post-Free Trade Agreement 1990s where continental capitalism promises a personal environmental salvation through "green" groceries and blue garbage boxes, there will be an ever greater need for a thoughtful political economy critique. It is clear from our brief survey of some of our central texts on resource production that until now the new Canadian political economy has not given the environment the attention that it merits. This is a situation that indeed holds considerable irony. It was revulsion against an unplanned, growth-before-human-values, wasteful and irrational economic system that first stimulated many of us to generate our critiques of continental capitalism. What previously has been implicit in our analysis must now become explicit.

ENDNOTES

This article is a revised version of a paper prepared for a Conference on Canada-U.S. relations at Queen's University of Belfast, October 1989. My thanks for the helpful comments of Wallace Clement, Rianne Mahon, Michael Whittington and the *Studies in Political Economy* reviewers and editors.

1. To illustrate, our 1989 collection of essays which survey the Canadian political economy literature does not include a chapter on the environment. W. Clement and G. Williams (eds.), *The New Canadian Political Economy* (Montreal: McGill-Queen's, 1989).

2. For an overview, see R. Neil, *A New Theory of Value: The Canadian Economics of H.A. Innis* (Toronto: University of Toronto Press, 1972), Chapters 3 and 4.

3. See H.A. Innis, *The Fur Trade in Canada*, rev. ed. (Toronto: University of Toronto Press, 1956), or "The Lumber Trade in Canada" in *idem*, *Essays in Canadian Economic History* (Toronto: University of Toronto Press, 1956). While sensitivity to the environment was, at best, a subtheme in his work, Innis nevertheless recorded how the technology characterizing "European civilization" created environmental havoc in North America. His first major study, on the fur trade, documents how ever more advanced trapping technologies exterminated the beaver in successive regions of Canada and concludes with the statement that "...one cannot predict for the production of wild fur in Canada, without an immediate and thorough investigation with consequent regulations, a happy future." (*The Fur Trade*, p. 379.)

4. For a classic account of native views on the environment and economic development, see the Berger Royal Commission, *Northern Frontier, Northern Homeland: The Report of the Mackenzie Valley Pipeline Inquiry* (Ottawa: Department of Supply and Services, 1977), especially vol. 1, Chapters 8-12.

5. For a discussion of several aspects of this process, see M. Redclift, *Sustainable Development: Exploring the Contradictions* (London: Routledge, 1987), Chapters 5 and 6.

6. "The Political Implications of Unused Capacity," in Innis, *Essays in Canadian Economic History*, p. 382.

7. André Gorz describes advanced capitalism's model of development thus: "Essentially this model derives from the principle that all problems and needs—even collective ones—must be answered by *individual* consumption of marketable goods and services. Growth of production and consumption depends on this quest for individual solutions to collective problems. But these individ-

ual solutions are more expensive than a collective response and moreover are increasingly ineffective. The case has been systematically proved in the fields of housing, transport and health." in (*Paths to Paradise: On the Liberation from Work*, trans. M. Imrie, London: Pluto Press, 1985, p. 16.)

8. Redclift, *Sustainable Development*, p. 40.

9. *Duck Soup*, Paramount Pictures, 1933.

10. See, for example, M. Clark-Jones, *A Staple State: Canadian Industrial Resources in Cold War* (Toronto: University of Toronto Press, 1987); and G. Williams, *Not For Export: Toward a Political Economy of Canada's Arrested Industrialization*, Updated Edition (Toronto: McClelland and Stewart, 1986).

11. For a more complete discussion of these points see G. Williams, "Regions within Region: Canada in the Continent," in M. Whittington and G. Williams (eds.), *Canadian Politics in the 1990s*, 3rd ed. (Toronto: Nelson, 1989).

12. See, for example, J. Brodie and J. Jenson, *Crisis, Challenge and Change: Party and Class in Canada Revisited* (Ottawa: Carleton University Press, 1988).

13. Canadian political discourse on the environment may become somewhat less regionally distinct during the 1990s as continental economic, political and media elites evangelize to the public their current view that the environment can be "saved" through the choice of appropriate behaviours by individuals—for example, the purchase of green consumer products and the sorting of recyclable garbage. From the self-serving vantage point of these elites, the eco-hostile basis of continental capitalist production as the antithesis of rational, social planning remains as hidden as ever.

14. Canada, House of Commons, *Debates* 12 May 1987, p. 6012, and 27 October 1987, p. 10470. However, as late as 1988, Atomic Energy Limited of Canada had neither participated, nor considered participating, in any research into the effects of bordering U.S. nuclear reactors on arable Canadian soils and waters. See *Debates*, 5 July, 1988.

15. *Montreal Gazette*, 25 April, 1988, p. A7.

16. *Montreal Gazette*, 22 April, 1988, p. B1. More recently, when asked to characterize the attitudes of the disputing parties, 46 percent of Canadians felt that their government was very or quite serious about confronting the problems of acid rain while 32 percent felt that the U.S. government was not serious at all. Canadian Institute of Public Opinion, *The Gallup Report*, 3 April, 1989.

17. *Montreal Gazette*, 26 April, 1988.

18. Namely, the 1909 *Boundary Waters Treaty between Canada and the United States*, Principle 21 of the 1972 *Stockholm Declaration on the Human Environment*, and the Economic Commission for Europe's *Convention on Transboundary Air Pollution* of 1979.

19. Canada, House of Commons, *Debates,* 23 March, 1987, p. 4450.

20. *Montreal Gazette,* 10 July, 1990, p. B1, and 14 March, 1991, p. B1; *Globe and Mail,* 14 July, 1990, p. A8. In yet another embarrassingly silly attempt to pump up Mulroney's nationalist credentials, Bush claimed that the pact had come about through the tenacity of Mulroney's emissaries in lobbying Washington. "They were on us like ugly on an ape," he claimed.

21. S. Clarkson, *Canada and the Reagan Challenge* (Toronto: Lorimer, 1982), p. 200.

22. P. Weller, "Drinking, Eating and Swimming as Part of a Complex Ecosystem," *Seasons,* Autumn 1987, pp. 42-45.

23. The burning of the Cuyahoga has become an archetype in North American popular culture of corporate environmental abuse—immortalized in bitter jokes, ecological rhetoric, and protest songs. Consider, for example, these angry lines from a popular mid-1980s song by the Georgia group R.E.M.:
"Let's put our heads together,
Start a new country up,
Underneath the river bed,
Burn the river down!
This is where we walked, swam, hunted, danced and sang.
Take a picture here, take a souvenir.
Cuyahoga! Cuyahoga!"
Berry, Buck, Mills, Stipe (Night Garden Music), "Cuyahoga," *Life's Rich Pageant,* R.E.M., I.R.S. Records, IRS-5783, 1986.

24. I. Cuthbert, "Toxins increasing in Great Lakes," *Alternatives,* 15/2 (1988).

25. M. Keating, "An Ecosystem Health Report," *Seasons,* Autumn 1987, pp. 35-40.

26. R. Malcomson, "Niagara in Crisis," *Canadian Geographic,* October/November 1987, pp. 10-19.

27. W. Clement and G. Williams, "Introduction," in *idem* (eds.), *The New Canadian Political Economy.*

28. Clarkson, *Canada and the Reagan Challenge*, Chapter 8, "Acid Rain and Environmental Dependence."

29. I am grateful to Wallace Clement for reminding me of the relevance of this point.

30. Unhappily, those who have written on topics such as industrialization have been equally deficient. I would critique my own work for the same shortcomings.

31. John Richards and Larry Pratt, *Prairie Capitalism: Power and Influence in the New West* (Toronto, McClelland and Stewart, 1979), p. 328.

32. *Ibid.*, p. 47.

33. Wallace Clement, *The Struggle to Organize: Resistance in Canada's Fishery* (Toronto: McClelland and Stewart, 1986.)

34. Wallace Clement, *Hardrock Mining: Industrial Relations and Technological Changes at INCO* (Toronto: McClelland and Stewart, 1981), p. 250.

35. Clark-Jones, *A Staple State*, p. 209.

36. *Ibid.*

37. Patricia Marchak, *Green Gold: The Forest Industry in British Columbia* (Vancouver: University of British Columbia Press, 1983), pp. 379-80.

38. *Ibid.*, p. 63.

39. Robert Paehlke, *Environmentalism and the Future of Progressive Politics* (New Haven: Yale University Press, 1989), pp. 189, 273.

40. M. Redclift, *Sustainable Development*, p. 46.

41. Paehlke, *Environmentalism and the Future*, p. 274.

42. *Ibid.*, p. 100.

43. *Ibid.*, p. 258.

44. D. Massey, *Spatial Divisions of Labour: Social Structures and the Geography of Production* (London: Macmillan, 1984), pp. 99-100.

45. A. Giddens, *The Nation State and Violence* (Cambridge: Polity Press, 1985), pp. 281-282.

46. See G. Stevenson, *Unfulfilled Union: Canadian Federalism and National Unity*, 3rd ed. (Toronto: Gage, 1989); and C. Offe, "Two Logics of Collective Action," in J. Keane (ed.), *Disorganized Capitalism: Contemporary Transformations of Work and Politics* (Cambridge: Polity Press, 1985.)

47. *Globe and Mail* 13 October 1981, p. 1. See also R.B. Byers (ed.), *Canadian Annual Review of Politics and Public Affairs—1981* (Toronto: University of Toronto Press, 1984), p. 289.

48. See surveys referenced in notes 15, 16 and 17.

49. P. Weller, "Great Lakes Water Quality: Miles to Row before We Sleep," *Alternatives,* 15/1 (1987), p. 53.

50. *Montreal Gazette,* 12 October, 1989, p. B1; and Canada, House of Commons, *Debates,* 11 October, 1989, pp. 4531-33. The report of the joint study was published the following year as *Great Lakes, Great Legacy* (Halifax and Washington: Institute for Research on Public Policy and Conservation Foundation, 1990).

51. See, for example, Isa Bakker, "The Political Economy of Gender," and Frances Abele and Daiva Stasiulis, "Canada as a 'White Settler Colony': What about Natives and Immigrants," in Clement and Williams (eds.), *The New Canadian Political Economy.*

	CHAPTER 12
REGIONAL TRADING BLOCS	JOHN LOXLEY

INTRODUCTION

Since the end of World War II, there has been a marked movement towards the internationalization of capital and greater integration of national economies within a rapidly emerging "global" economy. The basic patterns of trade and financial flows demonstrate this.[1] Globalization is assisted by the GATT process which seeks to reduce trade barriers through multilateral negotiations, and through the establishment of generally acceptable trade rules. The IMF and World Bank, via credit transactions, country consultations and, equally importantly, their influential publications, work to reduce impediments to both international trade and payments and to justify this in intellectual/ideological terms. The governments of all major industrialized capitalist economies also declare their commitment to open trade and payments systems with persistent regularity.

Notwithstanding this clear trend towards globalization and to facilitation and legitimation by international institutions, there are concerns in some quarters that the world economy may break down into a number of larger regional trading blocs, in which member nations within a bloc pursue liberalized policies towards each other but adopt neo-mercantilist policies towards countries of other blocs.[2] Such regional blocs might serve as obstacles to further globalization and could, indeed, reverse that process as blocs adopt protective measures and beggar-thy-neighbour policies, not unlike those observed in the collapse of the world system into currency blocs in the 1930s.

Three regions are envisaged, each centring around a dominant economic pole: the European Community revolving around Germany, a North American bloc dominated by the U.S., and an Asian bloc with Japan at its centre.

This paper examines why, in the face of such clear trends towards globalization, a breakdown into regional blocs is considered a possibility. It then looks at the likelihood of this happening given the current structure of world trade and investment.

WHY THE CONCERN?

There are three main reasons why some analysts fear that regional trading blocs might become a reality: a) tendencies to protectionism in Europe; b) the strengthening of neo-mercantilist inclinations in U.S. economic policy; and c) increasing difficulties in managing global trade and financial imbalances among the major capitalist powers. To begin with, the unification of the internal market of the European Community may strengthen tendencies towards autarky in that region. In the past intra-EC trade has grown at a much faster pace than EC trade with the rest of the world.[3] By 1987, intra-EC trade accounted for 59 percent of all EC trade (Table 12.1). European trade is, therefore, already regionalized and, in its internalization, is not unlike that of trade among states of the United States.

What makes this tendency to regionalization of Community trade worrisome to some observers are the neo-mercantilist policies the EC has been adopting towards non-member countries in recent years. There may be further strengthening rather than weakening of such restrictive trade policies as the Community builds its internal market. Tariffs remain much higher than the six to seven percent average most-favoured-nation level among GATT members for industries such as textiles, clothing, some petrochemicals, etc., and on one third of the items bearing tariffs, the most-favoured-nation rate in the EC is in excess of ten percent.[4] But the recent growth of non-tariff restrictions, and especially voluntary export restrictions (VERs)—or bilateral arrangements to restrain exports—is considered to be much more ominous.[5] Of 99 major VERs identifiable in 1986, the EC was responsible for 55 covering such diverse commodities as steel, agricultural products, automobiles and transport equipment, textiles and clothing, electronic products, footwear and machine tools. These restrictions were estimated to cover 38 percent of the exports of Japan to the EC in 1984 and also affected Taiwan, Korea, other developing countries and Eastern Europe.

Since 1984 the EC has adopted tough new anti-dumping legislation designed to offset "unfair" trade practices by trading partners and in 1988 initiated 92 anti-dumping cases.[6] These measures were aimed at middle-income Third World countries and Eastern Europe primarily, but have affected both Japan and the U.S. Since 1988 the EC has also taken steps to prevent evasion of anti-dumping charges through the establishment of "finishing touch" assembly plants, by the adoption of strict rules of origin. Though aimed primarily at Asian countries, especially Japan, Japanese plants in the U.S. are also affected and hence there is conflict over the issue between the U.S. government and the EC. The European community has also moved to prevent the absorption of anti-dumping duties by importers, so that such duties do indeed find reflection in prices.[7] The EC also maintains a variety of import quota restrictions, both through the Multi-Fibre Agreement and in other areas. The U.S. has expressed anxiety about whether national quotas, such as those imposed by the French on automobiles, will be applied EC-wide and there are concerns that unification of external restrictions might be achieved at the harshest prevailing national level rather than the most liberal.

The Common Agricultural Policy (CAP) of the EC is also very protectionist and consists of price supports to uphold and stabilise farmers' incomes, and monetary compensation amounts (MCAs)—in effect tariffs and subsidies—to offset the effects of exchange rate changes within the Community. While a unified market leads to the abolition of MCAs, the other components of the CAP remain in place. The impact of CAP has been to raise EC agricultural self-sufficiency and to create large surpluses in some agricultural commodities. It has, however, been controversial politically, absorbing the equivalent of two thirds of the EC budget.[8] While benefitting food importing countries such as Japan, Russia and such Third World countries as Korea and Pakistan, it has been costly to countries producing competing products and is a major source of tension between North America and Europe. Between a third and a half of all agricultural imports into the EC are subject to quota or monitoring arrangements.[9]

The major concern about extensions of the EC's internal market, however, stems from the Community's intention, outlined in the 1985 White Paper *Completing the Internal Market*, to seek both global and sectoral reciprocity from non-EC trading partners. Access to the enlarged European market will be obtained by outsiders, therefore, only if they are prepared to make trade concessions to member states. This approach is particularly worrisome to the U.S. and especially in the area of financial services. Unlike European laws, U.S. laws restrict interstate banking and the underwriting of securities by banks. Nevertheless, the U.S. government is anxious that the EC market be opened up to U.S. banks. Thus, when reciprocity provisions were built into a Community directive on banking, the U.S. issued a strong protest arguing, instead, for the principle of "national treatment" under which, whatever their country of origin, banks would be subject to prevailing host country laws. This protest did achieve a compromise as the EC defined the principle of reciprocity to mean national treatment plus "effective market access." Reciprocity in the financial area would be problematic for Japan too, which also separates banking and security business and limits equity ownership of banks in commercial enterprises.[10] Canada has also registered objections to the principle.[11]

Fears of "fortress Europe" stem, therefore, from the already high degrees of trade internalization and trade protectionism, as well as from the possibility that 1992 might heighten both features of EC trade. The economic and political strength of the Community is also likely to be enhanced in the near future by closer ties, membership or otherwise, with several Eastern European countries and with the European Free Trade Association (EFTA).

The second reason advanced for the possible emergence of regional trade blocs is the tendency in the U.S. towards neo-mercantilism. Like Europe, the U.S. has been very active in introducing trade restrictions in recent years. It has also adopted a bilateral approach to negotiating trade agreements, suggesting the possible emergence at some point in the future of a trading bloc encompassing the Americas.

U.S. protective measures mirror those of the EC. Seventeen percent of import items subject to tariff have most-favoured-nation rates in excess of ten percent while non-tariff barriers have proliferated in recent years. Of the 99 identifiable VERs in 1986, the U.S. was responsible for 32: 25 on steel, four on textiles and clothing and one each on automobiles, electronic products and machine tools. Japan, Korea, Europe and Brazil were the major targets.[12] Almost a third of Japanese exports to the U.S. are now covered by VERs.

In 1988 the U.S. initiated 76 anti-dumping and 26 countervailing duty investigations, aimed mainly at Japan, Canada, Singapore and Korea, and adopted an Act to prevent assembly operations being set up to circumvent anti-dumping duties. In the same year, it removed nine countries from preferential tariff treatment under the Generalized System of Preferences (GSP) and abolished duty-free treatment on $1 billion of imports. The countries mainly affected by these measures were Korea, Singapore and Taiwan.[13]

U.S. agricultural policy is also very neo-mercantilist and, as with trade policy generally, has been aggressively so since 1985. Between 1981 and 1985 the combination of the appreciating dollar and high domestic support prices for grain caused the U.S. share of the world wheat market to fall from 47 to 29 percent. The Export Enhancement Program (EEP) was introduced in 1985 specifically to enable the U.S. to compete with EC subsidies, in order to restore world market share and to provide for export subsidies for grains and oilseeds.[14] Since then the mandate of the EEP has been extended to that of raising the U.S. market share of other products. By 1987-88 the U.S. share of world wheat exports had recovered to 41 percent.

The U.S. subsidises its farmers heavily, using deficiency payments (as opposed to the price supports favoured in the EC) import quotas and VERs. In total, these subsidies have been estimated to be the equivalent of 28 percent of producer income, compared with 40 percent in the EC and 39 percent in Canada.[15] It can be said, therefore, to be a fundamental feature of agricultural trade policy on both sides of the Atlantic. Trade restrictions in agriculture have increased in the past two years leading to increased friction between the U.S., Canada and the EC[16]

Overall, the proportion of U.S. imports affected by barriers such as quotas and anti-dumping duties, or subject to more indirect restrictions (complicated customs procedures or advertising restrictions, for instance) rose from 36 percent in 1966 to an estimated 45 percent in 1986. In the EC, these proportions rose from 21 to 54 percent over the same period.[17]

Behind the rhetoric of commitment to liberal trading regimes lies a reality, therefore, of pervasive neo-mercantilist interventionism designed to protect the interests of specific sections of capital within regional or national boundaries.

The Canada-U.S. Free Trade Agreement (FTA) lends further credence to the view that such neo-mercantilist policies might, in future, be exercised within the context of regional trading blocs. That a North American bloc will emerge becomes even more likely with the NAFTA negotiations. The Caribbean Basin Initiative of 1983 already provides trade preferences for the Caribbean and Central America with the U.S., albeit one-way preferences, completing the geographical trade entity.

The third factor which might heighten protectionist policies and hasten a retreat to regionalism is the problem of addressing global trade and financial imbalances between the three major capitalist countries. In recent years these difficulties have been reflected in the U.S. balance of payments deficit which rose to $133 billion in 1986 (from a surplus of $8 billion in 1981), with counterparts in the Japanese and German balance of payments surpluses which reached $86 and $39 billion respectively in that year. The U.S. *trade* deficit with the four East Asian Newly Industrialising Countries (NICs) also reached more than $40 billion by 1987.[18] The origins of these imbalances are complex and owe much to the impact of profit decline since the late 1960s, to changes in international competitiveness, to the global restructuring of industry and to the varying approaches to domestic policy management in the 1980s, all of which are interconnected. The Reagan government's attempt to restore the profitability of U.S. capitalism by pursuit of tight money and lax fiscal policies, with tax cuts for the wealthy and a huge expansion in military spending, led to a $200 billion fiscal deficit, high interest rates and a dollar which appreciated in real terms by over 45 percent between 1980 and 1985. The latter led to a fall in U.S. exports, compounding the negative impact of the debt crisis on export sales to Third World countries, and resulted also in a rise in imports. The subsequent military-Keynesian-led recovery of the U.S. economy stimulated yet further demands for imports and persistent record levels of payments imbalances. The changing patterns of external trade had a profound structural impact on the U.S. economy so that, even when the dollar appreciation was reversed by an almost equal percentage real depreciation between 1985 and 1987, the *trade* deficit actually rose from $122 billion to $160 billion. It fell subsequently but remained high.

The persistence of trade and balance of payments deficits suggests that trading partners and, in particular Japan and the four East Asian NICs, have been able to offset the effects of dollar depreciation by raising productivity, or by absorbing price increases in reduced profit margins, or because of consumer loyalty. What is more, even if the trade balance reacts with a time lag to exchange rate changes, it is becoming increasingly obvious that exchange rates themselves are set more by capital flows than by trade flows. Ironically, despite the persistence of a large negative trade imbalance with Japan, the

ollar appreciated relative to the yen. Thus it moved in exactly the opposite
irection of that needed to narrow the trade deficit, despite official interven-
on to prevent it.

It is for these reasons that the U.S. government resorted increasingly to
irect controls over imports. Furthermore, sustained deficits prompted the
J.S. to negotiate bilaterally with Japan in a bid to reduce the trade imbalance
nd obstacles to U.S. companies investing and operating in Japan. In this
Structural Impediments Initiative," the U.S. called for no less than 200
hanges in Japanese economic policy and structure. In what some Japanese
escribed as an effort to "remake Japan" the U.S. demanded an increase in
ublic works spending and increased access by foreign companies to this,
neasures to reduce monopoly and restrictive trade practices, and steps to
educe land prices, *inter alia*. The Japanese responded by suggesting that, to
elp reduce the trade deficit, the U.S. should raise taxes, restrict credit card
se, raise savings and investment and increase competitiveness externally.[19]

The EC and the U.S. have both attacked Japan for protecting and insulat-
ng its domestic market and warned that unless it takes corrective measures it
isks losing investment and trade access to Europe and the U.S.[20] In this way,
esponsibility for global imbalances is shifted largely onto the shoulders of
apan. It is apparent, however, that Japan alone is unlikely to absorb the huge
xpansion in U.S. exports that would be needed to avoid a recessionary solu-
ion to the external deficit, and the current recession has not so far been deep
nough to eradicate these imbalances. Europe too, and especially Germany,
vould need to absorb more U.S. goods and hence would probably need to
oth expand domestic income growth *and* appreciate their currencies relative
o the dollar. Expanding the domestic market would, however, contradict
Germany's tendency to conservative economic policies which, incidentally,
ontrol growth to modest proportions in the rest of the EC. It is to be noted,
owever, that unification has had the unintended effect of doing this to some
xtent.[21]

Even if Japan and Europe were to co-operate fully, rectifying global imbal-
nces would also require that the U.S. deal with its own domestic imbalances.
ndeed, some observers feel that without prior strong initiatives in this direc-
ion, international co-operation will not be forthcoming, especially if the U.S.
ontinues to shift responsibility for external imbalances onto the shoulders of
rading partners. Thus, as Drysdale and Garnaud have concluded, "there
vould seem to be no reliable prospect for addressing current international
rade tensions independently of U.S. progress in moderating domestic
lemand, in pursuit of balance in current external payments."[22]

The significance of 1992 for the European Community is that most instruments of trade policy cease to be wielded by national governments in Europe and, like the external tariff, are ceded to a supra-national entity. Conflicts with non-member countries will, therefore, be mediated through the Community, although specific national interests are likely to shape the detail of external trade policy in possibly, as some fear, a lowest common denominator fashion. In short, the deepening of the European Community does not mark the eradication of economic conflict between nation states. On the contrary, it renders such friction more difficult to manage, thereby creating pressure for defensive realignment of the global economy into trading blocs.

Co-ordination of national policies in order to achieve global stability continues, therefore, to be an elusive goal. It is feared that if large imbalances in external payments and related domestic disequilibria persist, they may heighten tendencies towards protectionism and regionalization, hastening the breakdown of the global economy into a series of relatively inward-looking trading blocs.

COUNTERVAILING FORCES
AND ALTERNATIVE INTERPRETATIONS

A major restraining force against the development of regional blocs is the fact that the global economy is already highly integrated across regions. Thus while Table 12.1 does suggest that trade *within* the three regions is in all cases larger than trade *between* each region, it is only in the case of the EC that this tendency is a marked one. For North America, trade with Japan and Asia is almost as large as trade between Canada and the U.S. while trade with the EC, at 19 percent of the total, is very significant. Likewise, trade with North America is only slightly less important for Asia than is trade within Asia and, although much smaller, trade with the EC is not unimportant. On the whole, trade outside the region accounts for 46 percent of the total external trade of the three regional groupings. Such data have led some observers to conclude that the emergence of trade blocs "is improbable, since the pattern of trade is global rather than regional."[23] "The dominant trend is towards a more integrated global economy" and hence "substantial regionalization of the global political economy is unlikely."[24] The guarded nature of this conclusion reflects, of course, the ambiguities and uncertainties in global trade developments.

TABLE 12.1

VALUE AND RELATIVE IMPORTANCE
OF REGIONAL TRADE 1987

$US BILLION AND %

	United States/ Canada	European Community	Japan[2] Asia	Total
United States/ Canada	$ 258 (30%)	$ 161 (18.6%)	$ 243 (28.2%)	$ 863 (100%)
European Community	$ 161 (8.4%)	$ 1,122 (58.6%)	$ 118 (6.1%)	$ 1,913 (100%)
Japan/Asia[2]	$ 243 (28.3%)	$ 118 (13.7%)	$ 305 (35.6%)	$ 857 (100%)

1. Figures for each region are the sum of imports and exports.
2. Asia includes Hong Kong, Singapore, Taiwan, Korea, China and other ASIAN countries.

Source: IMF Direction of Trade Statistics

Those who fear the emergence of inward-looking regional trading blocs are silent on what this might mean for flows of international direct investment. On the one hand, one might expect a movement towards more restricive trade relations to encourage an increase in direct foreign investment, as foreign capital seeks to "jump over" trade barriers. Trade and investment flows might move, therefore, in opposite directions. On the other hand, since persistent trade surpluses often have a counterpart in increased foreign ownership of assets in the deficit country, with resulting friction from this source too, trade barriers might also be accompanied by restrictions on direct foreign investment. Implicit in the literature, but unstated, is this latter view that regional blocs would move towards autarky in investment. To be consistent with this, our assumption in what follows is that in the long run international capital has a vested interest in open trade regimes and that countries relying heavily on international capital are less likely to impose restrictions on trade with countries which are the source of foreign investment.

Global patterns of investment are as ambiguous as trade patterns but differ in some important structural ways. Though data are incomplete and tend to underestimate capital reinvested from profits, Table 12.2 suggests that there is considerable cross investment between North America and Europe and that, over the decade in question, investment both ways rose rapidly. North American investment in Europe rose threefold in nominal terms or by about 60 percent in real terms (deflated by an index of capital goods prices), and EC investment in North America increased fivefold in nominal terms and almost threefold in real terms. Of the 1985 stocks, Canada accounted for less than five percent of North American investments in Europe and nine percent of European investment in North America.

TABLE 12.2

REGIONAL PATTERNS OF REPORTED STOCKS OF DIRECT FOREIGN INVESTMENT 1975-1985

	Recipient							
$U.S. B	United States/ Canada		European[1] Community		Japan[2] Asia		Total	
SOURCE	1975	1985	1975	1985	1975	1985	1975	1985
United States/ Canada	34,629	72,421	51,366	161,883	3,339	9,246	124,212	250,722
European Community	25,294	133,223	33,929	66,345	317	1,514	74,485	263,557
Japan	3,721	26,726	2,395	10,797	—	—	15,942 214,639	83,649 597,928
Total	67,294	253,550	87,690	239,025	3,939	12,576	158,923	505,151

1. Sources for intra EC cover Germany, Netherlands and U.K. only, for 1978 and 1984.
2. There are discrepancies in data for Japan between recorded inflows and receipts by other regions. The larger of the two figures was taken and totals adjusted accordingly.

Source: Calculated from UN Centre on Transportational Corporations: *Transitional Corporations in World Development: Trade and Prospects*, New York 1988.

Almost two-thirds of North American direct foreign investment is in Europe while 50 percent of European direct foreign investment is in North America. The huge excess of foreign investment assets over liabilities of North America with Europe has closed substantially in relative terms in recent years. EC investment in North America is now much more important than intra-North American investment and North American investment in Europe appears to have grown much more rapidly than intra-European investments. Indeed, investment relations between the two regions are unique in being almost twice the magnitude of trade relations; in all other inter- and intra-regional relations annual trade flows are greatly in excess of the stock of investment.

What is most striking about Table 12.2 are the magnitudes and structures of Japan's foreign investment relationships. Firstly, in spite of experiencing many years of balance of payments surpluses, Japan's direct overseas investments are less than a third those of North America and Europe. This is explained by the preference of Japanese financial institutions and especially insurance and pension companies—the main repositories of Japan's high level of personal savings—for the purchase of long-term foreign securities.[25]

Secondly, however, Japanese investment abroad grew more rapidly than any other source of foreign investment over this period. This trend continued in 1985-87, when it increased by $346 billion or 40 percent. Nonetheless, the attraction of overseas securities continues, as their purchase rose by $189 billion over the same period.[26]

The third point to note is that, though relatively small, Japanese investment in North America and Europe is over three times North American and European investment in Japan, while Japanese overseas investment in total is almost seven times that of foreign investment in Japan. With Japan's strong savings and foreign surplus performance, these differentials are likely to grow in future and are already a major source of friction between Japan and its major international competitors.

Regional trade and investment relations are to some extent, then, asymmetrical. Europe and North American trade integration is of less importance than investment integration and cross investments are reasonably balanced. Japan's trade links to Europe and, especially, North America, however, are of much more importance than investment ties while cross investments are grossly imbalanced thereby providing much scope for friction. These trade and investment patterns suggest that retreat into regionalism would be resisted by powerful trading and investment interests in all three centres.

Nowhere is that resistance likely to be greater than in Japan and, indeed, in Asia generally, where the obstacles to a "natural" regional bloc are immense as evidenced by the numerous proposals which have been advanced for Asia-Pacific Rim trading arrangements, all of which are problematic. The most widely proposed variant has Japan linking up with the four East Asian NICs, the other ASEAN (Association of South East Asian Nations) members and the Peoples Republic of China, but there are many difficulties standing in the way of such a regional grouping becoming a reality. To begin with, though these countries have close trade relations, there is a good deal of overlap in their production and export structures, in such fields as textiles, electronics and electrical products, machinery and transport equipment, so that replacing exports to the EC and North America by intra-regional trade would be difficult structurally.[27] Secondly, Japan has the same problem of trade imbalances with these countries as it has with the EC and North America, and currently enjoys a trade surplus with them of $21 billion.[28] Concern about the inequality in trade relationships is likely to be as great for Japan's Asian neighbours, therefore, as it is for the EC and North America. Finally, with the exception of Hong Kong and Singapore, trade protectionism and resistance to liberalization are rife in this region.

Most ASEAN countries have high tariffs on manufactures, in the 30 percent range and are likely to be resistant to suggestions of freeing up regional trade because the main impact of tariff removal within the ASEAN itself has been trade diverting rather than trade creating.[29] Although Japan has low tariffs on industrial goods, the institutional impediments to market penetration are considerable. China would be crucial to such a regional arrangement, but the peculiarities of its internal pricing system are thought to inhibit regional integration.[30] The average industrial tariffs in Korea (23.5 percent) and Taiwan (13.8 percent) are also high. Protective tariffs in some Asian countries on agricultural products such as rice are among the highest in the world. The average rate of protection on agriculture generally in the early 1980s was 144 percent in Japan and 166 percent in South Korea.[31] By 1986 the cost of supporting Japanese agriculture was the equivalent of 69 percent of the gross value of agricultural production.[32] Such protectionism is as much a source of friction within the region as it is with the U.S.

Thus, there are considerable obstacles to an Asian Free Trade bloc along the lines of the EC or North America. Such a development is highly unlikely, the more so since in Asia "political resistance to Japanese dominance is widespread, and confidence that an open global market is in the best overall interest is equally widespread."[33]

A second possible voluntary regional trade arrangement for Japan is one which would include Australia and New Zealand. These countries would offer much greater complementarity in terms of products and, since Australia and New Zealand have had a free trade arrangement since 1966 and also have recently reduced tariffs on manufactured imports from the outside world, this regional arrangement might be more easily negotiated. At the same time, Australia does maintain restrictions on labour intensive products such as clothing, textiles and footwear, greatly affecting Asian exports. It also has high tariffs on cars,[34] while Japan, Taiwan and Korea maintain protective barriers against Australian agricultural products. Furthermore, U.S. success in 1988 in negotiating greater access to the Japan beef market was at the direct expense of Australian exports. For these reasons, there is hesitancy on the part of Australia and New Zealand to pursue contractual arrangements with Asia.[35] Instead, they have begun studying the possibility of a free trade agreement with Canada.[36]

A further indication of the difficulty of getting Asia into a neat geographical trade bloc is the proposal for a Japan-U.S. Free Trade Agreement. It has been argued that this might be a way of minimising structural imbalances in Japan-U.S. trade and investment relations, which might make possible a non-recessionary solution to the problem of the U.S. external deficit. Recent calls for an agreement modelled on the lines of the Canada-U.S. FTA are, in effect, revivals of proposals made twenty years ago.[37] Their aim is not to create a trading bloc but, on the contrary, to prevent the emergence of such blocs by promoting the expansion of world trade as a whole. Clearly such an arrangement might serve as a powerful lever to discourage further protectionism in Europe.[38] But if the barriers to entry in Japan stem from deeply institutional and cultural practice, as it is claimed, it is unlikely that a bilateral free trade agreement, with emphasis on tariff and quota removal, would go far enough. Moreover, some have argued that removal of U.S. restrictions on Japanese imports might actually lead to a deterioration in the U.S. trade balance with Japan. For these reasons, an influential group of advisors, including Cyrus Vance, Henry Kissinger, Lester Thurow and Clyde Prestowitz call instead for more managed trade with Japan, perhaps involving quotas, in order to rectify the imbalance, a strategy also advocated by some academics.[39]

A movement towards bilateral trade management of this kind, in which results rather than rules are emphasized and in which specific reciprocity is carried to the extreme, would be a logical extension of recent U.S. policy towards Japan.[40] Such a development would suggest that the GATT system of multilateralism and "diffuse reciprocity" was unequal to the task of rectifying fundamental global trading imbalances. To the extent that a major source of these imbalances lies, however, in the structural imbalances of the U.S. domestic economy, "specific" reciprocity is unlikely to provide a long run solution either.

Some critics of the Canada-U.S. FTA see it also as an abandonment of the GATT system while its proponents deny that it undermines multilateralism or that it in any way threatens global free trade through the formation of a regional bloc. On the contrary, they would argue that the FTA is consistent with GATT rules, conforming fully with Article XXIV which permits the negotiation of free trade areas provided they cover most of the trade between the countries involved, are implemented within a reasonable length of time, are designed to expand trade rather than restrict it and do not result in a raising of barriers to (including tariffs on) trade with non-members. Indeed, the official U.S. view of bilateral free trade arrangements is, in the words of George Schultz, that "they can stimulate trade and strengthen the multilateral system.... they can promote freer trade than the multilateral system is currently prepared to accommodate."[41] They are seen, therefore, as a powerful lever, but a positive and expansionary one, against protectionist policies of trading partners and in 1984 were provided for in the Trade and Tariff Act as instruments of official U.S. policy.

It would be more accurate to view Canada's interest in the FTA as stemming, in part at least, from a desire to avoid being a victim of the trend towards increasing protectionism in the U.S. itself. That is, it was to some degree a defensive reaction by Canada rather than by the U.S. The asymmetrical trade dependence between the two, with Canada being much more dependent on trade with the U.S. than *vice versa*, and the widening of this asymmetry in the past 20 years as the Canadian portion of U.S. imports has fallen from 30 percent to 19 percent meant that Canada was not only very vulnerable to restrictive U.S. trade policies, but that it also had considerably less negotiating power than the U.S.[42] Critics of the agreement would say that this finds expression, in particular, in the concessions granted to the U.S. in terms of guaranteed access to Canada's energy and natural resources and in the area of investment.

There is no doubt that the FTA goes considerably farther than the current round of GATT talks are likely to go in terms of the depth of tariff cuts and the dismantling of non-tariff barriers (the precise extent of which is yet to be negotiated). This applies to almost all sectors, but is especially so in those to which GATT has only recently turned its attention—for instance services and agriculture—or which it has left to other negotiating arrangements, for example textiles.[43] Opponents of free trade who are concerned about Canada's reduced ability to pursue national economic policies do not, of course, see this as a virtue, as they correctly view the recent GATT agenda as being set largely in the interests of U.S. capital. But at the other extreme, the most ardent proponents of global free trade object strongly to the bilateral free trade agreement approach. They see it as a cumbersome, time-consuming process which does more to prevent an increase in protectionism than it does to dismantle existing barriers. They argue that enormous complications would arise if a series of FTAs were to be put in place as this would undermine the value of trade concessions granted to those in earlier bilateral agreements. Even the much heralded Canada-U.S. FTA dispute mechanism is seen by them to be too unwieldy to be replicated in deals with any significant number of other countries. Finally, they believe that the bilateral process deflects resources and attention from, and reduces the commitment to, the multilateral process.[44] These criticisms, it will be noted, are levelled more at the replication of free trade agreements as a means of achieving global trade liberalization than they are at the specifics of the Canada-U.S. FTA which most people, including its opponents, would now accept is consistent with both the letter and the spirit of GATT.

This is not to downplay the threat to the national integrity of Canada inherent in the FTA or to suggest that GATT provisions are the appropriate yardstick by which to judge the desirability of international economic policy. On the contrary, the loss of sovereignty implicit in the FTA and in the positions being pressed in GATT negotiations by the U.S. is a major cause of concern. The issue being addressed here is the much narrower one of whether or not the regionalization of trade relations contravenes GATT multilateralism, which it would need to do if it were to give rise to the emergence of blocs in the sense in which we are using that term.

The Canada-U.S. FTA does not in itself suggest a collapse of multilateralism; nor does it presage necessarily the creation of a North American trading bloc. The very asymmetry in trade dependence which helped pressure Canada to negotiate also implies that there are clear limits to the degree to which the FTA *per se* could propel North America into an autarkic economic unit. Given the small size of Canada and its already high degree of integration with the U.S., the FTA itself does not create a radically larger North American economy. Extending the agreement to Mexico would, likewise, not in itself lead to the emergence of a North American bloc in the sense in which that term is being used in this paper. The U.S. already dominates Mexican trade, accounting for more than 70 percent, so that in an important sense the North

American trading region is already a reality. Trade dependence is equally asymmetric, with Mexico accounting for only about four percent of U.S. trade. This again underscores that U.S. trade interests extend well beyond this region and are likely to do so for some considerable time to come. A U.S.-Canada-Mexico agreement is likely to lead much more immediately to industrial restructuring within North America than to a reduction of trade with other parts of the world (although there will undoubtedly be some diversion of U.S. imports from Brazil and Asia). Indeed, Canada's main reason for wishing to participate in the NAFTA was the essentially defensive one of protecting industries said to have derived benefits from the Canada-U.S. FTA such as automobile parts, chemicals, petro-chemicals, steel, metal products, natural gas and paper.[45]

Until very recently the consensus was that a U.S.-Mexico agreement along the lines of the U.S.-Canada FTA was highly unlikely because of political opposition in both countries. It was felt that, at most, a series of sectoral agreements or a less demanding general agreement might be possible and even this would take a considerable time to negotiate.[46] Events have moved, however, more quickly than anticipated. Under pressure of the debt crisis, Mexico abandoned long-standing and deeply entrenched policies of national ownership, control, and economic integration. It entered GATT, reduced import controls and tariffs, drastically devalued the peso, privatized the large state sector and deregulated foreign investment. Mexican interest in a trade agreement, which originated almost solely as a defensive reaction to U.S. pro-tectionism against Mexican goods in the mid-1980s, is now driven also by the conscious pursuit of a development strategy of export orientation based on attracting U.S. capital investment.[47] Drawn by the prospects of access to resources, especially oil, and cheap labour, and seizing the possibility of mak-ing inroads in the areas of investment, services and intellectual property rights, the U.S. put the negotiations onto the "fast track" basis, which also served to mute political opposition from the segments of both capital and labour most likely to be adversely affected by an agreement.

The rapidity of these developments suggests that caution is in order in projecting the future. The trend in North America is clearly towards greater regional integration through bilateral negotiations although the precise nature of economic interrelationships remains to be negotiated. The degree of co-operation will, however, fall far short of that envisaged in Europe and, even if Mexico manages to obtain preferential access to the U.S. market for some of its manufactures, is not likely in the immediate future to threaten North

American trade with other regions to a degree that would imply the emergence of "fortress America."

CONCLUSIONS

The significance of the post-1984 U.S. trade policy is that if large trade and payments imbalances persist and if the Uruguay Round of GATT negotiations fails to produce significant progress, one can expect an even more pronounced shift from multilateral to bilateral negotiations. Competition between the three major capitalist poles will increase, based not on "the impersonal rules of liberal economic behaviour" but rather on strength and bargaining power.[48] Given the existing patterns of regional integration, and their underlying economic and political logics of proximity, a continued retreat from multilateralism will undoubtedly strengthen regional relationships and could, indeed, lead to the emergence of regional economic blocs which are inwardly liberalized and outwardly protectionist. We have argued, however, that there are countervailing forces at work that militate against the emergence of a neat and tidy tripolar regionalization. Instead, economic blocs with a more complex geographical base might arise. One scenario has the U.S. "crisscrossing the world with bilateral free trade areas and mutually beneficial ties beyond its regional sphere." The EC would then be forced to emulate the U.S. with the result that "the two trading giants, polarizing parts of the world around them, would fragment the international economy to the detriment of all nations, small and large."[49]

This Eurocentric view of bi-polarization dismisses too easily the economic strength of Japan and even the possibility of an Asian regional bloc, but it is suggestive of the type of cross-regional bilateralism that might arise in the future.

All of this suggests that nation-states continue to wield enormous influence in the world economy and that the decline of U.S. hegemony and the diffusion of world power have resulted in the world trade system being subjected to neo-mercantilist policy pressures. This has not halted the internationalization of the global economy; on the contrary, in some areas, such as capital markets, there has been rapid liberalization over the last decade, and world trade is now at record levels. Rather, the very process of internationalization characterized, as it is, by unevenness and lack of symmetry, has created or heightened national economic imbalances, generating domestic and international pressures that, in the absence of effective global political structures, must be addressed by national governments. These pressures are unlikely to be ameliorated, and may even be heightened, by closer integration in Europe.

Neo-mercantilism and the threat of trade blocs, regional or otherwise, suggests that we are far from a situation of "ultra-imperialism" in which the interdependence of nations through ties of production, trade and finance is a more powerful force than competitive struggles between them.[50]

ENDNOTES

This Paper draws on material developed as part of a larger project on South-North Interdependence initiated by the International Development Research Centre, Ottawa. The financial assistance of the Centre and the research assistance of Ian Hudson are gratefully acknowledged. Ann Weston provided useful comments on an earlier draft. The usual disclaimer applies.

1.   Some basic statistics are as follows. Since the mid-1950s world trade has expanded 30-fold in current dollar terms, more than six-fold in real terms (International Monetary Fund, *Direction of Trade Statistics* (Washington, D.C.: IMF, 1988). Comparable financial and investment data are less readily available. Nevertheless, between 1960 and 1985 the stock of foreign direct investment in the world rose 11-fold while by 1986 total U.S. assets abroad had reached $1.1 trillion and foreign assets in the U.S. totalled $1.3 trillion. Between 1973 and 1987 the foreign assets of deposit banks rose 12.5 times to $4.7 trillion. Transnational corporations play an important role in this process, accounting for three quarters of the exports of countries such as the U.S. and U.K.; and intra-firm trade itself accounts for 30 percent or more of the exports of the major industrial powers (United Nations Centre on Transnational Corporations *Transnational Corporations in World Development: Trends and Prospects*, (NY: United Nations, 1988), p.92. Transnational banks oversee global capital markets which, assisted by new information technologies and the generalized financial liberalization of national markets since the 1970s, are now more than 20 times as large as global trade markets (Maurice Allais, "The Economic Science of Today and Global Disequilibrium," (paper presented at Conference on Global Disequilibrium, McGill University, 1989).

2.   Michael B. Smith, "Bilateralism's Role in Trade Liberalization," *Economic Impact*, 4 (1989), p. 25.

3.   Between 1958 and 1985 intra-EC exports grew from 35 to 53 percent of total EC exports, their share rising from 4.9 to 14 percent of GNP. See A. Lopez-Claros, "The European Community: On the Road to Integration," *Finance and Development*, September 1987.

4.   Clemens Boonekamp, "Industrial Policies of Industrial Countries," *Finance and Development,* March, 1989.

5.   Information on VERs is not easily come by but their number seems to have grown dramatically in recent years, from about 50 in 1978, to 135 in 1987 and 260 in 1988. Boonekamp, "Industrial Policies of Industrial Countries," p. 15.

6.   International Monetary Fund, *Developments in International Exchange and Trade Systems,* (Washington, D.C.: IMF, September 1989).

7.   IMF, *Developments in International Exchange and Trade Systems.*

8.   Lopez-Claros, "The European Community: On the Road to Integration."

9.   IMF, *Developments in International Exchange and Trade Systems.*

10.   Gita Bhatt, "Europe 1992: The Quest for Economic Integration," *Finance and Development*, June, 1989.

11.   Mary Ann Smythe, "The Three Pillars of Canadian Trade," *The New Federation*, February/March, 1990.

12.   Boonekamp, "Industrial Policies of Industrial Countries."

13.   IMF, *Developments in International Exchange and Trade Systems.*

14.   Peter Winglee, "Agricultural Trade Policies of Industrial Countries," *Finance and Development*, March, 1989.

15.   Winglee, "Agricultural Trade Policies of Industrial Countries."

16.   Naheed Kirmani, "The Uruguay Round: Revitalising the Global Trading System," *Finance and Development*, March, 1989.

17.   Sam Laird and Alexander Yeats, "Nontariff Barriers of Developed Countries, 1966-86," *Finance and Development*, March 1989.

18.   John Loxley, "Economic Interdependence: Global Disequilibria and Growth," (Ottawa: IDRC, 1990).

19.   Winnipeg *Free Press*, March 25, 28, 1990.

20.   Toronto *Globe and Mail*, Feb. 5, 1990.

21.   Alain Lipietz, "The Debt Problem, European Integration and the New Phase of the World Crisis," *New Left Review*, 178 (November-December, 1989).

22.   Peter Drysdale and Ross Garnaut, "A Pacific Free Trade Area?" in Jeffrey Schott (ed.), *Free Trade Areas and U.S. Trade Policy* (Washington, DC: Institute for International Economics, 1989), p. 249.

23.   Joyce Kolko, *Restructuring the World Economy* (NY: Pantheon Books, 1988), p. 368.

24. Stephen Gill and David Law, *The Global Political Economy* (Baltimore, Maryland: John Hopkins University Press, 1988), p. 368.

25. Akira Ariyoshi, "Japanese Capital Flows," *Finance and Development*, September, 1988.

26. Ariyoshi, "Japanese Capital Flows."

27. Ulrich Hiemenz, "Expansion of ASEAN-EC Trade in Manufactures: Pertinent Issues and Recent Developments," *The Developing Economies*, XXVI/4 (December, 1988).

28. IMF, *Direction of Trade Statistics*.

29. Mohamed Ariff, "The U.S.-ASEAN Free Trade Area Option: Scope and Implications," in Jeffrey Schott (ed.), *Free Trade Areas and U.S. Trade Policy*; and Drysdale and Garnaut "A Pacific Free Trade Area?," p. 245.

30. Drysdale and Garnaut, "A Pacific Free Trade Area?"

31. Anandarup Ray, "Trade and Pricing Policies in World Agriculture," *Finance and Development*, September, 1986.

32. Winglee, "Agricultural Trade Policies of Industrial Countries."

33. Ernest H. Preeg, "The Growth of Regional Trading Blocs," *Economic Impact*, 4 (1989).

34. Richard H. Snape, "A Free Trade Agreement with Australia," in Schott, *Free Trade Areas and U.S. Trade Policy*.

35. Drysdale and Garnaut, "A Pacific Free Trade Area?"

36. Preeg, "The Growth of Regional Trading Blocs."

37. Makato Kuroda, "Strengthening Japan-U.S. Co-operation and the Concept of Japan—U.S. Free Trade Arrangements'"in Schott, *Free Trade Areas and U.S. Trade Policy;* and Kiyoshi Kojima, *Japan and a Pacific Free Trade Area* (London: MacMillan, 1971).

38. Kuroda, "Strengthening Japan-U.S. Co-operation."

39. Robert Z. Lawrence, "Comments on Makoto Kuroda," in Schott, *Free Trade Areas and U.S. Trade Policy* and Stephen D. Krasner, "Trade Conflicts and Common Defence: The United States and Japan," *Political Science Quarterly*, 101/5 (1986).

40. Robert O. Keohane, "Reciprocity in International Relations," *International Organization*, 40/1, (Winter 1986).

41. Quoted in Smith, "Bilateralism's Role in Trade Liberalization."

42. Jack L. Hervey, "Changing U.S. Trade Patterns," *Economic Perspectives*, Federal Reserve Bank of Chicago, March-April, 1990, vol. XIV, Issue 2.

43. Richard G. Lipsey, and Murray G. Smith, "The Canada-U.S. Free Trade Agreement: Special Case or Wave of the Future?" in Schott, *Free Trade Areas and U.S. Trade Policy*.

44. Anne O. Krueger, "Comments on Snape" in Schott, *Free Trade Areas and U.S. Trade Policy.*

45. *The Financial Post*, April 14-16, 1990.

46. Gerardo Bueno, "A Mexican View" in William Diebold, Jr. (ed.), *Bilateralism, Multilateralism and Canada in U.S. Trade Policy* (Cambridge: Ballinger, 1988); Preeg, "The Growth of Regional Trading Blocs."

47. Ignacio, Trigueros, "A Free Trade Agreement Between Mexico and the United States?" in Schott (ed.), *Free Trade Areas and U.S. Trade Policy*; Michael Hart, *A North American Free Trade Agreement; The Strategic Implications for Canada* (Ottawa: Centre for Trade Policy and Law, 1990).

48. Robert W. Cox, *Production, Power and World Order* (New York: Columbia University Press, 1987), p. 249.

49. Paul Luyten, "Multilateralism Versus Preferential Bilateralism: A European View," in Schott (ed.), *Free Trade Areas and U.S. Trade Policy*, p. 278.

50. K. Kautsky, "Ultra-Imperialism," *New Left Review*, 59 (January-February, 1970).

NEW LOCAL ACTORS: High TECHNOLOGY DEVELOPMENT AND THE RECOMPOSITION of SOCIAL ACTION	CAROLINE ANDREW FRANÇOIS HOULE J. YVON THÉRIAULT

Local political spaces and, along with them, local political actors are enjoying a renewed importance as centres of economic, social and political development. Urban centres are seen as important actors on the international level. Boston in Massachusetts, Cambridge in England, and Toulouse in France are world leaders in the high technology (high tech) field. This reconsideration of the importance of the "local" is, at least in part, related to the retreat of "senior" governments from social or economic interventionism and the resulting quasi-obligation on the part of local leaders to take up the challenges of economic development, the quality of life and the construction of social solidarity.

Local economic development strategies are increasingly independent of those formulated at national or regional levels. In many cases such development strategies have been oriented to bringing together leading edge economic sectors (centred around high technology), a quality living environment (the urban centre but also the local community) and self-confident local actors working together to respond to community initiatives. This vision of a green high tech community is being elaborated in a large number of places, both internationally and within Canada. We have been involved in looking at two specific examples: the Ottawa-Hull and the Waterloo-Kitchener-Cambridge-Guelph areas. This chapter focuses on the relationship among key institutions in these two areas: universities, business and governments. It situates what is novel in the current situation and suggests how it can be understood.

What do we find when we look at these two areas? The most obvious answer is that we find a complex, highly particular and socially ambiguous situation. New phenomena are emerging, but within ongoing structures. Relationships between business, universities and governments are structured in specific ways in each area. Synergistic relationships exist but they obey independent and even contradictory logics. Two examples illustrate this.

Open Text is a small high-tech enterprise in Waterloo. It develops and markets an integrated text management program which permits the treatment of large written texts and the extraction of relevant information. It sorts through 60 million words in less than a second. This text-search system was developed for the *Oxford English Dictionary* but can be applied to any large text. The system was developed by a research team in the Department of computer science at the University of Waterloo. Initially, the president of the university informed several professors of computer science that Oxford University Press wanted to computerize its dictionary. They began to work on the project and developed the search program. Then the professors and the university's Director of Research created the company *Open Text*, which now contributes to the development of software and markets other research results. The professors conduct much of their research through the spinoff company, which they also use to fund their basic and applied research.

Here we have an example of synergy which started primarily because of the expertise of the professors and of the reputation of the University in the area of computer science, facilitated by the contacts of the University President and Research Director. The collaboration led to the creation of this small company which uses the expertise of the professors and helps them develop saleable products. Although the professors have research contacts with other companies, *Open Text* works only with the researchers who created it.

In the Ottawa-Hull region, *Bell Northern Research* (BNR) occupies a dominant position in the field of high-tech research. Because of its national stature, BNR has research links with university researchers outside the Ottawa-Hull region. Nevertheless, the research links within the region are especially well-developed. Indeed a specifically regional dynamic is apparent, characterized by more spontaneous contacts originating in both the company and the universities. The mediating organizations operating in the region are relatively well known by those involved in the university-business link and are seen as useful. This has the effect of creating a stronger regional network in the high-tech field than that observed in the Waterloo area.

Our study shows, however, that independent of the relative strength of these regional networks, the synergistic relationships are established in basically the same ways in the two areas, through highly informal, personal contacts.

As these examples suggest, new types of social networks relating to economic development are being created at the local level. These networks involve not only university researchers and private companies, but also local government actors. For instance, the Waterloo area has created Canada's Technology Triangle (CTT). It began as a joint marketing strategy by the four Economic Development Commissioners of Waterloo, Kitchener, Cambridge and Guelph. The CTT sees itself as having successfully "sold" the region, nationally and internationally, by stressing the advantages of synergy. As a publicity document asserts:

> The C.T.T. area is home to a long list of advanced and high technology industries, three of Canada's top Universities, extensive research and development facilities, a strong service sector, technology centres, centres of excellence and a superior life style. These features working in harmony make the Technology Triangle a dynamic centre for business and investment.

The CTT is now moving slowly from a purely marketing strategy towards the development of strategies for involving the private sector more directly in its operations and for increasing links between the local universities and local business.

Are these examples merely smoke and mirrors? Are they the continuation of strategies of social control, merely transferred to new terrains? Do they represent the construction of new progressive social spaces around local high-tech development strategies? Are they simply survival tactics of local governments faced by the inability of senior governments to assure any kind of development and to maintain even a minimum of universality in welfare programs? Do these strategies represent a new fragmentation of development that will bring about greater inequalities both within these local areas and between those urban centres that succeed and those left behind?

This chapter explores the ambiguity of these local development processes. Such local activities and relationships are not easy to analyze given the categories that were used to apprehend the processes of industrial society and national states. In order to understand the examples of Ottawa-Hull and Waterloo-Kitchener-Cambridge-Guelph, it is important to reflect at a more abstract level on the nature of current social transformations.

That there are profound changes in the socio-political realm of western societies is confirmed both by recent events and by the studies that attempt to interpret and explain these changes. The idea that we live in a society that is "post-industrial," formulated during the 1960s by thinkers as different as Daniel Bell and Alain Touraine, has been taken up in a variety of forms.[1] The "post" hypothesis suggests that existing models of social action and social regulation are no longer operative and that society is now being influenced by new logics. The term "post" suggests that while the past is over, the future remains as yet undefined. Politics, economics and socio-cultural phenomena are seen to be more and more difficult to understand using the old categories of analysis. Previously central actors and models of development are disappearing, but it is not clear who and what will replace them.

Our aim is not to clarify or to confirm the hypotheses of post-industrialism, post-Fordism, post-Keynesianism or post-modernism. Rather it proposes to use the idea of the deconstruction of social reality to evaluate the appearance at the local level of social actors involved in practices that can be interpreted in terms of a recomposition of the social universe. We feel that it is possible to read directions from emerging social practice that at least allow us to suggest certain interpretations. It is through the examination of local settings and particularly the synergy developed in the area of high technology between economic entrepreneurship and university research that we propose to identify the existence of new social actors and the direction(s) / meaning(s) / sense(s) of their actions.

THE RECOMPOSITION OF SOCIAL ACTION: FROM HARDWARE TO SOFTWARE

There are a variety of ways, indeed, in which looking at the regional dynamic created around the development of the high-tech sector allows us to look at social space. Going beyond the analysis of the fragmentation of societal logics it appears possible to see the emergence of certain forms of recomposition. For example, whether the focus is on the economic sphere with its post-Fordist logic, the political post-Keynesian realm or the post-modernist socio-cultural domain, the movement from a social world structured around bureaucratic, rigid and centralized apparatuses to a social world marked by flexible, adaptable and decentralized networks is underlined. The "hardware" of industrial society has been replaced by the "software" of the "post-..." society.

In strict economic terms, the disintegration of the Fordist model leads to a process of economic reconstruction that breaks with the classical model of hierarchical and bureaucratic communication at the same time as it develops a tendency to regional agglomeration.[2] This emerges partly as the consequence of a consumption-based industrial logic rather than a production-based one. Post-Fordist industrial strength is a function of capacity to gain control over a part of the consumer market rather than its capacity to manage a production process. Research and development then become crucial for the never-ending creation of new products and new needs. Instead of the traditional hierarchical patterns, communications and interdependencies develop on a lateral basis.[3] These horizontal communication links begin to structure a new local economic space, defined not as a region in the sociological sense but as a network of interconnected energy. At the same time, these communication links are also structuring a new world space which, by eclipsing the old national identities, takes the global international space as partner and as market. Economic reconstruction comes about under a banner of economic liberalization, but can take a variety of forms, from an anti-state appeal in favour of the new entrepreneur to one favouring "yeoman democracy."[4]

Certain authors argue that post-Fordism is "better seen as one ideal-typical model or strategy of production and regulation, co-present with others in a complex historical ensemble, than as a valid totalizing description of an emerging social formation here and now."[5] If this implies that post-Fordism and the use of new technologies are only a strategy of capital to go beyond the rigidities of the Fordist labour process and to initiate new patterns of consumption, however, it underestimates the radical character of the social transformations underway in our advanced societies. In fact, the new technologies go along with a transformation in the whole of social relations. This is reflected "in the dwindling power of trade unions, changes in consumption patterns, deregulation, the stepping aside of government and the revitalizing of market powers."[6]

Without implying a causal relation, the emergence of this new economic space is accompanied, at the political level, by new attention to the local. The crisis of the welfare state has led civil society to pick up some of the functions that had been taken over by the Keynesian state. The notion of the autonomy of social actors has given rise, as well, to a rearticulation of the meaning of the idea of democracy. Many argue in terms of "de-centring the state" and of the importance of specificity and of locality.[7] The re-emergence of the local means that the image of local government, of local officials, and even of local politics has in the course of this process become more visible if not more noble. The city as the level of government closest to people and as an autonomous social actor has gained legitimacy. This movement can perhaps be interpreted as part of a neo-liberal process. One must look at the particular local circumstances, however, to see whether the return to civil society is reproducing at the local level the notion of competitive entrepreneurship that lies behind privatization, or whether, on the contrary, it is creating new solidarities, both intra- and inter-regional. One must look specifically at concrete cases to see in practice what the links between the renewed significance of local politics and the locally-organized network of the high-tech universe actually are.

A cultural dimension helps to clarify this relationship between the political and economic dynamic in "post-..." societies. The importance of sociological identities (of class, sex, ethnicity, etc.) diminish and are replaced by the development of an individuality with multiple partial identifications.[8] The recomposition of identities and social actors comes about through *ad hoc* groupings through networks that are sometimes created out of patterns of daily life and sometimes constructed through the invention of new communities of identity going beyond national borders (the internationalization of collective action).[9] The role of conflict within social relationships is also modified as the point is no longer to impose one final outcome but rather to enlarge, through public debate, the choices available to citizens. Social action is not defined in terms of a single central conflict but rather organized around diverse poles and against an ever-moving opposition. Even the entrepreneur and the company have been reinterpreted. Touraine argues that, in a world where the workplace no longer represents the site of the principal social conflict, the entrepreneur has no longer necessarily the same social connotation as before.[10] Previously condemned to be the clear and consistent enemy of progressive social action, the entrepreneur has now been reinterpreted as, under some conditions, the ally of cultural innovation. If one adds to this list the growing consciousness of the environmental crisis and the questioning of industrialization in the name of post-materialism, the vitality of the new social movements and the demands for autonomy and democracy emerging from civil society, one cannot reduce the transformations under way to a simple mutation of capitalist logic. Indeed the modern reinvention of democracy is putting into question our traditional ways of viewing social conflict.

These elements that bring about the recomposition of social action—flexible economic structures, local political space, individual democratic rights—appear plausible in the context of high-tech economic development linked to the restructuring of post-Fordist industry. Cannot high-tech enterprises be seen as part of the destruction of the hierarchies and solidarities of industrial society? Are they not central actors in a society perpetually restructuring itself, a society marked by the intricate interrelations of locally specific identifications and international networks? At least this is the modern triumphalist image that high-tech entrepreneurs would have us believe. But, in fact, it is important to see whether the milieux of economic and technological innovation are, in reality, milieux of cultural innovation. Does the rigid separation between science and technology on the one hand and social change on the other that marked industrial society really disappear in the local organization of high technology? In order to answer this question, we must look more closely at the way in which synergistic relations between different sectors are conceptualized and operationalized. The economic aspects of the mechanisms of reconstruction that are at work in the practices of business-university synergy as well as the political dimension of the processes of redefinition of regional and local actors will be the central foci of the next section of the chapter. Understanding these dynamics will lead us, in conclusion, to look at the political-cultural dimension of these modifications.

THE LOCAL HIGH-TECHNOLOGY UNIVERSE: THE ECONOMIC RECONSTRUCTION

The new technological revolution is central to the debates surrounding post-Fordism and flexibility. Without the dynamism of new technologies we would not be in the "post-..." era. The way in which high technology is to be understood varies greatly, of course. For certain authors it appears as a key factor in our economic problems.[11] For others high tech is the source of beneficial changes, or the necessary condition of improved possibilities.[12] Each of these all-encompassing visions contains both elements of truth and falsehood.

The emergence of a new technological paradigm is at present indissociable from the development of new core technologies (in particular, micro-electronics, biotechnology, new materials) which bring about important modifications in the labour process, in industrial structure and in the location of growth spaces. At the level of the organization of work, the introduction of new technologies (flexible types of automation, robots, CAD-CAM, vision control, etc.) are primarily intended to achieve productivity gains. In addition, the application of these technologies favours better quality control, cost reduction and greater product differentiation aimed at highly segmented markets. As Castells shows, this has allowed the transformation of the capital-labour relationship by restoring the initiative to capital.[13] At this level the change represents one more step in the direction of the control of workers, in what Parker and Slaughter have called "management-by-stress."[14] New technologies however, are not inevitably linked to one particular form of social relations and, indeed, they can be associated with a variety of different patterns of social relations.

At the level of industrial structure, the application of new technologies would appear to permit certain traditional Fordist sectors to withstand the competition of the newly industrializing countries. Such application avoids relocation and, in addition, develops new enterprises in the high-tech areas (electronics, micro-electronics, semiconductors, computer hardware and software, biotechnology, robotics). These sectors all share an accelerated rate of innovation and a high level of spending on Research and Development (RandD).[15] For this reason high-tech industries have "a common dependence (directly or indirectly) upon advanced scientific and engineering knowledge."[16]

The crisis of the Fordist regime of accumulation is linked, according to the theorists of the regulation approach, with a new regime of accumulation. The new regime of flexible accumulation

> is founded preeminently on three major ensembles of industrial sectors. These are a) revivified artisanal and design-intensive industries producing outputs largely but not exclusively for final consumption, b) various sorts of high technology industries and their associated phalanxes of input supplies and dependant subcontractors, and c) service functions, and most especially business services.[17]

The risk of this new growth model is that it will lead to a pattern of dualistic development, excluding a wide variety of social groups from the new norms of consumption and in which only a minority of workers will have access to well-paid jobs. "The remaining core workers will not be paid for their achievement or degree of training but for their reliability (reliability wage) because the company is assured that they will not be tempted to stop or sabotage the production process over discontent with the work or low wages."[18] This may lead to the development of new values or norms that are in opposition to the work ethic and that may indeed benefit communities through the development of new forms of solidarity. Such changes would reinforce the possibility of the development of new social relations associated with the new technologies.

New technologies and new models of growth are also associated with the increased importance of new actors and spaces of industrialization. Local actors come to the forefront and industrial agglomerations are created as new technologies allow dramatic changes in the space-economy. Scott and Storper consider that the forces behind new growth centres "reside primarily in the division of labor in production, the structure of inter-establishment transactional activity, and the different agglomeration economies that arise endogenously out of localized forms of development."[19]

The development of these new spaces of industrialization is also tied to actions by local governments and local actors. Municipalities and local governments play the role of entrepreneur in relation to high-tech industries by highlighting the qualities of the region, particularly those qualities likely to attract people who work in the high-tech field. The importance of local actors can be seen in the various structures and networks established by local governments and universities in order to encourage the development of high-tech enterprises and to maximize the potential of scientific collaboration between companies and researchers. Concrete examples of this in the areas we studied include the Ottawa-Carleton Research Institute (OCRI) which brings together representatives of universities and colleges, business and government, and the efforts by Canada's Technology Triangle to bring about closer links between business and universities in the area. Preliminary results from our study would seem to suggest that these efforts do work and do produce results, particularly in the already existing areas of regional specialization. This is true for the areas of telecommunications in Ottawa and of computer science and design, biotechnology and earth sciences in the Technology Triangle of Waterloo-Kitchener-Cambridge and Guelph.

High tech would appear to be associated with locational factors different from those which dominated in the Fordist period. Indeed, certain authors go further in arguing that flexible production "tended to flourish most actively at places where the social conditions built up in Fordist industrial regions either could be avoided or were not present."[20] This occurs not only in an effort to establish new relations of production but also because factors such as the environment, residential attractiveness, recreational activities, the need for highly qualified researchers, engineers and managers, educational opportunities and close access to an international airport play a determining role in the development of new industrial spaces. Studies of Silicon Valley, Route 128, Orange County, M4 Corridor, Cambridge, the Southern Paris region and Toulouse all insist on the centrality of environmental considerations and research capabilities. Keeble and Gould found the same thing, that entrepreneurs "had been greatly influenced in their choice of the area by its high residential amenity and environmental attractiveness as a place in which to live."[21] So do our interviews in the Waterloo and Ottawa areas, which are considered "liveable," with easy access to the country for outdoor recreation and pastoral appreciation. In both cases, the concentration of research institutions is also considered a key factor.

At the same time, one should not universalize a model by suggesting links of direct causality between the development of new high-tech industrial spaces, the existence of an environment having certain characteristics and technically-oriented universities.[22] Joseph argues that although one finds a concentration of high-technology companies near universities, "this is about as far as it goes. Firms remain isolated from the university."[23] The Canadian model of university-entreprise relationships may have more in common with Joseph's analysis of Australia than with the ideal types of Silicon Valley, Route 128 or Cambridge. The simple co-existence of high-tech companies and universities in the same physical space does not of itself lead inevitably to synergistic relationships. Patterns of university and company behaviour must be taken into account.[24] It is, then, important to keep in mind that synergy is being encouraged by the universities in a period of fiscal difficulties, in which granting bodies are increasingly specifying private matching of public funds and in which new governmental programs, such as the Ontario program of centres of excellence, call for partnerships between private companies and university researchers. The suspicion that synergy is being called for as a way for governments and university administrations to reduce expenditures is certainly a perception shared by wide numbers of researchers.

It is also clear, according to our interviews, that synergy comes much more from inter-personal and informal relationships than from any role played by formal liaison organizations or structures. A university attitude that encourages and rewards professors who are developing new contacts, working with private firms and earning extra money does more to stimulate the development of a process of synergy than well-structured organization at the local government level. Segal attributed the Cambridge phenomenon to the university's "loose contractual relationships" with its professors and, as well, to the fact that the university did not want to be involved itself in these industrial linkages.[25] At the same time, university research offices are seen by professors and private companies as useful in facilitating co-operation. These offices act as a focus for information, allowing professors to get information on how to organize links with the private sector and allowing the private sector a visible access point within the university. Their real importance emerges at the moment when the researcher-company relationships are formalized by way of legal contracts or when researchers are going into the market. They can best be understood as networks and communication linkages, rather than as formal structures.

THE LOCAL HIGH-TECHNOLOGY UNIVERSE: POLITICAL RECONSTRUCTION

There is, therefore, an economic dimension of these new local moves to create synergistic relations between universities, companies and local government actors. But what are the political trends currently operating in Canada that might lead to, or favour, the emergence of new social actors at the local level? To what extent do these trends actually operate in Ontario and what is their impact?

In the era of mass production and national economies the central political role was played by the federal and provincial governments. This may well already be less true today and may be clearly so in the future. This change, if it occurs, will erode traditional support for the institutionized compromise specific to monopolist regulation.[26] As a result, it will be from the local level, and not the national, that new forms of solidarity will emerge. These new forms may be marked by attempts to establish social solidarity and cohesion as a basis of building support for strategies of economic growth and modernization rather than as a basis to achieve social redistribution of economic growth. Solidarity is seen as a way of achieving development rather than its result.

Three interrelated trends are important to explore in order to understand the reduced role of the "senior" (note the hierarchical language) levels of government; their concern with budget reduction, decentralization and privatization. All involve an effort to reduce the size of government but each of them operates in a somewhat different manner and each is motivated by a somewhat different set of ideological preoccupations. All have been much discussed in recent debates on state responses to the economic crisis and the rise of neo-liberal and conservative strategies. What remains to be examined is the extent to which they are indeed operative at the level of the federal and the Ontario government.

The argument here is that these trends are in operation but that at the same time the federal—and also in its own sphere the Ontario—state have been reluctant to abandon their claim to political direction or to the maintaince of certain policy goals. Governments want to cut spending or to shift responsibility for spending on to other groups, but, at the same time, they do not want to lose control over the shape of public intervention. These states, however, have neither the tools nor even the vision to see themselves as part of the solution, either as interventionist or as non-interventionist.

It would be possible to say that there is both an economic and a political reading of this reaction. From an economic perspective, the role of the state in capital accumulation means that the federal government is concerned to maintain control over certain policy directions. But political considerations also exist. Much has been made of the efforts of governments to reduce expectations, yet if governments are going to be held responsible for certain areas, they want to continue to keep a certain level of influence or control over them. The need to build electoral and political clienteles also sustains governments' interest in maintaining visibility and influence in crucial policy areas. Being re-elected is seen by most politicians as the most urgent goal, and public opinion surveys indicate that the public looks, with despair, for state leadership. Research and development is seen as being a key area for the future, and therefore governments are hesitant to abandon it.

Nevertheless, pressures for reducing the size of government exist. Once again, these can be analyzed in economic and political terms. Budget deficits do create problems of reduced margins of manoeuvre, and politically the appeal to the dynamism of the civil society is attractive.

Faced with these conflicting pressures, one of the emerging strategies of the federal and Ontario governments is to look for other competent social actors in order to divest themselves of responsibility for certain activities. The emergence of such social actors will enable the governments to reduce their direct involvement (and therefore their own costs) but without having to admit that they, like the Emperor, are without clothes. But as these governments also fundamentally doubt the competence of many, if not all, of the possible social actors, their strategy has been to look to the multiplication of these actors and therefore to networks of social actors. In this way there can be a concerted effort of many social actors working together. From the point of view of "senior" governments the competency of the social actors is increased by the networking of a range of social actors. Two kinds of networks have been particularly apparent: spatially-defined networks (i.e., communities) and subject-defined networks (as, for example, the program of centres of excellence). Defining communities in terms of networks is illustrated by the Science Council's report on the Round Table on National Technology Policy. "Le terme 'collectivité' désigne une localité où vivent et évoluent des gens et envers laquelle les résidents éprouvent un sentiment d'appartenance... Cela dépend surtout de la mesure dans laquelle les voies de communication parmi les principaux intervenants locaux sont actives et organisées."[27] A community is therefore defined in terms of links between actors; it is a network that is spatially located and the links make it a social actor.

Subject-defined networks also have the capacity of concentrating and therefore maximizing resources. Indeed, given the very strong sectoral orientation of "senior" governments, subject-defined networks more often correspond to sectoral definitions of policy. University-industry links are primarily of this type; they are only sometimes, and secondarily, spatially defined. Subject-defined networks can sometimes be also spatially-defined. For instance, a program proposal is being studied in the Department of Justice relating to urban security.[28] Stemming from the Department's concern for crime prevention through social development, there are now links with the Federation of Canadian Municipalities and with a number of large cities. As the Department looks to develop possible programs, communities are seen as legitimate participants, with communities defined as those municipalities that have made efforts at broad community participation.

There are certain indications, both from the federal and Ontario governments, that this shift is occurring. At the same time, it is important to see how timid the moves are. The calls for new social partners, and particularly the calls for these social partners to be local social actors, can be found primarily in studies made for the senior governments or reports of committees established by these governments, rather than in concrete actions. For instance, the Canadian Labour Market and Productivity Centre established a series of task forces to examine the new federal Labour Force Development Strategy. Their conclusions were resolutely local.

> Until we recognize that decisions about the appropriate mix and delivery of training and adjustment programs are best made at the

local level with the involvement of all the labour market partners, business, labour, community groups and educators alike, Task Force members are convinced that real reform will not be possible. It is at the local level where our individuals and institutions most directly share a sense of community and can best shape a common purpose.[29]

In areas of significance for overall Canadian economic growth, such as the development of high technology, the enthusiasm for finding actors outside the "senior" governments is more limited, however. An Economic Council document on local government illustrates this hesitation. The initial definition is community-oriented, but serious reservations are expressed about the competence of the community. "The common thread among these experiences is that local action can work. But is essential to build a new kind of infrastructure, composed of leadership, management skills, and information networks."[30] The conclusion limits still further the significance of these moves.

These community development efforts are fragile. They depend on good luck as well as good economic and business skills, but they offer a hopeful avenue for development to many of Canada's smaller communities that could easily go unnoticed in the blur of global trends.[31]

In this document communities end up as useful actors in marginal, and relatively rural, sectors of the economy. Or, in the words of the Council, "this approach can revitalize the economies of small and isolated communities."[32]

The position taken jointly by the Science Council and the Canadian Advanced Technology Association is more optimistic about the possibility of locally-led development strategies. In *Firing up the Technology Engine*, the two bodies reported on the National Technology Policy Roundtable and argued strongly in favour of community-based economic development strategies.

Traditionally, innovation policy has been the prerogative of higher levels of government. However, a broad concensus is emerging in Canada, the United States, Europe and parts of the Pacific Rim regarding the importance of building innovation policy instruments into local and subregional economic development strategies. Innovation policies are being decentralized to make them more responsive to regional and local concerns and aspirations. Successful national and regional strategies are those that build on local strengths, pool public and private resources, and enjoy the support of local public and private decision makers.[33]

If "senior" governments appear slightly more willing to consider local action, is it also true that there is a corresponding will on the part of local communities to take on more dynamic political responsibilities? The twentieth century had been marked by the relative decline of the local state, but it is now possible to see indications of a growing dynamism on the part of some local communities, particularly on the part of some of the large urban communities with more agressive political leadership.[34] Three areas are particularly important here—economic development, international contacts and local corporatist strategies.

Economic development strategies are currently being developed at the local level in a more forceful way than during the centralizing period of the 1960s and 1970s.[35] The recession of the early 1980s and the inability of federal and provincial governments to play a role in the restructuring of the economy pushed local governments to become active. Economic development officers were hired by municipalities. They set up programs and administrative units and gave more importance to the establishing of economic development strategies. To cite the example of Ottawa, the first administrative structure was developed in 1982 and by 1986 the service had acquired an autonomous status. The promotion of the high-tech sector was given a central position in Ottawa's strategy.[36] In part, this can be seen as going back to the municipal "boosterism" of the 19th century and the socially progressive nature of even the most progressive of these campaigns is certainly debatable. Indeed debate is occurring within Canadian municipal circles, as it did within British municipal circles, as to how municipal economic development policies can contribute to the creation of new growth spaces, of new social actors, of new solidarities.[37]

Municipalities, especially the large cities, are developing international contacts in order to position themselves in the increasingly global economy and society.[38] Programs of twinning cities are expanding and mayors are increasingly seeing the development of international links as an important part of their overall political strategy. Several mayors in Canada have made major commitments to international contacts.

Finally local political strategies have been using corporatist stategies to create broad social consensus for local action. Léveillée has described the policies of Montreal, building economic development strategies through joint public-private collaboration.[39] In another area, all of the major Canadian cities are active in the "Healthy Communities" program, whereby municipalities establish broadly based community projects in the area of health.[39]

One can therefore see some examples of increased activity and initiative on the part of local government actors. This activity has been provoked or stimulated by specific actions taken by "senior" governments and also by the lack of political leadership from the federal and provincial levels. At the same time it relates to the increased political will and technical competence at the local level, especially in the largest cities where financial resources, administrative expertise and political will are more easily concentrated. Without overstating the local renaissance, it is possible to see signs of post-Keynesian political restructuring, and to understand local activism as a response to the emergence of a new regime of accumulation and new possibilities resulting from global restructuring.

NEW CULTURAL PARADIGM AND NEW POLITICAL CULTURE

High tech and its applications have enormous present and potential effects on the organization and reorganization of the work process, on the economic growth of certain regions, on the role of actors at the local level, on the norms of consumption, etc. The culture of the high-tech environment, as with certain currents within the feminist movement, the ecology movement and the peace movement, fit well within the post-national state era with the rallying cry of "think globally, act locally." As well, the lateral networks defined on a local basis and the openness to world markets that is characteristic of high-tech spaces are in conformity with the political necessity of finding new social actors capable of assuring economic development and social solidarity.

As indicated at the beginning of the chapter, we are clearly conscious of the ambivalence of the processes at work in these new spaces of development. Flexibility in the labour process can mean greater creativity and innovation; it can also mean work that is increasingly precarious within a dualistic labour market. The never-ending search for new products and for new outlets for products can lead to an altered relationship between science and technology that would be part of a post-materialist society less predatory in its relationship to nature and less linked to the control of those who control capital. It can also accentuate the consumerist manipulation of our lives as it can increase disparities of wealth between classes, sexes, regions, etc. The fragmentation of hierarchical bureaucratic structures in favour of flexible networks is perhaps a sign of the emergence of new patterns of social relations based less on dependence and alienation. It can also be the source of an even more perverse development for those social categories already marginalized in the Fordist model of development. Finally, the paralysis of the national state can allow one to hope for the realization of the old utopian dream of a local participatory democracy corresponding to a local socio-economic reality that is, at the same time, flexible and open to the universal. It can also indicate the obsolescence of the present state structures, with the local sphere having few alternatives other than individual entrepreneurship and the privatization of the management of solidarity.

CONCLUSIONS

It is difficult during a period of transition to distinguish clearly between the exhaustion of the old models and the constraints inherent in what is coming into being. Even if preliminary, the results of our study of the socio-political dynamic of the spaces of high-tech development indicate that nothing has been definitely played out yet. The ambivalence of the new paradigm can lead the existing economic and political dynamic towards a new definition of solidarity, a new social contract founded on flexible links and a greater focus on individual autonomy, just as it can assure the triumph of a civil society understood essentially as a market space—with all the consequences that that implies.

Transition periods open possibilities. Social actors, multiple and fragmented as they are in current society, must accept the responsibility of orienting change. They will orient it according to their own social projects insofar as they are able to position these projects in the present cultural dynamic. The local space of high technology becomes an important interpretor of the cultural modifications going on in our societies. A new political culture is being developed before our eyes. The notion of solidarity, if it is to remain a significant concept, cannot remain unconnected to this development. Can the challenge be met of elaborating a new definition of the social contract adapted to the exigencies of a "post-..." universe? It is through the study of new local actors and the recomposition of social action that we have attempted to find a thread to a fuller understanding of what could well be the new social realities.

ENDNOTES

1.   Daniel Bell, *The End of Ideology* (New York: Free Press, 1965) and Alain Touraine, *La Société post-industrielle* (Paris: Denoël, 1969).

2.   Michael Storper and A.J. Scott, "The geographical foundations and social regulation of flexible production complexes," in Dennis Hayes (ed., *Behind the Silicon Curtain* (Boston: South End Press).

3.   Michael Rustin, "The politics of post-Fordism: or the trouble with 'new times,'" *New Left Review*, 175 (May-June, 1989).

4.   For the former see Robert Reich, *The Next American Frontier* (New York: Penguin Books, 1984). For the second see Michael Piore and Charles Sabel, *The Second Industrial Divide: Possibilities for Prosperity* (New York: Basic Books, 1984).

5.   Rustin, "The politics of post-Fordism," p. 61.

6.   Hirsch, quoted in A.J.M. Roobeek, "The crisis of Fordism and the rise of a new technological paradigm," *Futures*, 19:2, 1987, p. 142.

7.   See for example, Warren Magnusson and Rob Walker, "De-Centring the State: Political Theory and Canadian Political Economy," *Studies in Political Economy*, 26 (Summer, 1988).

8.   Christoper Lasch, *The Culture of Narcissism: American Life in an Age of Diminishing Expectations* (New York: Norton, 1979); G. Lipovetsky, *L'ère du vide, essais sur l'individualisme contemporain* (Paris: Gallimard, 1979); and Blanka Vavakova, "Éclairages américains sur l'individualisme," *Esprit*, 2 (1990).

9.   For the first see Alberto Melucci, "Mouvements sociaux, mouvements post-politiques," *Revue internationale d'action communautaire*, 10/50 (1983). For the second see M. Maffesoli, *Le temps des tribus, Le déclin de l'individualisme dans les sociétés de masse* (Paris: Méridien, 1988).

10.   Alain Touraine, *Le retour de l'acteur, Essai de sociologie* (Paris: Fayard, 1984).

11.   See, *inter alia* Göran Therborn, *Why Some Peoples are More Unemployed than Others* (London: Verso, 1986), and Manuel Castells, "High technology, economic restructuring, and the urban-regional process in the United States," *Urban Affairs Annual Reviews*, 28 (1985).

12.   For example, André Gorz, *Adieux au prolétariat* (Paris: Editions Galilée, 1980) and E. Malecki, "Hope or hyperbole? High tech and economic development," *Technology Review*, 90 (October, 1987).

13.   Castells, "High technology, economic restructuring, and the urban-regional process."

14. Michael Parker and Jane Slaughter, *Choosing Sides: Unions and the Team Concept* (Boston: South End Press, 1988).

15. A. Markusen, P. Hall and A. Glasmeier, *High Tech America* (Winchester: Allen and Unwin, 1986).

16. A.J. Scott and Michael Storper, "High technology industry and regional development: a theoretical critique and reconstruction," *International Social Science Journal*, 112 (1987), p. 215.

17. A.J. Scott, "Flexible production systems and regional development," *Research Paper* 168, Centre for Urban and Community Studies, University of Toronto, 1988, p. 11.

18. Schmitz, quoted in Roobeek, "The crisis of Fordism and the rise of a new technological paradigm," p. 144.

19. Scott and Storper, "High technology industry," p. 220.

20. Storper and Scott, "The geographical foundations and social regulation of flexible production complexes," p. 27.

21. Quoted in D.E. Keeble, "High-technology industry and regional development in Britain: the case of the Cambridge phenomenon," *Environment and Planning C: Government and Policy*, vol/7, (1989).

22. R. Oakey, "High technology industries and agglomeration economies," in P. Hall and A. Markusen (eds.), *Silicon Landscape*, (Hempstead: Allen and Unwin, 1985) and S. Macdonald, "British science parks: reflections on the politics of high technology," *RandD Management*, 17/1 (1987).

23. R.A. Joseph, "Technology parks and their contribution to the development of technology-oriented complexes in Australia," *Environment and Planning C: Government and Policy*, vol. 7 (1987), p. 187.

24. Blanka Vavakova, "Technopole, des exigences techno-industrielles aux orientations culturelles," *Culture technique*, Revue de l'École Nationale des Mines, 18 (1989).

25. N. Segal, "The Cambridge Phenomenon," *Regional Studies*, 19/6 (1985).

26. Robert Delorme and Christiane André, *L'État et l'économie* (Paris: Seuil, 1983).

27. Science Council of Canada and the Canadian Advanced Technology Association, *Firing up the Technology Engine* (Ottawa: Science Council, 1990) p. 8.

28. Caroline Andrew, "Federal Urban Policy Post-MSUA, or is there Really Nothing There?," (paper presented at the Conference on the Changing Canadian Metropolis, York University, 1990).

29. M. Flumian, (speech at 2nd Annual Business and Education Conference, Ottawa, 1990), p. 9.

30. Conseil économique du Canada, *La relance locale* (Ottawa: Conseil économique, 1990), p. 3.

31. Conseil économique du Canada, *La relance locale*, p. 3.

32. Conseil économique du Canada, *La relance locale*, p. 5.

33. Science Council, *Firing up the Technology Engine*, p. 4.

34. John Taylor, "Urban Autonomy in Canada: Its Evolution and Decline," in Gilbert A. Stelter and Alan F.J. Artibise, *The Canadian City* (Ottawa: Carleton University Press, 1984); M. Gottdiener, *The Decline of Urban Politics* (Newbury Park: Sage, 1987); and P. Hamel and M. Mormont "De l'espace pour le local," *Revue internationale d'action communautaire*, 22/62 (1989).

35. P. Filion, "Dépendance locale et développement économique," *Revue internationale d'action communautaire*, 22/62 (1989).

36. Caroline Andrew, "L'individu et le communautaire: impasse au nouveau modèle de développement," *Revue internationale d'action communautaire* 22/62 (1989).

37. For the British debate see M. Boddy and C. Fudge, *Local Socialism?* (London: MacMillan, 1984).

38. P. Smith, "Foreign Policies and the Canadian Metropolis," (paper presented at the Conference on the Changing Canadian Metropolis, York University, 1990).

39. J. Léveillée, "L'action économique de la ville de Montréal," in Jean Bouinot (ed.), *L'action économique des grandes villes en France et à l'étranger* (Paris: Economica, 1987).

40 Andrew, "Federal Urban Policy Post-MSUA."

	CHAPTER 14
FINANCIAL DEREGULATION: DISARMING THE NATION STATE	MANFRED BIENEFELD

INTRODUCTION

Despite its critical importance and its pervasive impact, the financial system has been relatively neglected in recent political economy debates, probably because it is the least well understood and least well documented part of the economy. This is a grave mistake both tactically and analytically since financial liberalization has been a central driving force behind the severe social and economic problems currently emerging in Canada.

Financial liberalization has been espoused by the Mulroney government as part of a high risk strategy based on the assumption that deregulation and exposure to competition will suffice to ensure the future welfare of Canadians. Unfortunately, this strategy is more likely to produce an increasingly polarized society in which the majority will suffer sustained welfare losses and in which the goal of a more humane, caring and leisure-oriented society will soon be dismissed as a hopelessly unrealistic dream. The truth is that financial liberalization significantly disenfranchises Canadians by reducing their ability to make social and political choices. The dream of a caring society can only be kept alive if it is possible to restore a degree of effective national control over the finance sector. If that seems politically unattainable today, it will not remain so as the bankruptcy of present policies becomes ever more apparent.

FINANCE AND CANADIAN DEVELOPMENT

The Canadian political economy debate asks whether, at various stages of Canada's development, different policies could have produced a more humane, prosperous and equitable society and, if so, why this did not happen. The radical or nationalist view emerged in opposition to a mainstream argument which links Canada's relative economic success to its liberal foreign investment policies and regards its periodic nationalist policies as unfortunate aberrations reflecting the power of special interests to appropriate rents to the detriment of national welfare.

This mainstream perspective did not historically regard Canada's financial system as a problem. Although its concentration was occasionally noted with concern, a strong national banking system was widely regarded as a valuable asset whose efficiency could be ensured by domestic competition and effective regulation. It was only in the eighties, in the context of a general neoconservative demand for deregulation, that this pragmatic view gave way to strident demands for financial liberalization.

Against this mainstream view, many political economists have argued that Canada's most serious economic problems stem from its failure to develop a more sufficient capacity to earn and to appropriate technological rents through high value manufactured exports. The explanation of why Canada did not implement a more complete industrialization strategy has frequently focused on the alleged failure of its financial sector to play a leading political and entrepreneurial role in that process.

The experience of other late industrializing countries suggests that the centralized and oligopolistic structure of Canada's financial sector would have been well suited to the task of financing and steering a more complete industrialization strategy,[1] which makes its failure to do so more puzzling. The most common explanations are that Canadian financial institutions were dominated by merchant interests or that they lacked entrepreneurial drive, but such explanations neglect the more important fact that political support for a comprehensive industrialization strategy was bound to be weak in Canada because its resource sector allowed it to attain a relative degree of prosperity, even in the absence of a technologically sophisticated manufacturing sector.

In fact, in the short term a more comprehensive industrialization policy would have entailed significant risks and costs and these would have been difficult to accept when Canada's early survival as a nation depended on its ability to contain the steady outflow of labour to the high wage U.S. So long as the "soft option" of dependent industrialization could meet that objective, there was unlikely to be strong support for a more comprehensive industrial policy from capital, from labour, or from the farming or resource sectors. In the absence of that "soft option", political support for a comprehensive policy would have been greater, but Canada, like Mexico, might still have emerged as a poor peripheral economy, despite its proximity to the U.S. Indeed, as Canada's resource base loses its capacity to underwrite the high living standards of a growing population, that same possibility confronts Canada today. It is a sobering thought that in 1913 Argentina had the fourth highest per capita income in the world.

There is, thus, no guarantee that Canada will now be able to meet the challenge of completing its industrialization process at this late stage, especially since it begins with a historical legacy that includes a weak technological base, a weak and divided national business elite, and a frequently inappropriate set of institutions, including a financial sector with little expertise in long term industrial lending.

The Mulroney government has sought to meet that challenge by exposing all sectors of the economy, including finance, to more direct international competition. It has done so at a time of stagnant domestic markets, heavy accumulated debts, high real interest rates, and a strong Canadian dollar. At the same time the federal government has been content to sit on the sidelines. Maybe it should come as no surprise that bankruptcies are soaring, manufacturing is faltering, trust in government is at a low ebb and Canada's sense of nationhood is evaporating faster than a drop of Petrocan Unleaded on a hot prairie blacktop in July.

FINANCIAL MARKETS: A TRANSITION TO WHAT?

Historically, Canada's financial system has been remarkably stable. As Rod McQueen notes, "During the depression, when 5,522 banks went out of business in the U.S., no Canadian bank failed."[2] This contrast with the U.S. remained strong in the 1980s as U.S. bank failures multiplied, and as the cost of rescuing the deregulated Savings and Loans soared to incredible levels.

The 1964 Royal Commission on Banking and Finance (Porter Commission) clearly regarded the financial sector's stability as a valuable asset but was concerned about the level of competition. The 1967 revision of the Bank Act therefore sought to increase competition without jeopardising stability or undermining the effectiveness of national regulation. It did so by reducing the compartmentalization of domestic financial markets and terminating the "open-entry policy" which had allowed the virtually unrestricted entry of foreign banks.[3]

Unfortunately, this attempt to strengthen Canada's financial institutions did nothing to alter the economy's systematic reliance on the U.S. for its long-term capital needs, even though it was a net exporter of short-term capital. The resulting external debts harboured significant risks for an economy whose future capacity to export was a matter of concern. By 1970, an official with the U.S. Federal Reserve warned that

> Canadian capital markets were structurally deficient,... that Canada was too reliant on the U.S. long-term bond market... [and] that it was in the U.S. interest, as well as Canada's, for Canada to switch some of its long-term borrowing back into the Canadian market-place.[4]

Some economists dismissed such concerns by arguing that this pattern of external borrowing had to be efficient because it resulted from market forces and therefore reflected investors' risk-adjusted preferences.[5] However, as one critic pointed out, "this efficiency-inefficiency debate is completely beside the point," which was that the economy's debtor status could become "self-perpetuating."[6]

Between 1970 and 1974 the federal government issued guidelines urging long-term borrowers to explore domestic sources of funds before turning to foreign issues.[7] Given the level of foreign ownership in the Canadian economy, however, such moral suasion was never likely to succeed. In the event, the effort was simply overwhelmed by the explosive increase in international financial flows that accompanied the oil crisis and the rapid expansion of offshore financial markets.

By 1982 renewed demands to curb the growth of Canada's external debt were overtaken by the economic crisis and the threat of financial collapse. Such longer-term concerns were now displaced by the urgent need to stimulate economic activity and this strengthened demands for a general lowering of prudential standards and for easier access to foreign funds as over-extended and financially distressed investors, speculators and governments sought access to credit at almost any cost.

A crisis that had been partly created by financial deregulation now fuelled the demand for more deregulation. As prudential standards were lowered, more and more credit was extended to speculative or distressed borrowers willing to pay high rates for credit. The tautology that equates market outcomes with efficiency was now used to justify even the most desperate survival strategies and the most speculative Ponzi schemes,[8] including the excesses of the U.S. Savings and Loans and the junk-bond markets. Eventually the process became self-perpetuating because policy choices were now determined by what a senior London banker called "the stranglehold that deregulated financial markets are increasingly coming to have on government monetary policy."[9]

Financial deregulation now came to be widely regarded as a technologically determined, irreversible fact of life which governments had to accept, if only because refusal would lead to capital flight and exclusion from international capital markets. Acceptance, on the other hand, would lead to efficiency and welfare gains, though not without risk and at the expense of some national sovereignty. The Mulroney government's enthusiastic acceptance of deregulation undoubtedly raised growth rates a little in the mid-eighties, but the result was such an explosive growth of external debt that, by the end of the decade, a financial sector economist wrote that Canada had "suffered a massive loss of economic sovereignty over the past two decades—especially since early 1986—and it is no comfort that the wound was largely self-inflicted."[10]

Although financial deregulation has accelerated under the Mulroney government, some significant regulatory changes had been introduced earlier. Quebec had opened up its provincially regulated securities industry to foreign competition as early as 1973. The 1980 revision of the Bank Act had allowed foreign banks to incorporate subsidiaries in Canada, with the result that such banks had increased their share of all bank assets from 3 to 12 percent by 1988 despite some continuing limits on their operations.[11]

However, the internationalization of Canada's financial services took a giant step forward with the Free Trade Agreement (FTA). This has been described by the International Monetary Fund (IMF) as "one of the most comprehensive bilateral trade agreements ever... (which) breaks new ground, particularly in respect of services, investment and technology transfer."[12] An Economic Council of Canada (ECC) study summarized some of its implications for the financial sector.

> [The FTA] introduced a new set of legal parameters into the domestic banking situation. The agreement gives U.S. banking almost automatic entry into Canada and removes the limits on their asset growth. Their Canadian subsidiaries are no longer required to obtain the approval of the Canadian authorities before opening branches here, so that in effect, they enjoy the same opportunities as Canadian banks. With those barriers now removed, there is every reason to anticipate that Canadian institutions will, in future, face a much tougher challenge in their efforts to retain their share of the domestic market.[13]

Once again, deregulation immediately created a demand for further deregulation since the banks now complained that government was exposing them to international competition but "seems unwilling to give us full freedom to respond."[14] In response, the government introduced its long awaited reform of the financial sector, which further reduced its domestic compartmentalization and increased its integration into the global financial system.

Although some financiers have warned that these changes will force Canadian institutions to assume dangerously high risks in order to remain competitive, such warnings have been readily ignored as institutions struggle to adapt to these new rules in a difficult economic climate.

In any event, the Mulroney government continues to support financial deregulation, apparently oblivious to the associated risks and unmindful of the resulting constraints on Canada's sovereignty. In fact, it appears to regard these constraints as desirable because they will tie future governments to its neoconservative agenda. Pat Carney, then Minister for International Trade, once justified the government's pursuit of the FTA on the grounds that it "wanted to ensure that in future there is not the kind of anti-investment policies of other governments"! Greater exposure to "the stranglehold of deregulated financial markets" achieves the same objective.

Such behaviour is not only fundamentally undemocratic, it is also indefensible in its own terms. The policies to which the country is being committed are not likely to be efficient and they are not inevitable, while the policies being foreclosed are not inherently undesirable. This is especially so in finance where strong national institutions remain important instruments for any serious attempt to complete Canada's truncated industrialization.

THE BENEFITS OF FINANCIAL DEREGULATION

Since financial deregulation is generally advocated on the grounds that it is both efficient and inevitable, the argument is immune to empirical evidence since the policy prescription remains unchanged even when the evidence fails to support the efficiency claim. This section will examine the empirical and theoretical foundations for that efficiency claim (the "carrot"); the following section will consider the argument that deregulation has to be accepted because it is inevitable (the "stick").

A recent ECC study lists the many economic benefits typically said to result from financial deregulation.

> Internationalization and innovation have resulted in increased competition, greater specialization, and new services. They have given institutions new opportunities to compete in wider markets and an added capacity to specialize in particular activities. Borrowers have gained access to competitive markets and an enhanced capacity to obtain financing that meets their specific requirements. The new trends also offer the potential for better risk management and for an overall improvement in the worldwide allocation of resources.[15]

Such strong and relatively unqualified statements could be duplicated many times over but their empirical and theoretical foundation is extremely weak. Indeed the available empirical evidence does not support a general statement to the effect that financial deregulation increases efficiency and welfare. Thus, one recent review of that evidence concludes that "the basis for supporting financial liberalization is weak" and adds that "the benefits of financial liberalization can at best be described as unproven."[16] Another such study, by Paul Krugman of MIT, reaches an even stronger conclusion.

> At this point belief in the efficiency of the foreign exchange market is a matter of pure faith; *there is not a shred of positive evidence that the market is efficient, and...similar results obtain for other asset markets*...that is, both the bond market and the stock market... The bottom line is that *there is no positive evidence in favour of efficient markets*, and if anything a presumption from the data that [these] markets are not efficient. [emphasis added][17]

Evidence linking financial deregulation to corporate efficiency is equally weak. Colin Mayer of London's City University Business School concludes a recent review of that evidence by suggesting that the apparent agreement on the desirability of deregulation and financial innovation "is founded on a limited understanding of financial theory and practice." Having pointed out that the evidence appears to support the hypothesis that closely involved financial institutions are more successful than dispersed shareholders in effecting corporate reorganization, he concludes that

> before...trying to encourage increased dispersion of shareholdings and greater competition in financial systems, *perhaps we ought to have accumulated some reliable evidence to the contrary.* [emphasis added][18]

The World Bank also acknowledges that the recent experience of both industrial and developing countries with financial deregulation has been rather ambiguous. It cites numerous instances in the developing world where financial liberalization ended in disarray,[19] and warns that premature deregulation can lead to volatile financial flows that may intensify domestic imbalances.[20] Moreover, in urging developing countries to learn from the experience of the industrial countries, it warns that

> some of the lessons are cautionary. One lesson is that competitive financial markets...can still make mistakes—witness the excessive lending to developing countries that took place in the 1970s and the current savings and loan crisis in the United States. Another is that market-based financial systems can be unstable and susceptible to fraud.[21]

The Bank also accepts that two of the most successful developing economies, namely South Korea and Taiwan, liberalized their financial sectors more gradually and less comprehensively than most other developing countries.[22] Meanwhile the IMF confirms that, in the industrial world, financial liberalization has also frequently failed to live up to expectations and warns that it "may ...result in destabilizing and inefficient capital market speculation."[23]

In short, the confident claim that financial deregulation will yield significant efficiency gains cannot be based on the available empirical evidence. Many nevertheless continue to advocate such deregulation on the grounds that the problems encountered in the past were not due to deregulation, but to the way in which it was implemented. They frequently suggest that these problems can be avoided so long as liberalization is accompanied by "adequate regulation" and so long as different types of markets are deregulated in the proper sequence.

The injunction that financial deregulation must be accompanied by "adequate regulation and supervision"[24] is not very meaningful or very helpful. It is not very meaningful because it borders on being an empty tautology to say that you must "adequately regulate" while you deregulate. It is not very helpful because it fails to acknowledge that "adequate regulation" becomes increasingly difficult as financial sectors are deregulated and integrated into the global financial system. This is partly because "internationalization means giving up a large degree of autonomy in domestic fiscal and monetary policy,"[25] and partly because that global system has become much less transparent[26] and is now no longer effectively under anyone's control.

> The increasing complexity and volume of contemporary financial intermediation, its international scope, the speed with which disturbances spread, and the breakdown of geographic and functional barriers that potentially insulate markets, are now leading supervisory authorities...to reassess the adequacy of prudential arrangements both nationally and internationally.[27]

Unfortunately, it will be all but impossible to establish adequate controls in a world in which financial innovation is constantly allowed to create new and untested financial instruments whose "risk characteristics...cannot be appreciated until experience has been gained of how they function over the long term or during an economic downturn."[28]

The argument that the problems encountered with financial deregulation can be managed with proper sequencing is no more convincing. It suggests that problems have arisen because highly responsive, deregulated financial markets have been forced to interact with inflexible, regulated labour and goods markets and that such problems could be avoided so long as these markets were deregulated first (and in correct sequence, i.e. labour, then goods). This is, of course, merely a theoretical hypothesis whose plausibility can be no greater than that of the theory from which it is derived. However, one has to wonder, at this stage, whether one can present these choices in such an ahistorical and apolitical way. Surely, financial markets were deregulated first, not because someone made a "wrong choice", but because the evasion of existing regulations was relatively easy and relatively invisible in this sector. Moreover, initial political resistance was often low because short term effects on production, income and employment were often positive. Surely, the full deregulation of labour or goods markets would have entirely different implications and cannot simply be treated as interchangeable alternatives to financial deregulation.

In any event, the current popularity of this argument is not due to the value of these rather unworkable prescriptions for the future sequencing of deregulation. It is due to the fact that this argument has allowed the acknowledged failures of past deregulation to justify a demand for more dereg-ulation. The IMF achieves this result by asserting, without further explanation, that its analysis does "not imply that capital controls should be retained or reintroduced,"[29] even though this might be the most obvious response to a situation in which financial deregulation is said to have gone too far in relation to the conditions in other markets. Having rejected this possibility, the IMF is left free to conclude that its analysis "reinforces the case for accelerating the completion of comprehensive structural reforms of all markets."[30]

The argument is both implausible and disingenuous. It is implausible because clearly no amount of liberalization could ever make labour or goods markets as responsive as financial markets, so that their relative rigidity would always remain as a trigger for destabilizing and inefficient capital market responses. It is disingenuous since the comprehensive reform of other markets is, at best, a long term proposition that has little bearing on the urgent ques-tion of whether controls should be reintroduced to deal with the acknowledged and serious problems being generated by deregulated capital markets today.

An objective observer would have to conclude that this attempt to rescue the case for financial deregulation from the adverse empirical evidence is unsuccessful. However, this conclusion will not be shared by those who derive the case for deregulation from a body of theory whose validity they regard as having been demonstrated beyond reasonable doubt. From such a perspective, a single contrary piece of evidence cannot overturn that theory, but must be reconciled with the expectations of that theory in some way. In this case the lack of fit was said to be due to improper sequencing, but many other explana-tions could have been used, including among others: insufficiently rapid or rad-ical implementation; insufficient time to show results; market imperfections distorting the outcome. There is also recourse to the conclusion that alterna-tive outcomes would have been worse. In other words, when the case for deregulation is derived from theory and not from experience then empirical evidence once again becomes powerless and discussion must focus on the assumptions and the limitations of that theory.

Given the nature of the evidence, there can be no doubt that the general-ized demand for financial deregulation is derived from a rather crude version of neoclassical theory which effectively equates deregulation with efficiency by defining an efficient outcome as the outcome produced by unregulated mar-kets. This literally assumes that financial deregulation will increase efficiency and "make it possible to improve risk management, both for those who seek protection and for those who wish to profit from risk-taking."[31]

However, such general statements about the real world cannot really be derived from that theory but go far beyond what that theory is actually able to say.[32]

Neoclassical theory can only be said to predict that financial deregulation will yield efficiency and welfare gains if and when a highly restrictive, and frequently unrealistic, set of conditions are met. Some of these, like that requiring all actors to have perfect information available instantaneously and without cost at all times, cannot ever be met in the real world. Others, like that requiring atomistic competitive processes in which no single actor can influence prices, are often not met in the real world. Moreover, the theory of the second best has shown definitively that in a world of many imperfections the effect of removing some of these through deregulation is strictly indeterminate in the sense that the theory cannot say whether the net effect on efficiency and welfare will be positive or negative.[33] The general claims made on behalf of deregulation cannot therefore be derived from neoclassical theory.

In fact, neoclassical theory would actually expect financial deregulation to enhance instability, inequity and inefficiency under certain conditions. This could include situations where: deregulation corrupts or impedes information flows; those pursuing short-term, speculative profits are given a disproportionate advantage because financial managers are judged by short-term results or because there is reason to believe that the longer-term risk implicit in their activities will be borne by society as a whole; or the expectations of investors can be systematically distorted by waves of "sentiment" (or "animal spirits") generated by volatile deregulated markets. Moreover, the empirical evidence from the eighties suggests that these are not merely hypothetical possibilities but plausible descriptions of many real world situations. Indeed, Krugman has suggested that if we understand that evidence then

> we are freed from Friedman's...argument...that an efficient market could not exhibit destabilizing speculation... *Now we know that in fact no evidence supports this hypothesis—that it is one maintained purely on faith.* [emphasis added][34]

If one accepts these alternative assumptions as plausible descriptions of the real world, then the expectations of neoclassical theory can be reconciled with the actual experience of the eighties in quite a different way. The theory would now predict that financial deregulation would produce exactly the sorts of volatile and frequently destructive results that have actually been observed. It would also allow the turbulent events of the past twenty years to become far more intelligible, though no more reassuring.

The mechanisms through which deregulation can impede information flows were brilliantly discussed by two conservative monetarist economists studying offshore Eurodollar markets. In considering the claim that such markets are efficient because they have "a superior capacity to adapt to the changing needs of depositors and borrowers," they suggest that these hypothetical advantages are unlikely to be realized in practice. Dealers in these markets have strong incentives to corrupt and obscure information in order to maximise trading volumes and short-term profits, often at the expense of longer-term economic rationality. The market's success, as measured by growth, thus,

> usually means...that the Eurodollar is adept at finding means to make a bad lending proposition look like a good one. However poor the prospects of the borrower, and however doubtful his capacity to repay, some way will be found to persuade the owner of cash to accept the risk, usually by hiding it.... this does affect the real economy [in that] borrowers and lenders can be generated who would not otherwise be borrowers or lenders. Money can be channelled into the wrong projects. Lenders can be induced to pass on funds to finance spending that they would not think of supporting if they knew the facts, and if, knowing the facts, they were required to carry the risk unsupported by the underwriting bank. In consequence the rate of interest is maintained higher than it otherwise would be, crowding out, perhaps, more productive (and safer) spending elsewhere.[35]

This also helps to explain why real interest rates have remained so high even when financial systems were awash with money. In effect, deregulation has allowed people to assume greater risks and has also provided them with incentives and opportunities to obscure and spread those risks to the point where they are effectively socialized by being turned from investment risks into "systemic risks".

An understanding of why deregulation has simultaneously produced high real interest rates and a rapid expansion in the money supply is crucial to understanding the current economic crisis. It is this paradoxical combination that has so dramatically enriched financial asset holders while creating mountains of unserviceable debt that weigh down the world economy: enforcing shorter time horizons on investors; bankrupting otherwise viable firms; devastating entire developing economies; holding mortgage holders, tenants and consumers to ransom; undermining the ability of governments to finance education, infrastructure and welfare services; and shifting income distribution patterns to such a degree that, in the U.S., the proportion of Gross National

Income accruing as interest payments rose by an incredible 150 percent (from six to 15 percent) during the course of the 1980s.

Some of the reasons why deregulation would raise real interest rates have been set out in the quotation from Hogan and Pearce. However, in the early stages of deregulation, those factors will tend to be reinforced by an explosive growth of credit which expands the opportunities for generating short term capital gains through Ponzi schemes designed to inflate all manner of asset prices ranging from real estate, to junk-bond companies, to antiques or Van Gogh paintings.[36] The high returns initially available from such activities allow participants to bid aggressively for credit, thereby raising interest rates, distorting resource allocation, displacing other borrowers and reminding us that "high interest rates make speculators a bank's best customers."[37]

Of course, once enough Ponzi schemes run into trouble, as they eventually must, this source of upward pressure on interest rates will abate. However, for a short time it is likely to be partially replaced by pressure reflecting a general increase in risk and uncertainty and the proliferation of distressed debtors prepared to borrow at any cost to stave off collapse, and able to borrow from desperate lenders willing to lend so that borrowers can service their bad debts. These last expedients are soon exhausted, however, and at this point interest rates will fall. By then, even low interest rates may be unable to revive investment and spending because accumulated debts, bankruptcies and uncertainty combine to stifle consumer and investor confidence, as in Keynes's liquidity trap.

In late 1991 the U.S. economy was approaching this point as the White House urged financial regulators to relax already low prudential standards because falling interest rates were not restoring investment and spending. At the same time the American Bankers' Association was advising the White House that "their real problem is finding creditworthy customers," while a senior banking official suggested that "the borrowing binge of the past decade is the key reason why lending is tight."[38]

Paradoxically, while the banks cannot find customers for their money, mainstream analysts continue to call the problem a credit crunch, that reflects tight money policies. But how "can you have a crunch on something for which there's no demand?"[39] The truth is that there is no credit crunch. In fact, there is a glut of financial assets relative to commercially viable investment opportunities under current market conditions. There is a real economy crunch.

So much for the link between deregulation and interest rates. Let us now consider the link between deregulation and the money supply. This also appears as a paradox because mainstream commentators consistently accepted and validated monetarist government claims that they were pursuing tight money policies, and they have continued to do this even though these governments have actually presided over an unprecedented global explosion of money and credit. They do so because they tend to equate high real interest rates with tight money policies, which is a reasonable proposition *when all other things are equal*. However, as has been shown, under deregulation all other things were most decidedly not equal. Indeed, interest rates could rise despite massive increases in the money supply precisely because deregulation was dramatically altering prudential standards, the perception of risk, the pooling of credit markets and credit instruments and the ability to create credit itself.

In any event, the explosive growth of credit under the monetarists is an incontrovertible fact. Although it had begun in the 1970s, when "the Euromarket sprang up, [in] a wonderful country called Offshore...where there were no rules at all because there was no country,"[40] financial deregulation under the monetarists who came to power in the U.S. and Britain in 1979/80 massively accelerated this process. By 1984 the Eurodollar market was dealing in accumulated international debts valued at U.S. $3,000,000,000,000— "five times the entire stock of money in the U.S." and a sum larger than the value of that country's Gross National Product.[41]

As deregulation proceeded, control of the money supply became all but impossible since borrowers could always obtain credit from abroad or from new sources of "near money" springing up as a result of financial innovation. The "explosion of money and credit" made "the sheer volume of money loosed upon the world harder and harder to control."[42] In the U.S., "after decades of trendless stability, the credit ratio began an unprecedented climb in 1982 which ha[d] not stopped as of [1988]."[43] The IMF spoke of "a pyramiding of financial transactions on a relatively small base of real transactions."[44]

How is one to explain this apparently paradoxical outcome? It is possible that these monetarist governments were genuinely concerned about controlling the money supply and that the explosive growth of credit was an unintended outcome of their policies. This is most unlikely since these results were both clearly predictable and widely foreseen. In fact the governments in question persisted with those same policies long after these "perverse" results had become evident.

The explanation suggested by the evidence is that these governments were, in fact, primarily concerned to restore the real value of the mass of financial assets that had been created in the seventies and whose value was being rapidly eroded by inflation at the end of that decade. The control of the money supply was the instrument through which they ostensibly set out to achieve that objective, even though it must have been obvious that financial deregulation would destroy the effectiveness of this instrument. Moreover, when the futility of targeting M2 and M3 became evident, control of the money supply was quietly abandoned in favour of policies that fuelled the growth of financial assets while sustaining high real interest rates—a rentier's paradise. Finally, it is clear that these outcomes were considered acceptable since the policies that produced them have been fiercely defended for over a decade, while attention has been turned to the task of forcing real economies to adjust to the facts of economic life, thus defined. In this sense structural adjustment is the legacy of that earlier financial deregulation.

Our discussion of the benefits of deregulation thus leads to the conclusion that financial deregulation carries large and incalculable risks and that acceptance of these risks cannot be justified on efficiency grounds. The promise of large efficiency gains is not supported by the available evidence and cannot legitimately be derived from theory. The case for further deregulation can, therefore, only rest on the claim that it must be accepted, even though it may not be good for us, because it is inevitable. Let us examine this argument.

IS FINANCIAL DEREGULATION REALLY INEVITABLE?

Given the above discussion it is not surprising that the supporters of financial liberalization should emphasize its alleged inevitability. The ECC's support rests heavily on this claim. Indeed,

> the Council is convinced that the world of finance has been fundamentally transformed by the forces of internationalization and innovation—*and that there is no looking back.* [emphasis added][45]

However, somewhat surprisingly, the Council's main reason for declaring these developments irreversible is not technical, but political. Thus it argues that:

> [i]f governments were to re-impose barriers or to ban ... specific instruments, they would undoubtedly meet resistance from borrowers, investors, and financial institutions, who would not willingly give up the benefits produced by the recent changes and who, in all likelihood, would seek to avoid any restrictions; with the use of modern technology, that would probably not be too difficult.[46]

This conclusion would be defensible if the costs of an attempt to break "the stranglehold of international financial markets" could be shown to be greater than those of accepting it as a *fait accompli,* but this has not been done. In any case, the political balance of forces on which such a judgment must rest will change over time and the ECC accepts that economic crises have reversed earlier processes of globalization after they, too, had appeared to be irreversible. However, it is confident that such crises will not recur, because they will be averted by timely joint international action.[47]

It is not easy to share this confidence given the similarity between current international efforts and those employed in the 1920s with such singular lack of success. In the 1980s each threat of crisis has been met by "turning on the money taps."[48] Yet the policies of the 1920s have been described as "futile" because

> the only remedy applied was the same old nostrum—more credit. As we survey the monetary situation in this period we discover that the distortions and convulsions which developed were the result of a people relying increasingly upon money to facilitate its commercial exchanges, while at the same time progressively weakening and deteriorating its monetary system.[49]

The problem is that credit creation will generally provide short term relief but may deepen the underlying crisis if it contributes to the accumulation of bad debt by encouraging relatively speculative investment, excessive consumer spending on credit, or investment in production capacity that can only survive by displacing existing capacity. It is possible to argue that the repeated turning on of the money taps in an increasingly deregulated world has produced the long sequence of debt crises that began with the Third World debt and then extended to real estate, to public finance, to consumer finance and to corporate finance. As is now clear, this has not solved the crisis. Indeed it may lie at the heart of it.

Ironically, the ECC's belief that joint international efforts will succeed in averting economic crises actually contributes to their creation by further encouraging the imprudent behaviour that financial deregulation permits. In any event, at this time there is all but unanimous agreement that the global financial system must be more effectively regulated. Even the IMF accepts that there is now an urgent need for regulators "to review their controls over the risks to the entire financial system that may originate in securities markets."[50]

Unfortunately such declarations of intent do not help to contain the irrational, speculative pressures that flourish today as deregulation proceeds in the absence of adequate "prudential arrangements." Under these conditions the ECC's confidence in joint international action is quite misplaced. Moreover, given the chaotic, volatile and dangerous conditions that now characterize the global system, it is quite impossible to argue that one should treat deregulation as irreversible. Indeed, since deregulation which occurs outside of "adequate regulatory standards" clearly enhances the risk of economic crisis, with all its incalculable social, political and economic costs, one can only conclude that regaining a degree of politically accountable control over the financial system is critical.

Occasionally it is argued that national regulation of finance has become impossible for technological reasons, but this is not so. While technology certainly poses serious problems for regulators, the issue is ultimately a political, not a technical, one. This is implicitly acknowledged by the various advocates of deregulation. Thus, when the IMF, the World Bank and the Bank of International Settlements call for more effective global regulation, or when the World Bank advises developing countries to be cautious "in opening up the capital account...to avoid the destabilizing capital flows that proved so difficult to manage in several countries attempting deregulation,"[51] they all imply the possibility of overcoming the technological aspects of this problem.

Nor is it plausible to argue that such regulation is possible internationally, but not nationally. Ultimately effective global regulation will be impossible without effective national regulation, since monitoring and enforcement has to occur at the national and local levels. In any event, national financial regulation is clearly still a fact of life, extensively and effectively practised in some of the most successful NICs to this day. The truth is that regulation is primarily a political—and not a technical—problem that turns around the sorts of controls and sanctions a society is prepared to establish. Moreover, the fact that perfect enforcement will not be possible is no argument against any law.

DEREGULATION AND THE NATIONAL QUESTION

The inescapable need to regulate financial systems at some level raises the issue of sovereignty, partly because regulation is more likely to be feasible within a relatively coherent national society and partly because regulatory systems embody social and political choices which must be legitimated through a meaningful and effective political process. Financial regulation is an inherently political task because it determines: how effectively a society can mobilise resources to serve its collective concern with the welfare of future generations and that of its more disadvantaged members; where a society will maintain the delicate balance between the need to encourage entrepreneurial risk taking, the need to protect society from speculation and the need to encourage a concern with long term outcomes; how easy it is to sustain a viable domestic compromise with respect to the sharing of rewards between labour and capital; and to what extent a society can really choose between efficiency and leisure, or between growth and stability, social harmony or environmental protection.

The political content of financial regulation is usually entirely neglected when the multilateral agencies stress the importance of international regulation while advocating national deregulation even though this "means giving up a large degree of autonomy in domestic...policy."[52] This omission either implies that international regulation is viewed as a purely technical issue or that the implicit political content of international regulatory regimes is being effectively obscured. This is quite unacceptable. Indeed, the discussion of international regulation can only be taken seriously if it explicitly addresses the question of how the political choices implicit in such a regime are made and politically legitimated.

This issue is reflected in the ECC's discussion of the potential for conflict between the objectives of national and international actors in Canada's financial sector.

> The stimulating effects of foreign entry (and liberalization) must be balanced against the desirability of maintaining a strong Canadian-controlled financial sector in the home market. Because the quality of information on which all financial decisions must rely tends to deteriorate with distance, institutions headquartered in Europe, Asia, or the United States are often less familiar with the needs of Canadians than are domestic institutions. In addition, the corporate objectives of foreign financial institutions may, at times, be more attuned to conditions and policies in the home country than to Canadian circumstances. Financial institutions that are rooted in Canada are also more likely to support the financing of Canadian exports than would an institution with its home base elsewhere.[53]

One can only agree with the ECC that strong Canadian financial institutions are important if the financial sector is to be significantly influenced by democratically determined social and economic priorities, since compliance with the rules and laws expressing these priorities is far more likely if those institutions see their long term interests being linked to the long term stability and prosperity of Canada. Not only will international institutions be less concerned with such matters, but they will often have greater opportunities to evade national regulations and they will use their influence and power to oppose governments seriously interested in implementing such priorities.

The ECC ultimately sets aside its nationalist concerns but not before trying to soften the blow by suggesting that the entry of foreign financial institutions might increase the stability of Canada's financial sector and improve the provision of "services to all regions."[54] However, the inclusion of these very weak arguments merely casts doubt on the argument as a whole.

The claim that the entry of foreign financial institutions may enhance stability is quite implausible, especially given the historic stability of Canada's financial sector. In fact, deregulation will almost certainly increase instability because regulation will become more difficult, because many foreign entrants will be relatively small, mobile and elusive firms, like the now infamous BCCI because the size of a global operation does not guarantee the viability of any one of its subsidiaries, and because size is not a guarantor of stability when the greatest risks may be "systemic risks" resulting from a lack of effective international regulation.

The suggestion that the entry of foreign financial institutions might improve services to Canada's regions is even more difficult to take seriously. The same study argued that "the quality of information on which all financial decisions must rely tends to deteriorate with distance [so that] institutions headquartered...[abroad] are often less familiar with the needs of Canadians,"[55] and had also noted with concern that past entrants into the financial sector had only located in larger towns and cities.[56]

Given these shaky foundations, the ECC's strong support for financial liberalization is surprising, but it becomes doubly so when one discovers that it advocates these policies despite acknowledging that "Canadian institutions... have been losing ground" internationally[57] and despite recognizing that

> if Canadian institutions continue to lose market share and to reduce their international operations, they may eventually find it difficult to retain their traditional Canadian customers in the face of competition from better-capitalized and more internationalized institutions.[58]

The truth is that the ECC's apparent concern with the potential importance of national financial institutions had no chance of being taken seriously since the analytic framework within which it develops its argument allows no significance to be attached to the nationality of capital. After all, if one assumes that in order to survive, Canada's financial institutions have to become fully internationalized in their activities and their orientation then they must either perish or cease to be Canadian in any meaningful sense of the word, their Canadian origins soon being of interest only to historians.

The fact is that if Canadian financial institutions are to be "made" internationally competitive simply by opening domestic markets to competition, then they must perish or become international firms. This is in sharp contrast to a model like that of Japan, where strong national financial institutions were encouraged and allowed to build on their domestic strength to become efficient national actors on the international stage.

THE IMPLICATIONS
FOR CANADIAN POLITICAL ECONOMY

The attempt to regain a meaningful degree of sovereign control of Canada's financial system faces formidable opposition from an international financial system that is now dangerously unstable and that has grown enormously powerful as a result of deregulation, the FTA and Canada's heavy past reliance on external long-term capital.

Within these constraints there is little scope for the development of an internationally competitive manufacturing sector, especially when real interest rates remain high, when the FTA limits our ability to support the development of promising Canadian firms, when the dollar remains high because, in an unstable world, it is seen as a safe currency in the short term, and when domestic (and U.S.) demand is constrained by a multitude of debts. It would be a miracle if, under these conditions, financial deregulation and greater exposure to international competition were to prove an adequate stimulus for the economic transformation that is needed. And even if that miracle were to occur, there is no chance that the competitive firms that emerged in that process would have any special interest in sharing their technology rents with Canadian governments seeking to invest in Canada's long-term future. Hence, even such a success might not prevent a steady decline in social and welfare services, in economic infrastructure, in the development of skills, in labour relations, and in working conditions.

If that decline is to be arrested or reversed, the rebuilding of a strong national financial system must have the highest priority, since only that would allow democratically determined social and political priorities to influence patterns of resource allocation, income distribution and risk management. This seems politically impossible today, but it may be less so tomorrow. It is critical that people come to understand more clearly that the speculative excesses of interlocking, deregulated financial systems are at the heart of the current economic crisis in which debt, asset price inflation and high interest rates are combining to destroy governments, businesses, jobs and farms. In this crisis the historic gains made by working people in the industrial world over the past fifty years are being systematically attacked, while in much of the developing world the social fabric is literally tearing apart, even though productivity levels have never been higher!

If people simply try to cope with the irrational conditions generated in those unregulated global financial markets by working harder or tightening their belts, or if they focus their anger only on symptoms like tax increases, spending cuts or factory closures, they will not find a solution. Indeed they will be ground down and they will end up fighting each other, as one person's tax cut becomes another's job loss. Meanwhile their dreams of a stable, prosperous and just society will turn into a neoconservative nightmare in which billion dollar fortunes grow as rapidly as the soup kitchens and the armies of the homeless. These are the long term costs of failing to restore a degree of control over our financial system and they must be set against the short term costs that will be incurred in the process of regaining that control.

Success will require a political coalition capable of taking the longer view and of focusing its energies on two complex and difficult objectives: first, that of restoring a degree of effective, democratic control over our financial system; and second, that of finding a relatively swift and painless way of liquidating or devaluing a significant proportion of those financial claims that currently prey parasitically on the global economy, reminding us why Keynes concluded that a socially desirable capitalism would require the "euthanasia of the rentier."

Unfortunately, since Keynes wrote those words, the power of the rentier has become so institutionalized and entrenched that as one London banker observed, "the old solution of ruining the rentier no longer seems to be available." Moreover, in the absence of such a liquidation of assets, he suggests that the debts will eventually crush the debtor societies.[59]

The political coalition needed for these tasks has to be strong enough to resist the retaliation of global financial markets; it has to be based on a clear understanding of the problems to be conquered; and it requires commitment, skill and an ability to compromise, both because it has to include those Canadian financial and business interests who understand the potential importance of functioning as part of a strong, stable and coherent national economy, and because those global markets cannot and should not be openly confronted but must be engaged through policies and negotiations capable of exploiting what little room for manoeuvre there is, to the maximum.

Our situation may have been best summarized by a western Canadian farmer describing, on TV Ontario, his desperate efforts to stave off foreclosure by his creditors. While setting out his plans for planting, weeding and spraying in the current season he suddenly pauses to say: "Of course I'm destroying this soil, but it's my only hope of survival."

If we as a nation simply accept the challenge of becoming competitive within the parameters determined by today's unregulated global economy, we will either fail, or we will succeed through actions that will destroy most of that which is worth preserving, including our environment, our welfare system, our social stability and even our compassion and humanity. Acceptance of such a situation would be both inefficient and immoral and would constitute a craven abdication of responsibility.

ENDNOTES

1.   A. Gerschenkron, "Economic Backwardness in Historical Perspective" in *idem*, *Economic Backwardness in Historical Perspective* (Cambridge: Cambridge UP, 1962).

2.   R. McQueen, *The Money-Spinners* (Toronto: Macmillan, 1983), p. 5.

3.   Economic Council of Canada [ECC], *A New Frontier: Globalization and Canada's Financial Markets* (Ottawa: 1989), p. 24.

4.   A.W. Donner, *Financing the Future: Canada's Capital Markets in the Eighties* (Ottawa: Canadian Institute for Economic Policy, 1982), p. 157.

5.   E.P. Neufeld, "The Relative Efficiency of the Canadian Capital Market: The Consequences of Canadian-United States Financial Relations," in The Federal Reserve Bank of Boston, *Canadian-United States Financial Relationships*, (proceedings of a Conference held at Melvin Village, New Hampshire, September 1971).

6.   Donner, *Financing the Future*, p. 162.

7.   *Ibid.*, p. 151.

8.   For a full discussion of Ponzi schemes see H.P. Minsky, "The Financial Instability Hypothesis: A Restatement," in P. Areshis and T. Skouras, *Post-Keynesian Economic Theory: A Challenge to Neo-Classical Economics* (Sussex: Wheatsheaf Press, 1985).

9.   J. Toporowski, "Why the World needs a Financial Crash," *Financial Times*, February 1986, p. 21.

10. D. Best, "Budget confirms international debt has put new masters in the house," *The Globe and Mail,* 24 February, 1990, p. B1.

11. ECC, *A New Frontier*, p. 24.

12. International Monetary Fund [IMF], *International Capital Markets: Developments and Prospects* (Washington D.C.: April, 1989), p. 50.

13. ECC, *A New Frontier*, p. 24.

14. G. Ritchie in *The Globe and Mail*, 24 March, 1990, p. B2.

15. ECC, *A New Frontier*, p. 16.

16. P. Collier and C. Mayer, "The Assessment: Financial Liberalization, Financial Systems, and Economic Growth," *Oxford Review of Economic Policy*, 5/4 (Winter, 1989), p. 10.

17. P. Krugman, "The Case for Stabilizing Exchange Rates," *Oxford Review of Economic Policy*, 5/3 (Autumn, 1989), p. 65.

18. C. Mayer "The Assessment: Financial Systems and Corporate Investment," *Oxford Review of Economic Policy*, 3/4 (Winter, 1987), p. xvi.

19. World Bank, *1989 World Development Report* (Washington D.C.: World Bank, 1989), p. 5.

20. *Ibid.*, p. 131.

21. *Ibid.*, p. 4.

22. *Ibid.*, pp. 4-5.

23. International Monetary Fund [IMF], *Staff Studies for the World Economic Outlook* (Washington D.C.: IMF, August, 1989), pp. 8-9.

24. World Bank, *1989 World Development Report*, p. 4.

25. *Ibid.*, p. 131.

26. ECC, *A New Frontier*, p. 31.

27. IMF, *International Capital Markets*, p. 12.

28. *Ibid.*, p. 12.

29. IMF, *Staff Studies*, p. 8.

30. *Ibid.*, p. 10.

31. ECC, *A New Frontier*, p. 31.

32. F.H. Hahn, "Reflections on the Invisible Hand," *Lloyd's Bank Review*, April, 1982.

33. R.G. Lipsey and K. Lancaster, "The General Theory of the Second Best," *Review of Economic Studies*, Vol 26 (1956-57).

34. Krugman, "The Case for Stabilizing Exchange Rates," p. 66.

35. W.P. Hogan and I.F. Pearce, *The Incredible Eurodollar* (London: Unwin, 1984), pp. 85-86.

36. Minsky, "The Financial Instability Hypothesis."

37. M. Mayer, *The Bankers* (New York: Ballantine, 1974), p. 444.

38. *Globe and Mail*, 8 October 1991, p. B6.

39. Alan Abelson, "The Stirrings of Panic Become Evident," *Globe and Mail*, 14 October, 1991, p. B7.

40. A. Smith, *The Roaring Eighties* (Toronto: Summit Books, 1988), p. 19.

41. Hogan and Pearce, *The Incredible Eurodollar*, Frontispiece.

42. Smith, *The Roaring Eighties*, p. 211.

43. M. Friedman, "Lessons on Monetary Policy from the 1980s," *Journal of Economic Perspectives*, 2/3 (Summer 1988), p. 63.

44. IMF, *International Capital Markets*, p. 1.

45. ECC, *A New Frontier*, p. 16.

46. *Ibid.*, p. 16.

47. *Ibid.*, p. 15.

48. Smith, *The Roaring Eighties*, p. 211.

49. E. Groseclose, *Money and Man: A Survey of Monetary Experience* (Norman, CA: UCLA Press, 1934), pp. 234-235.

50. IMF, *International Capital Markets*, p. 15.

51. World Bank, *1989 World Development Report*, p. 5.

52. *Ibid.*, p. 131.

53. ECC, *A New Frontier*, pp. 24-25

54. *Ibid.*, p. 24.

55. *Ibid.*, p. 23.

56. *Ibid.*, p. 24.

57. *Ibid.*, p. 20.

58. *Ibid.*, p. 23.

59. Toporowski, "Why the World needs a Financial Crash," p. 21.

Chapter 15

NEW WINES, NEW BOTTLES: REGULATION OF CAPITAL ON A WORLD SCALE

HARRIET FRIEDMAN

Neither do men put new wines into old bottles:
else the bottles break.   (Matthew 9:17)

INTRODUCTION

Present restructuring in Canada, Europe, the former Soviet Union, and elsewhere challenges political strategies based on the national state and national economy. Capitalist restructuring is taking two different directions. One is global accumulation centred on transnational financial institutions, and the other is the formation of continental economic spaces in North America, Europe and Asia. At the same time, "post-Fordist" decentralization has created some examples of regional economies that relink production and consumption, and the natural and social bases of production, which had been so drastically separated by the capitalist division of labour. An effective political strategy, then, must focus on two levels of politics, the regional and international, where the potential for action has been strengthened by the weakness of national states. My subject is the second level, the institutional political regulation of capitalism on a scale larger than the national state.

Capital has always been larger in scope than any state's jurisdiction.[1] The nation-state and the national economy are taken to be natural objects of study and comparison, but their history is more recent and more tenuous than the history of capitalist accumulation. National states have been only one form of capitalist regulation, and only briefly. Analysis must be appropriate to the historical scale of regulation, and, therefore, must be wider than national.[2]

Capital has never been fully global, because it has never created the organizational capacities to regulate relations between capital and labour, or competition among capitals. Yet "national capital" has always depended on political institutions that are international, or transnational. Analysis must therefore focus on the political structures that organize distinct spaces for capitalist accumulation in specific historical periods.

The political structure encompassing all states, then, is the regulative framework of the world economy. In this essay I explore the political history of world capitalism since the free trade era of the mid-nineteenth century. Using the concept of *blocs*, I specify distinct forms and boundaries of regulation. This allows me to analyze, not internationalization of the state in general, but historical structures of domination among specific states.[3] By making transnational regulation more concrete, it is possible to understand the political conflicts and choices presented at moments of restructuring, both past and present. Remembering that nations are historical in their extent and powers, we can see that both sovereignty and transnational regulation are *strategies* of national and transnational fractions of capitalist classes, allied with and opposed by other classes and political movements.[4]

The international division of labour has always been bounded and shaped by political rules, especially those governing money, and military structures. My argument is that national states and economies were created in parts of the world under the military and monetary *relations* of the *Pax Britannica*. They existed in a contradictory relation with mercantile rules. Political nationalism took a new form within these states, which paradoxically revived colonialism. The new colonialism of the national era created *imperial blocs*, a specific partitioning of the world into competing hierarchies of metropolitan and colonial states. Imperial blocs expressed contradictory principles of citizenship and sovereignty on one side, and of racism and rule on the other. Colonialism in turn generated national liberation movements.

However, while the number of national states multiplied once independent of imperial blocs, the oldest national state-economies became unified into new blocs dominated by capitalist and socialist superpowers. The *Atlantic bloc*, provided the regulatory space for transnational capital. Its existence depended on an antagonistic relationship with the *Soviet* (or *party-state*) *bloc*, with a parallel regulative space for transnational central planning. The antagonistic social system blocs shaped actually existing capitalism and actually existing socialism. The contradictions within each system have been expressed in large measure as competitive links across blocs which have ultimately led to the collapse of the bloc structure itself. The disarray of Atlantic capitalism, no less than the collapse of the Soviet bloc, creates specific dangers for democracy and peace, but also possibilities for new economic rules and spaces.

Free Trade: Liberal Wine in One Mercantile Bottle

The "free trade era" lasted about three decades, from the first abolition of British tariffs in 1846 until the 1870s, when all major states introduced or raised tariffs, and began a competitive scramble to consolidate and enlarge overseas empires. Free trade consisted of three elements. The first was a unified, politically regulated world market. Commodities circulated through new commercial instruments, such as bills of exchange, ultimately regulated through British guarantees of payment in sterling. Second, new states emerged or consolidated the rule of national capitalist classes. They adopted constitutional forms which defined national sovereignty and rights of citizens. Third, the states organized national markets in commodities, including land, labour and money. Together, these implied that the "cell" of the world market was the "national economy," and world commerce for the first time took the form of inter-national trade—what I shall call liberal wine.

Paradoxically, the United Kingdom established free trade in pursuit of mercantile monopoly. As the uncontested "workshop of the world" for much of the nineteenth century, Britain realized the mercantile ideal, which defined a division of labour between a manufacturing metropolis and an overseas "farm" supplying both temperate and tropical products to the motherland.[5] The difference between mercantilism and free trade, as McMichael argues, was the military defeat of competing "workshops" which created a mercantile monopoly for Britain. After defeating its main rival, France, in the Napoleonic Wars in 1815, Britain could enforce the mercantile division of labour through trade rather than direct rule.[6]

Victory over competing European colonial powers allowed Britain to pour liberal wine into its mercantile bottle. The *Pax Britannica* "broke through the limits of mercantile capital accumulation, reconstructing a truly global economy."[7] Only three decades later, in 1846 and 1849, the British state uni-laterally introduced free trade by dropping its own tariffs. For a time, textile manufacturers in Manchester drove out artisans at home and abroad. English merchants induced settlers, landlords, slaveowners, and peasants throughout the world to supply great quantities of cotton and wool to English factories. Their monopoly allowed capitalists to accept state limits on exploitative prac-tices which threatened to destroy the British working class. Merchants readily obtained from the settler states and colonies bread, sugar, tea and opium to sustain and mollify new industrial workers.

But along with liberal wine, the mercantile bottle contained a genie: co-mpeting workshops created by British trade, overseas investment, and migration. The world market soon undercut British industrial monopoly by encouraging the formation of truly *national* states and *national* economies. Since it was still a mercantile bottle, it was colonial. Far from disappearing in the liberal era, the colonies were key to Britain's attempts to put the genie back into the bottle.

Apart from the United Kingdom, the *national economies* of the free trade era were a new phenomenon. The mercantile pattern combined locally provisioned towns and villages on one side, with long-distance trade in luxuries on the other; rent and other forms of appropriation from direct producers provided the ruling classes with goods for long-distance trade. In contrast, what we mean by a national economy is a politically demarcated territory whose material life has three characteristics. First, it is capitalist: it is an inte-grated territory which functions as a framework for national labour markets, national currencies and national circulation of goods. Second, it is relatively self-contained. Most products are circulated internally, so that there exists a coherent set of "balanced" sectors linked primarily to one another. Within national economies, the division of labour is based on exchange between agri-cultural and industrial sectors. Third, it is linked to other economies through international trade. As a result, circulation of commodities is at once nationally bounded and potentially global.

The world economy, especially the trans-Atlantic economy,[8] provided the basis for the formation and reproduction of national economies. European settler states were founded from the outset on commodity circulation, both internally and externally, and were the first national economies.[9] Although subsistence production underpinned export agriculture,[10] the commercial imperative distinguished settler agriculture from that of the agrarian regions of Europe. After brutally displacing precapitalist societies, commercial settler agriculture developed in tandem with industry and with markets in labour ower. The intersectoral connection contained within the national economy provided an internal dynamic for commodity circulation and the rise and decline of industries.[11] This is precisely the reason why the shift in historical reference points from England to the United States has been very fruitful for Marxist theory.[12]

Paradoxically, therefore, national economies were the consequence of, rather than the basis for, inter-national trade. As Radice writes, "It is only against Britain's economic and military hegemony that "the national capitalist economy" becomes the primary framework of capitalist development, first in the U.S. and then in continental Europe."[13] Agricultural exports underpinned settler states, including their industrial sectors. When these exports flooded Europe, they undermined precapitalist agriculture. In response, most states introduced tariff protection and other means to facilitate the commercial transformation of agriculture.[14] Both settler states and European states eventually introduced tariffs to protect national industries against British exports. Both created the inter-sectoral linkages underpinning a national economy.

Politically, the national states of the free trade era adopted liberal principles of citizenship and sovereignty. Thus the principles of the American and French Revolutions became grounded in capitalist property relations, which in turn depended on international trade. Trade and investment created conditions that enabled the revolutionaries of 1848 to struggle for independence from the rickety empires in Russia, Eastern Europe, and Turkey, and for settlers to struggle for self-government in the British Empire. Trade and investment gave a material basis to the first anti-colonial revolutions which formed liberal states throughout Spanish America.

Built on a contradiction with mercantile monopoly, the classical free trade era contained further contradictions that shaped the blocs of the subsequent period. First of all, England never became a national economy like the others. In providing the mercantile pivot of international trade, it sacrificed its own very productive, commercial mixed grain and livestock farming.[15] Because it lacked these internal sectoral links, Britain responded to competing national economies, which undercut its monopoly, by turning back to Empire in the late 19th century. Second, the formal and informal empire of free trade was split between settler states, whose geographical characteristics made their exports *competitive* with domestic production in England, and colonies, whose climate provided Britain (and other imperial metropoles) with *complementary* tropical products. Third, British demand for cotton reinforced slavery in the U.S. South, and various forms of extra-economic coercion of direct producers in colonial India and Africa. Finally, the Empire sustained Britain's balance of international payments. The massive outflows of investment capital that created the international economy were possible only because Britain included India in the "national" (imperial) accounts.[16]

Thus when economic competition became military in the closing decades of the 19th century, Britain provided the model to other European states and even the United States for pouring the capitalist wine, created through international trade, back into colonial bottles. These were imperial blocs.

IMPERIAL BLOCS:
CAPITALIST WINE IN COLONIAL BOTTLES

Imperial blocs grew out of the military competition of nation-states, and adapted the colonial division of labour of the mercantile era to industrial capital—capitalist wine in colonial bottles. As extensions of the metropolitan state colonial states were sites of contradictions between modern statebuilding especially between administration and civil service, on the one side, and the racial exclusion of colonial peoples from liberal institutions of sovereignty and citizenship on the other. Ultimately, however, liberation struggles aimed at sovereignty and equality destroyed the imperial blocs and created new nation-states.

A. New colonial bottles

Under British world hegemony, other centralizing states benefited from free trade which not only fostered the prosperity of national capitalists, but also enhanced their competitiveness as *states*. In particular, unification of Germany and of the United States (through the Civil War) created strong states with rational administrations and major armies. State demand for armaments stimulated technical advance and new types of production in heavy industry. Competition among states led all the major industrial powers to develop their armies and navies competitively.

Just as Britain's mercantile monopoly created the global space for international trade and competition, so Britain's retreat into Empire provided the model for imperial expansion of competitive *states*. Britain retreated into Empire—first to finance trade imbalances with the U.S. and Latin America, and then to substitute colonial products, for instance Punjabi wheat, for international imports.[17] National states responded with a competitive revival of colonial and mercantile practices. They created an epoch of competing *imperial blocs*. In each of these the colonial branch of the metropolitan state ruled the colony through appointed governors. However, two changes made this old form into something completely new. First, it was not absolutist monarchies, but rather national states which, with the new technical might and new interests associated with capitalist economies, conquered colonies. The development of taxation, administration, and state intervention into conditions of production at home and abroad was affected by the political structure of imperial rule. Second, national states created a new division of labour organized not through international trade, or through trading outposts, but through policies aimed at securing labour and raw materials for an imperial economy, based on complementarity of temperate and tropical regions. *Imperial blocs* reorganized capitalism through the competitive overseas territorial rule of national states. The new national empires created in Africa and Asia drew on the state-building projects of national capitalism, not only in France and Holland, which could revive their archaic colonial practices, but also in Belgium, Italy, Germany and even the United States. For the new imperial powers, nationalism formed the cohesive basis for state expansion to conquer distant peoples and territories.

Each imperial bloc was defined by military rule, and created an integrated hierarchy of states co-ordinating distinct and unequal territories. Superficially the blocs mimicked older mercantile empires in their territorial sweep and racial ideologies. However, whereas the latter empires were based on trading outposts and private rule by merchant companies, the new empires created colonial states with prefectural administrations adapted from the administrative apparatus created during a more recent phase of European state-building.[18] Indigenous peoples, considered inferior to those of imperial origin, were, in law as well as in practice, subject to autocratic rule by overseas departments. This rule was qualitatively different from the government of either metropolitan citizens or settler colonies. Racist ideologies legitimated coercive labour practices which were not applied, for instance, to European settlers in Canada as opposed to forcibly dispossessed indigenous peoples).[19] This was the political basis for the division of labour within the imperial bloc.[20]

Again, Britain was both at the centre of the imperial movement and an archaic exception to it. It kept its colonies through universalizing its mercantile monopoly, and because of this, it both delayed its own development as a modern state and initiated an administrative transformation of colonial rule. Responding to political problems, notably but not only the uprising of 1857, Britain established in India a Civil Service whose form (and even its name) became significant in the reform of the British state itself.[21] The reform of the Indian Civil Service "represents a precedent rather than an offshoot of the main branch of administrative development" of Britain.[22] The practices developed to selectively "Indianize" the colonial administration may account for at least part of the particularly class-based practices of recruitment favouring Oxford and Cambridge graduates embedded in the apparently universalistic recruitment to the home service well into the twentieth century.[23]

B. Capitalist wine

The metropolitan division of labour, created through a *national* principle, was extended to the imperial bloc. Paradoxically, the "national" economy incorporated unequal and distant territories and peoples through its hierarchical political structure.[24] The continental European states had created national economies with internally linked sectors only by protecting agriculture from settler state imports. These internal linkages between industry and agriculture were founded on coalitions of classes and sectors that promoted social order and "national interest" above the criterion of cost.[25] Britain's reorganized empire, which had financed Britain's accounts under free trade, became the model for competing imperial blocs. Imperial blocs extended the effective economic borders of the nation to include sources of tropical products.[26]

The economic organization of imperial blocs was hierarchically co-ordinated through rule by the metropolitan over the colonial state, the very opposite of inter-*national* trade. The economic, administrative and military resources of national-imperial states allowed them to more effectively restructure colonial production into a bloc-wide division of labour. Colonial administrations were generally required to raise their own taxes.[27] The specifically economic dimension of nation-state imperialism, which distinguished imperial blocs from earlier empires, included an integration of the colonial with the metropolitan economy. Not luxuries for princely consumption, but raw materials for industry and articles of consumption for growing working class markets were the object of 19th century imperial blocs.[28]

The rationale for imperial conquest derived from the new uses for tropical products, both in mass consumption of coffee, tea, vegetable oils, and sugar, and, more significantly, as industrial raw materials. In prevailing technical conditions, there were no economical substitutes. In contrast to wheat, meat, and the other primary exports of the settler colonies, as well as to manufactures, it was theoretically possible to gain secure supplies and to prevent access by competitor states through military control over tropical territories.

C. Contradictions

Together, imperial blocs produced contradictions both in the principles of rule and in the organization of territorial economies, which ultimately led to the formation of new national state/economies within and against the blocs. When the national principle took the form of anti-colonial mobilization, it was the downfall of the new empires of Africa and Asia. At the same time national movements were undermining the old empires of Eastern and Southern Europe. Nationalism thus turned on itself; the impulse of conquest became the impulse for independence.

The imperial division of labour contradicted the national principle of integrated sectors organized through national markets in labour power and capital. Internal circulation of commodities had been the achievement of centralizing states with the will and capacity to suppress local barriers imposed by local powers. This gave them the power to impose an internal integration first within the nation, then through imperialism. The latter created a new economic space, which was not contiguous or uniform in principle. This imperial economic space was ideologically appropriated as part of the "national economy." It was so deeply rooted that even progressive political thinkers included the overseas territories in their post-World War II ideas for national planning.

Imperial blocs integrated temperate and tropical regions into a trade pattern that is only a century old, but has come to be seen as "traditional" and until recently, sometimes as inevitable.[29] Yet the importance of tropical products for industry and for working class consumption was specific to the period 1880-1945. In the postwar agro-food complex, there was considerable investment in scientific invention of substitutes for most tropical products.[30] Especially since these products have increasingly become industrial raw materials rather than final consumer goods, technical substitution was an important factor in the decline in the terms of trade between advanced capitalist exports and so-called traditional exports from former colonies. It has removed technical-economic incentives to secure the sources of many tropical products through direct rule.[31]

The antagonistic, racist dimension of nationality, which fostered conquest and subordination, became the political basis of empire. The relations among formally equal national state/economies, expressed through the inter-state market, gave way to domination by imperial powers over subject peoples. Just when workers, women, and others were struggling to make universal the franchise and other political rights in metropolitan states, those same states reasserted racist, colonial principles in the colonies.[32] Even the emancipation of black slaves in the United States, followed by the denial of their constitutional rights, ran parallel with the development of free trade liberalism and imperial blocs.[33] Yet imperial blocs exposed the peoples of the colonies to exactly those liberal principles that it denied them through colonial rule; anti-colonial movements eventually claimed the principles of equality and national self-determination for themselves, and dismantled the imperial blocs.

The contradiction between the blocs and capital shaped the conflicts between classes and the problems of accumulation. That is why the demise of imperial blocs did not prove fatal for capitalism, which rose from the ashes of empire to greater heights of accumulation—and a renewal of inter-national trade. On one side, capitalism was revived and expanded by incorporating new national state/economies which formed after the dissolution of the imperial blocs. However, from the outset this renewal and expansion of national state-economies was shaped by the antagonistic relation between two new blocs. The origin of the Cold War blocs was the Russian Revolution which, like the First World War, was the beginning of the end for the imperial blocs.

NO BOTTLES: THE INTER-WAR PERIOD

The collapse of the world economy in the 1930s followed a decade of experimentation in re-establishing elements of the pre-1914 structure. The gold standard was abandoned, re-established, and abandoned again. International commodity agreements and barter arrangements expressed the contradictory attempts to build on the imperial blocs and to construct international trade. Anti-capitalist revolutionary movements everywhere coincided with experiments in new forms of production, and the creation of new cultural forms designed to create a social base for accumulation in mass consumption of standard goods, particularly consumer durables. These are the processes which Gramsci labelled as Fordism and Americanism.[34]

Three explicitly *national* experiments of this period were the U.S. New Deal, fascism in Germany and Italy, and Soviet "socialism in one country."[35] The second was defeated in war by the others. These two became in turn the core of new types of blocs based on antagonistic social systems. The Soviet Union became the national base for a centrally planned division of labour which ultimately was extended by force and manipulation to a larger "party-state bloc." The New Deal institutions, together with other American innovations of the interwar period, such as modern advertising,[36] laid the basis for mass consumption and mass production organized by the national states. The creation of a bloc of capitalist states centred on the U.S. involved the active introduction of the "American model of accumulation," or "Fordism" in Europe.

Cold War Blocs:
Different Wines in Military Bottles

Before imperial blocs dissolved, a different type of bloc structure was defined by military alliances around two "superpowers," in the new terminology of the period: the *Soviet* (or *party-state*) *bloc* and the *Atlantic bloc*. The Cold War military alliances were the institutional framework for hierarchical, transnational forms of both capitalism and socialism. The Cold War was a great *economic* division of the world into two political-military blocs, with parallel, mutually exclusive divisions of labour. The Warsaw Pact and NATO provided the political/military core for two distinct regulative spaces of two international economies, centred on the superpowers. The dam between the "socialist" economic bloc and the "free market" economic bloc led to parallel divisions of labour organized through the Council of Mutual Economic Assistance (COMECON) on one side, and on the other, the panoply of Western institutions centred on the Bretton Woods monetary system.

The existence of the Soviet bloc is evident from the direct force used to create and maintain it, and its collapse is also evident. What is less often noted is that the military space of the Warsaw Pact created an economic space for an extended "socialist division of labour." That particular space was dominated not by any of the national projects of Eastern Europe, but by Soviet central planning extended throughout COMECON. Soviet rule over formally sovereign bloc states, like state rule over formally free citizens in each state, was substantively guaranteed by the (contradictory) legal monopoly of power by Communist parties, and by rule of the Soviet Party over the other national parties.

By contrast the existence of the Atlantic bloc is less evident. Economic integration is widely studied, especially the integration of "national" subsectors into Atlantic economic sectors by transnational corporations.[37] However, the Atlantic economy is rarely linked to the military structure of NATO.[38] The Atlantic bloc was the pivot of a combined economic and military tribute system. Its existence depended on political power exercised in each European member country by class fractions favouring Atlantic unity over both national models of regulation and international links to Eastern Europe. In postwar circumstances, the victory of those favouring Atlantic integration could be achieved only through a combination of economic leverage and specific violations of sovereignty and civil rights, which undercut the moral posturing of the "free world" by mimicking in kind, if not in degree, the specific forms of tyranny of the Soviet bloc.

Within each European country that entered the Atlantic or Soviet bloc in the late 1940s, political forces favouring the alliance triumphed over alternative projects. The principal alternative was nationally planned capitalist economies, which would have built on historical ties with colonies and on trade between Western and Eastern Europe. This project would have involved a different relation between the state and the society—planning in Western European capitalism and capitalism in Eastern European planning. International trade would have been negotiated on the basis of national plans rather than national economies adjusting to international trade. Instead, the blocs constructed historically specific, transnational forms of capitalism and socialism based on the division between West and East Europe.

A major expression of political conflicts within blocs took the form of competitive state relations across blocs. New states were created through national liberation from the old imperial blocs, through the conquest of national states by Communist parties (in China, Cuba, and elsewhere), and through the rise of national capitalist state-economies at the margins of the blocs (first Japan, then the NICs). While these were shaped by the Cold War blocs, they also created tensions within them.

A. The Atlantic bloc: capitalist wines in a military bottle

The "free world," organized through a panoply of military, monetary, and other institutions, shaped actually existing capitalism.[39] Postwar military and economic arrangements were an unprecedented renunciation of sovereignty by former great (and lesser) powers in favour of the American "superpower." Through NATO the U.S. controlled the key military forces of Europe, and through the Bretton Woods monetary system Western Europe was forced to accept the economic power of the U.S. to finance military expenditures and foreign investments beyond the limits of its exchange balance. The rules of the system, particularly convertibility of national currencies against the dollar, opened Europe (and European colonies) to foreign investment by U.S. corporations. These corporations became fully transnational through branch plant production, which in turn integrated production subsectors throughout the Atlantic bloc. Superpower status rested on a match between an integrated military hierarchy and an integrated monetary system.[40]

The Bretton Woods monetary system established fixed exchange rates against the dollar, and between the dollar and gold. After the War, the U.S. held most of the world's gold as well as its dollars, and Bretton Woods could only work if other countries could earn export dollars in sufficient quantity to allow their currencies to be freely convertible with the dollar. Without U.S. aid, Europe would have no dollars to buy U.S. exports, and recovery would have to follow the nationalist and protectionist plans favoured by the dominant political coalitions emerging from the war effort. In Europe after World War II there was a strong consensus in favour of the only apparently practical project: national capitalist planning. All anti-fascist parties, including Christian Democrats, favoured large state-run sectors of the economy; Britain, France, and Italy undertook comprehensive socialization of major industries and infrastructures, and only a veto by the Occupation authorities prevented it in Germany.[41]

Beginning in 1948, the rules which opened European and colonial economies to U.S. (and eventually all) foreign investment were entrenched in a complex web of regional military alliances centred on NATO. From the beginning the construction of combined economic and military hierarchies centred on a new invention, foreign aid, and from the beginning, economic and military aid were completely entangled.[42]

The eventual form of Marshall aid represented a compromise between two U.S. political positions: one emphasized the Bretton Woods monetary system, sought to derail nationalist economic policy by left governments in Europe, and feared German militarism; the other promoted West German reconstruction as an anti-Soviet measure.[43] The Marshall Plan, according to Block, eventually "made it possible for the United States to respond simultaneously to a whole range of interrelated problems. It provided a means of financing a large export surplus and influencing Western Europe's economic course."[44]

The Marshall Plan sought to reconstruct international trade in two ways. First, aid was to facilitate investment opportunities for U.S. corporations, and was never to substitute for it. As a result, no Marshall aid went to Latin America, where U.S. investment was firmly established, and political regimes offered sufficient stability to sustain its flow.[45] Second, Europe was to be diverted from nationalist, continental, or imperial projects which would exclude U.S. investment. Marshall aid allowed the U.S. to shape European economies in conformity with a U.S. model by imposing deflationary policies and Fordist labour discipline. It gave a double leverage through the extraordinary mechanism of counterpart funds, which later became central to U.S. aid to the Third World. Counterpart funds required each recipient government to establish a fund of inconvertible domestic currency equivalent to U.S. aid. The counterpart fund could be used only in agreement with the Marshall administration in that country. Thus the first leverage came through conditions attached to receiving the aid. The second leverage came through conditions on the use of the same amount of national currency in counterpart funds.[46]

The Marshall Plan strategy of rebuilding trade around U.S. investment included European colonies in Africa and Asia. The strategy was to integrate the countries of Western Europe and their colonies into a triangular trade. The plan was built on imperial trade and accounting practices, in which colonial powers counted surpluses of colonial primary commodity sales against deficits in domestic trade. The U.S. hoped the triangular trade would give it access to colonial products (and investment in the colonies) and, through the dollars generated for the colonial power, allow Europe to import U.S. goods. The danger of reinforcing imperial blocs was met by forced devaluations in Europe, which prevented the raising of currency barriers against U.S. imports, and by directing the use of aid in the colonies so that U.S. trade and investment would be favoured.[47]

However, Marshall aid was not sufficient to the task. What consolidated the Atlantic bloc as the centre of actually existing capitalism was a combination of political intervention in Europe and other countries, and the permanent mobilization of economic aid under the rubric of the Cold War. Leverage through Marshall aid did consolidate political control of European states by parties and fractions of capital favouring the Atlantic alliance,[48] and established a pattern of overt and covert intervention that continued to be practiced in Third World countries. The Cold War brought McCarthyism at home and political intervention into working class movements in Europe which opposed Marshall policies, splitting them along "Communist" and "anti-Communist" lines.[49] It put overt and secret pressure on political parties throughout Europe which favoured Atlanticism over national economic projects,[50] and later used these tactics with less restraint to support even the most brutal dictators against nationalist parties and elected governments in the Third World. Even the Civil Rights movement to extend the franchise to citizens of all races within the U.S. was opposed in the language of anti-Communism.

Before turning to the NATO framework for Atlantic economic integration, it is important to see the costs to Europe (and the world) of the Bretton Woods monetary rules. With the dollar established as world currency, the U.S. became the effective—but unaccountable—central banker of the world economy. It used this power to get the rest of the world to finance foreign investment and military expenditures on a scale so great that it produced chronic deficits in its balance of payments in spite of its overwhelming surplus in trade.[51]

The postwar boom rested on the unequal inter-state structure of the Atlantic bloc. The monetary system encouraged transnational capital investment, first through aid and then through capital flows which, by rule, were unimpeded by national capital or currency restrictions. The agents and beneficiaries of sectoral integration were transnational corporations. After World War II the free movement of capital, especially U.S. investment in Europe, gave a solid basis for the development of transnational production capitals. These capitals, by investing in subsectors of the U.S., Canada, and Western Europe, integrated Fordist sectors (consumer durables and heavy industry) across the Atlantic economy.[52] Transnational industrial capitals have internalized many transactions previously conducted through markets, including international markets. Intra-firm transfers are difficult to trace and measure, but they can sometimes constitute as much as 80 or 90 percent of international trade, for instance in aluminum or in copper and tin.[53] Through regulative institutions, investment relations, commodities, production systems, and mass communication, Europeans and Americans came to produce and consume many of the same standardized goods. Along with the U.S. political culture of economic liberalism, the popular culture of consumption permeated the diverse historical cultures of Europe.[54]

The political framework of the Atlantic economy was the North Atlantic Treaty Organization. NATO became the framework for West European military co-operation in the early 1950s, when the Western European Union, created in a 1948 agreement among France, Britain, and the Benelux Countries, relinquished its operational functions to the Atlantic alliance.[55]

NATO sealed the U.S. ideology of "containment,"[56] which triumphed over opposition to the emerging Cold War in the presidential election of 1948. Containment extended the notion of "security" first developed in Roosevelt's New Deal as *social* security against impoverishment in the Great Depression, to Western (capitalist) security against the Soviet bloc *and* against unions, parties, and even ideas actually or allegedly linked with the recent wartime ally, the Soviet Union. Schurmann interprets the policy as a resolution of the longstanding conflict between "internationalist" and "nationalist" factions of American politics. A consensus was forged between Democratic and Republican parties on foreign policy. Within NATO this was expressed as a shared perception of threats from Soviet expansion.[57]

Between the treaty signed in 1949 and the Korean invasion of 1950, NATO quickly changed "from a transatlantic mutual assistance treaty into an integrated military alliance, run by the United States."[58] In practice, the political institutions have little authority over the military machinery under the

Supreme Allied Commander who "has never been the first servant of the [NATO political] Council, but the viceroy of the American president."[59]

However, the costs of the U.S. military, first as a consequence of the Vietnam War in the 1960s and 1970s, and then Reagan's Star Wars expenditures in the 1980s, eventually became too heavy to finance by creating more dollars. It put too much strain on allied countries and caused chronic inflation. One U.S. response was to try to get Canada and Western Europe to pay more for NATO. Calleo describes the system as a protection racket:

> There is something to the view that we are rather like the rich man who regularly persuades his timid neighbours to loan him money, on the grounds that his spending creates a high demand for goods and services in the neighbourhood, and his bankruptcy will ruin them all. A part of the loans maintains a body of armed retainers. Most of the rest buys up mortgages on the houses of the creditors. More specifically, neither America's peacekeeping nor its foreign investment is universally popular.[60]

B. Contradictions in the Atlantic bloc

Before looking at how links across blocs expressed some of the major contradictions of Atlantic capitalism, I shall outline the contradictions within the bloc. Most significantly, transnational capitals, especially money capital, expanded beyond the regulative capacities of the Atlantic bloc which had spawned them. Through overseas investments, transnational sectors were extended beyond the Atlantic bloc and former colonies. The transnationalization of industrial capital through branch plants of Atlantic corporations, especially in the Latin American NICs, led to competition with Atlantic economies. "Export oriented industrialization" was introduced by foreign investment in the Cold War period, and institutionalized as "conditions" for turning over debt in the 1980s. This put an end to varying interludes of "national development" between colonial rule and the 1970s. It created a new division in the Third World, between so-called newly industrializing countries and countries not favoured by transnational capital.

In finance, the monetary system ceased effectively to be regulated with the rise of Eurodollar markets in the 1960s. These arose when European bankers lent dollars, which they held as reserves, for investments in Europe or elsewhere, creating dollars outside the control of U.S. monetary institutions. As the U.S. lost control over the supply of dollars, its continued foreign investment and military expenditures led to inflation. The U.S. responded unilaterally and aggressively in 1971 by taking the dollar off gold and thus ending the

Bretton Woods system. This contributed to the spread of unregulated money markets to other continents and other major currencies. It was compounded by two major shocks in 1973. The oil crisis shifted dollars away from industrial capital (which had to pay more for energy) and into the banking system as petrodollars. The food crisis was precipitated by massive Soviet purchases, partly paid for by exports of Soviet oil and gold, vastly expanding liquidity in the whole system. Thus Atlantic capitalism, and therefore world capitalism, went through three interconnected crises in the early 1970s: oil, food, and especially money.

The dollar crisis was compounded by the emergence of a U.S. trade deficit with its competitors not only within the Atlantic bloc but also outside. In addition to its internal contradictions, Atlantic capitalism came under competitive pressure from outside, as a result of exports from the truly *national* capitalisms of Asia. Japan, and later Korea and Taiwan, produced cheap industrial exports through a highly state-controlled process of capital accumulation. Japan's success was based on postwar policies set by the Allied Occupation forces, dominated by the U.S. After the Chinese Revolution of 1949, the U.S. reversed the balance between strategic and economic goals in favour of the former. In place of early attempts to destroy the prewar industrial conglomerates, the Occupation forces supported reconstruction through aid in ways that rebuilt the prewar relations between them and the state. Ironically, by retaining the constitutional ban on a Japanese military, and providing military forces in the Pacific, the U.S. allowed all Japan's resources to go into export-orientated industrialization. The Asian NICs, particularly Korea and Taiwan, became frontline states in the Pacific theatre of the Cold War. For strategic reasons, U.S. aid was large and exempted Korea and Taiwan from rules applied to other aid recipients. They created highly dirigiste national economies, much like Japan's, and with similar export success.

After 1971 especially, money, investment and trade ceased to be effectively regulated by Atlantic (or perhaps any) institutions. These changes led to a growing disjuncture between the military framework and the regulative space of capital. One dangerous result was an explosion of the international arms trade in the 1970s, mostly as a result of Third World purchases financed through petrodollars whether earned or borrowed. This was followed in the 1980s by intense export competition with many new suppliers in addition to the superpowers, and the growth of a large clandestine trade. Finally, many Third World countries began producing arms for export.[61]

Military and economic integration within the Atlantic bloc existed in constant tension with historic ties among European countries. The division of

Germany and of Europe in the construction of the Atlantic and Soviet blocs never entirely nullified the historic pull towards European unity and autonomous European relations with (former) colonies. Despite intra-European conflicts—between Germany and France, and between Britain and the Continent—tensions persisted over U.S. dominance in the Atlantic bloc. They were expressed through European economic (and now political) integration, opposition to NATO by DeGaulle and by popular political movements. Most of all they were manifested through competitive U.S. and European economic links with the Soviet bloc.[62]

The breaches of the economic dam between Cold War blocs became significant in the early 1970s. The new opportunities for eastern European countries to borrow from western banks, trade with the West, and even join the International Monetary Fund, were offered by private banks, Atlantic states, and Atlantic bloc quasi-state institutions at a time of crisis. The debt regime, based on extravagant loans and levered credit, began not only in the Third World, but also, with acute results, in the East. Thus the virtual abandonment of *capitalist* transnational regulation, especially monetary regulation, was implicated in the collapse of the party-state bloc.

The European Economic Community has always expressed the tension between Atlanticist and European projects, and it is now the basis for an extended continental renationalization of economic ties centred on (West) Germany. Anticipated by Canadian wheat sales to China, which helped to fray the socialist bloc,[63] competitive bridges to the Soviet Union initiated by West German Chancellor Brandt's "Ostpolitik" in 1967, and eventually matched by U.S. President Nixon's "Detente" in 1972, expressed contradictory movements within the capitalist bloc.[64] The crisis of Atlantic capitalism, therefore, is also a crisis of the antagonistic blocs which shaped it. Now incorporation of fragments of the former party-state bloc is a major terrain for contesting alternative institutions of regulation, either for capital, or for democratically organized ways to embed economic life in society.

C. The Soviet bloc: proletarian wines in a military bottle

More than two decades of economic links across blocs were the material basis for the strong capitalist orientation of economic reform, now being tested and opposed in democratic and nationalist politics in Eastern Europe and the former Soviet Union. What is being transformed is actually existing socialism, defined by the Soviet party-state bloc.

The Soviet bloc was an economic space at once separate from the capitalist world, and distinct in its use of central planning. It created an integrated economic space in the bloc through the "socialist division of labour." COMECON extended Soviet central planning into a bloc-wide plan. In some respects, it was similar in intent and effects to the "capitalist division of labour." In particular, it embraced a rationality leading to both spatial and social concentration of production, which paralleled specialization through trade in the West. For example, the agricultural equipment industries of both Canada and Hungary were phased out, despite the continuing importance of the agricultural sector in each "national" economy. In other respects it was different. If explicit planning gave the "socialist division of labour" an appearance similar to imperial blocs, the allocation of sectors within the bloc had nothing of the mercantile about it. The Soviet Union specialized in raw materials, notably oil, as well as high technology, and its terms of trade often favoured the politically subordinate nations of the bloc. The key characteristic of "central planning" was that political and strategic criteria could override efficiency or cost in allocating production among national economies. The most dramatic example came with the switch of Cuba from the capitalist to the socialist bloc between 1959 and 1961. The Soviet bloc phased out East European beet sugar despite the chronic costs to the bloc of permanently guaranteed purchase of Cuban cane sugar exports.

The hierarchical structure of rule by the Soviet Union over formally sovereign states in Eastern Europe (and more tenuously elsewhere) was organized as a *party-state bloc*.[65] It consisted of nominally independent states, with formal sovereignty over domestic and foreign relations. Formally sovereign states entered into economic and military alliances, COMECON and the Warsaw Pact. Formal sovereignty, like the formal guarantees of civil rights, were denied in practice by Communist Party rule, which, contradictorily, was also constitutionally guaranteed.

Real domination by the Soviet Union worked through the overarching hierarchy of Communist parties. In practice, the Communist Party of the Soviet Union (CPSU) ruled the other Communist parties. Just as the constitutional monopoly granted to Communist parties overrode the rights of citizens, the real domination of the Soviet Party over the supposedly "national" parties of the East European states overrode the sovereignty implied by the economic and military treaties which formally defined the bloc.[66]

Although COMECON defined the bloc economically, its real basis was the Warsaw Pact military alliance. Tensions within the bloc hinged on the struggles over sovereignty within the hierarchy of ruling parties. Communist parties sometimes tried and even succeeded in acting autonomously. However, only the Warsaw Pact countries, that is, the party-state bloc, were crucial to the bloc structure.

The success of the Chinese party and state in opposing the Soviet Union stands in stark contrast to Hungary in 1956 and Czechoslovakia in 1968. Despite the importance of the Chinese Revolution of 1949 in consolidating the Cold War (and shifting U.S. stance towards Japan from victor to ally), China was never part of the Warsaw Pact or COMECON. The Sino-Soviet split occurred in the early 1960s, after the capitalist and socialist superpowers had consolidated their blocs. Stabilization of the nuclear stand-off through "peaceful coexistence" led to a conflict between China and the Soviet Union. The conflict in turn led Khrushchev to harden the Cold War, provoking a crisis in Berlin and in Cuba, while extending support for national liberation struggles, notably in Southeast Asia. He also acted to show the Chinese that, in Schurmann's words, "the solidarity of the socialist camp, based on opposition to American imperialism anywhere and everywhere, demanded complete submission of all its members to Moscow."[67] The split precipitated the first crisis in the bloc structure over the incipient Chinese nuclear capacity. This was paralleled in the Western bloc by the withdrawal of France which wished to create an independent nuclear arsenal from NATO. Yet despite China's ideological fervour and the alarm bordering on panic which it caused in both superpowers, its response to economic weakness was autarkic. This allowed the superpowers to stabilize their competition in the underdeveloped world, especially in Asia, by supporting regional struggles for national liberation opposed by "counterinsurgency."[68]

Although COMECON included Cuba, Mongolia, and Vietnam, the core of the "socialist division of labour" was bounded by the Warsaw Pact military alliance. To understand the collapse of the bloc, it is crucial to see that the link between formal sovereignty and real subordination was the unequal integration of national ruling parties, and thus the integrated control of bloc military force. Thus, in Hungary in 1956 and Czechoslovakia in 1968, the Warsaw Pact was the means of forcibly suppressing *national* Parties threatening to depart from the *Soviet* Communist Party line. The 1968 invasion followed economic overtures between Czechoslovakia and West Germany, which led to fears by the USSR about the solidity of the Warsaw Pact.[69] By contrast, the repression of Polish Solidarity in the 1980s was accomplished through a national military coup. This was a crucial departure from both Party rule and Warsaw Pact enforcement. It was the first moment in the collapse of the party, and the hierarchy of parties, as the principle of rule within the bloc.

The political monopoly of the rest of the parties of Eastern Europe ended from below, through a combined struggle for democracy and against Soviet party domination of the whole bloc. Both parts of the struggle depended on links *across* blocs. Politically, in contrast to the violence usually necessary to abolish explicit foreign rule and racism in imperial blocs, the possibility of peaceful revolution was inherent in the constitutional form of party-state rule. The latter allowed for politics demanding enforcement of existing constitutional rights and abolition of contradictory provisions for party rule. However, it was international support, especially by West European peace movements, which allowed the peaceful possibility to be realized by oppositional movements.[70] At the same time, the party-state bloc almost required opposition movements seeking to distance themselves *economically* from the USSR during the 1970s and 1980s to establish alternative trade and financial ties with capitalist corporations, states and institutions, such as the International Monetary Fund. Despite the importance for popular movements of links to Western peace movements, state links to the West pushed East European independence in a capitalist direction.

The collapse of the Soviet bloc, like the earlier imperial blocs before them, has again multiplied national states. Ironically, however, just as it is becoming universal, the national state may be cast into irrelevance by the larger restructuring of international capitalism, which calls into question the very future of national economies.

After the Cold War: Which Wines? Which Bottles?

Early in this century, on the eve of war between imperial blocs, Lenin and Kautsky had a famous debate over the nature of larger-than-national capitalist accumulation. Kautsky's position, labelled "ultraimperialism" by Lenin, was that the transnational capitals of the day—trusts and cartels—were integrating the world economy to such an extent that it would contain competition among states, and make war unlikely. Lenin's position was that states still organized capital, and that trusts and cartels would give way to war between states competitively carving out spheres of influence. History, in the shape of World War I and the Russian Revolution, has usually been thought to have proved Lenin correct: competing states overwhelmed unifying capital.

However, now we can see that "ultraimperialism" and "spheres of influence" are expressions of two *aspects* of capitalism which constitute a *contradictory unity*. As van der Pijl has shown in great detail, after World War II the classes and class fractions, political parties and factions, which favoured

Atlantic integration (bloc ultraimperialism) contended successfully, but never definitively, against those which favoured national capitalism and the integration of the whole of Europe. The contest continued through complex politics over the shape and pace of West European integration, and even more complex politics of forging economic and political ties with East Europe and the Soviet Union. The latter have given new strength to the interests, particularly in Germany, asserting a European sphere of influence against Atlantic integration.

Both ultraimperialism and spheres of influence define two possibilities opened by the end of the Cold War blocs. Both are strategies of capital. Both pose distinct dangers for peace and democracy.

First, global accumulation has achieved much greater organizational and sectoral integration than a century ago. In the 1970s and 1980s, transnational capitals burst the bounds of Atlantic regulation, and overseas investment in the Third World disarticulated not only national economies, but also the Atlantic bloc. Transnational investment went far in integrating productive sectors and standardizing consumption across nationally organized economies and even across Cold War blocs. Moreover, with the combined crises of the early 1970s, accumulation shifted from industrial capital to mineral rents, and via petro-dollars, to banking capital. Abandonment of Bretton Woods in the face of Eurodollar markets, and later multiple currency money markets in many financial centres, set banking loose.

McMichael and Myhre, updating Kautsky, argue that transnational finance capital (in which global banks organize accumulation for transnational capital as a whole) now regulates accumulation. The Paris Club, for instance, represents the transnational banks directly in negotiations with debtor governments. Multilateral institutions, such as the IMF and World Bank, indirectly shift power away from states and towards private regulation. The three rules imposed on all states—maximize exports, reduce state social spending, and end state economic regulation—enhance the power of private capitals to reorganize aspects of national economies as parts of transnational economic networks. This does not so much undercut the power of states, however, as change and redirect it. Social ministries shrink while trade and finance ministries grow. The enhanced economic ministries are tied to capitals and outside agencies, and the reduced ones to civil (national) society. The effect is a "transnational state," composed of many "national" ministries linked to international institutions. It creates a "global wage relation," in which production everywhere, no matter what its form, is regulated by value relations operating on a world scale. Post-Fordist states and economies, according to McMichael and Myhre, are transnational.[71]

The political implications are potentially serious. Private, transnational regulation leads to social conditions quite different from national regulation by the state in the Fordist era. Instability of employment, and downward pressure on private wages and the social wage (transfer payments, public provision of goods and services) have already led to social unrest. In the Third World, structural adjustment policies have created the now common phenomenon of "IMF riots." Although these lead to some modification of conditions in each case, they so far do not threaten the debt regime itself. These were precisely the policies judged to be politically unacceptable in postwar Europe.[72] Marshall aid led to the alternative construction of a politically regulated Atlantic bloc and later aid shaped decolonization. Now enforced openness to a world economy, which is increasingly regulated privately if it is regulated at all, is politically managed through the police and military apparatuses, which continue to grow alongside trade and finance ministries. Ultraimperialism may be the nightmare of social war.

The second aspect of capitalist restructuring is reassertion of (transformed) states through competing spheres of influence. It is likely that capital continues to require regulation through political institutions which set and enforce rules about the relations between capital and labour, about competition among capitals, and (as Polanyi said almost half a century ago) about the "fictitious" commodification of land and money, as well as labour.[73] A major contradiction of Atlantic capitalism in the 1970s, one which is becoming stronger, was competition from truly national and statist capitalist economies. Japan was first, followed by the Asian NICs. These statist, export-oriented economies followed policies encouraged by the U.S. for Cold War strategic reasons. Together with the internal challenge of competitive German/U.S. links across Cold War blocs, the external challenge of Asian national capitalism caused a rift between economic and political/military organization of the Atlantic bloc. Although Japan was one of the Group of Seven major industrial countries which began to meet in regular "summits" to negotiate common responses to the chronic crisis of Atlantic—and consequently world—capitalism, its divergent interests became starkly clear in its reluctance to participate in giving aid to the ailing and flailing countries of the socialist bloc. The reassertion of Germany's historic sphere of influence in Eastern Europe is simultaneously a threat to the Atlantic bloc (and thus U.S. hegemony), and the basis for a bloc to rival Japan's (re)emerging sphere of influence in Asia. Like tectonic plates, while Atlantic bloc institutions remained in place, economic dynamism shifted to the Pacific, and a rift opened in the Atlantic.

Competing blocs have already brought two world wars in this century. The situation is now more complex and dangerous. Under the peculiar peace between blocs sustained by nuclear terror, "globalization [became] as true in military as in economic matters."[74] The vast network of military bases created (unequally) by the two superpowers, the international arms trade (of which almost half goes to five Middle Eastern countries), and military training in developing countries by major powers (often from both blocs), have left a dangerous legacy of militarism permeating the entire world. At the same time, the U.S. military has been as prone as other major industrial sectors to national disarticulation through transnational integration. The U.S. military has increasingly come to depend on components produced abroad by U.S. or foreign-based corporations.[75] If the U.S. continues to sustain a military monopoly, the tribute it exacts from its allies will be increasingly visible as the military hierarchy diverges from spheres of economic organization. If, by contrast, a future European state realizes plans for an integrated European military, it conjures familiar scenarios of world war, made unpredictable by the new technological and territorial scope of military power.

The third alternative is to find a way out of the dangerous impasse between direct rule by capital and wars between blocs. Capital, by enlarging both ultraimperialism and spheres of influence, is weakening national sovereignty. Other things being equal, this also weakens individual rights guaranteed by states.

The metamorphosis of national states opens possibilities as well as dangers. A democratic and peaceful alternative must reclaim the economy from capital, and re-embed it in nested levels of integrated social relations, from the community to the global. The history of the contested project to create Atlantic capitalism reveals that it was a multi-faceted struggle over political organizations, social movements, and culture. The alternative may build on the two levels which become more important as national states lose regulative capacities: act locally and act globally; act to increase democracy as sovereignty moves upwards and downwards. Regional economies which relink work and life, production and consumption, are the only comprehensive solutions to ecological, employment, land use, and consumption problems created by capital organized on a global or even a bloc scale. Municipal and regional governments are the appropriate place for pursuing democratic self-government, which organizes much material and social life already, and can facilitate democratic reorganization of regional production and commerce, through credit, technical research and assistance, infrastructure, and other services.[76] At the national level, politics may direct the loss of sovereignty, negatively by reducing military expenditures and fostering conversion to peaceful uses, and positively by working for genuinely multilateral institutions to regulate money, trade, and investment in ways that foster self-governing communities and regions.

ENDNOTES

I acknowledge support of the Social Sciences and Humanities Research Council of Canada. I have benefited from critical comments from Fred Bienefeld, Linda Briskin, Michael Dolan, Jane Jenson, Jeanne Laux, Rianne Mahon, Philip McMichael, David Myhre, Barry O'Neill, Bob Ross and discussions with Metta Spencer and participants at the Conference on Canadian Political Economy in the Era of Free Trade, Carleton University, April 1990.

1. Immanuel Wallerstein defines the "capitalist world-economy" as the "arena larger than that which any political entity can totally control." See Wallerstein, *The Capitalist World-Economy*, vol. 1 (New York: Academic, 1974), p. 348. However, this leaves no space for the partial and provisional regulative arrangements studied by the regimes school of international political economy. Two studies which combine sociological analysis with a regimes approach are Robert E. Wood, *From Marshall Plan to Debt Crisis: Foreign Aid and Development Choices in the World Economy* (Berkeley: University of California Press, 1986) and Fred L. Block, *The Origins of International Economic Disorder* (Berkeley: University of California Press, 1977).

2. For an excellent critique of the national focus of the regulation approach, see Philip McMichael and David Myhre, "Global Regulation vs. the Nation-State: Agro-Food Systems and the New Politics of Capital," *Capital and Class, 50* (1991), pp. 3-6. For a parallel critique of world systems analysis, which derives all explanations from an unvarying totality during the history of capitalism, see Harriet Friedmann, "Rethinking Capitalism and Hierarchy," *Review Journal of the Fernand Braudel Center*, 13/2 (1990).

3. This makes more concrete both Cox's concept of "internationalization" of the state, and McMichael and Myhre's concept of the "transnational state." See Robert W. Cox, *Production, Power, and World Order* (New York: Columbia University Press, 1987), pp. 253-65, and Philip McMichael and David Myhre, "Global Regulation vs. the Nation-State."

4. Richard Bryan, "The State and the Internationalization of Capital: An Approach to Analysis," *Journal of Contemporary Asia* 17/3 (1987), p. 274. Also Philip McMichael, "State Formation and the Construction of the World Market," *Political Power and Social Theory,* 6 (1987); and Kees van der Pijl, *The Making of an Atlantic Ruling Class* (London: Verso, 1984).

5. George Canning, Prime Minister in the post-Napoleonic period, stated this vision for Latin America. This was cited by A. Aguilar Monteverde, *Pan-Americanism from Monroe to the Present* (New York: Monthly Review Press, 1968), p. 23 and quoted in Giovanni Arrighi, *The Geometry of Imperialism* (London: Verso, 1978), p. 64.

6. McMichael, "State Formation," p. 191. and *passim.*

7. *Ibid.,* p. 192.

8. Brinley Thomas, *Migration and Economic Growth, A Study of Great Britain and the Atlantic Economy* (Cambridge: Cambridge Univ. Press, 1973).

9. See H. Friedmann and P. McMichael, "Agriculture and the State System: The Rise and Decline of National Agricultures, 1870 to the Present," *Sociologia Ruralis,* 29/2 (1989). For Canada see Vernon Fowke, *The National Policy and the Wheat Economy* (Toronto: Univ. of Toronto Press, 1957) and for Australia, see P. McMichael, *Settlers and the Agrarian Question, Capitalism in Colonial Australia* (Cambridge: Cambridge Univ. Press, 1984).

10. See Marjorie Griffin Cohen, *Women's Work, Markets, and Economic Development in Nineteenth-Century Ontario* (Toronto: University of Toronto Press, 1988) for an excellent critique and revision of staples theory.

11. Charles Post, "The American Road To Capitalism," *New Left Review,* 133 (1982).

12. M. Aglietta, *A Theory of Capitalist Regulation* (London: NLB, 1979).

13. Hugo Radice, "The National Economy: A Keynesian Myth?," *Capital and Class,* 22 (1984), p. 117.

14. Michael Tracy, *Agriculture in Western Europe: Crisis and Adaptation Since 1880* (London: Cape, 1964).

15. And ecologically superior. See Colin Duncan, "The Centrality of Agriculture," (PhD Thesis, York University, 1989).

16. E.J. Hobsbawm, *The Age of Empire, 1875-1914* (London: Wiedenfeld and Nicholson, 1987), p. 69.

17. Harriet Friedmann, "World Market, State and Family Farm," *Comparative Studies in Society and History,* 20/4 (1978).

18. The term comes from the French Corps of Prefects created by the Napoleonic reforms of the early 19th century. For a brilliant analysis of the "bureaucratic dialectic" of this form, especially as it underlay the colonial state, see Bruce Berman, *Control and Crisis in Colonial Kenya: The Dialectic of Domination* (London: Currey, 1990), pp. 73-127.

19.   See Richard Wolff, *The Economics of Colonialism: Britain and Kenya, 1870-1930* (New Haven: Yale, 1974), pp. 68-110. By contrast, the colonial adminis-tration accepted its failure to induce Canadian farmers to introduce new crops needed in Britain. Australia began as a penal colony with coerced British labour, but as a setter colony it was central to the formation of the international econo-my constituted by liberal states in the mid-19th century. Imperial bloc practices were not conceivable there by late in the century. See Philip McMichael, *Settlers and the Agrarian Question*.

20.   In Hobson's terms, the hierarchical expansion of the metropolitan state was the "new imperialism." To follow Arrighi's interpretation, it represents expansion of the State rather than of the Nation. See *The Geometry of Imperialism*.

21.   See Berman, *Control and Crisis* especially p. 98, and Rudolf von Albertini, *European Colonial Rule, 1880-1940: The Impact of the West on India, Southeast Asia and Africa* (Westport, CN: 1982), pp. 13-20.

22.   Cited in Berman, *Control and Crisis*, p. 98.

23.   R. Keith Kelsall, *The Higher Civil Servants in Britain* (London: Routledge, 1955).

24.   This is what Immanuel Wallerstein calls a "world-empire." For a brief, clear exposition, see "The Rise and Future Demise of the World Capitalist System: Concepts for Comparative Analysis," *Comparative Studies in Society and History*, 16/4 (1974). By definition a world-empire is a world-system and can-not be one component of it. Thus following this logic, which is in my view essentialist and functionalist, Arrighi has treated the socialist sphere as a variant of the periphery. See Jessica Drangel,"The Stratification of the World-Economy: An Exploration of the Semiperipheral Zone," *Review*, 10/1 (1986). In my view the idea of empire should not be restricted in this way, and Arrighi's 1981 analysis (*Geometry*) is the best evidence for my argument. I make this argument in greater detail in criticizing Wallerstein in "Rethinking Capitalism and Hierarchy."

25.   Peter Gourevitch, *Politics in Hard Times: Comparative Responses to International Economic Crises* (Ithaca: Cornell University Press, 1966), pp. 71-123.

26.   Plans of the Left for national capitalism after WWII included colonies.

27.   See Wolff, *Economics of Colonialism* and Berman, *Control and Crisis*.

28.   Hobsbawm, *Age of Capital*, and Jack Wayne, "Capitalism and Colonialism in Late Nineteenth Century Europe," *Studies in Political Economy*, 5 (1981).

29.   The term "non-traditional exports" has been coined, not very helpfully, to describe agricultural exports which are not uniquely tropical. They include fruits and vegetables, fish, timber, fresh cut flowers, and so on. The idea that bananas, sugar, coffee and tea were the destiny of former colonies was common in underdevelopment theory until it began to take into account industrial exports from NICs.

30. David Goodman, B. Sorj, and J. Wilkinson, *From Farming to Biotechnology* (Oxford: Blackwell, 1987). The other tendency is "appropriation" of those parts of agriculture that can be subordinated to capitalist production.

31. See Friedmann, "Agro-food Industries," and Friedmann and McMichael, "Agriculture and the State System."

32. See, for example, Uday S. Mehta, "Liberal Strategies of Exclusion," *Politics and Society,* 18/4 (1990), and Judith Whitehead, "Deconstructing Caste: British and French Images of India in the Late Nineteenth Century." (MS 1990).

33. Victory in the Civil War strengthened the U.S. state and allowed it to integrate the South economically and politically into the national economy. Following abolition of slavery, the Constitution was amended to proclaim universal rights for (male) citizens. However, beginning in 1873, court decisions incrementally supported the powers of Southern state governments to nullify these rights through "Jim Crow" segregation laws. Eric Foner, "Blacks and the U.S. Constitution, 1789-1989," *New Left Review,* 183 (1990), pp. 69-71.

34. Antonio Gramsci, *Prison Notebooks* (New York: International, 1971).

35. Karl Polanyi, *The Great Transformation* (Boston: Beacon, 1957).

36. Stuart Ewen, *Captains of Consciousness* (New York: McGraw-Hill, 1976).

37. For instance, Michel Aglietta, "World Capitalism in the Eighties," *New Left Review,* 136 (1982), and Mike Davis, "From Fordism to Reaganism: The Crisis of American Hegemony in the 1980s," in Ray Bush, Gordon Johnston and David Coates (eds.), *The World Order: Socialist Perspectives* (Oxford: Polity, 1987).

38. A major exception is Kaldor, "After the Cold War," *New Left Review,* 180 (1990).

39. Kaldor, "After the Cold War"; van der Pijl, *Making*; Block, *Origins*; Franz Schurmann, *The Logic of World Power* (New York: Pantheon,1974); E. P. Thompson, *Exterminism and the New Cold War* (London: Verso, 1982).

40. Kees van der Pijl, "The International Level," in T. Bottomore and R.J. Brym, *The Capitalist Class: An International Study* (New York: Harvester, 1989).

41. Alfred Grosser, *The Western Alliance: European-American Relations Since 1945* (London: Macmillan, 1980), pp. 51-58.

42. See Wood, *From Marshall Plan to Debt Crisis.*

43. Schurmann, *Logic*, pp. 117-23, and Block, *Origins*, pp. 70-108.

44. Block, *Origins*, p .87.

45. Wood, *From Marshall Plan to Debt Crisis*, pp. 44-47.

46. Block, *Origins*, pp. 89-92.

47. Wood, *From Marshall Plan to Debt Crisis*, pp. 40-60.

48. van der Pijl, *Making*, pp. 138-77.

49. David Caute, *The Great Fear* (New York, Simon and Schuster, 1978), and Block, *Origins*, pp. 89-92.

50. van der Pijl, *Making*, pp. 138-212.

51. David Calleo, *The Atlantic Fantasy: The U.S., NATO and Europe* (Baltimore: The Johns Hopkins Press, 1970), pp. 84-85.

52. Aglietta "World Capitalism" and Davis, "From Fordism to Reaganism."

53. Gerald K. Helleiner, *International Economic Disorder: Essays in North-South Relations* (Toronto: University of Toronto Press, 1981), p. 38-39.

54. Stephen Gill, *American Hegemony and the Trilateral Commission* (Cambridge: Cambridge, Univ. Press, 1990), pp. 89-121.

55. Willem van Eekelen, "WEU and the Gulf Crisis," *Survival* (1990), p. 519.

56. However, George Kennan "found the whole enterprise a misguided perversion" of the concept he is thought to have invented. Calleo, *Atlantic Fantasy*, p. 25.

57. *Logic*, p. 65-68.

58. Calleo, *Atlantic Fantasy*, p. 24.

59. *Ibid.*, p. 27.

60. *Ibid.*, p. 90.

61. Michael T. Klare, "Deadly Convergence: The Perils of the Arms Trade," *World Policy Journal*, 6/1 (1988).

62. van der Pijl, *Making*.

63. Schurmann, *Logic*, pp. 331ff.

64. van der Pijl, *Making*, pp. 252-58.

65. I cannot tell the story of the creation of Soviet bloc institutions parallel to that of Marshall Aid and NATO. See Fernando Claudin, *The Communist Movement, From Comintern to Cominform* (Harmondsworth: Penguin, 1975), and Schurmann, *Logic*.

66. F. Claudin, *Eurocommunism and Socialism* (London: NLB, 1978), pp. 32-33.

67. Schurmann, *Logic of World Power*, p. 314.

68. *Ibid.*, pp. 310-27.

69. Calleo, *Atlantic Fantasy*, p. 69n. cites de Gaulle, who actually blamed Germany for provoking the Soviet invasion.

70. Mary Kaldor, "After the Cold War."

71. But not equal. McMichael and Myrhe, in "Global Regulation," focus on North-South relations rather than Atlantic/Pacific or East/West, as I do here. They argue convincingly that Northern states are able to use multilateral agencies, such as the GATT, to improve the flow of capital from the South, that is, to affect the location of socially (relatively) beneficial investments in their favour.

72.   Wood, *From Marshall Plan to Debt Crisis*, pp. 27-28.

73.   Polanyi, *The Great Transformation*.

74.   Ruth Leger Sivard, *World Military and Social Expenditures, 1987-88*, p. 13.

75.   Moran, "Globalization."

76.   Several models of regional economies are worth attention. I am most familiar with the Emilia-Romagna region of Italy, which has achieved a highly efficient, dynamic, and prosperous economy through several decades of democratic planning.